International Political Economy Series

General Editor: **Timothy M. Shaw,** Professor of Human Security & Peacebuilding, School of Peace & Conflict Management, Royal Roads University, Victoria, BC, Canada

Titles include:

Kees Kingma
DEMOBILIZATION IN SUBSAHARAN AFRICA
The Development and Security Impacts

Vijay S. Makhan
ECONOMIC RECOVERY IN AFRICA
The Paradox of Financial Flows

Clever Mumbengegwi (*editor*)
MACROECONOMIC AND STRUCTURAL ADJUSTMENT POLICIES IN ZIMBABWE

Nana Poku
REGIONALIZATION AND SECURITY IN SOUTHERN AFRICA

Howard Stein, Olu Ajakaiye and Peter Lewis (*editors*)
DEREGULATION AND THE BANKING CRISIS IN NIGERIA
A Comparative Study

Peter Vale, Larry A. Swatuk and Bertil Oden (*editors*)
THEORY, CHANGE AND SOUTHERN AFRICA'S FUTURE

International Political Economy Series
Series Standing Order ISBN 0-333-71708-2 hardcover
Series Standing Order ISBN 0-333-71110-6 paperback
(*outside North America only*)

You can receive future titles in this series as they are published by placing a standing order. Please contact your bookseller or, in case of difficulty, write to us at the address below with your name and address, the title of the series and one of the ISBNs quoted above.

Customer Services Department, Macmillan Distribution Ltd, Houndmills, Basingstoke, Hampshire RG21 6XS, England

Neoliberalism, Civil Society and Security in Africa

Pádraig Carmody
Lecturer in Geography, Trinity College Dublin,
Ireland

First published 2007 by
PALGRAVE MACMILLAN
Houndmills, Basingstoke, Hampshire RG21 6XS and
175 Fifth Avenue, New York, N.Y. 10010
Companies and representatives throughout the world

PALGRAVE MACMILLAN is the global academic imprint of the Palgrave
Macmillan division of St. Martin's Press, LLC and of Palgrave Macmillan Ltd.
Macmillan® is a registered trademark in the United States, United Kingdom
and other countries. Palgrave is a registered trademark in the European
Union and other countries.

ISBN-13: 978-0-230-52159-9   hardback
ISBN-10: 0-230-52159-2   hardback

This book is printed on paper suitable for recycling and made from fully
managed and sustained forest sources. Logging, pulping and manufacturing
processes are expected to conform to the environmental regulations of the
country of origin.

A catalogue record for this book is available from the British Library.

Library of Congress Cataloging-in-Publication Data

Carmody, Pádraig Risteard.
    Neoliberalism, civil society and security in Africa/Pádraig Carmody.
        p. cm.
    Includes bibliographical references and index.
    ISBN-13: 978–0–230–52159–9 (cloth)
    ISBN-10: 0–230–52159–2 (cloth)
    1. Africa—Economic conditions—1960- 2. Neoliberalism—Africa.
        3. Democratization—Africa. 4. Civil society—Africa.
        5. Africa—Politics and government—1960- I. Title.

HC800.C265 2007
    320.96—dc22   2006048055

10   9   8   7   6   5   4   3   2   1
16   15   14   13   12   11   10   09   08   07

Printed and bound in Great Britain by
Antony Rowe Ltd, Chippenham and Eastbourne

For my family

Contents

List of Figures

Acknowledgments

Thanks to Eric Sheppard, Joel Wainwright, Francis Owusu, Scott Taylor, David Simon, Ben Fine, Jo Beall, Brian Pratt and John Grindle for comments on parts of the book, and the journal referees and the editorial boards of the *Journal of Southern African Studies* and of *Africa Today* for their comments on papers which appeared in those journals, and reappear in revised form here. Thanks also to Tim Shaw and an anonymous referee for Palgrave Macmillan for their comments on the proposal and manuscript, and to Philippa Grand, Hazel Woodbridge, and the editorial and production staff of Macmillan India Ltd. Many thanks also to Anne Pender for her help with the formatting of the book and editorial suggestions. To Christopher Clapham, Chris Alden, Ian Phimister, Jean Somers, Andy Storey and Abdi Samatar for useful articles and papers, and to Gerry O'Reilly and Emma Mawdsley for helpful conversations, and Kidane Mengisteab for contacts in Ethiopia. I owe a particular debt to Abdi and Eric for their advice and inspiration over the years, and to Abdi for helping me with the logistics of fieldwork in South Africa. Thanks to David Doyle for his research assistance on the sections on civil society, funded through a grant from the Advisory Board of Irish Aid, as part of the Centre for International Studies, Dublin City University project on 'Civil Society Engagement for Poverty Reduction.' Thanks also to the staff of the Advisory Board and of Irish Aid in Dublin and Addis Ababa, and in particular to Mary Sutton and Fiona Quinn. The views expressed here are of course independent and do not reflect those of any organization. Other elements of the research were funded by the Committee on Research and Scholarship at the University of Vermont, and the Research Committee of St Patrick's College. Their support is gratefully acknowledged. Thanks also to my colleagues in the Geography Departments at St Patrick's College, Boston University, the University of Vermont and the Centre for International Studies, Dublin City University for providing congenial and provocative working environments. Of course, the book would not have been possible without the much-appreciated co-operation and insights of the people I interviewed in Zimbabwe, South Africa and Ethiopia. Any errors of fact or interpretation belong to the author.

List of Abbreviations

9/11	September the 11th, 2001 (terrorist attacks on the United States)
ACOTA	African Contingency Operations Training and Assistance Program
ACP	African, Caribbean and Pacific Countries
ADLI	Agriculture-Development Led Industrialization
AGOA	African Growth and Opportunity Act
AIDS	Acquired Immuno-Deficiency Syndrome
ANC	African National Congress
BONGO	Bank Organized NGO
BRAC	Bangladesh Rural Advancement Committee
BWIs	Bretton Woods Institutions
CBO	Community Based Organization
CCM	Chama Cha Mapinduzi
CFA	*Communauté financière d'Afrique*
CFU	Commercial Farmers Union
CONGO	Co-opted NGO
CRDA	Christian Relief and Development Association
CSO	Civil Society Organization
CUD	Coalition for Unity and Democracy
CZI	Confederation of Zimbabwe Industries
DAG	Development Assistance Group
DBS	Direct Budget Support
DCNGO	Donor Created NGO
DFID	Department for International Development
DPCC	Disaster Prevention and Preparedness Commission
DRC	Democratic Republic of the Congo
EAVOS	Ethiopian Association of Voluntary Services
EPAs	Economic Partnership Agreements
EPRDF	Ethiopian People's Revolutionary Democratic Front
ESAP	Economic Structural Adjustment Program
FDI	Foreign Direct Investment
GDP	Gross Domestic Product
GEAR	Growth, Employment and Redistribution
GONGO	Government Organized NGO
GRINGO	Government-Run NGO

GRO	Grassroots Organization
HD	Human Development
HIPC	Heavily Indebted Poor Country
HIV	Human Immuno-Virus
IFI	International Financial Institution
IMF	International Monetary Fund
INGO	International Non-Governmental Organization
INTRAC	International Non-Governmental Training and Research Center
I-PRSP	Interim-PRSP
IRI	International Republican Institute
JSE	Johannesburg Stock Exchange
MCA	Millennium Challenge Account
MDC	Movement for Democratic Change
MDG	Millennium Development Goals
MEC	Minerals-Energy Complex
MNC	Multinational Corporation
MO	Membership Organization
MONGO	My-Own NGO
MOSOP	Movement for the Survival of Ogoni People
NAI	New Africa Initiative
NCA	National Constitutional Assembly
NDNGO	Northern Development NGO
NEDLAC	National Economic Development and Labor Advisory Committee
NEPAD	New Partnership for African Development
NGDO	Non-Governmental Development Organization
NGO	Non-Governmental Organization
NICs	Newly Industrialized Countries
NNGO	Northern NGO
NRM	National Resistance Movement
ODA	Overseas Development Assistance
OECD	Organization for Economic Cooperation and Development
OPEC	Organization of Petroleum Exporting Countries
PANE	Poverty Action Network
PEAP	Poverty Elimination Action Plan
PEPFAR	President's Emergency Program for AIDS Relief
PO	People's Organization
PPA	Participatory Poverty Assessment
PREM	People's Rural Education Movement
PRSP	Poverty Reduction Strategy Paper

PRSC	Poverty Reduction Support Credit
PSAC	Programmatic Structural Adjustment Credit
PSIA	Poverty and Social Impact Assessment
PWC	Post-Washington Consensus
R and D	Research and Development
RDP	Reconstruction and Development Program
REST	Relief Society of Tigray
ROSCA	Rotating Savings and Credit Association
SADC	Southern African Development Community
SAP	Structural Adjustment Program
SAPRIN	Structural Adjustment Participatory Review Initiative
SDI	Spatial Development Initiative
SDPRP	Sustainable Development and Poverty Reduction Program
SME	Small and Medium Sized Enterprise
SMME	Small, Micro and Medium Enterprises
SNGO	Southern NGO
SWAPs	Sector-Wide Approaches
TNC	Transnational Corporation
TPLF	Tigrayan People's Liberation Front
UN	United Nations
UNCTAD	UN Conference on Trade and Development
UNDP	United Nations Development Program
UNESCO	UN Educational, Scientific and Cultural Organization
USAID	United States Agency for International Development
WTO	World Trade Organization
ZANU-PF	Zimbabwe African National Union-Patriotic Front
ZCTU	Zimbabwe Congress of Trade Unions
ZESA	Zimbabwe Electricity Supply Authority
ZNLWVA	Zimbabwe National Liberation War Veterans Association

Introduction

Security, the chief pretence of civilisation, cannot exist where the worst of dangers, the danger of poverty, hangs over everyone's head.

(Shaw, 1905, cited in *Economic Focus,* 2002)

Africa at the start of the new century reveals an apparently disturbing paradox: an encouraging growth in both formal democracy and civil society, yet simultaneously, an increase in conflict which seems to revive and reflect divisions over ethnicities, regionalisms, religions, etc.

(T. Shaw, 2003, p. 186)

The number of people living in absolute poverty in Africa is projected to increase from 380 million in 1998 to 451 million in 2015.

(Economic Commission for Africa and Economic Policy Research Center, 2003, p. 3)

Neoliberalism, the synthesis of 'free market' economics and liberal democratic theory, has been the dominant force in African political economies during the last three decades. Neoliberalism as philosophy has been forged in Western think tanks and in international civil society groupings, such as the Trilateral Commission. It values market exchange as an ethic capable of guiding human action (Treanor, n.d., cited in Harvey, 2005) and has penetrated African political economy through World Bank/International Monetary Fund (IMF) programs and political conditionality from bilateral donors.

In terms of the sequencing of neoliberal reform on the continent, the market has been given primacy, as civil society and democracy are sometimes thought to be conducive to the development of distortionary distributional coalitions. Market discipline is thought to dissolve these coalitions, laying the groundwork for the emergence of genuine 'market democracies,' which can then be embedded through the development of liberal civil society. However, as the introductory quotes above make clear, sub-Saharan Africa's problems of poverty and conflict have deepened, rather than being ameliorated during this time.

Given the diversity of African social formations in terms of ideology, kinship, ethnicity, nationalism and economic structures, the application of neoliberalism on the continent has been particularly problematic. Neoliberalism and continued clientelism have proven to be mutually compatible. Partly because of its general lack of success, the theory and practice of neoliberalism on the continent has evolved in important ways during recent decades.

There has been a substantial debate about the causes of Africa's problems and whether they are internal or external, political or economic, historically driven or the result of recent policy choices. Such binary oppositions are largely unhelpful, however. There is now an emerging consensus that the causes of these problems lie in the interaction between the continent's politics, economics and perhaps its sociology; its political economy, of which neoliberalism is now a central component.

Neoliberalism has not reversed, but has arguably deepened Africa's marginalization in the global economy.[1] The statistics on this are well rehearsed (see Cheru, 2002). The proportion of global trade that it accounts for has fallen consistently. It attracts negligible amounts of foreign direct investment (FDI), heavily concentrated in the oil sector, and many countries have experienced negative per capita economic growth over the last two decades. 'Although Africa's share of world trade declined during the 1980s and 1990s, the volume of exports increased, while the value of sub-Saharan exports was cut in half relative to the value of imports from the North' (Toussaint, unpublished, cited in Bond, 2002a, p. 54).

The number of violent conflicts doubled during the 1990s (United States Institute for Peace, 2001, cited in Toulmin and Wisner, 2006), before falling back in the early years of the new millennium. Almost 70 percent of all conflict related deaths around the world from 1994–2003 occurred in sub-Saharan Africa (UNDP, 2005). Whereas the World Bank sees war as 'development in reverse,' in Africa it is intimately tied up with patterns of (primary) accumulation (World Bank, 2003b, cited in Cramer, 2006).

Neoliberalism's disastrous economic record in Africa has fed different types of insecurity on the continent. In part this is by design. 'A security problem arises when someone – a person, gang or group, or state – threatens another's life, limb, or livelihood' (Kolodziej, 2005, p. 1). However, a security problem may originate not only with actors but also from other social forces, such as markets (Kirby, 2006).

The central thrust of neoliberalism is the commodification of labor (people's work) and the application of the law of supply and demand to society. This creates both inclusion and exclusion. In the ideology of the 'free' market, the creation of insecurity (competition) in the labor market is meant to be beneficial to society. However, inclusion is dependent on there being sufficient demand in the market to absorb available job seekers; very far from the case in sub-Saharan Africa. In addition to the freedom to vote, neoliberalism may also mean the freedom to be unemployed and at its most extreme, the freedom to starve.

Neoliberalism and conflict interact in country specific ways, depending on preexisting conditions and institutions. In some instances neoliberalism has been associated with state strengthening; in others with state collapse. However, neoliberalism attempts to embed the market logic in society through the state. This disembedded logic creates human and sometimes national security problems, as regionalized poverty may fuel irredentism. Poverty and insecurity also feeds 'poor governance' and 'war economies.'

Exclusion and conflict are intimately related. Across sub-Saharan Africa, neoliberal policies have tended to produce, on the one hand, weaker states,[2] and on the other, deeper poverty and social exclusion for (informal) workers, peasants and women. Where there are scant or shrinking economic resources, the state may become the primary locus of accumulation. This may politicize ethnicity and make politics a zero sum game. Excluded ethnicities and regions may have incentives to try to dissociate or secede from the central state. Together these conditions have sewn the seeds of widespread economic insecurity and ethnic division, and struggles to control the state as a site of extraction, as opposed to development strategy-building. However, it is also important to recognize that the so-called new wars are a continuation of a historical pattern of plunder of the African continent by outsiders and elites, rather than a novel feature of neoliberal globalization (Cramer, 2006).

Conflict may become a form of social equilibrium, as accumulation and force intertwine, and 'war economies' develop their own dynamic. Destitution associated with conflict may, in turn, feed economically motivated violence (Keen, 2000). The failure to provide for human security may thus also spill over into not only state but international insecurity, with failing states providing high quality operating environments for transnational terrorists (Rotberg, 2005). These forces of fragmentation are today unfolding in the context of a post-9/11 era of securitization,[3] with potentially even worse implications for state–civil society relations. The very conditions needed to overcome neoliberalism – state–society linkages rooted in a national development strategy and social contract – are being uprooted.

Despite this record, the dominance of neoliberalism at the level of state politics is largely unchallenged on the continent, and indeed is undergoing further revision and institutional embedding. This book examines how neoliberalism has been revised and reinvented over these decades in order to allow for its perpetuation, despite its massive failings; and how to transcend it.

The evolution of neoliberalism

The initial response to the economic and debt crises in Africa in the late 1970s and early 1980s on the part of the 'international community' was to enforce programs of free market economic reform in Africa. As it was originally formulated, neoliberalism was concerned with state retraction and letting the 'free' market determine prices – 'getting the prices right.' However, these 'structural adjustment programs' (SAPs) failed to reverse, and arguably deepened Africa's economic problems.[4]

The other 'blade' of the neoliberal (counter)revolution during the 1980s, in addition to free market reform, was the increased prominence and importance given to nongovernmental organizations (NGOs). NGOs were initially meant to play two associated roles in this revolution in Africa: (1) to substitute for state services, and (2) to ease the transitional social costs of economic adjustment. However, they were to assume greater political significance in the evolution of neoliberal development policy in the 1990s with the elaboration of the theory of 'good governance.'

The failure of orthodox SAPs was initially blamed on their subversion by political elites. The International Financial Institutions (IFIs), such as World Bank and International Monetary Fund, attempted to enforce stricter conditions and attach additional governance conditionality on loans in response to this. However, ultimately it was felt that the IFIs did not have the coercive power to make elites conform to their dictates. Consequently as stricter conditionality was found to be ineffective, new approaches were tried (Killick, with Gunatilaka and Marr, 1998). Given deepening poverty and intensifying conflict in much of the continent, often originating in civil society, state elites and much of society remained uncommitted to neoliberal reform.

In the 1990s, the question for IFIs and donors became how to embed neoliberalism socially. Different neoliberal approaches are sometimes in tension, sometimes in harmony with each other. Another 'bypass the state' approach, complementary to service delivery funding to NGOs, which emerged in the mid-1990s focused on the development of trust or 'social capital' in African society. This was meant to be a developmental elixir. However, as will be discussed later this did not stem the economic crisis either.

Neoliberalism underwent a social crisis of legitimacy in Africa and parts of Latin America in the 1980s and 1990s, contributing to instability. As these regions were global peripheries, however, their exclusion could be policed and regulated, in part through funding to international NGOs (INGOs). However, neoliberalism underwent a global legitimation crisis in the wake of the rolling East Asian, Brazilian, Russian and Argentinean financial crises at the turn of the century. It was renovated in a variety of important ways during the late 1990s and early 2000s to take account of these developments in an attempt to establish a new hegemony, and solve some of the problems of the previous regime.

The third neoliberal approach in Africa was to try and achieve the 'lock-in' of economic reform through the development of (liberal) civil society and its participation in policy formulation and implementation processes, coupled with social investment. The failure of reform was explained through 'poor governance,' combined with external constraints, and lack of investment in health and education. This new strategy was pursued through national Poverty Reduction Strategy Papers (PRSPs), introduced by the World Bank in 1999. The emphasis here was on strengthening the state to provide services, particularly free or subsidized primary healthcare and education to enable people to compete in the market. The choice of expenditure levels across services is meant to be determined, in part, with civil society participation. However, institutional embedding was also to take place at a regional level.

A fourth neoliberal approach emerged in the early 2000s. One of the themes and values underlying the new development aid regime and architecture is 'partnership' between different actors; NGOs, donors and states. This infuses the discourse at different levels, such as social capital (local), PRSPs (national) and the United Nations Millennium Development Goals (MDGs) (global). It also informs African regional initiatives, particularly the New Partnership for African Development

(NEPAD) launched in 2001, which is meant to dovetail with the PRSP and MDG agendas. Whereas other approaches were globally inspired, NEPAD is a regional initiative.

Much has been written about NEPAD from both celebratory and critical perspectives.[5] It is a contradictory document combining, discursively at least, an eclectic mix of modernization and dependency theory (Pretorious and Patel, n.d., cited in Mathews, 2004). Governance is one of its leitmotifs. African states are meant to take responsibility for this and monitor it through a process of peer review. In return the developed countries are to catalyze Africa's deeper, but more productive, engagement with the global system through increased aid and foreign investment flows, reductions in trade barriers and debt relief. The overall unregulated integrationist terms of engagement with the global system are not questioned, however. As such it is somewhat doubtful this new approach will meet with more substantially more success than other approaches, as will be discussed later.

A further evolution of neoliberalism has emerged in the wake of the attacks of September 11, 2001 on the United States. While this event is often taken to mark the beginning of a reversal of globalization through a reassertion of state power, the argument presented here is different. Rather than being reversed, neoliberal globalization is in the process of being transformed through securitization, as global forces penetrate not only economic but also security policies. This represents an attempt to assert order in the face of the chaos of individual interests (Harvey, 2005). Securitization has been particularly evident in Africa, given the strategic priority which the United States now attaches to African oil supplies.

This book traces the evolution and impacts of neoliberal theory as applied in Africa; particularly attempts to embed it by socializing, depoliticizing and securitizing it. Attempts to depoliticize neoliberalism, so that it becomes an accepted 'common sense' have failed; consequently the need to securitize it. The book explores the impacts of neoliberalism through case studies of Ethiopia, Zimbabwe and South Africa and concludes with suggestions on how to transform globalization so that it meets both human and state security needs.

Structure of the book

The first chapter of the book explores the theory and practice of 'civil society' from the 1980s, from both liberal and radical perspectives. The different theories are grounded by looking at types of civil society organizations, and the political economy of the relationship between donors and NGOs is then explored. Initially donors viewed NGOs as having a palliative function, however, as the next chapter elaborates they became more interested in their transformative potential after the collapse of the Soviet bloc, as civil society was seen to have played a central role in this. The implementation and impacts of 'good governance' are then traced through concrete examples. The discussion also pays attention to the tensions and complementarities between service delivery and advocacy functions, and the accountability of NGOs.

By the mid-1990s, it was increasingly clear that the economic reforms of the 1980s, even when combined with the spread of liberal democracy in Africa in early 1990s, were not reversing Africa's marginalization. The next chapter looks at the evolution of international antipoverty policy in the 1990s in response to this, and the theory of social capital in particular. It begins by contextualizing the concept by looking at the evolution of development theory, particularly the increasing prominence of human and social development concepts. The theory of social capital itself is then assessed.

'Social capital' serves powerful interests in the global political economy by displacing the locus of poverty production from the global to the local, and thereby negates claims for global income redistribution, or for preferential treatment for the productive sectors of developing country economies in international trade. The chapter concludes by discussing alternative ideas on how to link civil society and the state to promote poverty reduction. The following chapter explores the neoliberal approach to linking society to the state.

The fourth chapter looks at the way in which the market/state/civil society relationship has recently been reconceptualized by the World Bank through PRSPs. Whereas the theory of social capital could fit with an antistate agenda, the new participatory turn in development strategy is focused on the renovation and increased accountability of the state. This can be read as: (1) a push for greater participation as a source of information failure reduction to make neoliberalism more efficient and (2) making domestic civil society an institutionalized source of accountability for African states, as debt stocks have lessened and donors now have less leverage. In the new logic, liberal civil society's restraint of the state serves to embed the market. Consequently, PRSPs attempt to embed, constrain, legitimate, enable and empower African states along different dimensions. This represents a synthesis of Anglo-American and corporatist continental European approaches to development, to the exclusion of (East Asian) developmental and (Scandinavian) welfare statist approaches, which may be more appropriate. The following chapters examine the evolution and impacts of neoliberalism through a series of case studies.

The fifth chapter is a case study of the PRSP process. It begins by overviewing the changing nature of African civil society, in order to understand the context in which PRSPs are being implemented. Then, based on documentary analysis and interviews, it explores the development and impacts of (liberal) civil society in Ethiopia on the formation and success of the PRSP.

Ethiopia is the second most populous country in sub-Saharan Africa, after Nigeria. It is a key ally and strategic partner for the United States in the Horn of Africa and in the 'war on terror.' It has also, until recently, been held up as an exemplar of successful political and economic reform. As such Ethiopia is a key country in terms of the current development moment, and its experience also has important lessons for other 'postconflict' societies.

The roots of liberal civil society in Ethiopia are weak and its influence on the policy process has been limited. Whether the new participatory mechanisms in the PRSP can be considered an element of political liberalization, or are coincident with authoritarian economism is open to debate. Despite the rhetoric, participation, as it is currently constituted in the programs of the IFIs may serve to bypass parliamentary democracy and legitimize programs of neoliberal economic reform and governance, while allowing for (security) state strengthening and the continuing, and sometimes brutal, repression of dissent, as shown after the recent Ethiopian election. By bypassing parliamentary institutions, PRSPs may therefore be compatible with securitization and state repression.

The failure of neoliberalism to transform economic structures reinforces the importance of control over the state as a site of (power) accumulation; (re)politicizing ethnicity in the process. Attempts to displace domestic tensions in Ethiopia have resulted in 'saber rattling' along the Ethio-Eritrean border. The chapter concludes by arguing that civil society, by itself, offers limited potential to achieve human security, which is dependent on the transformation of broader politico-economic structures and a reconceptualization of the relationship between (global) state, market and civil society. The following chapters examine the impacts of neoliberalism on the political economies of Zimbabwe and South Africa, and what the security implications have been.

During the 1980s, Zimbabwe was hailed internationally as an African success story, with a stable economy and 'good' governance. It was, in theory at least, a multiparty democracy that had transcended the legacy of racial division and grown its economy, while extending social services to the majority of the population. All of this was to tragically change in the 1990s. This chapter looks at why this has been the case, with a particular focus on the interaction between the presidency of Robert Mugabe, neoliberalism and the contradictory nature of resistance to the neoliberal state in civil society, among both 'war veterans' and trade unions.

While in the international media, it is the land question which has received the most attention, this chapter argues that Zimbabwe's economic crisis, military adventurism in the Democratic Republic of the Congo, and descent into authoritarian violence and electoral manipulation can be explained through a focus on the deindustrializing effects of neoliberal economic reform, and the resistance this engendered in different elements of civil society to the political structure. In particular, it argues that Robert Mugabe sought to undermine resistance to his rule in civil society through the development and co-optation of 'semi' or 'uncivil' society in the form of the war veterans and youth militias. The attempt to merge civil society and the state represents a 'neo-feudal' strategy, where land is presented as the economy. The implications of this strategy for Zimbabwe are then explored.

South Africa is the main country involved in its promotion of NEPAD, and the purported economic 'engine' of continental renewal. Zimbabwe is often held up as a test case for NEPAD, as the nostrums of 'good governance' are blatantly and repeatedly violated there, and yet Robert Mugabe continues to receive tacit support from the South African government through economic backing and political cover. This can only be understood in reference to the regional context. In order to deepen regional market access for South African business, the government of Thabo Mbeki must remain in step with the sentiments of political leaders in the region in relation to Mugabe, who are supportive of him.

Given the relative size of its economy, what happens in South Africa affects not only Southern Africa but the entire sub-continent. The relatively peaceful liberation of South Africa from white apartheid minority rule in 1994 has been widely acclaimed as a 'miracle.' However, the expectations of liberation have not been met; with the reality of worsening unemployment and deteriorating living conditions for much of the population. This chapter explores why this has been the case through a focus on the interaction between the lingering socio-structural effects of apartheid and the globalization of the economy.

South Africa does not have a World Bank/IMF program, but its adoption of neoliberalism was largely to do with the internal structure of class power in South Africa. Whereas most developing countries have experienced globalization from the 'outside in,' in South Africa's case it has been substantially internally generated by the major business groups that dominate the economy, and the state. Large-scale business and state interests coincided in this project in that the opening up of the economy allowed divestment, which opened up space in the domestic economy for 'black economic empowerment.' Externally this imperative is expressed through NEPAD, as a form of regional neoliberalism. The social and spatial distributional impacts of these developments for South Africa and the region are then assessed.

Since the events of September 11, 2001 in the United States, neoliberal globalization has entered a new phase. This is marked by securitization; an attempt to strengthen the state along certain dimensions and repress elements of civil society. The final chapter examines the changing nature of globalization and US–Africa relations post-9/11. It argues that attempts to construct a new hegemony based on overt coercion and force in Africa are likely to fail because, investments in primary health and education under PRSPs notwithstanding, it underplays social reproduction. Chinese support of repressive governments in Zimbabwe and Sudan, is also further enflaming conflict on the continent.

The securitization of neoliberalism has taken two forms: (1) where the international community restores order in failed states and a PRSP is then adopted (as in Sierra Leone or the Democratic Republic of the Congo) and (2) where there is military cooperation to ensure continued 'free trade' in natural resources, particularly oil.

Neoliberalism attempts to embed the market logic in society through the state. This disembedded logic, however, creates security problems. Thus in order for globalization to be sustainable, it is a social logic that should be embedded in the market. Attempts to securitize neoliberalism are consequently also destined to fail.

Solutions to Africa's problems will, in an era of increased globalization, necessarily be multiscalar. The book concludes with suggestions on how to transform globalization to transcend the current development/-security impasse. This must proceed through the reform and integration of the current development architecture by adding a strong social welfare dimension to it, coupled with local reforms such as participatory budgeting, and more freedom for developing countries in determining their own economic priorities. A by-product of this approach would also be the recapacitation of the African state, central to development and the fulfillment of its military and police functions. Only through the redistribution of power and the transcendence of neoliberalism will there be security and development on the continent and more widely.

1
The Rise of Non-Governmental Organizations and the Civilization of Neoliberalism?[1]

Enter civil society. But precisely what has ventured upon the stage? Is this truly an actor, organically constituted? Is its corporeal being only an illusion of distant perception, dissolving as one approaches? Is it merely a metaphor masquerading as a player? Is it yet another child of the anthropomorphic fertility of the social scientific imagination? Or do we spy a redemptive spirit, providentially dispatched to right a political world gone awry?

(Young, 1994, p. 43)

Global development and civil society

Major changes are currently underway in global development. While some World Bank officials celebrate state collapse in parts of Africa as enabling the creation of genuine market economies *de novo* (Bayart *et al.*, 1999) as juridical sovereignty was threatened in parts of the continent, 'underdevelopment turned dangerous' (Duffield, 2001). This created negative externalities for the international system in terms of crime, unwanted migration, the spread of AIDS, terrorism and a variety of other 'public bads'; and this, combined with the global economic crisis in the late 1990s (Brenner, 1998) and transnational activism, necessitated a new approach to development and a widening of the concept of security. Consequently at the end of the last millennium there were significant, but evolutionary, changes in both the global discourse of development and in the global aid architecture and regimes. This new architecture is comprised of five elements. According to Simon Maxwell (2003, pp. 5–6) these are:

(i) the Millennium Development Goals (MDGs), with poverty reduction at their heart;
(ii) international consensus on how to reduce poverty, best summarized in the World Bank's *World Development Report 2000/2001: Attacking Poverty*;
(iii) a mechanism for operationalizing the strategy at country level, in Poverty Reduction Strategy Papers (PRSPs);
(iv) technologies for delivering aid in support of PRSPs, notably Medium-Term Expenditure Frameworks, Sector-Wide Approaches (SWAPs) and Poverty Reduction Support Credits (PRSC), all associated with budget support rather than project funding; and
(v) underpinning the other four, a commitment to Results-Based Management.

This new architecture is underpinned by particular philosophies, values and concepts. The new watchwords and metrics are now civil society, social capital, participation, partnership, policy coherence, good governance and democracy. All of these are concepts derived from Western historical experience; however, they are applied as if they are unproblematic, unequivocal, trans-geographical and historical concepts (Mercer, 2002). Whereas up until the early 1990s, the development debate was posed in terms of 'states or markets' (Colcough and Manor, 1991), the answer was found during that decade 'outside the (political) box' – civil society.

For Howell and Pearce (2001, p. 1) 'civil society has established itself at the beginning of the twenty-first century as a significant, even paradigmatic concept in the field of development policy and practice.' Björn Beckman (1993) goes further and argues that '"the liberation of civil society" from the suffocating grip of the state has become the hegemonic ideological project of our time.' Civil society is now thought to be the 'missing middle' between citizens and the state (Garrison, 2000), whereas social capital is the 'missing link' in development for the World Bank (Grootaert, 1997). However, the problem noted above applies in relation to the concept of civil society; namely that

> underpinning the notion of civil society are principles central to Western political thought, such as the presumed existence of a public sphere bound together by universal citizenship, the recognition of

individual autonomy and rights, and a collective conception of justice and moral order.

(Encarnación, 2000, p. 12)

Part of the reason for the change in discourse and practice has to do
with the failure of the previous system to deliver its anticipated benefits. Poverty in some regions, particularly in sub-Saharan Africa, has
continued to increase markedly (White and Killick, 2001). Bi-lateral
donors, international financial institutions and the United Nations realized that previous modalities of development planning were both exclusionary and, consequently, ineffective because they were seen to be
externally driven and insufficiently 'country-owned' by both domestic
states and civil societies. The failure of previous structural adjustment
programs (SAPs) was blamed on 'recalcitrant' and/or 'recidivist' states,
leading donors to impose new governance conditionalities, with civil
society acting as a watchdog (Howell and Pearce, 2001). The new aid
regime seeks to accelerate market penetration by engendering the social
stability required for this to happen (Fowler, 2004a).

Events outside Africa also contributed to this changed direction. The
growth of civil society was seen in Western policy circles as central to
the collapse of totalitarian regimes in Eastern Europe, and this is one of
the reasons for its new prominence in development policy (Chandhoke,
2001). This conjuncture, combined with 'global civil society' pressure
around the issue of debt in particular, led to a re-evaluation of the global
aid and development architecture and an attempt to re-embed the
development policy formation process more firmly in domestic soil
(Inter-Africa Group, 2002). A key element of this new agenda is the
greater use of participatory methods and greater civil society engagement in the development policy formulation and implementation
processes. This chapter will assess the etiology and theory behind this
shift in neoliberal development strategy toward civil society in the
1980s and 1990s, focusing particularly on the role of non-governmental
organizations (NGOs).

Defining civil society

Development, poverty, state, society and civil society are all contested
terms. Some neoliberals and Marxists argue 'there is no such thing as
society,' as Margaret Thatcher famously opined. For Michael Mann
(1986) there are only social networks. However, people often refer to
'capitalist societies,' in which what unites society is the imbrication of

its component members and households in innumerable webs and networks of market exchange. In this sense the economy and its structuration are constitutive of society. This is a paradox because despite being embedded (Boyer and Hollingsworth, 1997), markets also tend to be individuating.

There is a large literature on the nature of civil society. It means different things to different people and agencies. However, there are common intersubjective understandings of the term among different groups, organizations and 'epistemic communities' (Haas, 1992). As such civil society is an ideational/organizational and political concept with multiple, geographically differentiated and shifting meanings, but with political force.

The idea of civil society in development policy is tied up with the idea of 'good governance,' which has its origins in the new institutional economics. Good governance is equated with political and economic liberalization in World Bank publications (World Bank, 1996c), and rose to the fore with the end of the Cold War. In part this reflected Western countries' 'natural preference' for democracy (Sandbrook, 1993). However, political conditionality also served as a cover for dramatic reductions in aid with the end of the Soviet bloc (Duffield, 1993). The reincarnation of the World Bank as a self-proclaimed 'knowledge bank' may also speak to this (as well as to the rise of the global information economy).

It is important to get a sense of the diversity of the different meanings of the term 'civil society' in order to be able to assess the ways in which it is deployed, the ways in which it is used to crystallize power and its material effects. The term civil society has its origins in the Latin term *civilis societas*, dating from the 1400s (Van Rooy, 1998). It gained greater currency in Europe in the eighteenth century as it was during this time that the Industrial Revolution was taking hold in the Continent, and the economy, society and state came to be seen as separate spheres of activity (Teivainen, 2002).

The traditional liberal definition of civil society sees it as a sphere of intermediate associations that is autonomous from the household and the state. Different liberal definitions have somewhat different inflections, but share this core. Examples of definitions in this tradition include the following:

1. Civil society refers to those groups, networks and relationships that are not organized or managed by the state (Narayan *et al.*, 2000, p. 129).
2. Civil society is generally understood as 'the population of groups formed for collective purposes primarily outside of the State and the marketplace' (Van Rooy, 1998a cited in Lewis, 2002, p. 570).

3. The realm of organized social life that is voluntary, self-generating, (largely) self-supporting, autonomous from the state, and bound by a legal order or set of shared rules (Diamond, 1994, p. 5).
4. An arena where manifold social movements . . . and civic organizations from all classes . . . attempt to constitute themselves in an ensemble of arrangements so that they can express themselves and advance their interests (Stephan, 1988, pp. 3–4).
5. That area of organized human activity concerned with the exercise of state authority which functions between the state and the family (Barkan, 1994, p. 92).

It is important to note the different emphases in these definitions. Definition 1 includes private sector firms. Definition 2 excludes market institutions but claims that civil society is outside of the state. Definition 3 notes the importance of legal order and hence the dependence of civil society on the state. Definition 4 may seem an odd inclusion as it brings in the notion of class, but it does not posit a definite relation with the state, whereas definition 5 posits that the *raison d'être* of civil society is to influence the state. Others working in the liberal tradition would also add that civil society is a space of voluntary, as opposed to ascriptive, association. However, for scholars working in a more critical tradition the strict separation of state and civil society in liberal definitions is a fatuous one.

In the alternative genealogy of civil society, the history of mutual support and solidarity is given greater emphasis (Howell and Pearce, 2001). Most people might agree that human nature has both selfish and selfless dimensions and that which of these achieves prominence is, in part, culturally determined. Liberal interests and institutions are built around the individual. However, societies are more complex than that.

Some commentators put civil society in quotation marks to emphasize the tentative and liminal nature of the concept (Rothchild and Lawson, 1994). For Jurgen Habermas (1990, quoted in Ehrenber, 1999), 'its institutional core comprises those non-governmental and non-economic connections and voluntary associations that anchor the communication structures of the public sphere in the society component of the life-world'. In this definition the relation between civil society and the state is hinted at. It is the contribution of civil society to the public realm, and hence its democratic function which is foremost in this definition. Following on from this civil society can also be seen as 'a space or realm defined by newly constituted norms about what the state should and should not do and by the rules of politics in that space, including politics by non-state actors' (Callaghy, 1994).

In the Gramscian tradition, civil society is the ensemble of 'institutions, ideologies, practices and agents . . . that compromise the dominant culture of values' (Carnoy, 1984, p. 70). In this conceptualization, capitalism is dependent on its domination of state, market and civil society for its reproduction. In particular the power of the state is bolstered and structured through the workings of civil society. This capitalist 'hegemony' is achieved through framing the discursive rules of the public sphere to achieve an accepted 'common sense' (Ruppert, 2000). However, civil society is itself fractured along class, ethnic, regional, religious, gender, clan and other lines. It is a site of different, overlapping social forces; some are oppositional to the state and others are deeply imbricated with it. Civil society is thus a 'space which reflects the social divisions of society as a whole' (Pearce, 1997b, p. 72). It is an arena where citizens can organize to defend or contest existing power distributions in society (Kohn, 2002). Thus capitalism may give rise to civil society, rather than civil society giving rise to capitalism, as many donors would have it.

For Gramsci, the degree of structuration (organization and ideological coherence) of civil society determined its nature. However, in this conception the more structured civil society, the more conservative it is; and its development becomes a hegemonic, rather than a counter-hegemonic, project. Where civil society is 'gelatinous' and 'primitive' it neither serves the interests of bourgeois hegemony (coercion informed by consent) nor resists the intrusions of the (colonial) predatory state. According to Crawford Young 'not the least tribute to the originality of the Italian communist theoretician is international aid agencies' unacknowledged (and unconscious) appropriation of his reading of civil society as being defined by structuration' (Young, 1994, p. 36).

The Gramscian definition of civil society is not hegemonic in critical theory, however. For example, for Jean-Francois Bayart (1986, cited in Young, 1994, p. 44), who is sometimes referred to as a 'rational choice Marxist,' civil society is

> society in its relation to the state . . . in so far as there is a self-consciousness of its existence and of its opposition to the state . . . the process by which society seeks to 'breach' and counteract the simultaneous 'totalization' unleashed by the state.

This definition speaks to the 'over-developed' nature of the African state, inherited from colonialism (Alavi, 1972).

This idea of civil society as a space is further developed by constructivists for whom it is an idea and discourse.

'Civil society' is the outcome of the process in which the idea of civil society is discursively constructed and used by donor agencies, international NGOs, the . . . government and . . . social organizations to legitimate their actions.

(Whitfield, 2003, p. 379)

As such it is both an idea and a process, 'conceptualized as a field of struggle between organized social groups' (Whitfield, 2003, p. 380). For Lindsay Whitfield the idea of civil society may be hegemonic, counter-hegemonic or tactical, in which it is used for instrumental purposes, such as donor support for the construction of 'autonomous civil society.' Some also distinguish between 'latent' and 'active' civil society depending on the level of engagement with/opposition to the state (VonDoepp, 1996). Where the state has substantial influence, but does not control, we may talk of 'semi-civil societies' (Boagang, 1997).

Civil society is used by donors as a universalizing discourse. 'For all donors civil society is defined predominantly in sociological fashion as a sphere of intermediary organization, which unlike the market is "not-for-profit" and unlike the state is "non-authoritative"' (Howell and Pearce, 2001, p. 112). Civil society is meant to have a solidaristic ethos to complement the public ethos of the state and the private one of the market. Thus although mutually imbricated and constituted, and sometimes infused with overlapping values, the three spheres remain analytically distinct. Paradoxically, part of the problem is that the African state, in some cases, has become a market for private influence (Lemarchand, 1991). Neoliberals do not address why the same should not happen to civil society, particularly in the context of substantial aid flows. Also the extent to which civil society is nonauthoritative is open to question, particularly in an African context, as will be discussed later.

Different donors use definitions with somewhat different emphases. For example, the United Nations Development Programme (UNDP) equates civil society with social movements constructed around ideals (Riddell and Bebbington, 1995). For the UNDP (1993), 'civil society is the sphere in which social movements become organized.' However, as will be discussed later, the UNDP's engagement in the construction of the new hegemonic development discourse may serve to coopt and demobilize these social movements.

Some argue that the donor preoccupation with action (an 'operational approach,' in the language of the United States Agency for International Development – USAID) over analysis has led to such an impoverished conception of civil society that it can be used as an 'analytical hatstand' to their political agenda (White, 1993). Given the complexity of development, an organizing concept like civil society is very appealing but by oversimplification it may lead to flawed policy and action (Roper-Renshaw, 1994). This in turn has discursive and ultimately material effects, as will be discussed later.

According to McIlwaine (1998b, p. 652),

> There are no precise definitions of what civil society actually means, which in turn, relates to a lack of recognition of the theoretical complexities surrounding the term. The upshot has been the reification of civil society and a tendency to hail it as the answer to many of the ills of the South. Second, while criticisms of the concept have been largely made on ideological grounds, few writers have highlighted the need to account for geographical diversity. The call for recognizing this differentiation can be made at a range of spatial scales; perhaps the most obvious has been the imposition of the concept of civil society onto societies of the South with little attempt at contextualization.

Geographic diversity in the definition of civil society is revealed by the fact that Southern participants at a seminar in 1995 rejected the 'cookie-cutter' transfer of the concept as a form of cultural imperialism, which whitewashed away the long history of social struggles for civil, political and social rights across the world (Van Rooy, 1998). For McIlwaine (1998b, p. 652), however, 'the key to what constitutes civil society rests on some form of coordinated activity beyond the sphere of the individual and household, and beyond the confines of the state.' As such it is a trans-historical sphere of social reproduction, rather than an entity in itself.

While there is little agreement on the meaning of the term, Mary Kaldor (2003, p. 10) argues that there is a common core around all definitions of civil society as 'a rule governed society based on the consent of individuals.' For her, civil society includes the 'third sector,' social movements and neo-traditional groupings. On the other hand, for Alison Van Rooy (1998) there are six viewpoints on what constitutes civil society: value, collective noun, historical moment, space for action, anti-hegemony and antidote to state. Which of these achieves prominence is geographically contextual, with anti-hegemony in civil society evident in Mexico and Thailand, but civil society broadly supportive of neoliberal hegemony in Vietnam, for example (Hakkarainen *et al.*, 2002). This speaks to the often oppositional nature of civil society to the state, with reactions against the neoliberal state and free market in Mexico and Thailand to the fore, and against the Communist State in Vietnam.

Theories and types of civil society organizations

There are two main types of social movement theory: new social movement theories and resource mobilization theories. New social movements, such as the women's movement, arose in Europe and the US in the 1960s. There were also new peasant and urban social movements in parts of the developing world. In the urban context these were often around what Manuel Castells (1983) has called the 'collective means of consumption,' or social infrastructure. There are also other theories of civil society, such as the regime and associational schools, which see civil society as a transmission belt from the individual to the state (Mohan, 2002).

Gramscian theory is linked to research on social movements which seek to transform structures of power and identity, and the state (Lewis, 2002). In the Gramscian tradition social movements refer to three converging components: 'to the actors (groups) involved; to the values, beliefs, and claims (issues) articulated; and to the actions (events) carried out' . . . 'A social movement implies a dynamic in a given direction and a core set of overriding values that binds different actors to the same broader goal' (Ndegwa, 1996, p. 5).

Resource mobilization theory, based on a methodological individualism,[2] was developed by Mancur Olson. His question was, why do individuals come together to achieve collective goals? For Olson, social collectivities are 'distributional coalitions.' Contrary to popular perception, the most effective of these have limited membership, as this reduces coordination problems. In an African context, Bates (1984, 1987) applied this framework to show why the peasantry were numerous, but ineffective in influencing government policy.

While everyone has many overlapping identities, e.g. feminist, African, worker, 'soccer-mom' (Castells, 1997), many of these do not find overt political/associational expression. In Africa, only where the interests of the peasantry are coterminous with ethnicity, as in Sudan or Rwanda, are there likely to be vocal demands made on the state (Chazan *et al.*, 1999). Thus, in Africa, 'rather than being interpreted as fixed, rigid, and exclusive categories, class and ethnicity seem more accurately viewed situationally – in terms of social, economic, and political context in which various groups interact and attempt to achieve their collective purposes' (Chazan *et al.*, 1999, p. 127).

There are also many different types and structures of civil society organizations (CSOs). Depending on one's definition of what constitutes civil society, different organizations will be included/excluded. In talking about actors in development, Nederveen Pieterse (2001, p. 10) draws a distinction between structures and infrastructures. He considers formal NGOs and International NGOs (INGOs) to constitute 'structures' and 'people, social movements, trade unions, parties, firms, churches, etc.' to constitute 'infrastructures of power'. This approach allows for actor-orientation, agency and institutions and the idea that development is discursively constructed, with material effects (Lee, 2003) that interact and coevolve in dialectical fashion.

More specifically, van de Walle (2003, p. 6) defines NGOs as 'any private organization involved in development activities in which generating profit is not the only or primary purpose.' This definition is sufficiently broad to allow a focus 'downward' on service delivery to the poor or 'upward' to advocacy activities focused on the state. There are many different types of NGOs, such as those focused on development (NGDOs), INGOs and 'non-operational' Northern NGOs (NNGOs), which do not provide services directly, but may serve as a conduit for donor funds to Southern NGOs (SNGOs).

What about the distinction between NGOs and social movements? Perhaps one way to think about this is that NGOs tend to work in 'partnership' with the state, and may strive to be 'watchdogs' on the state, to ensure that it fulfils its functions. For Edwards and Fowler, 'NGDOs belong "in" civil society, but they are not solely "of" civil society because they purposefully work in the spaces between civil society, state and market' (Edwards and Fowler, 2004, pp. 8–9). On the other hand social movements seek a transformation in the nature of state power. However, 'it is more difficult to alter the behavior of those who feed you and NGDOs are not renowned for hunger strikes. In this light, non-aid related social movements might be a better bet in terms of changing the system' (Fowler, 2004b).

The transformative potential of social movements may be contrasted with NGOs. For example, a study for the World Bank (Narayan *et al.*, 2000, p. 130), drawing on participatory poverty assessments (PPAs) worldwide, found that while the 'potential for scaling up by working complementarily with the state is beginning to be tapped, especially in the delivery of basic services such as primary education, forest management, and drinking water . . . *there are few examples of NGOs addressing basic structural inequity'* (emphasis added). Furthermore a PPA in Kenya found that 'there was little or no evidence that any groups formed or assisted by NGOs had achieved any level of autonomy. Nor had they evolved into larger groups or diversified their activities' (Narayan *et al.*, 2000, p. 141). Perhaps as a consequence of this 'the poor invest heavily and place their trust much more readily in their own CBOs (community based organizations)' (Narayan *et al.*, 2000, p. 130). Consequently this report argues under the heading 'redistributing power is not high on the agenda', that 'organizations that help to increase the bargaining power of the poor, or to correct the fundamental power inequities at the household, community or state level, are conspicuous in their absence from the PPAs' (Narayan *et al.*, 2000, p. 131) perhaps as a result of state repression. This would appear to confirm Tarrow's (1994, cited in Hilhorst, 2003) insight that collective action doesn't come about as a response to deprivation, but to changes in political opportunity structure. Might this suggest that the World Bank and other donors should be funding groups such as the landless movement in Brazil?[3] However, the oppositional agenda may be submerged by donor funding. David Korten has argued that 'the surest way to kill a social movement is to throw funding at it' (Korten, 1990, cited in Nederveen Pieterse, 2001, p. 82).

Social movements are not necessarily counter-hegemonic, however. As Sklair (2001) has noted, probably the most powerful social movement in the world is the one in favor of global neoliberal capitalism. Phillip McMichael (2000) sees the neoliberal project as driven by a global social movement against social protection, organized through the World Economic Forum, World Trade Organization (WTO) and other venues.[4] Elite consensus is also forged in less public, transnational civil society groups such as the Bilderberg Group, the Trilateral Commission and the Council on Foreign Relations.[5] This brings out clearly the dialectical and class-divided nature of civil society.

Other types of CSOs include popular economic organizations, which may seek alternatives to the 'neoliberalization of space.' Fuller and Jonas (2003) draw a distinction between 'alternative oppositional,' 'alternative additional' and 'alternative-substitute' economic and social institutions. More work needs to be done on the definition and boundaries of these institutions. While some popular economic institutions, such as micro-finance or local exchange trading systems, may operate on a different logic to the individual profit maximization one, they may nonetheless serve to fill in structural holes in the capitalist market economy and thereby serve a legitimating function in the broader social formation. This perhaps speaks to the contradictory nature of civil society in that capitalism binds together the fragments of civil society. As such civil society is a 'crucial, yet double edged, element of the superstructure of capitalism' (Meiskin-Wood cited in Howell and Pearce, 2001, p. 71).[6]

Other important CSOs are 'community-based organizations [which] are grassroots organizations managed by members on behalf of members' (Edwards and Hulme, 1992) or 'organizations that originate within a community to meet its specific needs' (Michael, 2004). These are also sometimes referred to as People's Organizations (POs). The term 'sectoral movements' refers to 'grassroots' peasant or indigenous people's movements, POs of the urban poor or thematic movements, such as those around human rights (Hilhorst, 2003).

Mari Tripp (2003) notes in relation to local informal associations that the fact that they do not attract official attention may help them retain their self-help spirit but also prevent them from scaling-up and becoming more influential organizations. While Narayan *et al.* (2000) view informal associations as palliative, rather than transformative, Hilhorst's (2003) work in the Philippines shows that there may not be a clear separation between different types of CSOs, as the NGO she studied grew out of and remains part of a movement for regional autonomy. Local POs may also become social movements.

An interesting example of CBOs turning into a social movement and influencing the policy process is the Federations of Indigenous Networks in Ecuador. According to a PPA in Ecuador (1996 cited in Narayan *et al.*, 2000, p. 152):

> Building bridging networks is a long-term process that requires patience and nurturing. Rural people, including indigenous communities in Ecuador, have strong traditions of mutual support and labor exchange, strengthened by blood or ritual kinship ties. Over a period of two decades organizational capacity has been strengthened at the community level and linked to organizations at higher regional and national levels based on representation and common interest. Thus, at the lowest level, the unions link as many as 20 communities in one canton. These organizations, in turn, belong to a federation that operates on a provincial basis. The provincial networks combine into a national network. A community organization can approach the national-level organization directly. As a result of a proven ability to organize, including the 1993 March of Quito, indigenous organizations

are now part of the governance debates and decision-making at the local and national levels. They played a key role in defining the new Agrarian Law and ensuring rural bilingual education and have gained a significant degree of participation in municipal and national government. This organizational effort by indigenous people on their own behalf has been supported by a range of outsiders on a sustained basis over a period of 20 years.

'The fact that these organizations are "informal" and work according to gender, age or kinship ties rather than "interests" in the liberal sense has left academic researchers generally poorly equipped to make sense of the interactions of this "rural civil society" and the state' (Harrison, 2002, p. 96). For most donors '"modern" organizations are deemed to transcend in purpose and action any primordial attachments, mobilize people around common interests of a professional, economic or welfare kind and draw people out of the private into the public' (Howell, 2000, p. 14). However, informal, grassroots CSOs, such as burial societies, have also served political functions, expressing anti-colonial demands in Africa, for example (Makumbe, 1998 cited in Howell and Pearce, 2001). They continued to serve political functions under repressive postindependence developmentalist and revolutionary regimes (Mamdani, 1996). However, it is important not to romanticize CBOs and the local. As Nederveen Pieterse (2001, p. 66) argues,

> culture and development discourse in its strong form pleads for an alternative development based on local culture. In the process it attempts to erect boundaries – in a time of boundary crossing. It welcomes crossing disciplinary boundaries in order to strengthen the case for erecting cultural boundaries. As such it reflects a politics of nostalgia.

Others are equally skeptical of this 'postmodernism,' arguing that 'their evocation of local, small-scale solutions to massive social ills that can replace the "grand narratives" which provide systematic analyses of the causes of social problems as well as comprehensive solutions . . . It is difficult to see how the critical social needs of millions of people can be effectively addressed through ambiguous proposals of this kind' (Midgley, 1998, p. 98). However, as in the example of Ecuador above, CBOs can network and become social movements, and influence the state. Social movements are explicitly political and seek to bring about social change, although Hilhorst (2003) argues that social movements always 'dig their own grave' as they are coopted. However, some recent social movements, such as the Zapatistas, do not target the state as their object of attention, but rather internal community transformation to resist unwanted external intrusion (See Esteva and Prakesh, 1998).

Some argue that the poor are particularly vulnerable to social sanctions by power holders and there is therefore a critical need for intermediate institutions to represent their interests (Engberg-Pedersen and Webster, 2002). However, while trade unions tend to have democratic structures, many NGOs are characterized by 'personal rule' (Ndegwa, 1996). In Bangladesh, the Grameen Bank went to court to prevent the organization of its workforce (Stiles, 2002). Joseph Hanlon (2000) distinguishes between 'real' membership-based civil society struggling against governments and international organizations and 'contract' NGOs being paid to do things for other people.[7] Membership organizations (MOs), such as unions and women's organizations, often serve both representational and operational functions, thereby having the linkages which some donors purport to value (Bebbington and Riddell, 1997). An example where MOs have had a direct impact on poverty are the 'popular kitchens' and the Glass of Milk program, which were originally organized through women's organizations in Peru (Friedmann, 1992). However, many NGOs have a genuine commitment to the betterment of the human condition, and partnerships between NGOs and unions perhaps can be effective in poverty elimination (Gallin, 2000).

The political economy of donors and 'civil society': the rise of NGOs

The enormous rise in the number of development NGOs in the 1980s led some to speak of an 'associational revolution' (Salamon, 1994). Indeed NGOs accounted for over 5 percent of total employment in a survey of 22 countries (and substantially more if volunteers are included). The number and proliferation of INGOs roughly corresponds to the number of transnational corporations. There were 28,900 INGOs by 1993 and 35,000 by the end of the decade (United Nations Commission on Global Governance, 1995; Edwards, 2000). The United Nations Conference on Trade and Development (UNCTAD) calculated that there were 39,000 parent-company transnational corporations (TNCs) in the mid-1990s (UNCTAD, 1996). As such they can be thought of as different, but in some senses complementary, 'arms' of neoliberal globalization, with INGOs fulfilling the global legitimation required to offset the effects of global accumulation.

Nederveen Pieterse (2001, p. 49) argues that 'one of the questions that looms in the background is whether social movements and NGOs should serve as buffers against globalization, providing shelter from the storm and shielding local culture and local identity, or whether their role should be to help connect regions and communities to the global-ized economy.' The growth of NGOs globally is a response to the dys-functions of the market and state liberalization, meaning that it is itself constitutive of globalization. As John Toye (1987) notes, the increased prominence given to NGOs is part of the neoliberal counter-revolution in development, although also compensation for it, perhaps thereby neutralizing popular resistance to structural adjustment. Some go fur-ther and argue that NGOs act as 'Trojan horses for global neoliberalism' (Wallace, 2003 cited in Harvey, 2005). Taking a dialectical approach, Craig and Porter (2006, p. 61) argue that

> The rise of NGOs . . . is a fascinating example of Polanyi's 'enlight-ened reactionaries' at work, pitching themselves as both effective representer of the 'grassroots' and civil society (and thus as a coun-terbalance to both market and state failures), and a market-reliable deliverer of services to the marginal.

The rise of INGOs, along with economic liberalization, could also be seen as part of a double movement to hollow out the third world state, the principal node of resistance to neoliberalism in the 1980s and early 1990s. International NGOs look to boost local development and global reform, but often do not have a clearly stated position on how they see the articulation between the two.

The associational revolution was, in part, the taming of new social movements within the frame of global governance (Kaldor, 2003). NGOs' societal legitimacy is based on both the provision of substantial employment and services. Thus the political economy of neoliberalism may undermine the empowerment function of NGOs (Dicklitch, 1998). Nonetheless Ndegwa (1998, p. 2) found that in Kenya 'a clear effect of NGO grassroots development work is to enable local commu-nities to independently engage in political actions, with important implications for democratization.' This speaks to the dialectical nature of this development.

Substantial amounts of money are now channeled by donors through NGOs for service provision to the poor. Nederveen Pieterse (2001, p. 75) notes an 'enormous increase of development funds being channeled or re-channeled through NGOs during the past two decades (which now exceed the total annual disbursements through the IMF [International Monetary Fund] and World Bank).' In 1997, the Organization for Economic Cooperation and Development (OECD) estimates that INGOs managed the equivalent of a fifth of aid flows to Africa (Harris, 2003). Some 85 percent of Swedish aid is channeled through NGOs, versus 10 percent for the UK (Kaldor, 2003). Although with the new aid modality of direct budget support (DBS) to governments gaining prominence, this trend is now changing.

Overall *et al.* (cited in van de Walle, 2003) estimate roughly 30 percent of Northern development NGOs (NDNGOs) funding comes from official donors, making them much less dependent than SNGOs, where dependency rates typically vary from 80 to 95 percent. This raises the important issue of autonomy from donors and whether or not NGOs can influence donor policies (McIlwaine, 1998b). This will be discussed later in reference to Africa.

Africa has the largest number of World Bank projects involving NGOs (Gibbs *et al.*, 1999), although in the past the Bank has given more funding to CBOs, perhaps because they were deemed not to be 'political.' NGOs are better able to target the poor than traditional aid modalities, government or commercial institutions, but not the poorest (Riddell and Robinson, 1995, cited in van de Walle, 2003; Smillie and Helmich, 1993; Farrington and Bebbington, 1993, cited in Hulme and Edwards, 1997b). While the Bangladesh Rural Advancement Committee's (BRAC) programs in health and nutrition reach almost 30 million people, the largest NGOs in Bangladesh (including the Grameen Bank) together reach less than 20 percent of landless households (BRAC, 1999, cited in Michael, 2004; Farrington and Lewis, 1993).

Some NGOs, such as the People's Rural Education Movement (PREM) in India, demonstrate high impact at low cost (Edwards, 2004a), but, at most, NGDOs reach 20 percent of the world's poor, thereby suggesting an important role for advocacy (Fowler, 2000). This 'fourth position' sees the role of NGDOs as multi-sector negotiators, promoting and exacting compliance of their duties from power holders to deliver rights (Fowler, 2004c). However, this should be done in ways which do not compromise the social or horizontal politics of CSOs, concerned as they are with self-governance (Cheru, 2002). Some argue that in any case NGOs are not well positioned to perform this role, but that there must be political organizations for the poor that are autonomous from states and donors that can press to eradicate poverty (Gibbon, 1992). Also Edwards and Hulme (1996, p. 359) argue that much of the case for emphasizing the role of NGOs/GROs [grass roots organizations] rests on ideological grounds rather than empirical verification. In addition, although the evidence is inconclusive, there are signs that greater dependence on official funding may compromise NGO/GRO performance in many areas, distort accountability and weaken legitimacy.

Specifically, they argue (p. 361) that official funding

- encourages NGOs to become providers of social and economic services on a much larger scale than hitherto, even though their long-term comparative advantage in this field is doubtful;
- compromises the performance of NGOs and GROs in other areas of development activity, such as institutional development and advocacy;
- weakens the legitimacy of NGOs and GROs as independent actors in society;
- distorts the accountability of NGOs and GROs away from grassroots and internal constituencies, and over-emphasizes short-term, quantitative outputs [based on 'logical frameworks'].[8]

The more donor funding is the dominant factor in the development of NGOs, the less NGOs are likely to be representative of the values and aspirations of local populations, particularly of traditionally excluded social categories. NGO staff, even when they do not emerge from the civil service, are typically from the same elite educational and social background (van de Walle, 2003, p. 28).

Donor funding also has other impacts. 'The reasons for lackluster NGO performance vary, but the PPA reports and other literature on NGOs suggest that uncertain funding and limited management capacities hinder effectiveness and independence of NGOs' (Narayan *et al.*, 2000, p. 139). 'Some NGOs, fed up with their dependency, now consider their highest priority to be achieving financial independence for themselves and their clients' (Narayan *et al.*, 2000, p. 137).

Both states and NGOs are now expected by donors to conform to private sector organizational imperatives such as competition and 'efficiency.' According to some, this new managerialist regime risks making good governance 'privatization by another name' (Mawdsley and Rigg, 2003). Thus many African NGOs become 'managers of foreign aid money, not managers of local African development processes' (Nyang'oro, 1993), as attacking the structural drivers of poverty cannot be addressed using market principles (Edwards, 2004b). Nonetheless many donors favor the model of poverty alleviation through individual enterprise and self-employment ('promotion'), through micro-finance schemes for example, rather than through the public provision of basic needs ('protection') (Hulme and Edwards, 1997a). This is mirrored among some CSOs, such as Silveria House, a Catholic charity in Zimbabwe which shifted from supporting cooperative development to micro-enterprise and credit support in the 1990s (Sylvester, 2003). Donor funding of micro-finance can thus be seen as a form of 'public–private partnership.' As Hulme and Edwards (1997a, p. 10) note:

> NGOs are analyzed as non-profit private agencies accountable through the forces of competition in an open market. Beneficiaries and members become 'customers' (as BRAC in Bangladesh now terms the poor) and claims to be strengthening civil society become redundant. As with the private sector, 'empowerment' in such organizations is confined to leaders and managers.

Such provision may undermine the link between citizens and the state, reducing voice and accountability and thereby political rights, the central feature of good government (Wood, 1997).

Civil society is not a free-floating, feel-good sector with a nonmaterial existence; it must have an economic base. Parts of civil society in Africa, such as trade unions, have been hollowed out by the continent's economic crisis. The nature of this economic base will in part determine the nature of civil society 'outputs.' It may be a case that where aid provides this base there may be a 'he who pays the piper' or donor inputs => donor outputs (DIDO) syndrome.

> Yet as long as the assumptions that donors uncritically make about the compatibility of civil society with capitalism are left unexplored, it is unlikely that civil society strengthening programs can yield the results that donors might wish. . . . Should civil society function mainly as a way of compensating for market and state failures or can it also serve as a counterweight to market despotism? Whom within civil society should and do, donors support?
>
> (Howell and Pearce, 2001, p. 87)

'Donors' are unwilling to problematize the relation between capitalism and civil society, however. In the case of USAID, it gives untied funding to prospective client NGOs on the condition that they do not have major alternative sources of funding, creating what a review of its programs in South Africa called 'AID-dependent NGOs' (Hanlon, 2000). Such donor-created NGOs (DCNGOs) may then feed into the PRSP process. American NGOs that receive USAID funding have been told to regard themselves as 'an arm of the US government' (Interaction, 2003, cited in Michael, 2004).

In addition to increased social need and the availability of large amounts of funding for their operations, there are other forces driving the formation of domestic NGOs. 'The founders of NGOs are the victims of economic recession who see the establishment of an NGO as the solution to their financial and employment problems' (Narayan *et al.*, 2000, p. 139). In some cases they are members of a displaced elite, excluded from access to state patronage.

While many NGOs are characterized by personal rule, nonetheless 'beneficiaries' may also have structural power to represent NGOs in particular ways through discourse and action, and thereby to make NGOs conform to them (Hilhorst, 2003). This highlights the contested and negotiated nature of power relationships. Likewise, donors are dependent on NGOs, to some extent, as NGOs may choose donors, and this means the social interface between the two is subject to negotiation, as well as coercion. Hilhorst (2003, p. 193) notes that 'while strong critique is often voiced against the direct interference of donors in NGO policies . . . the more damning objection to donor influence may be that it frames the very terms of what constitutes NGOs, society, development and social change.' In support of this, an analysis of a meeting between UN representatives and an NGO in the Philippines found that UN staff took up 80 percent of the speaking time (Hilhorst, 2003). Donors exercise infrastructural power by getting NGOs to 'willingly' rethink their priorities to fit with donor agendas (Michael, 2004).

Power is thus crystallized and constituted in NGOs. Donor funding for NGOs may stem partly from the fact that they are often thought to be apolitical; however Hilhorst argues that 'everything happening in and around NGOs has a bearing on the politics of power within the organizations, the politics of organizational legitimation and, finally, the politics of (local and global) development,' and that they do make ideological choices (Hilhorst, 2003, p. 4). For her the question is not what an NGO is, but how 'NGO-ing' is done. As Michael Barnett and Raymond Duvall (2004, p. 10) note 'if power is in social relations of constitution, it works in fixing what actors are as social beings, which, in turn, defines the meaningful practices in which they are disposed to engage as subjects; constitutive power, then shapes behavioral tendencies.' Designating themselves as NGOs is thus a claim-bearing label. They can at times close down alternative discourses[9] – thereby engaging in what has been termed 'discursive violence.' Of course NGOs present different faces to different stakeholders, and there may also be subversive 'hidden transcripts' at play within the organization.[10] However, how effective these are at bringing about material change is open to debate.

2
Civil Society, Governance and Transformation

The World Bank's total lending in 1993 was the equivalent of the amount transferred by international capital
markets in the space of nine minutes. The idea that aid,
can, will or does 'make a difference' to world development or the distribution of poverty is illusory; far larger
forces are at play.

(Fowler, 2004d, p. 296)

It was from within civil society that the opposition to
authoritarian rule emerged and therefore it was imperative to 'penetrate civil society and from therein assure
control over popular mobilization. . . . Robinson continues . . . 'The composition and balance of power in
civil society in a given Third World country is now just
as important to US and transnational interests as who
controls the governments of those countries. This is a
shift from social control "from above" to "social control
from below."'

(W. Robinson, 1996a, p. 94 quoted in Hearn,
2000, p. 816)

There is a distinction between immanent (world) development and
imminent (managed) development. 'Imminent development, led by a
belief in the "makeability" of society, emerged over the past two centuries
largely as a means of managing those "surplus populations" that have
either been excluded from or "adversely incorporated" into processes of
immanent development' (Cowen and Shenton, 1996, cited in Hickey and
Mohan, 2004b, p. 10). In this context there is a fundamental question

about whether the role of civil society in development is palliative or transformative. Initially the donor emphasis on direct funding for NGOs for service provision was palliative, particularly during the 1980s, and very few NGOs have well-developed theories of why poverty arises (Fowler, 2004d). Increased funding from donors partly arose because donors view NGOs as more accountable, and have to negotiate less detailed programs with them than they do with national governments (Stiles, 2002). However, as noted above, there were also political impacts to this funding. The emphasis of donor funding, particularly with the collapse of the Soviet bloc, subsequently moved on to governance and transformation.

Many scholars have noted the shift from government to governance as state–society relations have become less authoritative. Governance is a mode of rule through which diverse actors are incorporated into 'action-centered networks' (Carley and Christie, 2000) with defined rules of membership and engagement. As such governance, in this sense, is the enactment of globalization (McGuirk, 2005). It is reflective of the structural power of transnational corporations; perhaps the dominant governance institutions on the planet (Korten, 1995). Indeed rather than thinking of the global economy as deregulated, we may see society as being in an era of 'market regulation' (Standing, 1999).

According to Tom Young (1995) it is the 'liberal project' which needs a suitably defined civil society. This is because

> for it to flourish, and in its flourishing, civil society thus requires a state which is limited, non-interventionary, and which furthers the 'freedoms' of individual citizens, notably their market freedoms.
>
> (Allen, 2004, p. 266)

The idea of civil society, in its current most common usage, is thus bound up with the notion of liberal democracy. It may even be a source of competitiveness, as for some there is a correlation between democracy and technological development and advancement. Given structural changes to the world economy, Cardoso argues that 'either the South (or a portion of it) enters the democratic-technological-scientific race, invests heavily in R and D [research and development] and endures the "information economy" metamorphosis, or it becomes unimportant, unexploited, and unexploitable' (Cardoso, 1993 quoted in Nederveen Pieterse, 2001, p. 47).

The increased interest in the role that civil society can play in improved governance and poverty reduction is a revival of modernization theory

(Barkan, 1994). As mentioned earlier, civil society is a Western concept and its transplantation to Africa may be both ahistorical and aspatial. According to Barkan (1994, p. 89):

It is a permutation of the modernization paradigm, however, that places less emphasis on central institutions and the elites that control them than the original formulation of three decades ago and more emphasis on how organized interests in society seek to establish linkages with the state to make it more responsive to their needs.

The theory is that 'the more the members of society organize themselves into groups to advance their particular interests, the less likely the state can function in an autonomous and unaccountable manner' (Barkan, 1994, p. 91). While this may be true, what types of particularistic interests should be advanced: business associations (cartels) or organizations of the poor? The teleological assumption of a strong civil society leading to development is flawed (Howell and Pearce, 2001).

The modernization perspective sees political and economic liberalization as mutually reinforcing as political freedoms allow a more liberal and flexible economy, which results in higher growth, thereby bolstering democratic governance. It is also argued that market economies disperse social power, reinforcing pluralist politics. The exact channels through which this 'virtuous circle' are created are, however, unspecified, particularly as free markets have an inherent tendency to undercut their own competitive bases, through the concentration and centralization of capital (Krugmann, 1995), leading to the necessity of anti-trust legislation and competition authorities. In its new incarnation, the neoliberal virtuous circle is established by social investment and social capital getting the economics right, NGOs and social capital righting society, and civil society participation getting the politics right, as will be explored later. Thus civil society is meant to play a central role in the transformation of societies, economies and polities, from which donors are 'autonomous.'

There is a dialectical tension between the different elements of the neoliberal agenda, however. Adam Przeworski (1991) has noted contradictions between economic and political reforms as it may take 'strong' governments to undertake politically unpopular economic reforms. 'The successful experiences of the newly industrializing countries (NICs) of East Asia and the economic reform efforts of authoritarian governments in Uganda and Ghana provide support for this view' (Chazan *et al.*, 1999).

In fact the 'capacity of these [latter] regimes to resist or to remain adamant in the face of popular opposition to economic reform policies is part of "good" governance' (Kankwenda, 2004, p. 13). Thus Thomas Callaghy (1994, p. 247) argues that

> democratic politics require a viable economic base. Yet their very existence may make the creation and consolidation of such a base even more difficult than it is already.

This is because democracy and capitalism operate on different logics; one public, the other individual (Terreblanche, 2002). Hence the paradox that the embedding of the global market requires a 'capable state' to manage local social instability (Craig and Porter, 2006).

Some refer to the new regime type, in Uganda for example, as 'low-intensity democracy – a compromise between psuedo-democratic institutions and dictatorships that enjoy little popular support' (Adedeji *et al.* [1997] cited in Anon., 2004b, p. 235). However,

> who can reasonably object to 'good governance', 'democracy', 'civil society', 'transparency'? Of course each of these can be unpacked. Thus, embedded in 'good governance' is the contentious idea that the free market and democracy go together.
>
> (Nederveen Pieterse, 2001, p. 164)

Thus partly what is at issue is the definition of these terms. Whereas donors see a strengthened civil society as a way of ending inefficient and corrupt political economies, many Africans view it as a way of protecting them from the ravages of neoliberal economic reform (Callaghy, 1994).

The increased emphasis on civil society by donors could be seen as a new '*mission civilatrise,*' with Yash Tandon (1996) referring to NGOs as the 'missionaries of the new era.' Meanwhile, the emphasis on governance could be read as an attempt to save neoliberalism from itself (Munck, 2005).

Beckman (1993, p. 57) puts it thus:

> It is in this contest that the neo-liberal project intervenes, prodding the state to be more responsive to interests of capital and private property. The intervention is made in the name of civil society as opposed to the state, while its consequences are to intensify state intervention in suppressing existing forces of civil society, including those converging

within the public service nexus; it is also an intervention on the side of capital within the capital-labor relations. In either case, the existing civil society is portrayed as 'vested interests' which need to be combated in the interest of a civil society yet to come.

The organized social groups that most actively articulate the defense of the autonomy of civil society vis-à-vis the state can be found within and around the public service nexus, e.g. teachers, students, doctors, lawyers and journalists.

Thus civil society is an arena where different class, ethnic and gender projects, and associated NGOs and social movements confront each other.

Governments may pursue a twin-track strategy to repress and co-opt civil society groups opposed to economic liberalization (Bangura and Beckman, 1993; Jega, 1993), whereas groups that are not supportive of the neoliberal project are often defined out of civil society by donors. The World Bank has not undertaken any research on the role of trade unions in African development, for example (Sender, 2002). This is because in the neoliberal schema organized labor are 'rent seekers,' engaging in market distortions. To correct this in neoliberal discourse labor is depoliticized as 'human capital.' 'Laborers [become] . . . autonomous entrepreneurs with full responsibility for their own investment decisions . . . They are entrepreneurs of themselves' (Lemke, 2001 cited in Sinha, 2005, p. 166). Indeed Thandika Mkandawire (2004) argues that PRSPs are opposed to existing social movements, especially the labor movement, preferring instead to incorporate a few NGOs, who benefit as service providers. Although it is important to note that an important discursive shift is underway at the Bank in its 2006 World Development Report, *Equity and Development*, it is praiseful of unions, participatory budgeting and even the Kerala model of development, where a Communist government has long held sway.[1] Indeed another World Bank report argues that if natural resource losses as a result of export-orientation are taken into account, much of Africa is poorer than it would be otherwise (World Bank, 2005d, cited in Bond, 2006). However, power is crystallized in the World Bank, as its policies must be attractive to the international bond market, and developing country governments were successful in stopping the Bank using the term 'primary stakeholders' for those living in poverty most affected by development projects (Chambers, 2006).

As noted earlier, the concept of good governance also extends to the creation of appropriate regulatory institutions, legal environments and the implementation of neoliberal economic policy. Graham Harrison

(2004b) argues that some African states, particularly Uganda, Tanzania and Mozambique have internalized the nostrums of good governance becoming what he terms 'governance states.' In Tanzania there is even a Ministry of Good Governance (Shivji, n.d.). The question here is 'good for whom?' As noted earlier, in this formulation 'good governance' and the insulation of key economic ministries and institutions from society can transcend democracy (Harriss, 2002). In Tanzania, user fees are still in place for primary health care, raising about US $12m a year (Rajani, 2004). Meanwhile former President Mkapa bought a personal jet and £40m was spent on a controversial and unnecessary military radar system, bought from the UK with Tony Blair's approval (Porteous, 2005). Governance can indeed be good, for some.

In Cameroon an unaccountable and unelected board made up of state, donor and civil society representatives was set up to monitor and supervise debt relief expenditure (Brown, 2004). In this way 'good governance' becomes a way of 'subordinating politics and political actors to the demands of the orthodox structural adjustment model in the belief that it is a model that is essentially coherent, settled and inevitable, the only challenge being left being to (re)orient politics and public administration in its support' (Olukoshi, 2003, p. 230).

However, these new undemocratic structures are not immune from rent-seeking and corruption. Recently it emerged that the British government had paid £712,000 of 'aid' money for hotels and meals, through a US consultancy company, for Malawian members of parliament and members of NGOs. The purpose of this wining and dining was 'to debate the establishment of committees that would scrutinize the work of the Malawian government' (*BBC News*, 2005b).[2]

'Good governance' is tied up with the new public management theory of 'joined-up government,' accountability, competition, and also involves using targets and indicators. New public management theory does have a 'social control' current, but in general citizen-consumers can express their preferences through market mechanisms and exit from state services in favor of private ones (if they can afford it) (Ackerman, 2004). However, residualism and withdrawal from the public realm may undermine social capital and citizenship (Cunill, n.d.; Wallis and Dollery, 2001, cited in Ackerman, 2004). Nonetheless, this issue is elided in the new aid regime as participatory democratic institutions are meant to transform state–society linkages to establish synergies and erode the basis of the patrimonial state.

As Adrian Leftwich (2000, p. 151) argues 'there have been some democracies and some non-democracies that have been developmentally

successful, and it is therefore crystal clear that regime type (that is democratic or not) has had little to do with it.' However, he suggests that
one of the features of developmental democracies, and developmental
states more generally, is a 'weak and subordinated civil society.' This has
been the case in rapidly industrializing countries such as China, and in
what is widely accepted to be mainland sub-Saharan Africa's most successful country, Botswana. (Edge and Kekorwe, 1998, cited in Hope,
2002; Howell and Pearce, 2001) There the state integrated rural society
through the village *kgotla*, which served as a forum for consultation and
reinforcement of customary authority (Holm and Molutsi, 1992).[3] On-
the-other-hand, some of the poorest countries in the world, such as
Bangladesh, have vibrant associational sectors. This speaks to a broader
problem with liberal-democratic theory.

> It puts more weight on good governance procedures than on pro-
> poor governance results [thereby violating one of the nostrums of
> the new public management theory] . . . discusses state reform with-
> out discussing reform of the wider social-political power relations
> and . . . discusses changes in the relationship between 'non-poor' and
> 'poor' in terms of positive sum games and not in terms of redistribu-
> tion of economic and political resources.
>
> (Braathen, 2000, p. 40)

However, a weak civil society may also provide conditions for developmental disasters as documented by Scott (1998). Where social development, understood in the narrow sense of improving social indicators,
is a prime concern, through redistributionist and community initiatives, this may be compatible with liberal democracy. Thus it is important to examine the multi-dimensionality and differences between
developmental regimes.

Governing civil society and state through 'partnership'

Before its poverty refocusing/branding in the mid-90s the World Bank
was skeptical of the power of NGOs which 'by definition . . . are peripheral to the systems they are trying to change and lack the leverage necessary to maintain their influence when there are other, more powerful
interests at work' (World Bank, 1991, cited in Edwards and Hulme,
2004, p. 62). They may, however, serve a useful role as junior partners
in the constitution/legitimation of the emergent transnational historic
bloc and its hegemony. As the Bretton Woods Institutions (BWIs) have

no direct public constituency in developing countries, hence the importance of NGDOs and religious organizations engaging in 'partnership' with them (Fowler, 2004c). While donors tend to refer to CSOs as 'partners,' CSOs themselves tend to refer to their funders as donors rather than partners (Hakkarainen *et al.*, 2002).

The World Bank (2000c) envisages civil society playing a watchdog role in relation to the state.[4] However, this neglects the fact that civil society needs the state for its protection (Hall, 1995, cited in Van Rooy, 1998). 'The growth and good health of associational life is unlikely unless those in control of the state conclude that it is in their interest – that it will enhance the legitimacy of their rule – to give associational life free rein' (Barkan, 1994, p. 111). Again this contradiction is resolved discursively through the notion of 'good governance' which opens the door for the rehabilitation of the state, and its elites.

> Through the notion of governance, the Bank managed to argue the case for a complementarity between state elites – properly motivated – and adjustment. On the tails of good governance arrived a new vocabulary more closely focused on the power relationship between state and donor: partnership, participation, principal-agent issues, incentives, decentralization and so on.
>
> (Harrison, 2002, p. 71)

Although as development processes are nonlinear, not subject to full knowledge and consequently partly unpredictable in their outcomes, this is fraught with danger. May more fractured social formations be the result, rather than more cohesive ones in this new agenda? Is it time to start talking about 'actually existing or empirical civil society?' Alexander (1998, p. 3) suggests that it is 'only by understanding the "boundary relations" between civil and uncivil spheres can we convert civil society from a normative into a "real" concept which can be studied in a social scientific way.' How much power, and along what dimensions do donors have power?

To speak of partnership given unequal power relations is apolitical. What is required is for NGOs and civil society to 'perform partnership' (Mercer, 2003). Donors prefer a weak version of partnership where there is policy dialogue, but not multi-annual funding commitments, thereby enabling continued micro-management (Maxwell and Riddell, 2002). While the majority of NGOs are excluded from policy-making circles, the elite national and international ones' performance as the 'voices of the marginalized' enables them to continue to attract donor funding.

Thus, 'the relationship generally turns to be that of between the donor and the beggars, the rhetoric of partnership notwithstanding' (Hakkarainen *et al.*, 2002, p. 44).

Donor funding may encourage CSOs to focus on influencing the state, as for example in Guatemala, rather than building their grassroots organization (Howell and Pearce, 2001). The state may in turn respond by setting up its own proxy CSOs, making civil society a battlefield for influence where state and donors contest for hegemony.[5] Accountability by NGOs to their base is lost in this. Furthermore, 'NGOs exercise strategic pragmatism, framing what few challenges they make to the political order in a depoliticizing discourse in order to make themselves acceptable to their colleagues and the state. In short, NGO's are often constrained from taking on the roles imputed to them by the civil society theorists, by virtue of having a stake in the . . . system' (Dorman, n.d., cited in Dorman, 2001, p. 40).

There is also a serious urban bias at play with 'charisma, command of the English language, social ease with Westerners and class [having] important influences on donor choice of partner organizations and individuals' (Howell, 2000, p. 13). In some cases draft PRSPs have only been made available to civil society groups in English, for example (Whaites, 2002). 'One would therefore expect the expansion of civil society to be led by and to accrue to the advantage of, social classes well positioned to exploit economic opportunities in a capitalist economy. These would include the industrial, commercial and professional middle classes, large peasant farmers, and the unionized "aristocracy" of labor' (Bratton, 1989a, p. 418).

The growth of urban over rural civil society has been particularly noted in Ethiopia, Uganda and Vietnam (Campbell, 2001; Mercer, 2002). Thereby donor funding may reinforce elitist tendencies within civil society, and may, paradoxically, actually extend state power into civil society. The actors who are empowered are those capable of 'jumping scale,' with access to contacts, information and other resources at different levels of the aid industry (Gould, 2005a). However partnership is a logical concomitant of a global political economy, rather than just serving an instrumental function.

The theme of development partnership at present serves an ideological role as part of a neoliberal new policy framework which papers over contradictions and the rollback of government. . . . However, the underlying significance is much more profound: just as sectoral approaches and disciplinary boundaries have been losing their relevance, sectoral agendas are now too narrow. The ideological use that is being made of this conjuncture should not obscure the significance of the trend itself.

(Nederveen Pieterse, 2001, p. 17)

Nonetheless, donors may currently be involved in the creation of 'virtual civil societies' which are structurally disembedded from the values, identities and interests of the groups in society which they purport to represent. Whereas African states are increasingly characterized by 'negative autonomy' from domestic social forces (that is where the state appears autonomous, but that autonomy is the obverse of embeddedness and dependence on transnational forces), liberal civil society may be characterized by 'negative/virtual embeddedness' where it appears embedded in the preoccupations of domestic society, but the 'capillary power' in its networks run from top (donors) to bottom (society). According to Giles Mohan (2002), SNGOs claim to represent local communities but often have patronizing attitudes toward them and so thereby actually impede democratization and good governance.

Samantha Gibson argues that donors may be creating the democracy and governance sector in African countries. In 1996 there were 120 democracy and governance groups working in Kenya, with the vast majority based in Nairobi. Hardly any of these existed before 1993, and only nine out of that 120 did any local fund-raising (Andreassen *et al.*, 1996, cited in Gibson, 1999). It should be noted however that there is also a 'reverse flow' of ideas and influence from NGOs to donors, particularly in the areas of participation and process (Edwards, 2004d), although the precise form this reverse flow takes is mediated through circuits of power.

Michael (2004, p. 15) in her study of African NGOs found that it was not so much the state crowding out space for NGOs which was the problem but,

the fight for space, financial independence, international links and access to political issues within development, often indirect and involving actors other than government, that had prevented local NGOs in Africa from achieving power.

While there are many INGOs and GROs, there is a 'missing middle' of powerful local NGOs in Africa, with some notable exceptions such as the Green Belt Movement and Women's World Banking.

Studies also have shown that there is 'no minimum degree of democracy' necessary for NGOs in achieving policy influence (Thomas *et al.*,

2001, cited in Michael, 2004). Thus the more pressing issue would appear to be the extroversion and external dependence of civil society on donor funding, which can often be withdrawn at short notice, rather than the excessive power of the state. Indeed Gould (2005b) has argued that populist neoliberalism, in the form of PRSPs, is the rhetorical device deployed by external actors to legitimate their interventions in the name of the poor. Were donors willing, this could be countered through a 'seller's market for aid' in which the work of local NGOs holds the key to legitimacy of Northern aid agencies (Fowler, 1998, cited in Michael, 2004). Excessive donor influence could be countered by funding being channeled through local endowment funds (Bebbington and Riddell, 1997).

Donors also favor funding of CSOs, rather than private sector firms' capability development, which would compete with their own companies, because of their palliative nature, not their potential for structural transformation. USAID's charter explicitly prohibits funding of foreign firms in 'sensitive sectors,' such as textiles, which would compete with US production, but in which low-labor cost economies are meant to have a natural comparative advantage (USAID official, in conversation, Zimbabwe 1995). Most aid to sub-Saharan Africa tends to go to social infrastructure and program aid, rather than to the productive sectors (Abegaz, 2001). The new emphasis on 'pro-poor growth' occludes the 'real stuff' of economic development, such as industrialization and land reform (Gould and Ojanen, 2005). The World Bank is more autonomous in this, recently proposing to shift billions of dollars of funding for infrastructural development from the International Development Association to the International Finance Corporation, which lends exclusively to the private sector (Fine, 2004).

Overall though INGOs may thus serve US and EU geo-economic interests in this context as

> The swelling phalanx of American-led – and mostly Western based – NGOs which have succeeded in advancing the 'governance, participation and environment' agenda . . . have shown little serious interest in economics and economic growth.
> (Wade, 2001, p. 136)

Although it should be noted some INGOs, such as Oxfam in particular, have shown a 'negative' interest in economics, in that trade and macro-economic policies should not hurt the poor.[6]

While the total amounts given by donors to civil society for 'capacity building' are relatively small in global terms, they nonetheless have substantial impacts in poor societies. By some estimates, in 1995 civil society and governance projects received 8.6% of overseas development assistance (ODA), with civil society projects receiving roughly a tenth of this amount (Van Rooy, 1998, cited in Howell and Pearce, 2001). The US is by far the biggest donor in this category, contributing 85% of the total (Van Rooy and Robinson, 1998, cited in Encarnación, 2000). In 2001–2003, 42% of US 'aid' went to this category (Hearn, 2000). Geographically, the majority of donor expenditure in this category shifted from Latin America in the 1980s to Africa in the 1990s (P. Robinson, 1996, cited in Gibson, 1999).

The three main approaches by donors have been institutional and capacity building; coalitions and partnerships, and approaches around financial sustainability (Howell and Pearce, 2001). In some cases US money is channeled through party affiliated organizations, such as the International Republican Institute (IRI). A US State Department official (cited in W. Robinson, 1996a, cited in Hearn, 2000, p. 817) put it bluntly in relation to democracy promotion: the US has a need to 'clothe . . . security concerns in moralistic language . . . The democracy agenda, in short, is a kind of legitimacy cover for our more basic strategic objectives'.

Pinpointing the state as the locus of the development crisis has allowed Northern states to intervene extensively in the South with perceived legitimacy (Howell and Pearce, 2001), although this is sometimes undertaken by intermediaries in civil society. As noted while the amounts given to civil society projects are relatively small, they may have substantial impacts through structuring the ways in which NGOs with substantial budgets work, or through the legal system. For example, in South Africa, USAID has funded groups to take legal challenges to government policies (Hanlon, 2000).[7] The rhetoric of partnership with business and civil society also enabled USAID to downsize its programs, while maintaining its influence (Howell and Pearce, 2001). As the director of a German political foundation in South Africa (cited in Hearn, 2000) put it, if you can influence the rules of the game, 'you don't have to play.'

Organizations promoting liberal democracy and economic liberalism are particularly favored by donors for funding (Hearn, 1999). Funding for NGOs also has the political attraction that their promotion has also been supported by those who see them as an alternative to the market (Chandhoke, 2001). Thus donor funding of NGOs serves a liberal normalizing function. The extent to which NGOs may pursue simultaneous 'inside/outside' strategies in relation to the state and donors is an empirical question, dependent on local context (Brecher *et al.*, 2000).

The US government views civil society in terms of system maintenance: 'the creation or strengthening of the democratic institutions that protect the rule of law, legitimate peaceful opposition, and the expression of dissent in acceptable ways' (Howell and Pearce, 2001, p. 59). Howell and Pearce, argue that this contrasts with the more radical European tradition which looks at how social and economic inequalities impinge on the exercise of citizenship; an idea incorporated into PRSPs as will be discussed later. Nonetheless, the opening of political space is a pre-requisite for the articulation of economic alternatives (Ake, 1996). One comprehensive study found that

> While development programs often leave a lot to be desired, clearly the investments made since the late 1980s are beginning to pay off as far as civil society is concerned. Not only do WIPs [well informed persons] feel that they increasingly can speak out and form groups, but in many countries there is a stronger link between exercising these rights and influencing the policymaking process.
>
> (Hyden *et al.*, 2003, p. 29)

However, there is a danger that by institutionalizing a certain type of stability the voices *and actions* of the poor are marginalized.

Funding and autonomy of NGOs

Foreign funding has made it easy for governments to dismiss NGOs as dancing to a foreign tune, and to enforce tougher regulation which may diminish NGO capacity (Bratton, 1989b, cited in Hulme and Edwards, 1997a). For example, in early 1997 the Tanzanian government de-registered BAWATA – the Tanzania National Women's Council, claiming that it was acting as a political party (Maina Peter, n.d., cited in Michael, 2004). Thus self-financing and popular support would appear to be pre-conditions for legitimate entry into domestic policy debates.

In Bangladesh some of the most successful large-scale NGOs are largely self-financing. Proshika, whose members' incomes and literacy rates nearly doubled from 1995 to 1999, aimed to be 100% self-financing by 2004. BRAC is 75% self-financing, and only takes a maximum of 20% of its donor funding from any one donor (Michael, 2004). Over time it partnered with the government in providing basic education services (Narayan, 2002). BRAC has also globalized and has a field office in East Africa (Hulme and Edwards, 1997a).

In many cases it is not a lack of funding for local African NGOs which is the problem. Michael (2004) found that among local NGO directors in Harare that she interviewed, over a quarter had more funding, or promises of it than they could use. However, donor dependency means there is a tendency to prioritize outputs over institutional development, whereas BRAC invests 7% of its annual salary budget in staff development (Smillie and Hailey, 2001, cited in Michael, 2004).

According to van de Walle (2003, p. 25) 'the most successful NGOs are the ones who can credibly claim to know the field well enough to be effective intermediaries to . . . [informal, village level] associations on behalf of the donors.' Others have a somewhat different perspective, with PREM in India 'working to put itself out of a job' by helping grass roots organizations (GROs) graduate into People's Organizations (Edwards, 2004c). Thus some see NGOs helping donors to penetrate informal CSOs, whereas others work to see their scaling-up to act as sources of countervailing power.

In the case of some donors, such as UNDP, the focus is less on funding and more on creating appropriate legal and financial frameworks. As a multi-lateral donor, rather than financial institution, UNDP has had a longer history of involvement and greater freedom in its relations with civil society and it has pioneered a variety of innovative techniques and approaches. One of the key findings from one of its missions in the mid-1990s was that CSOs in Africa were weak in making links between macro and micro levels, and it set up programs to address this deficit (Howell and Pearce, 2001). Thus it does not adopt an instrumental approach to civil society but views its strengthening as a benefit in its own right. UNDP launched its 'Civil Society for Poverty Reduction in Sub-Saharan Africa' Initiative in 1996 (African Development Bank, 2000) and has a board composed of NGO representatives to advise the administrator on 'issues involving firms, governments and civil society' (Streeten, 2002, p. 50). This could be seen as a pre-cursor of the PRSP approach. Donors had helped create a liberal civil society, which governments could now engage with. Many donors continue to treat NGOs as secondary actors, however. In part this is because one of the main targets of 'civil society strengthening' is constraining the state from 'interfering' in the market, where capital is sovereign. Indeed the World Bank sees improved governance and policy reform as the 'primary driving force' behind recent higher rates of economic growth on the continent (World Bank, 2001b, cited in Mkandawire, 2006).

Some donor funding also goes to umbrella organizations which can help offset problems of service duplication (Mari Tripp, 2003), but the skills required for efficient service delivery are very different to those required for advocacy. It may be expecting too much of NGOs to fulfill advocacy functions better suited to 'trade unions, professional bodies and groups representing women, students and youth' (M. Robinson, 1996, cited in Van Rooy and Robinson, 1998, p. 35). In Senegal the growth of the NGO umbrella organization has 'reduced the impetus for, or ability of, individual NGOs to seek space and power' (Michael, 2004, p. 109). These groups do not necessarily have links with people living in (absolute) poverty. Thus Howell and Pearce (2001, p. 2) argue that 'the constant slippage between civil society as a normative concept and civil society as an empirical reality conceals the intense, ongoing debate about its meaning and enables donors to fund "civil society" as if it were an unproblematic given.' Jenkins (2001, p. 253) goes further in elaborating this contradiction in donor policy:

> The main difficulty is that the definitions [adopted by donors to civil society] are not capable of producing, in a co-ordinated way, the three main outcomes that assistance to civil society is designed to produce: 1) transitions to competitive politics, 2) the 'consolidation' of fledgling democracies, and 3) the establishment of market-oriented economic policies, and subsequently positive developmental performance. . . . To put it slightly differently, in order to make the case for civil society's pivotal role in achieving one of the three objectives, the concept is defined in ways that preclude it from contributing to the other two. This disjunction is remedied by specifying, when referring to the other two objectives, alternative definitions of civil society that render its ability to achieve them more plausible.

Thus different units within USAID have different definitions of civil society (Howell and Pearce, 2001). In this way USAID is even willing to fund 'first-tier associations' based on kin, clan, ethnicity or religion to promote democracy (USAID, 1996, cited in Jenkins, 2001). A further contradiction is that donors expect civil society to serve a watchdog function, while also collaborating with the state (Garbutt and Pratt, 2003). Indeed official agencies are forcing CSOs to work with the state, by often making funding conditional on it (Garbutt and Pratt, 2003).

According to van de Walle (2003, p. 19) 'there is moreover, little evidence of an attempt by either donors or African governments to prioritize the activities of the state, or to plan for a division of labor with local governments or civil society actors.' He also argues that 'at least some in the donor community seem to believe that benign neglect of the state is a viable strategy in the long run. Rather than undertake politically difficult and expensive frontal public sector reform, why not allow the state to slowly die on its own' (van de Walle, 2003, p. 20). He concludes that this approach is incompatible with strengthening the technocratic core of the state, without turning it into an appendage of donor organizations. Also the neglect of central state institutions may poison relationships between states and NGOs as they come to be viewed as competitors for resources. Alternatively the capacity of states may be undermined as civil servants leave for the NGO sector or engage in 'straddling' strategies between the two. This pattern is unlikely to result in greater transparency or accountability. In Uganda many National Resistance Movement (government) officials are involved in NGOs (Dicklitch, 1998). Some of these then participate in the PRSP process, perhaps telling the government what it wants to hear, but serving an important legitimation function. There are also, of course, independent CSOs such as the Forum for Women in Democracy which is concerned with gender budgeting (Samatar *et al.*, 2006).

Jude Howell (2000) argues that 'donors need to be more realistic and modest in their goals and base their interventions on more refined analyses of the local dynamics of social and political change' as in the end civil society must grow locally.

> Donor attempts to operationalize the concept of civil society are innovative and imaginative, promising to open up new avenues of participation for otherwise marginalized voices. They also seek to resist an essentialist, conflictual approach towards relations amongst market, state and civil society, suggesting imaginations of cooperative rather than antagonistic forms of mutual engagement. . . . However supporting or in some cases manufacturing, civil society from the outside raises a number of practical problems and dilemmas. These include the illusion of plurality and inclusion, identifying the social forces of change, donor dependency, and assuming the universality of civil society and its institutional manifestations. These arise in part from a reluctance to interrogate the assumptions underpinning the liberal-democratic conceptualization of civil society and in part from a tendency to think normatively rather than empirically, that is to confuse the 'ought' with the 'is'.
>
> (Howell, 2000, p. 11)

Some, such as Hulme and Edwards (1997b), argue that donors should move toward multi-annual funding and have continual dialogue about objectives and strategies, rather than just targets and outputs. They also argue that donor funding to NGOs should be channeled through independent public institutions or umbrella organizations to reduce donor influence. Another suggestion, noted earlier, is for funding to be channeled through endowments (Stiles, 2002).

As Harriss (2002, p. 12) notes 'it is really not surprising to find that strong associational life can give rise to real and tangible, measurable benefits for people.' The question is, perhaps, how this can be aided.

> Foreign assistance to civil society organizations in Africa, and elsewhere, poses considerable predicaments which can be ameliorated if: (1) such organizations have total autonomy and the freedom to plan and conduct activities as they see fit; (2) funding renewals are based on thorough reviews and evaluation conducted by independent consultants to assess the work of the organizations – at least two assessments should be done by a group of consultants each respectively commissioned by the funders and the organizations concerned and working independently and separately from each other; (3) a period of time is specified beyond which a given donor will not provide funding, thereby lessening dependence; and (4) organizations actively seek funding from a wide array of foreign donors sources to prevent any single donor from dominating and trying to influence their work.
>
> (Diamond, 1997 and Hope, 1997, cited in Hope, 2002, p. 91)

Fowler (1997, cited in Kaldor, 2003) proposes empowering beneficiaries through interpretive forms of assessment. This does not of course address the issue of initial group selection and the opportunity costs of investment in civil society over other activities.

As noted earlier relations between state and civil society are characterized by both conflict and collaboration. The challenge is to enhance the 'win–win' potential of the interaction: to develop collective, rather than distributive (zero sum) power (Arrighi, cited in Harvey, 2003). This will necessarily take place in the context of a politics where different interests are openly expressed, rather than veiled. According to Howell and Pearce (2001, p. 234), donors need to recognize that 'their contemporary intervention forms part of a longer historical trajectory of intervention, which has often been violent, exploitative and oppressive.'

Consequently they need to 'clarify their own visions and make explicit their assumptions about what and how civil society can contribute to processes of democratization and economic development in their own societies. In this way they can ensure that donor support for their own activities strengthens rather than weakens or distorts their own agenda.' Specifically they suggest that International Financial Institutions (IFIs) and multi-lateral development organizations focus on dialogue with civil society, while leaving its strengthening to organizations that have a 'record of promoting progressive values and goals in their own and host communities' (Howell and Pearce, 2001, p. 236). Otherwise donor programs risk destroying the most important purpose of civil society, 'to imagine and engage in alternatives.' As Nederveen Pieterse (2001, p. 49) notes

> As NGOs are part of a globalizing ethos, what they do and can do is negotiate the kind of globalization they are willing to be part of. They can use their influence to make and shape the case for social development, not just as a matter of tinkering in the margins but as representing the cutting edge of contemporary development (Social development is here used in the substantive sense . . .). What NGOs have stood for, that development is for the people, now figures higher on the agenda than ever.

The private sector, labor and civil society

Associations are now so thoroughly entangled with states and markets, that trichotomizations tend to be misleading (Warren, 2001, cited in Akkerman *et al.*, 2004). Some also argue that donors form a fourth sector as they are very important providers of economic resources and policy influencers (Hakkarainen *et al.*, 2002). States provide the legal and institutional frameworks for markets and civil societies to develop. While it is possible to have informal markets and civil societies without states, it puts limits on their development (Little, 2003). However, some argue that the absence of a state, in Somalia for example, has enabled the development of synergy between markets and social capital. According to Colletta and Cullen (2002, p. 221):

> The penetration of markets into society can foster secondary networks of social capital. Globalization in the form of external market penetration and the spread of technology has facilitated peace efforts in Northern Somalia enabling expansion and economic growth . . .

Weak state penetration (especially in Hargeisa) has also enabled this development of market forces, for there is no longer the threat of overregulation.

Developed markets require a strong state regulatory presence, however. Developed markets (developed capital and labor) provide the state with tax revenues; some of which may be used to develop civil society, but it is labor which has played the key role in democratization historically (Rueschemeyer *et al.*, 1992). NGOs may out-compete private sector businesses by virtue of subsidies from donors and tax breaks from states. Thus private sector, particularly manufacturing, development, may strengthen civil society (trade unions and employers associations) and democracy. There are also other channels through which private sector development strengthens civil society.

Civil society indirectly is meant to create the conditions for the emergence of a vibrant private sector. However, in parts of Africa, such as Botswana and Ghana, the development of an indigenous business class has created alternative power centers to the state and opened up space for the funding of alternative parties and more associational possibilities (Molutsi and Holm, 1990; Holm and Molutsi, 1992; Chazan, 1992). However, there is a paradox here in that market forces are likely to be less accountable to the general public than the state. Accountability may come indirectly through the development of civil society. Thus Barrington Moore's famous dictum: 'no bourgeoisie, no democracy' (1966, p. 418) may have applicability in Africa, in as much as it is a productive and domestically embedded bourgeoisie. This suggests greater importance for fair and preferential trade, rather than aid (to civil society) in donor policy (Taylor, 2005a). Raising Africa's share in world exports to take up another 1% of the total would bring in $70 billion, five times what the continent receives in aid (Alagiah, 2005).

There are also, of course, counter-tendencies at play in the development of an indigenous bourgeoisie; with the risk that the state will be captured and behave in an instrumental, as opposed to a relatively autonomous fashion. The EU suspended some aid to Ghana recently, as a result of $100m in timber export tax going missing. President Kufor's family is involved in the lumber business.

Whether the 'straddling' of business and political interests is developmental or anti-developmental is context dependent, as it creates both opportunities for corruption, but also potential incentives against it if the rewards from private sector activity are sufficiently large.[8] Of course the other danger of political parties backed by business is that they bring unequal and superior economic resources and social capital to political competition, meaning that even 'a procedurally perfect democracy may remain an oligarchy: the rule of the rich over the poor' (Przeworski, 1991, p. 34, cited in Abrahamsen, 2000, p. 75).

In some cases civil society has effectively influenced economic policy, as in Mozambique where the trade unions and the employer's association, with the backing of a consultancy report, successfully argued, against the IMF, for the reintroduction of a cashew nut export tariff to revive the processing industry there (Harrison, 2002). It is interesting to note that it was not NGOs, which in Mozambique are between 80 and 90% dependent on donor funding, which brought about this change (Harrison, 1999, cited in Harrison, 2002).

The Mozambican economy has also been dramatically affected by the liberalization of capital controls in South Africa. With the end of apartheid, the South African government liberalized out-flows of investment to the rest of Africa first. Investment of South African based capital into Mozambique, supported by the Industrial Development Corporation and the Development Bank of Southern Africa, grew strongly in the late 1990s giving it, for a time, the fastest rate of economic growth in the world. This investment also catalyzed other investment, from Australia in particular.

Much of this investment has been concentrated in tourism, infrastructural development and mineral processing, such as the Maputo Iron and Steel Project and the Mozal aluminum smelter built outside Maputo at a cost of US $1.5bn (Mitchell, 1998).[9] Maputo Province has gotten 85% of the US $2.5bn of South African investment in the country (Palloti, 2004). Such investments may drive up the short-term rate of economic growth, but some commentators have noted that it is relatively easy to have a 10% p.a. economic growth rate off a per capita base of US $90 a year (Hanlon, 1996). However, these remain enclave activities with few linkage and multiplier effects for the local economy. South African investment has created only 31,000 jobs (Palloti, 2004). The high interest rate regime under structural adjustment also advantaged foreign investors able to raise capital on international markets, such as South African conglomerates (Cramer, 1999).

Mozambique's strict adherence to the policies of the 'Washington Consensus' was driven by its aid dependence. However, there have been some moves, as noted earlier, toward the partial deglobalization of Mozambique's economy. Cramer (1999) argues that increased autonomy from IFIs is a prerequisite for deepening agro-industrialization in Mozambique by up-grading the processing of primary commodities. For example, as noted earlier, the IMF's Executive Board has voted to allow Mozambique to protect its cashew nut and sugar industries (Hanlon, 2001). This could be read as evidence of a shift from doctrinaire free marketism. However, a 'bargaining approach' might see this as the IMF making a concession to keep the overall direction of neoliberal reform 'on track.'[10]

The protection of the domestic market and the fact that Mozambique could sell 16,000 tones of sugar to the EU per year (four hours of consumption) at preferential prices has attracted substantial South African investment into the sugar industry (Pocock, 2005). However, the recent reductions in price announced by the EU for sugar, as a result of a World Trade Organization (WTO) ruling will likely have a detrimental impact on the industry in Mozambique.[11]

Some CSOs, such as church organizations, have been in the forefront of resistance to neoliberal economic reforms, given their interest in the protection of the vulnerable. However, in the case of Mozambique progressive national reforms brought about by civil society pressure may be over-whelmed by reforms at global level; in this case by the WTO. Indeed Susanne Soederberg (2006) argues that the function of the WTO is to act as a buffer between states and more radical NGOs. The devastating floods of recent years in Mozambique have also again shown the dangers of agricultural dependence.

Governance and the accountability of NGOs

A democratic polity and civil society are mutually constitutive (Dicklitch, 1998), but according to Nederveen Pieterse (2001, p. 152), the current trend of 'strengthening civil society' by supporting NGOs is deeply apolitical, ignores contradictions within civil society, overrates NGOs and weakens state capabilities. He notes that the promotion of new development institutions by the donors has tended to weaken Africa's central states, not strengthen them. Whereas democratic states have institutions of accountability, this is not necessarily the case for NGOs.

According to Mari Tripp (2003, p. 140), NGOs:

Can set an agenda with little popular mandate and far fewer political consequences if they fail. In the late 1990s in Tanzania and Uganda, the World Bank and IMF were negotiating directly with what they refer to as 'Civil Society' (leading indigenous and foreign NGOs) regarding a Poverty Reduction Strategy Programme in Tanzania and

a Poverty Eradication Action Plan in Uganda. There was no involvement on the part of parliamentarians in these negotiations.
Although the NGOs do excellent work and their involvement constitutes popular participation, they are not, however, elected representatives of the Tanzanian and Ugandan people and are
self-appointed spokespeople for the citizenry in those countries. This
raises questions about who they are accountable to regardless of how
much one agrees with their goals.

In theory states are accountable to voters and public companies to
shareholders, but NGO accountability would appear to be most promi-
nently to donors. Hilhorst (2003, p. 126) defines accountability as 'a
process in which different actors negotiate the meaning and legitimacy
of NGO activities.' She contrasts moral and rational accountability, with
the former being both horizontal, within social groups, and the latter
being vertical. For her the mechanisms of moral accountability include
stories, gossip and ironic remarks. Jordan and van Tujil (2000, cited in
Kaldor, 2003) likewise differentiate between internal or functional
accountability and external or strategic accountability, whereas Kaldor
prefers the term 'moral accountability,' although it has a different connotation for her than for Hilhorst.
The lack of moral accountability may undermine empowerment.

> NGOs provide pure 'benefits', not entitlements in either the moral or
> the legal sense of the term. There is no moral or legal basis on which
> to organize to ensure that NGOs deliver what they promise. Equally
> important, NGO activities are invariably small scale and dispersed,
> and frequently experimental and in practice flexible, temporary and
> unstable. To NGO staffers and their funders, flexibility and experi-
> mentation are positive values that contribute to 'learning experi-
> ences.' To potential social activists these same values are disabling,
> for NGO implementation undermines the scope for mobilization of
> the poor around programmed implementation.
>
> (Joshi and Moore, 2001, pp. 44–5)

Also NGOs may shape funding proposals to fit the interests of donors,
marginalizing the concerns of intended beneficiaries. In order to counteract this, Mari Tripp (2003, p. 141) argues that NGOs should start by
'asking residents what they would like to see changed in a particular
area, how it should be transformed, and they should work with local
associations and resources for change' and that the state can ensure

accountability. In addition in some countries, such as Mozambique or Bangladesh, this issue is compounded by the fact that domestic and INGOs have more resources at their disposal than the government. The use of email and other information technologies may enable donors to take on the roles of 'proximate managers' (Hilhorst, 2003).

Mari Tripp (2003, p. 154) also argues that 'NGOs often have short-term agendas that are vulnerable to the vagaries of donor funding. The state needs to ensure that people are not left without services when unexpected changes occur.' Wood (1997, cited in Hilhorst, 2003) talks of a 'franchise state' where state functions are outsourced to NGOs, mediated by donor preferences and ideology. The outsourcing of social reproduction to NGOs, reduces risk for the state, may increase efficiency and hence legitimacy, at the same time as it undermines potential for patronage. Thus there are contradictory incentives for the state to adopt this strategy. If states were given additional resources, as they are in the new aid regime, they might become more efficient thereby breaking the self-fulfilling prophesy of weak state capacity. Thus the 'hollowing out' of the strategic state capacity, as opposed to 'rightsizing' may present formidable developmental problems which may take a long time to overcome. The notion of citizenship may also be compromised particularly as through the notion of social capital, people are encouraged to place their loyalties in organizations that further particularistic, rather than societal interests (Øyen, n.d.).

In terms of accountability to donors Hilhorst (2003) asks is it one-way (client/patron) or two-way (partnership). This idea of genuine partnership involving two-way accountability is potentially a radical one as it would open up the issue global poverty creation through debt, unequal trade and Northern protectionism and other mechanisms. For Nederveen Pieterse (2001, p. 90), 'the principle of people's sovereignty or popular legitimacy as the basis of sovereignty involves the redefinition of development cooperation as principally a matter of people-to-people relations in which governments play a mediating and enabling role. Development cooperation then needs to be redefined as a process of "mutual empowerment."' NGO accountability to stakeholders can be strengthened through methodologies such as Social Auditing (Pearce, 1997a) where performance criteria are negotiated with producers, staff, consumers and shareholders.

NGOs in the new development orthodoxy are meant to fulfill an intermediary governance role between national/local states and the poor. However, their ability to do this may be undermined by organizational bifurcation. In one NGO in the Philippines it was found that

'while new and often inexperienced staff had to deal with large numbers of village-based activities . . . management was largely absorbed in
report writing. International and alliance work often took them away
from the office, leaving little time to become personally involved in
village-based work' (Hilhorst, 2003, p. 57). The professionalization of
NGOs and their demands for formal education may also increase the
social distance between them and people living in poverty. This may
also serve to move the organization further away from its original political objectives. Some have defined this as a malaise of 'NGOism' defined
as 'a state of being engrossed in unholistic developmentalism leading to
bureaucratic tendencies in dealing with the people that the NGOs have
sworn to serve' (KMP, 1994, cited in Hilhorst, 2003, p. 62). This malady
is further defined as having seven components:

- Loyalty to donors over beneficiaries
- Socioeconomic work without class struggle and structural change
- Bureaucratism
- Corruption of service orientation
- Professionalism
- Adoption of corporate practices/standards
- Competition or 'turfing.'

In the NGO in Hilhorst's study this diagnosis led to internal NGO
reform, with a refocusing on grassroots mobilization. In some cases this
takes the form of *animateurs* or change agents conscientizing communities about the structural causes of poverty thereby enabling them 'to
critique and reject the value positions and discourse of dominant and
exploiting classes' (Rahnema, 1992, p. 125, cited in Parfitt, 2002, p. 157).
This jibes with the Marshallian conception of social rights as capacity to
struggle (Bustelo, 2001).

Power relations also infuse inter-NGO relations. As there has been a
decline in the authoritative power of states over economy, there has
been a shift from government to governance as a co-coordinating
mechanism/procedure. This has meant that NNGOs in particular serve
as sites where power is congealed, and have a disciplinary effect on
SNGOs. This trend has been accentuated by the growing number of
INGO mergers and alliances (Garbutt and Pratt, 2003). For example, in
Nepal, Oxfam stopped funding a local community development
organization when it shifted focus from organizing the 'poorest of
the poor,' to broader coalition building to address structural issues

(Hakkarainen *et al.*, 2002). Increased access to resources by CSOs from donors and INGOs thus plays an ambiguous role in democratization (Whitfield, 2003). For Ferguson (n.d., cited in Lewis, 2002, p. 577), NGOs rather than being an internal response to internal problems are 'horizontal contemporaries' of the wider institutions of transnational governmentality. In some cases INGOs have funded World Bank reports, for example.[12] Some have thus written of 'NGO governmentality,' (Mawdsley *et al.*, 2001, cited in Williams, 2004a) as they police multinationals codes of conduct for example (Harris, 2003).

NGO projects may also disrupt traditional social structures. For example, a NGO literacy project in the Philippines, by 'defining the women as lacking something – namely the ability to read and write – and by turning the project into a vehicle for education about modern values, the project contributed to an erosion of the status of older women and underlined a widening gap between educated professionals and peasant women' (Hilhorst, 2003, p. 100). Also the intervention model which many NGOs use require them to acquire a lot of power, without too much 'interference' from local communities. The solution to this may be for NGOs to reconceive their role as catalysts for organizing, rather than delivers of services. The sustainability of some NGOs may also be open to question as they are often founded by charismatic individuals.

The building of civil society may also contain another opportunity cost in that it may co-exist with a very uncivil political society. Brazil has one of the most vibrant associational lives in newly democratic countries, however initially at least, there was not a viable party system. This meant that at thriving civil society could co-exist with rampant state violence (Encarnación, 2000). Thus it may be the level of political institutionalization which is important in democracy and governance. McIlwaine (1998b) argues in El Salvador, division within civil society has promoted violence and undermined social capital formation and that consequently while promoting the fortification of civil society is a valid goal, it may be futile unless there is greater recognition of its context-specific complexities within and among individual nations, and the different roles which civil society can undertake.

There are also problems with the class nature of civil society. For example, in both Nigeria and India it was found that moderate and prosperous farmers control the co-operatives, thereby neglecting the needs of the most deprived groups and nonmembers (Narayan *et al.*, 2000, p. 155). Furthermore the view was expressed in a PPA in Venezuela that participation is ineffective unless you are a member of a political party.

This chapter has focused on the idea of governance. During the early 1990s donors promoted civil society capacity building as a way of attempting to influence/restrain the state. However, neither the previously dominant approach of funding NGOs for service provision, or better governance, by themselves, were likely to lead to substantially reduced poverty. Another concept seemed to offer hope for this: social capital.

3
The Theory of Civil Society in Poverty Reduction or the Social Capitalization of Neoliberalism

Poverty elimination is ostensibly the ultimate aim of development policy, however there is a debate about the combination of social forces, linkages between them and the instruments which can be used to achieve this goal. The evolving consensus is that power and poverty are intimately related: that there is excessive distance between the poor and the decision-makers in national government and it is this which is responsible for poor anti-poverty formulation and implementation. However, this is still a nationalized conception of poverty, focused on the excessive power of the state, rather than interrogating the global balance of social power more broadly and how this is constructed.

There are different approaches to the reduction of poverty. Empowerment of the poor might be seen as one way to reduce poverty, through supporting community-based initiatives. However there are also other ways to reduce poverty, particularly welfarist–productivist approaches. In this approach, originally pioneered in Scandinavia, poverty is targeted through structural transformation of the economy. This in turn yields resources for social investment in human capital formation, welfare and the third sector, reinforcing a virtuous cycle of growth. The causality could of course run in the other direction. Empowerment of the poor may reduce poverty and thereby yield a social surplus that could be used for investment in industry, although the marginal propensity for the poor to save is low. However, in the mid-1990s a new neoliberal approach was developed which downplayed economic issues, such as investment rates, in favor of an emphasis on the social: social capital.

The channels of civil society in poverty reduction

Thomas argues that civil society can exercise pro-poor policy influence through confrontation, collaboration, complementary activities and consciousness raising (Thomas, 1996, cited in Dicklitch, 1998). According to Temple and Johnson, (n.d., cited in Nederveen Pieterse, 2001, p. 123) 'a country's potential for rapid growth is strong not when it is backward without qualification, but rather when it is technologically backward but socially advanced.' There are three primary, and potentially overlapping, channels through which 'civil society' can influence levels of poverty and anti-poverty policy – promoting economic growth, equity and replacing waning state services (Van Rooy and Robinson, 1998). These take place at different, overlapping and socially constructed scales: micro, meso and macro.

The first mechanism is through the direct provision of economic and social services, which has been well described recently by Stephen Smith (2005). Economic services include rotating savings and credit associations (ROSCAs), known as *tontines* in West Africa.[1] These provide seed capital for micro-enterprises and also insurance against 'life shocks' such as deaths, through burial societies, and unemployment. As such they serve dual functions in people's livelihood strategies. These types of service providers are typically informal, but may also be formalized, such as the Grameen Bank in Bangladesh or Women's World Banking, started in Ghana, which has over 10 million clients worldwide, who suffered previously from financial exclusion (Barry, 2001, cited in Øyen, 2001). They may also engage in economic diversification, like the Grameen Telecom initiative (James, 2002).

Popular Economic Organizations (PEOs) (Friedmann, 1992) such as basket making co-operatives may also be formed. In some cases these may be engaged in significant exports such as the Dinesh Beedi or the Popadom co-operatives in India (Thomas Isaac *et al.*, 1998). What determines whether PEOs succeed or not in large part depends on their 'selection environments' – that is the historical–institutional legacy and market conditions of the area in which they are located (Boschma and Lambooy, 1999). The implications of this insight for policy are ambivalent. Whether successful replication is feasible is an empirical/practical and political, rather than a theoretical question.

Social services provided, typically, by NGOs include infrastructure, education, health, training, famine relief and infrastructure. It is often argued that NGOs can deliver these services more efficiently than African states. For example, 'church-affiliated entities represent probably the most visible and far reaching safety net presently operating in

Benin' (Participatory Poverty Assessment Benin, 1994, cited in Narayan *et al.*, 2000, p. 133). In some cases CSOs may serve hybrid economic and social functions such as in the case of Self-Employed Women's Association (SEWA) in India (Mitter, 1994).[2]

There is now a consensus among many orthodox and many hetero-dox social scientists that 'Africa's persistent economic crisis – severe as it has been – is but a consequence of the political crisis that manifests itself in a lack of democracy, accountability, good governance and a human-centered development paradigm' (Anon., 2004c; see also Ake, 1996). Kofi Annan, former Secretary General of the United Nations, stated that 'good governance is perhaps the single most important factor in eradicating poverty and promoting development' (UN, 1998, cited in Hyden *et al.*, 2003, p. 1) and 'donors increasingly articulate the view that . . . economic development is impossible in societies where the state is unaccountable for its actions' (Barkan, 1994, p. 112).

The second channel through which civil society can contribute to poverty reduction is through governance: holding the state accountable for its actions and expenditure, thereby increasing transparency and accountability and making the state more responsive to societal inter-ests (business, the poor), rather than state elites and office holders, or politically connected 'rent seekers.'[3] Flight capital from Africa, much of it taking place through political circuits, was estimated at $187 billion from 1960 to 1996, which is 145 percent of the value of public sector debt for the region.[4] Thus, 40 percent of African private wealth is held overseas, versus 4 percent for Asia (Commission for Africa, 2004).

Better governance has both equity and efficiency gains, as it is 'pro-poor' (creating a better balance between supply and demand for policies) and by creating institutional linkages for information sharing, states, through intermediate institutions, can reduce information and hence state failures. The theory is that NGOs through their direct contact with people living in poverty have expert knowledge and on the ground experience of the types of practical interventions which will reduce poverty. Also NGOs through this closer linkage are more easily able to establish trust and co-operation in their development interventions than government (Joshi and Moore, 2001).

Some authors outside of the neoliberal ambit, such as Joshi and Moore (2001) favor creating enabling environments for societal actors, rather than more authoritative state intervention. Governance has a central role to play in this. According to Nederveen Pieterse,

a social productivist approach might require an interventionist, developmental state, but this may be too heavy handed. A more modest approach in managed pluralism (Midgley, 1995) . . . Merging social and market concerns also involves the development of collective bargaining systems. This may be difficult to achieve in segmented societies.

(Midgley, 1995, cited in Nederveen Pieterse, 2001, p. 127)

He further argues, echoing Scott (1998), that 'where non-linear dynamics prevail, the counsel for policy is "gentle action"' (Elliot and Kiel, 1997, cited in Pieterse, 2001, p. 144) and that 'several components of the Washington agenda – public sector reform to achieve effective government, good governance, accountability and transparency – are part of the reform agenda' (Pieterse, 2001, p. 162).

Some see governance as 'government minus politics' (de Waal, cited in Lieven, 2004 cited in Lockwood, 2005). However, this is an unrealistic apolitical approach. Rather it is preferable to investigate the 'social relations of governance' (Gould, 2005b). For example, social movements may transform into political movements and capture state power, as has recently happened in Bolivia. Through the state they may then influence anti-poverty policy in myriad ways. This trajectory is not supported in neoliberal theory however, in which there should be a separation of civil society and the state.

The third mechanism through which civil society can reduce poverty in the neoliberal schema is through the development of the relatively abstract concept of social capital. This (American) communitarian (Midgley, 1998, p. 91)[5] vision of civil society is based on individuals coming together to achieve collective goals. This vision holds that communities, by virtue of their social capital, are more functional in caring for the disadvantaged than large-scale organizations, such as the state (Braathen, 2000, p. 40). This idea has resonance within the New Left too, although there is substantial disagreement about the appropriate institutions of community. Are they primarily a not-for-profit 'third sector' or would they include 'community corporations,' for example.[6]

Social capital is a politically catholic concept which can be adopted by either the right or the left to correct state or market failure. Robert Putnam defines social capital as 'networks of civic engagement and associated norms' (McNeill, 2000). It has many purported economic-catalytic benefits.

Similar to the notions of physical and human capital, the term 'social capital' refers to features of social organizations – such as networks, norms and trust – that increase a society's productive potential. Though largely neglected in discussions of public policy, social capital substantially enhances returns to investments in physical and human capital. . . . The implications for social and economic policy are far-reaching.

> (Putnam, 1994, cited in Ritchey-Vance,
> 2004, p. 308)

Another definition is that 'social capital, broadly defined, refers to the norms and networks that enable people to coordinate collective action' (Narayan *et al.*, 2000, p. 129) and thereby reduce enforcement and transaction costs, and share information. As Harris simply puts it 'its not what you know, its who you know!' (Harriss, 2002, p. 2) and he might have added how you know them (in an equal or dependent patron–client relation?). This hints at an older and more radical meaning of the concept developed by Pierre Bourdieu, where social capital (in the sense of 'old boy networks,' for example), is an instrument of class power.

Whereas Robert Putnam (1994) looks at associational membership and surveys which assess civic engagement through indicators such as newspaper readership, Temple and Johnson (n.d., p. 2, cited in Nederveen Pieterse, 2001, p. 123) define social capital narrowly as: 'the capacity of social institutions to assist in the adoption of foreign technology.' On-the-other-hand, James Coleman adopts a functionalist definition of social capital as 'any social arrangements that allow individuals more readily to achieve their goals' (Bourdieu and Coleman, 1991, cited in Fine, 2003, p. 137). Coleman did acknowledge the limited fungibility of social capital (its excludability) and hence that it is not a pure but perhaps a semi-public good, whose societal value is context dependent (Coleman, 1988 and 1990, cited in Harriss, 2002). In Robert Putnam's reformulation this nuance is lost and it is perceived as a pure public good.

For the World Bank, social capital is coterminous with social cohesion: it 'is the *glue* [emphasis added] that holds societies together and without which there can be no economic growth or human well-being' (I. Serageldin, Vice President of Special Programs at the World Bank, quoted in Fine, 2003, p. 138).[7] It is the social adhesive which offsets the individuating effects of market mechanisms. In this conception social capital is a value system which enables the reproduction of the social system by bringing about acquiescence to unequal class and power relations discursively, and through economic growth, but not through the redistribution of effective material claims.

Others have proffered yet different understandings of social capital. For some, social capital networks are characterized by 'structural holes' (Burt, 2000). Research on successful managers in the United States shows that those with the most social capital (e.g. contacts and interactions) who are able to bridge structural holes (link up and access information from different social networks) are the most successful. In this conception social capital is individually embedded in strategic brokers, rather than 'something in the air.' Here social capital is close to the idea of 'relational assets' developed by economic geographers (Morgan and Nauwelaers, 1999). However, the operational definition of social capital is the World Bank's one.

Narayan and Pritchett (1999, cited in Fine, 2003, pp. 140–1) argue that there are five mechanisms through which social capital can increase income:

> horizontal connections inducing more efficient government through better monitoring; co-operation for local problem solving; diffusion of innovations; less imperfect information and lower transaction cost; and informal insurance. It is accepted that these may only affect the level of income and not the growth rate (indicating the absence of any formal model relating social capital to income).

According to these World Bank researchers:

> The relationship between a flourishing associational life and economic development is confirmed by several recent studies. A national survey conducted in Tanzania as part of a PPA finds that, even after controlling for the standard set of economic and demographic variables, villages with higher social capital, as measured by membership in functioning groups, have higher incomes.
>
> (Narayan and Ebbe, 1997 and Narayan and Pritchett, 1999, cited in Narayan *et al.*, 2000)

In Tanzania it was found that one standard deviation increase in social capital raised incomes an average of 20 to 30 percent, versus only 4.8 percent for schooling (almost an additional three years) (suggesting that social capital is a 'high pay-off input') (Narayan, 1997 cited in Fine, 2003). 'This impact is as large as tripling either the level of education or stock of non-farming assets' (Narayan and Pritchett, 1999, cited in Harriss, 2002, p. 90). Other literature from Kenya to Italy also suggests that richer regions tend to have more developed associational life

(Putnam, 1994; Barkan 1994). However, these correlations are not explanatory, as has frequently been noted, and fit with a political agenda of public expenditure restraint.[8] Which comes first, social capital or economic development, or do they co-evolve?

Ben Fine (2003, p. 142) notes the problem of correlation versus causation arises in World Bank studies of social capital and 'this can only be disentangled by a more inclusive analysis, both in terms of exploring the relationships between the variables that are present, as well as incorporating those that are absent (above village level).' He notes further that the relationships estimated are non-linear and that social capital's impacts will be negligible at low levels, suggesting it will not have a dramatic impact on poverty alleviation.

Encouraging social capital is tantamount to social engineering by supporting the development of associations which will internalize externalities appropriately, and discouraging those that will not. There is also the issue of how social capital, which is based for the most part on a communicative, rather than an instrumental, rationality, might be promoted in-any-event (Habermas, 1990, cited in Drinkwater, 1991). Thus a foundational problem with the orthodox usage of social capital is its methodological individualism which

> gives it a distinct instrumental favor in which social capital is seen as a good in which individuals can invest and that yields a predictable rate of return . . . [this] is seriously flawed when it comes to understanding social relations in which mutual obligations and trust loom large.
>
> (Engberg-Pedersen and Webster, 2002, p. 16)

Nonetheless in World Bank studies there is a recognition that social capital is unevenly distributed across classes as

> The groups and networks of the rich, powerful, and elite are cohesive; they cut across communities, and their members are active in social, political, and economic affairs. The networks of the poor are more atomized.
>
> (Narayan *et al.*, 2000, p. 131)

'The PPAs indicate that CBOs and networks are indeed a key resource for the poor, but often only as a coping mechanism that substitute for the role of the state rather than as a complement to state efforts' (Narayan *et al.*, 2000, p. 130). Narayan *et al.* (2000, p. 130) in their World Bank report argue (in quite a radical fashion) that in order for these organizations to be transformative they must build 'bridging social capital' to social movements to 'challenge inequitable social norms, laws, or *distribution of resources*' (emphasis added) and 'facilitate new partnerships with the state that sustain improvements in economic well-being for the poor' (Narayan *et al.*, 2000, p. 130). This position was sailing very close to the wind indeed in the political economy of the World Bank and may have contributed to the controversy surrounding the *2000/2001 World Development Report*, into which this earlier report fed.

There are those that argue that external intervention in search of transformation has been the problem and what is needed is the maintenance of traditional institutions (see, in particular, Esteva and Suri Prakesh, 1998). This conclusion is perhaps indirectly supported by the World Bank *Voices of the Poor* study which notes that in Mexico 'those that have the least, the indigenous peoples of Oaxaca, are those that fear their present condition the least as well, for they, and only they, have traditional communitarian institutions (*tequio, guetza*) which provide them with support in times of need' (Narayan *et al.*, 2000, p. 146). Of course the reference to 'having the least' is a material one.

'Time poverty' may mean that the poor are constrained from fuller associational lives. Furthermore a study in the UK found that 'the concept of social capital is insubstantial without a material base: that is that the gains that can be achieved from co-operation alone, without material resources are limited,' (Cattell and Evans, 1999, cited in Harriss, 2002, p. 104) thus explaining why it tends to flourish in higher socioeconomic classes. Nonetheless, in World Bank reports social capital is meant not only to encourage economic development and efficiency, but also to be pro-poor as it 'has a disproportionate impact on lower income quintiles, and on small landholders rather than large landholders' (Narayan *et al.*, 2000, p. 129).

'Poor people invest heavily in social relations for psychological, cultural, and economic well-being. When communities are cohesive and their associational life is vital, they are better positioned to attract government and NGO resources,' with a social capital survey in Panama showing that communities with higher social capital receive up to five times more assistance from NGOs (Narayan *et al.*, 2000, p. 129). Thus while the purported benefits of social capital are partly internal to the community, its development can also be used in an exogenous development strategy.

Michael Woolcock and his colleagues at the World Bank developed the ideas of 'bonding, bridging and linking' social capital. Bonding social capital takes place within geographic communities. Bridging social capital links up people from different communities, while linking social capital links communities to state elites, educators and others. This idea of 'linking social capital' does not take any cognizance of differential power relations embedded in these relations, however, which may be reinforced in the process (Harriss, 2002). However, the idea of linking social capital can be seen in architecture of PRSPs.

Poor communities are meant to have substantial amounts of bonding (intra-community) social capital which allows for the maintenance of a low level socio-economic equilibrium. However, it is sometimes argued that in order to foster developmental, propulsive dynamics there is a need to build bridging and linking social capital. Woolcock (1999, cited in Harriss, 2002, p. 86) argues that 'a three-pronged approach by NGOs, firms and government agencies is essential to mobilize bonding social capital to markets [sic]; and to enhance linking social capital to public institutions.' His work suggests that 'getting the social relations right' is a technical rather than a political process (Harriss, 2002).

In theory, social capital accumulation, through the development of trust, allows for new intersubjective understandings and interests to emerge which will allow for a national consensus and shared commitment on how to achieve poverty reduction. However, Uma Kothari (2001, cited in Williams, 2004a) argues that participatory development programs bind people in poverty more tightly to structures of power, which they are then not able to question. Thus empowerment becomes elite-led, rather than directed by the poor, laying the basis for a reconstructed hegemony as the poor are integrated (glued) into the market society of the rich and civil society of the middle classes (Braathen, 2000).[9] Many peasants in Africa have rationally sought since colonial times to pursue '*la stratégie de la dérobade*' (the strategy of evasion) in relation to the state (Engberg-Pedersen, 2002). However, 'participation,' as currently constituted, may be a form of panoptic 'state simplification,' where subject populations become legible to states and donors, and thereby amenable to intervention and co-option (Scott, 1998, cited in Cornwall, 2004a).

Bridging social capital as a relational asset is something which is, in part, defined by its excludability. One person's social capital is another's social exclusion as the 'same ties that bind also exclude' (Narayan, 1999, cited in Harriss, 2002, p. 85). This excludability also speaks to what some people have referred to as 'anti-social (exclusionary) capital,' 'blinding social capital,' (Hyden *et al.*, 2003)[10] or the 'social capital of the felonious state' (Bayart *et al.*, 1999). Where the formal economy is under strain people experience 'adverse incorporation' into drug, crime, prostitution and other 'anti-social' networks (Wood, 1999, cited in Deacon, 2000). It is estimated that in Columbia the annual income of a petty criminal is about ten times per capita gross domestic product (GDP) (Rubio, 1997, cited in Narayan, 2002, p. 60). With returns to 'labor' such as this, little wonder there is honor among thieves. The militias which carried out the Rwandan genocide were called *Interahamwe* ('those who attach together' in Kinyarwanda) (Colletta and Cullen, 2002).[11] Care should be exercised in drawing too sharp distinctions between different positive and negative types of social capital, however. As Olukoshi (1998) notes, networks of mutual obligation and trust are celebrated as social capital in Western contexts, but are often seen as neopatrimonial in Africa.

The development of different types of social capital is in part dependent on the broader context or 'selection environment.' In a shrinking or stagnant economy, social and market interactions are often negative sum games, so people 'make hay while the sun shines' (Versi, 2004) through strategies of corruption and clientelism. Patron–client ties may provide a crude type of social security (MacGaffey, 1991). Indeed a number of studies have suggested that donors exacerbate corruption by giving more money to governments, as long as they implement neo-liberal economic reforms faithfully (see, for example Hanlon, 2004). Indeed creditors are willing to tolerate Ugandan involvement in 'Africa's World War' in the Congo rather than risk domestic disorder and the roll-back of economic reforms (Reno, 2002).

Horizontal and vertical corruption may become mutually reinforcing, with the saying 'a goat eats where it is tethered' reflecting this.[12] Low salaries in the police may force members to engage in corruption, for example, and make them less likely to investigate vertical corruption of political elites, for example. Political offices may then become 'feeding posts.'

However, it is important not to essentialize the African state as it still continues to discharge many of its legitimate functions in many places (Carmody, 2002; Samatar and Samatar, 2002b). Even in some of the more corrupt contexts, such as Congo-Brazzaville, where up to 30 percent of the government budget has been stolen, this means 70 percent is still spent legitimately (Blanq, 1994, cited in van de Walle, 1999). Also the African state is embedded in a global political economy, where transnational corporations often exercise direct power through bribery of government officials (Stiglitz, 2002).

Social capital can thus be conceived of as a form of socio-spatial competition between networks and communities, in addition to a form of co-operation. Which types of social capital are most prominent will depend on selection environments, path dependencies created by institutional development and popular mobilization, and state strategies. Empowerment in Kerala in India and Ceara in Brazil have meant that people demand proper public services and will not tolerate shirking or corruption (The Economist, 2005g; Tendler, 1997). However, 'under scarcity conditions [social capital may] also become an integral part of the structures of constraint created by gender, class, ethnicity.' . . . The relevance of social capital, then 'cannot be fully assessed unless one considers the power relations that mediate social interaction' (Pantoja, 1999, cited in Harriss, 2002, p. 106).

Social capital is Janus faced: it involves reciprocity, but also competition. The question is who is in and out of the network. In any network a member is expected to contribute either material or non-material resources. The fact that the poor have few material resources and that their non-material resources are not of interest to those in higher social classes contribute to their exclusion (Øyen, 2000b). Even if 'social capital' can be increased, by spreading it more widely, beyond ethnic business networks for example, (Barr and Toye, 2000) you may be reducing the returns from it and thereby undermining monetary capital accumulation, which is in part dependent on asymmetric information to generate rents. Economic growth may also disrupt networks enhancing 'economic capital accumulation for some, and social decapitalization for others' (Fox, 1997, cited in Howell and Pearce, 2001, p. 30). Thus, the channels may run in either direction. The effects of social capital are thus in need of further empirical research.

Øyen's conclusion that 'if a majority of the poor are neither able to develop useful networks for increasing their own social capital on a large scale, nor given entry into those networks where social capital flourishes, how can social capital then be an efficient instrument for poverty reduction?' is well founded (Øyen, 2000b, p. 29). However, she argues that it is nonetheless worthwhile to build social capital to achieve voice and hence political change and redistribution. Thus she sees social capital as a means to achieve rights, rather than a substitute for them.

Because of its supposed apolitical character, according to Ben Fine (2003, p. 136):

> Social capital is the dream concept for the new consensus. First, it incorporates all of the results of the information –theoretic economics – it can be seen as the non-market response to market imperfections . . . [It] is such a chaotic and all-embracing notion, that it can mean whatever you want it to, thereby granting extraordinary analytical discretion and power to the hands of those who use it.

It fails to address properly either capital or the social; it tends to set aside issues of power and conflict; it compartmentalizes capital into its economic and social components; and it places emphasis on civil society at the expense of state and politics.

(Fine, 2003, p. 137)

Thus there is no social capitalist nirvana where uneven development is reversed by everyone becoming nicer and more trustworthy. Social capital as a discourse represents a form of 'social inclusion lite,' without redistribution or job opportunities.

Social capital and the state

The good governance discourse has also been tied in with social capital. According to Michael Woolcock (2002), social capital can be measured using country-level trust and governance scores. Although it should be noted that high civil society governance scores (observance of the rules of the game) are also obtainable in nonliberal political regimes, such as in Jordan (Hyden *et al.*, 2003).

Deepa Narayan (2002, p. 60) argues that

Under conditions of good governance, the functioning state *compliments* the functions of the informal social groups. In societies in which primary social groups are connected through cross cutting ties economic prosperity and social order are likely.

However, she argues that where there is little bridging social capital and one group dominates, conflict is likely. One of the problems with this analysis is that it takes ethnic groups as primordial rather than examining how these identities come into existence, are 'invented' and changed.

Whereas Robert Putnam sees Northern and Southern Italy being locked in 'virtuous' and 'vicious' path dependencies, respectively, with their origins over a thousand years ago (see Harriss, 2002), others have argued convincingly that it is patterns of state building which heavily influence civic capacity (Tarrow, 1996, cited in Akkerman *et al.*, 2004). In particular prior to the unification of Italy, the Northern states penetrated the Southern ones, making the South into the 'Ireland of Italy' (Harriss, 2002). Thus the dependent integration of the South, into the industrializing ambit of the North and the creation of unequal trade, financial and productive relationships were implicated in the *Mezzogiorno's* lagging performance, rather than its inherent cultural characteristics (although Putnam does note that the unequal land holdings in the South created the conditions for the development of patron–client ties). It should also be remembered that fascism in Italy arose in the North of the country.

Taken to its extreme in an African context, and reminiscent of the diffusionist modernization theory, social capital theory can result in calls for 'cultural adjustment programs' (Chabal and Daloz, 1999).

According to these arguments, the cause of the weakness of development in parts of the Third World is 'lack of social capital. But if the absence of civic capacity is the by-product of politics, state-building and social structure, then the causes of the malaise (of development) are more likely to be structural. Then policy-makers who attack the lack of social capital would be attacking the symptoms and not the causes of the problem.'

(Tarrow, 1996, cited in Harriss, 2002, p. 1)

Thus for example, the Indian state of Kerala, which was long governed by the Communist Party, has the highest levels of social capital in the country (Mayer, 2000, cited in Harriss, 2002). Harriss (2002, p. 11) asks 'can this public action be understood except by taking into account the history of political mobilization in the state, which was also instrumental in bringing about India's most notable agrarian reform.' The history of militant labor organizing in Kerala also discouraged private investors and created space for the development of successful popular economic organizations (see Thomas Isaac *et al.*, 1998).

A high degree of associationalism in and of itself cannot explain the structural transformations that have underscored Kerala's social development. The redistributive thrust of Kerala's development has carried with it a direct attack on traditional structures of power [and entails] a fundamental realignment in the balance of class forces.

(Heller, 1996, cited in Harriss, 2002, p. 61)

Kerala's experiment with participatory planning was explicitly state-promoted, and combined a significant transfer of government resources with mass mobilization through the Kerala Popular Science Movement. The Maharashtra's EGS [employment guarantee scheme] was initially a welfare-for-work scheme that invited a degree of micro-level participation, but over time led to the wider politicization of rural unemployment as an issue.

(Williams, 2004a, p. 570)

Thus rather than looking at social capital, an alternative approach would ask 'under which social-structural and political governance conditions does collective self-organization of the poor contribute to effective poverty reduction?' (Braathen, 2000, p. 41). Social capital implies a lack of actualization and it might be better to speak of social capacities to address problems (Hokoo and Perkins, 1995, cited in Woolcock, 2002). Michael (2004), for example, argues that African NGOs need to focus on networking to build and transform their social capital into political capital. Social and political change is only likely to come about through social pressure and struggle, rather than 'participation.'

The tendency to reify communities as democratic is also a form of obscurantism. Indeed the definition and hence creation of communities is often undertaken as part of development projects (Williams, 2004a). Pantoja (2000, cited in Harriss, 2002, p. 113) argues that the promotion of social capital should be put in the context of democratization of community relations. This indicates that the most important priority is the redistribution of resources/power. However, this would undermine social capital's political utility to be able to talk about 'changing social relations – but without seriously questioning existing power relations and property rights' at local or global levels. While conscientization of state and donor officials is important, reliance on 'sympathetic individuals' will not bring about fundamental structural changes. Indeed whether it is within the power of third world state, or international organization officials, (remembering that globally power is concentrated within the developing capitalist transnational historic bloc, which is part of 'civil society' as discussed earlier) to bring these changes about is very much open to question.

By eliding questions of power, civil society and social capital are attractive concepts because they imply a solidarity with the aspirations of ordinary people. In practice they may be the converse: providing a cover for the roll-back of the state and its social reproduction functions.

> Notions such as social capital and the social market carry a double meaning: they refer to the socialization of the market and at the same time to the instrumentalization or commodification of social relations. The notion of 'trust as a commodity' exemplifies this double move.
>
> (Dasgupta, 1988, cited in Nederveen Pieterse, 2001, p. 125)[13]

This commodification of social relations may thus dovetail with the agenda of privatization.

Relatively equal distribution of income may be a prerequisite for the development of trust, but many developing countries in Latin America and Africa have very high Gini coefficients. As Alexis de Tocqueville (quoted in Reilly, 1995, cited in Edwards, 2004c, p. 290) put it, 'if men are to remain civilized or to become so, the act of associating together must grow and improve in the same ratio in which the equality of condition is increased.' While Putnam recognizes the potential for synergy 'between private organization and the government' (Putnam, 1994, cited in Howell and Pearce, 2001, pp. 48–9), the fact that most of the developing world is not characterized by these preconditions suggests that social capital is not a 'magic bullet.' The state has the central role in reducing inequality through land reform, transfer payments and other mechanisms. Nonetheless many NGOs are supportive of the idea of social capital, as it is seen to validate their own work in community work and participation (Øyen, 2000b).

Effective popular mobilization is facilitated by the enforcement of rights to free speech, assembly etc. As noted earlier, the Kerala 'model' has also experienced a 'crisis' more recently and so its lessons must be carefully evaluated.[14] Nonetheless its experience suggests that it may be the interaction between civil and political society[15] which is important. Thus the causality may not run from society to state, but derive from the interaction between state and society. As Peter Evans notes 'social capital inheres, not just in civil society, but in an enduring set of relationships that spans the public-private divide' (Evans, 1996a, cited in Harriss, 2002, p. 60). Particularly important is the infrastructure of legal and other governmental institutions in the development of trust in a society. Brehm and Rahm found a 'stronger relationship running from trust in institutions to interpersonal trust' than the converse (Brehm and Rahm cited in Foley and Edwards, 1999, cited in Harriss, 2002, p. 40). In relation to business, Poul Ove Pedersen (1998) found that the development of dynamic enterprise structures; ones where entrepreneurs continuously search out new market opportunities and shifting alliances, depend to a significant extent on what Mark Granoveter (1973) calls the *weak ties*. In particular he argues that such ties only develop when there is a basis for systemic trust underwritten by the state, large organizations or other large collectives.

The politics of scale and social capital

The obsession with social capital serves other useful functions in that it displaces the locus of poverty production from global to local processes ('poor countries do not have enough social capital'). This rescaling of the development/poverty problematic and the downplaying of the idea that poverty is a global responsibility in World Bank reports is traced by Mawdsley and Rigg (2003). However, while it serves an instrumental function, it may also be a practical recognition that 'on average development processes on a small scale and close to the direct needs of the poor were more successful in poverty reduction than ambitious large-scale projects' (Øyen, 2000a, p. 3). Although there is still the question about the operationalization of the concept.

Social capital was also implicated in particular *zeitgeist*. It is often argued that the integrative forces of corporate globalization generate ethno-nationalist and localist backlashes. Amitai Etzioni, the guru of communitarianism defines integration as 'a self-sustaining mechanism that helps a community to maintain itself, its existence and its form by its "own processes" without having to depend on external processes of its member units' (Etzioni, 1965, cited in Poku, 2001, p. 70). The mid-1990s were the era of the Balkan wars and the Rwandan genocide. Social capital provided an alternative vision of inter and intra-community co-operation to achieve productive global integration as the rise of ethnic conflict led to an interest in social capital and institutions (Woolcock, 2002).

The emphasis on civil society and social capital thus helps to 'legitimate a profoundly anti-democratic transnational politics' (Ferguson, n.d., cited in Lewis, 2002, p. 577). It obscures issues of class, economic inequality, politics and power and as such is an improved 'anti-politics' machine (Ferguson, 1994). Both social capital and liberal theories of 'civil society' are firmly 'internalist' in their explanation of underdevelopment. Social capital confines itself to local–national contexts, ignoring international associations and connection in an era of globalization (Fine, 2004). Also whereas 'market failure' suggests a corrective role for the state, 'civil imperfections' which detract from the workings of the market can be rectified through social capital (Fine, 1999). Through 'local organization' people living in poverty can 'pull themselves up by their bootstraps' (Williams, 2004b). Thus, there is no need for additional resources. Cut-backs in public services can be de-centralized and responsibility for them put on communities (Mohan and Stokke, 2000). However, World Bank authors do note that '"the application of social capital in development is not a distribution-neutral process [i.e. it may reduce or enlarge income gaps];" and that by themselves – without other resources – these associations may not make very much difference' (Grootaert, 1997, cited in Harriss, 2002, p. 9) – hence part of the importance given to decentralization in World Bank reform programs.

Social capital also has the political advantage of enabling the potential role of a developmental state not to be discussed, or to problematize the relationship between civil society and the market (Fine, 1999; Howel and Pearce, 2001). Gould and Ojanen (2003, p. 21) talk of the 'post-developmentalist' state. Another way of putting this is that civil society and social capital enable the World Bank to transcend the state–market dichotomy, while retaining an unwavering commitment to market policies (Howell and Pearce, 2001). Indeed civil society itself as a discursive construct is presented as a compromise between state and market logics. It presents itself as a pragmatic post-ideological idea to address both state and market failures through the delivery of services, and politically to address the disconnect between public and individual logics.

Whereas in the past it was primarily the (national) state which was seen to be the problem, now it is (local) society (lack of social capital) and the nature of the (national) state–society interaction. This has lead to the project of 'national development' being vigorously revived, globally (Weber, 2004). However, under globalization much 'power is located in global social formations and expressed through global networks, rather than through territorially based states' (Poku, 2001, p. 71). This renationalization of development thereby elides the question of the 'global reconfiguration of social authority which is not territorially based and which, indeed, transcends any spatial division of the world' (Saurin, 1995, cited in Weber, 2004, p. 191). As such it is a dialectical response to globalization.

Social capital and 'civil society' are concepts used by donors, in the manner of shifting cultivation, to explain underdevelopment, thereby eliding their responsibility in the creation of global poverty. Is there a historical cycle at play where the agents of modernization are seen to shift from the state to the market to civil society and social capital? Does the new pretender have clothes or will it be deposed before enthronement? Does this represent a theatrical 'permanent revolution' in development, with development a moving target, while the structures and (f)actors which perpetuate underdevelopment remain hidden off-stage?

In quick succession, donors have advocated state-led development, then marketization and the retrenchment of government from core functions, followed by democratization, decentralization, the establishment of autonomous agencies, the creation of public–private partnerships, and civil society participation in the delivery of core services. All of this has been imposed on poor countries, with weak institutions, many of them still in the process of basic state building, and in the context of a rapidly changing global environment.

(Center for the Future State, 2005, p. 1)

However, none of these fads have addressed the structural drivers of poverty, particularly the nature of the global economic system. In this context is prevention (eliminating the conditions which bring about poverty) not better than cure (mopping up poverty after it has been generated)? While the new discourse has succeeded admirably in asserting its hegemonic pretensions, it remains to be seen whether it will be sufficient to prevent state collapse and social revolts in the majority world.

Bringing the state back in

An active role for the state is critical in development. In an influential book van de Walle (2001) argued that it serves the interests of state elites to maintain Africa's economic crisis in order to continue to be able to gain access to international policy rents. Drawing on the East Asian experience, van de Walle (2003, p. 6) argues that the solution is to 'embed' the state in civil society. 'Mounting evidence suggests that states are most likely to be effective agents of development when they are "embedded" within a network of links to societal institutions and organizations' (van de Walle 2003, p. 4). However, in Taiwan and South Korea, the state was both autonomous and embedded, but not particularly with civil society, but with the private sector (Amsden, 1989; Wade, 1990).

While Ali Mari Tripp (2003, p. 135) argues that 'it is generally recognized that those countries that have the best linkages between central government and communities through a network of local institutions have fared the best in agricultural performance, in social indicators, and in achieving higher levels of welfare,' the first-tier Asian NICs were 'integral states' which penetrated and directed the private sector to achieve developmental outcomes. Some would argue that they were only able to achieve this outcome because of their favored geopolitical position, which enabled them to create 'developmental regimes' (Pemple, 1999). Thus the dynamic of economic structural transformation revolved around state–private sector interaction, and state investments in social infrastructure, (Hay Woo, 1991, cited in Midgley, 1998) not between the state and associational groupings. Indeed civil society, particularly trade unions, were actively suppressed in the NICs. Also might not the embedding of the state in civil society reduce the latter's oppositional function?

(Akkerman *et al.*, 2004). Thus civil society may not be able to emerge 'organically' in response to domestic issues, and its own rules and negotiations (McIlwaine, 1998a).

In terms of social development there is greater potential for synergy between the state and civil society groups, as Judith Tendler's (1997) work shows.[16] In Tanzania there has been notable success in joint government–NGO activities to tackle the AIDS crisis (Mari Tripp, 2003). Van de Walle (2003) is correct to argue that public and private actors should be seen as complementary rather than alternatives. Although it should also be noted that appeals to synergy may serve to cover co-optation, although this may not in itself be negative if it leads to previously marginal views being implemented (Nederveen Pieterse, 2001).

According to Nederveen Pieterse (2001) synergy does not require ideological consensus. NGOs and local governments require effective central states which supply adequate public goods. However, he goes further than this and argues that

> it is . . . generally recognized today that sustained development requires an interventionist and effective central state to spearhead the development process. Particularly in an environment characterized by both extreme resource scarcities and widespread market failures, state institutions must play a critical role.
>
> (2001, p. 29).

However, this raises the question of what types of interventions. Economic interventions are increasingly difficult, although still often possible for low income countries, under the liberal trade and international capital regimes (Lockwood, 2005; Gallagher, 2005). It would appear that the 'ingredients' for public–private synergy are a 'coherent dependable public institutions,' and a favorable political regime, characterized by political competition that is 'constrained by mutually acceptable ground rules,' in a context of a 'relatively egalitarian social structure' (Evans, 1996, cited in Harriss, 2002, p. 62).

Van de Walle (2003, p. 23) argues that 'donors should use the leverage of aid to forge cooperative behavior between . . . different agencies, by multiplying both formal links and creating incentives to collaborate.' Some authors have suggested linking public and societal associations through boards or trusts, or government organized NGOs (GONGOs) as in China where 'state control exists beside societal participation' (Mari Tripp, 2003, p. 135). Mari Tripp argues that there may be a case for delegation where the state determines what services are to be produced and where but delegates their provision to NGOs. As part of this she argues that state interventions could be targeted at poorer regions with weaker associational bases 'to ensure more even development' (Mari Tripp, 2003, p. 136).

Synergy and co-production do offer potential for developmental outcomes. However, they do not accord well with neoliberalism because they blur the distinction between the different spheres of state, market and civil society, each of which have very clearly defined roles in neoliberal theory. The market (capital), manages the economy, whereas the state serves both a 'night watchman' role, in addition to providing public goods; while CSOs serve as watchdogs on the state, as well as distributing charity. In a time of boundary crossing, however, synergy may be the most appropriate form of partnership, particularly for the production of collective goods which are central to capability development, but are being undermined by the global economic emphasis on knowledge driven accumulation (Evans, 2005).[17]

An active, economically directive role for the state is a bridge too far for the World Bank, however, and even a less directive 'co-productive' role with society characterized by 'synergy' is generally not favored by the Bank, with some exceptions among its staff (see Narayan, 2002). Production is for the private sector, as the World Bank's recent push for (disastrous) water privatizations makes clear;[18] outbreaks of cholera notwithstanding. Enclosure of the commons and commodification took on new meaning in the Bolivian city of Cochabamba in the early 2000s where water privatization was accompanied by legislation outlawing the collection of rainwater (Pilger, 2002). These privatizations, often to foreign companies, have been pushed as part of the Bank's Private Sector Development Strategy (PSDS), introduced in 2002. Arguably the PSDS has as substantial (negative) implications for poverty as the PRSP, but has received very little attention in comparison, showing the success of the World Bank's poverty rebranding.[19] We now move to a consideration of PRSPs.

4
Participatory Poverty: Poverty Re(pro)duction Strategy Papers

Participatory development is an indication of a larger change that is imperceptibly taking place in political systems and cultures. It reflects a relative disempowerment of states and political systems in relation to development and technological change, that takes the form of depoliticization and technocracy, and repoliticization through the emergence of subpolitics, manifesting itself in special interests, lobbying, social movements and localization, ethnic mobilization and religious resurgence. As both cause and effect of democratization, civil actors seek empowerment and the boundaries between political and non-political, public and private spheres have become increasingly fluid. Informalization and liberalization involve a transfer of responsibilities from government to NGOs and the emergence of parallel structures, for instance in welfare and public health. Thus in several countries in sub-Saharan Africa, much of the health care and welfare sector has been subcontracted to foreign-funded NGOs. But what are not being replaced are the procedures of accountability, inadequate as they are. Hence the new democratic culture of which participatory development is part also has new democratic deficits. The problems of participatory development are in part a function of the Washington hegemony. While 'participation' has become the leading development talk since the 1990s, it is a highly elastic term. The alternative platform matches the Washington consensus in the common theme of state failure, the trend toward privatization and informalization, i.e. a greater role for firms or NGOs; and the discourse of civil society and democracy. The new policy agenda of civil society building and 'NGO-ization', community development and self-reliance matches the new right agenda of government rollback and decentralization. Another problem is alternative dependency through foreign-funded NGOs. Accordingly, in the words of Michael Woost, 'we are still riding in a top-down vehicle of development whose wheels are greased with a vocabulary of bottom up discourse.'

(Grillo and Stirrat, 1997, cited in
Nederveen Pieterse, 2001, p. 166)

Is the new participatory myth acting more like a Trojan horse which may end up by substituting a subtle kind of teleguided and masterly organized participation for the old types of intransitive or culturally defined participation, proper to vernacular societies?

(Rahmena, 1997, cited in Williams,
2004a, p. 558)

By the end of the 1990s, the IFIs were facing sustained criticism from both left and right. The public criticism of the IMF's handling of the East Asian financial crisis also brought about a rethink of that institutions policies with the Fund's director in 1998 calling for '*higher* and more cost-effective spending on primary health care and education; [and] adequate social protection for the poor, unemployed and other vulnerable groups' [emphasis added] (Deacon, 2000, p. 10). After the financial crash, the IMF was concerned to ensure the stability of reform (Harrison, 2004a).

Also in 1998 Gordon Brown, UK Chancellor of the Exchequer, proposed a series of modernizing (neoliberal) reforms of the international financial institutions (IFIs). According to Brown 'by 1997, an increasingly turbulent and inadequately supervised international financial system threatened to create boom and bust on a global scale' (Brown, 1999, p. 2). For the Chancellor, 'untrammeled, unregulated market forces had brought great instability and even greater injustice' from the 1870s to the 1930s (Brown, 1999, p. 1). However, rather than dealing with the global economy's chronic demand side problems, most of the reforms Brown proposed centered on greater transparency, combined with World

Bank and IMF reforms preserving 'investment in the social, education and employment programmes which are essential for growth' (Brown, 1999, pp. 1–2). Thus PRSPs speak both to the structural power and contradictions of global capital and civil society, instantiated in international institutions and through states.

Also the global social justice movement was emerging at this time, with its 'coming out party'[1] at the WTO meetings in Seattle in 1999. Interestingly, PRSPs had been introduced earlier that year, as were the MDGs. Thus the global capitalist social formation is up-scaling its responses progressively from more local (social capital), to national (PRSPs), to weak global (such as MDGs and the International Financing Facility recently put into operation between the UK and France). However, as will be argued later, this dialectical displacement cannot succeed and calls for a 'strong global' response. The fact that the *2000/2001 World Development Report's* lead author, Ravi Kanbur, wanted to 'bring global actions to center stage' may have been one of the reasons for his (forced) resignation (see Wade, 2001).

It is from the World Bank, and to a lesser extent the UNDP, that the new hegemonic development discourse is emerging. 'Broadly speaking, the divide now runs between human and alternative development, on the one hand, and the number-crunching approach to development. . . . Institutionally this rift runs between the UN agencies and the IMF, with the World Bank increasingly – and precariously – straddled somewhere in the middle' (Nederveen Pieterse, 2001, p. 96). Indeed the increasing prominence of human development (HD) in the discourse can be seen as a form of recursivity as its main popularizer Muhbub al Haq of the UNDP had previously worked at the World Bank under Robert McNamara in the early 1980s (Hertz, 2004).

The new synthetic discourse promoted by the World Bank is not hegemonic in the sense that it is unchallenged, but that its statements are thought to have widespread relevance and that its key statements are valid (Latour, 1987, cited in Braathen, 2000). For a development theory to be significant, social forces must carry it. To be carried by social forces it must match their worldview and articulate their interests; it must serve an ideological function. However, to serve their interests it must also make sense and be able to explain things (Nederveen Pieterse, 2001). Braathen sees this new hegemonic discourse as legitimating future use of (monetary) force.

To keep the bank afloat Wolfensohn has to steer between two major constituencies. The first are the critics, the second is the US Treasury

(. . .) To save the Bank, and his own reputation it is essential that the Bank's policies and public pronouncements do not err too far from its main shareholder and political protector, the US Treasury.

(Focus on Trade, 2000, cited in Braathen,
2000, p. 32)

'Over time, the staff and management within institutions [IFIs] have increasingly become the source of new policy initiatives. While these initiatives do not necessarily coincide with the predispositions of the South, they do provide a counter weight to preferences from the North. If nothing more, IFIs insulate borrowers from Northern donors' (Krasner, 1985, p. 130). In part this reflects their role in promoting hegemony. It is very expensive for dominant states to rule through coercion, as compliance is much cheaper. Yet in order to be effective, a hegemonic regime must not be seen as merely an appendage of the dominant states. It must deliver wider benefits. Hence the role of PRSPs in the reconstruction of hegemony.

It had become clear that the hollowing out of the third world state had undermined its, and with it neoliberalism's, legitimacy. In parts of Africa there was a 'deinstitutionalization of the state . . . loss of territorial control and the pervasive spread of violence and insecurity' (Bach, 2003, p. 29). In dialectical fashion this called forth a need to strengthen and relegitimate the state, in order to allow for the perpetuation of neoliberalism. Whereas up until the late 1990s 'the failure of the state in Africa [was] so uncontested that both scholarly discussions and policy concerns . . . shifted to what is called civil society' (Samatar and Samatar, 2002a, p. 5), by the end of the decade civil society was to be called forth to serve state strengthening. This was the context in which PRSPs were introduced.

What then is the new theory of civil society engagement for poverty reduction? In order to understand the new hegemonic discourse in formation it is necessary to conduct a partial excavation of the evolution of development theory more generally.

Poverty and development discourse

The new hegemonic global development discourse is a synthesis of neoliberalism and HD. In 1999 Secretary General of the UN launched a 'global compact' between transnational business and the UN which would 'give a human face to the global market.' In return for support to the UN and signing up to voluntary human rights and labor and environmental standards, companies are allowed to use the UN logo. Annan chose these areas because 'they are the ones I feel that, if we do not act, there may be a threat to the open global market, and especially the multilateral trade regime' (Annan, 1999, cited in Hanahoe, 2003, p. 157). Others have gone further arguing for a World Development Corporation run by multinationals, with NGO support and under the auspices of the UN as the solution to global poverty (Lodge and Wilson, 2006).

The HD approach is fundamentally about capacitation and the enlargement of people's choices. It emerged, not coincidentally, at the same time as neoliberalism in the 1980s and authors in this school often make reference to the experience of the Pacific Rim, the importance of capabilities and the developmental state (Nederveen Pieterse, 2001). The UNDP began publishing its Human Development Reports in 1990. A recent evolution of this approach is the human security one, which pays attention to transnational social policy and a global social contract. The discourse on 'human security,' which emerges from the mid-1990s, represents a paradigm shift by focusing on individual, rather than state security (Grant and Söderbaum, 2003). As such a much broader range of issues, from poverty to disease, can be included in the study of security. It also recognizes the links between individual and state security, although the securitization of poverty or development may also pose problems (see Kirby, 2006). One of the key motifs of the human security approach is the idea of 'global public goods,' such as governance or education (Moore, 2004).

The UNDP now plays a pivotal role in civil society capacity building and linking the PRSP process with the achievement of the MDGs. The main recommendation of a report for UNDP in 2003 was that it should make the PRSP 'play a more central role in its country level operations' (UNDP, 2003a, p. 7). Thus the Bretton Woods institutions have been successful in further consolidating their hegemony in the aid cartel (Gould, 2005a). However, it is noted that 'UNDP has stamped PRSPs with its approach to the development process' (UNDP, 2003a, p. 3).

Both neoliberalism and HD share a focus on the individual. This approach has been characterized as growth with equity, with equal emphasis on both the 'social' and 'development' (growth) (Nederveen Pieterse, 2001, p. 116). In this approach there is a concern for the quality of economic growth; that it be broad-based and 'pro-poor.' This is seen by the World Bank (2004c) to be important in sustaining the political impetus for neoliberal economic reform.

Assuming the individual as the unit of development shows HD to have its roots in liberalism. However, this means that 'to the extent, then that HD does not challenge neoliberalism and the principle of competitiveness but endorses it, HD may enable development business-as-usual to carry on more competitively under a general "humane" aura' (Nederveen Pieterse, 2001, p. 121).[2] The fact that this synthesis is political/organic is evidenced by the fact that its main spokesman internationally is Jeffrey Sachs of Columbia University in the US, previously one of the main spokespeople for the neoliberal revolution.[3]

As Nederveen Pieterse (2001, p. 156) notes:

> Early development efforts concentrated on the hardware of development, such as infrastructure, capital inputs and technology. The recent trend is to pay equal attention to the software of development, to institutions, processes and management (e.g. World Bank 1997c), education and knowledge (World Bank 1998) or indeed to argue that development is essentially human software development, as in the human approach and the World Bank's aspiration to become a 'knowledge bank'. The emphasis on knowledge parallels the shift in the North towards the knowledge-intensity of production. It implies a major reorientation from a general preoccupation with the external dimensions and façade of development (infrastructure, capital inputs) to the 'inner' conditions: from a one-dimensional to a multi-dimensional understanding of development.

Much has been written about the nature and causes of poverty. White and Killick (2001) analyze poverty in terms of

- Interactive factors, which may be both cause and consequence of poverty.
- Primary causes, being the deep-seated underlying factors causing African poverty.
- Proximate causes, causes of poverty that are themselves outcomes of deeper sources.

For a long-time it was seen simply in policy-making circles as involving a lack of income. However, more recently the view that poverty is multi-dimensional has become commonplace, with some claiming that 'there is no question that there is now broad agreement that education and health outcomes are on par [sic] with income in assessing poverty and the consequences of economic policy' (Kanbur, 2005, p. 2). Drawing inspiration from Amartya Sen's (1999) capability approach, which argues that poverty in the result of lack of capability/power to access/create resources, the *World Development Report of 2000/2001* defined poverty as having five dimensions: lack of health, education, income, vulnerability and powerlessness (World Bank, 2000c, cited in Skirbekk and St. Clair, 2005). This new definition of poverty is also meant to draw inspiration from the 'voices of the poor' and the (European) ideas of social exclusion/inclusion. These terms are now found in World Bank literature. Indeed James Wolfensohn, former President of the World Bank opined that the 'challenge of inclusion' is what the Bank must meet (Wolfensohn, 1997, p. 1, cited in Bergeron, 2003, p. 157). However, social exclusion is seen to result from lack of individual capability/power, rather than systemic failures. The power to frame discourse is important in this. In some local languages, as in Burkina Faso in West Africa there is no word for 'poverty,' which is an outsider's concept (Engberg-Pedersen, 2002). Thus, the concept of poverty can be used as a cover for external intervention.

The recent redefinition of poverty also draws on the lineage of social development. Midgley (1998, p. 1) notes that 'social development's most distinctive feature is its attempt to harmonize social policies with measures designed to promote economic development.' Thus social policies are meant to promote economic development, and economic development is meant to be inclusive, thereby establishing a 'virtuous circle.' Human capital formation is meant to be subject to increasing returns (Romer, 1986 and Birdsall, 1993, both cited in Midgley, 1998), making social investment a win–win game for both the economy and society. It has been estimated that educational investments can generate rates of return of between 13 percent and 26 percent for governments, with primary education having the highest social rates of return (Psacharopoulos, 1992, cited in Midgley, 1998, p. 18; World Bank, 1995, cited in Mehrotra, 2001). In Madagascar, it is estimated that 90 percent of illnesses could be prevented or treated at primary level, if services were of good quality and accessible (World Bank, 1995, cited in Castro-Leal *et al.*, 2000).[4] This social rate of return logic feeds into PRSPs, where debt relief is tied to social investment. However, social development is still vulnerable to charges of economism, as those activities which have an 'economic pay-off' are prioritized over those which may have other intrinsic worth.

The HD approach extends the insights of social development, but redefines development to focus on capabilities rather than economic growth. In its 1996 *Human Development Report*, UNDP claimed that economic growth would not lead to development if it was jobless, associated with increased inequality, poverty, authoritarianism, the undermining of culture and unsustainability. It called these types of economic growth, jobless, ruthless, voiceless, rootless and futureless, respectively (UNDP, 1996, cited in Kanyenze, 2003). According to a report for the UNDP, 'the PRSP is but the most recent global manifestation of the view that people are the core of "development"' (UNDP, 2003a, p. 2).

> Alternative development in this sense claims a 'Copernican revolution' in understanding development. The key resource becomes not the country's aggregate GNP but people's creativity. This would also imply, for instance, that 'poverty' as such disappears as a clear-cut development indicator. Poverty as an indicator follows from the development-as-growth paradigm: 'the poor' are the target of development because they lack economic resources. But if development is not about growth but institutional transformation, then the concern is not merely with economic capital but as much with social, cultural, symbolic and moral capital and in these respects people can be rich. . . . Stereotypes of poverty as wholesale deprivation, the 'culture of poverty' etc, are disabling elements of development discourse. They evoke the notion of development as external intervention.
>
> (Nederveen Pieterse, 2001, p. 88)

However, there may be trade-offs between economic and social development. While 95 percent of Keralans, in India, over age seven are literate, the same as Israel (Douthwaite, 2004a), and it has infant mortality rates half those of countries nine times richer (Nederveen Pieterse, 2001), *The Economist* (2005g) notes that the unemployment level is three times the Indian national average. The economy improved in the late 1980s and early 1990s, however, putting it in a 'growth neutral category' (Heller, 1999, cited in Evans, 2004) compared to the rest of India. However, by the early 2000s the Communist government, which had ruled since independence, was voted out of power, and neoliberal style economic reforms introduced (Kumar, 2002).[5]

Social and HD, which were alternative developments, have become mainstreamed. This is part of the broader dialectic of development. For example, in the structuralist inspired African Alternative Framework to Structural Adjustment Programmers (AAF-SAP) it was envisaged that at least 30 percent of government expenditure would go to the social sectors (Tomori and Tomori, 2004). Subsequently the Organization for Economic Co-operation and Development (OECD) called for a 20/20 compact where 20 percent of aid and 20 percent of developing country government expenditure would go on the social sectors (Deacon, with Hulse and Stubbs, 1997). The inclusion of alternative development concepts thus serves both instrumental and objective functions. It allows for evolutionary learning, but also serves to minimize resistance to the status quo.

Whether a decreased emphasis on the material aspects of poverty is progressive or regressive is open to interpretation and ultimately dependent on the value system adopted. The failure of orthodox development approaches to raise living standards in Africa may not be so serious in the new orthodoxy if people are 'empowered.' It is to the nature of orthodox empowerment that we now turn.

Participation in neoliberalism

There are different patterns of interaction between states and civil societies or 'associational cultures,' (Pearce, 1997a, cited in Hilhorst, 2003), although the idea of 'associational patterns' may better capture the inter-institutional variation in relationships. Should a common template for associational cultures be globally transplanted through the PRSP and other processes?

Whereas social capital penetrated the global development discourse in the mid-1990s, participation became institutionalized in national development policies in the late 1990s with the development of PRSPs. What is the genealogy of PRSPs? In part it is the story of broader changes in immanent and imminent development, but also within the organizational culture of the Bank and the mainstreaming of participation.

Depending on the particular policy report there are different emphases, but according to the new development orthodoxy there are two sources of development failure: external constraints, such as debt and protected OECD markets, and the internal structures of domestic state/society complexes (e.g. World Bank, 2000a). The World Bank is progressive on questions of market access and developed country agricultural subsidies, but pays less attention to the fact that the regulations agreed under the WTO may in some cases take up to a year's entire development budget for African governments to enforce (Pogge, 2002). Market access is not necessarily the main problem for African countries with 97–98 percent of exports into the EU, even before the 'Everything But Arms Initiative,' entering at a zero tariff (Amjadi *et al.*, 1996, cited in Lockwood, 2005). Far more important is adverse movements in the terms of trade as a result of lack of economic diversification. In keeping with the Berg Report of 1981, however, the focus for the World Bank remains on what can be done at national level (World Bank, 1981).

Whereas in the past it was the nature of the neopatrimonial and prebendal African state which was seen to be the problem, this has now been rethought and the nature (weakness) of civil society and state-society linkages are now also perceived to be part of the problem. This may in part have been a recognition that 'in eradicating poverty and providing social services, NGOs are unlikely ever to play more than a complementary role' (UNDP, 1993, cited in Pearce, 1997a, p. 274). The challenge then is seen to be one of easing external constraints, while building civil society (and to a lesser degree the state) and facilitating new institutions to monitor performance and achieve synergies between these two arenas and actors, and the market.

In its 1993 *Human Development Report*, the UNDP argued that 'strengthening of the institutions of civil society [w]as the only appropriate policy response for increasing citizen participation' (McIlwaine, 1998a). However, the goal of this participation is an instrumental one to increase (individual) human capacity development, though education, for example. In 1994 a World Bank report called for the 'mainstreaming' of participation in Bank projects (World Bank, 1994, cited in Brinkerhoff with assistance from Kulibaba, 1996). The World Bank, 1996b, cited in Brinkerhoff and Goldsmith, 2003, p. 686) defines participation as 'a process through which stakeholders influence and share control over development initiatives and the decisions and resources which affect them.'

The World Bank has begun to see the state, market and civil society as strategic complements, with former President James Wolfensohn encouraging all World Bank country offices to appoint a civil society officer (World Bank, 1997c, cited in Howell, 2000). The links in the chain in this new triadic model of development are provided by institutions. As the World Development Report of 1997 notes:

> For good or ill, the state sets the tone. This chapter makes the empirical case for shifting the focus of our thinking about development toward the quality of a country's institutions and the capability of the state – for bringing institutions into the mainstream of our dialogue about development.
>
> (World Bank, 1997c, cited in Howell and Pearce,
> 2001, p. 66)

Institutions, including those of civic engagement are very much the focus in the rest of the report, while the active role of the state is downplayed, however. The report talks about the need to 'match [state] capability and role.' However, as state capacity is assumed to be lacking, a minimal role is envisaged, rather than interrogating how capacity can be created (see Moore, 1999 for a discussion of this). Thus the vision at that time was of a hollowed-out state, bolstered, but surveilled by a vigilant civil society, and donors.

The 1997 *World Development Report* also notes disparate interests, power differentials and the limitations of CSOs, while also arguing that strengthening CSOs may fend off anarchy (Howell, 2000; McIlwaine, 1998a), speaking to their social regulatory role, noted earlier. However, other World Bank publications note that NGOs are innovative and locally informed and consequently have the 'development software' (participatory methods, community organizing) to complement the state's 'development hardware' in macro-policies (Garrision, 2000, cited in Mercer, 2002).

The priority to 'strengthen civil society' has received new impetus as a result of the heavily indebted poor country (HIPC) initiative, introduced in 1997, and the more recently announced debt cancellation for some HIPC countries. HIPC is an 'accountability framework' to link debt relief to macro-economic and governance reform, and social policies (Craig and Porter, 2002). Debt relief is to be spent on health and education expenditures. As *ex ante* donor conditionality was found to be ineffective (on this, see Killick, 1998) and as debt stocks have lessened,[6] new sources of accountability in civil society have been sought (van de Walle, 2003; Elbadawi and Gelb, 2003). Thus PRSPs attempt to reduce principal (donor)-agent (state) problems through an intermediary (civil society).

> Critics argue though that in the new World Bank perspective 'any agenda for social and political change is lost in this technocratic discourse that essentially argues that NGOs be utilized to legitimize World Bank-sponsored attempts to foster widespread acceptance of the neoliberal . . . state' (Mercer, 2002, p. 18). Thereby 'in turning civil society into a technical project, donors not only impose a normative vision of civil society which is deeply embedded in the historical context of Western Europe and North America but also empty it of its political content and potential,' thereby making it potentially anti-democratic by restricting space for debate and its organic development.
>
> (Howell, 2000)

Thus,

> civil society is asked to participate in a new triadic model of development along with the state and the market, in which its primary

function is to counterbalance the power of the state. The model neither problematizes the relationship of civil society to the market nor
does it allow for civil society to have a role in defining what kind of
state there should be.

(Howell and Pearce, 2001, p. 2)

Furthermore,

To invest civil society with a moral dimension [as donors do] is not
only to misrepresent its historical role in the regulation of social and
political life, but also to deprive it of its capacity to express, and
thereby paradoxically to contain, the aspirations for power, influence, and control over truth which are defining features of politics.

(Jenkins, 2001, p. 266)

In this new architecture grass GROs may be by-passed by donor funding in favor of NGOs [renamed 'civil society' to avoid raising government hackles], thereby reducing space for oppositional voices to be
heard, and weakening democracy (Arrelano-Lopez and Petras, 1994,
cited in Mercer, 2002).

Global civil society and the World Bank

The World Bank pursues multiscalar strategies of engagement with
civil society, also operating at a global level. At an international level,
the World Bank favors certain types of CSOs over others. The
Structural Adjustment Participatory Review Initiative (SAPRIN), which
was set up in the late 1990s, comprised the representatives of the
World Bank and prominent national CSOs, many of whom were donor
funded. However, the World Bank backed out of the review when the
report was highly critical of SAPs, and produced its own report instead
(SAPRIN, 2002; World Bank, 2001a). The World Bank did not want a
critique of its neoliberal paradigm, but rather as its report put it to
embed 'adjustment from within.' This terminology is an attempted
discursive elision of the relativization of scale under globalization,
where no one scale is dominant, but are mutually constituted (Jessop,
2000). However, the World Bank wants 'rational'-national adjustment
to be internally owned by elites and civil societies. For an organization
promoting globalization, it does not follow through on its political
logic. However, according to Matt Coleman (2002, p. 518), the World

Bank is stuck between a statist understanding of geography and a 'genie out of the bottle' mapping of globalization which does not allow for 'a more dynamic, networked, relational and non-ontological notion of scale.' States cannot resist globalization, but it's their fault if it doesn't work!

The experience of SAPRIN shows, however, that the outcomes of participation are not predetermined. Challenging the state or international institutions may take numerous forms including accountability, transparency *and* their neoliberal form. The global justice movement may also provide a new rallying point for NGOs to become more oppositional as 'commitment to values that advance public and collective interests and that radically side with the poor will continue to be an important element in the ideological visions of many NGOs' (Hilhorst, 2003, p. 226). According to Alan Fowler (2004a, p. 357), what is needed are

> Tactics which draw on the principles of martial arts – such as judo and jujitsu – using the momentum and energy of the opponent to knock them off-balance and throw them in the direction wanted. The parallel in international aid is to identify and exploit contradictions and weaknesses in the aid system and economic system, its agents, and in the political system with its power holders.

More recently the World Bank has formed an alliance with the Tocquevillian inspired CIVICUS which has an emphasis on promoting an 'international civil society which is self-regulating, voluntary and promoting the public good' (Howell, 2000, p. 3) through a Joint Facilitation Committee which aims for more effective engagement between the World Bank and civil society (see, for example, Altangerel and Bae, 2004).[7] It has also sought to foster closer business–NGO ties through its Corporate Citizenship team. However even a multiscalar approach cannot paper over the contradictions of this project of alignment of state, market and civil society, because they do, to some extent, operate off different logics.

> The notion of a triadic unity glosses over the contradictory purposes of the three spheres and the degree of actual and potential conflict. The purposes and values of the market, state and civil society actors are replete with contradictions and tensions, which may not always be worked out in ways that strengthen civil society.
>
> (Howell, 2000, p. 9)

Mainstreaming participation

Participation has a long history in development discourse. The UN has promoted community participation since the 1970s (Midgley, 1998). However, it was only in the 1990s that the World Bank began to use participatory poverty assessments (PPAs) to contribute to country poverty assessments (PAs) which relied heavily on household survey data. The mixture of qualitative and quantitative methods has created a number of questions and dilemmas. There are indisputable advantages to PPAs, such as the stress on 'the right of the poor to participate in defining and analyzing the phenomenon and process of poverty as these affect them' (McGee and Norton, 1999, p. 28; Brock, 2002, p. 3). However, it is interesting that PPAs, which are local anthropological methods, have been adopted by the World Bank, but not methods from other disciplines, such as comparative case studies much used in Geography. Nonetheless even limited participation may open up space for previously marginalized groups to develop voice and thereby become 'policy shapers' over the longer-term (Cornwall and Gaventa, 2000, cited in McGee, 2002b).

For some the impacts of participatory development have been 'tremendous and truly salutary' (Onimode, 2004). Yet others have questioned the utility of participation without empowerment (Sunmonu, 2004). Educated elites may be more motivated and able to participate, thereby deepening the exclusion of the poor. Only through empowerment can the conditions of 'ideal voice,' where there is no fear of negative repercussions from participation, be met (see Parfitt, 2002). Thus effective participation may be dependent on more far-reaching structural reform and democratization, rather than the simple adoption of participatory research and planning methodologies. Opening up the core activities of the state to societal participation through co-governance may achieve empowerment, however, this is not on the agenda in the new aid regime (Ackerman, 2004). There are also issues around participation in the context of unequal gender relations (Cornwall, 2003).

Whereas for some

> The proliferation of the language of 'participation' and 'empowerment' within the mainstream is heralded as the realization of a long-awaited paradigm shift in development thinking. For others, however, there is less cause for celebration. Their concerns center on the use of participation as a legitimating device that draws on the moral authority of claims to involve the poor to place the pursuit of other agendas beyond reproach. According to this perspective, much

of what is hailed as 'participation' is a mere technical fix that leaves inequitable global and local relations of power, and with it the root causes of poverty, unchallenged.

(Cornwall, 2000, cited in Brock, 2002, p. 2)

Brinkerhoff and Goldsmith (2003, p. 695) argue that if managed properly that 'by subjecting policymakers to pressures from diverse interest groups, participatory processes can be a means to reinforce budgetary restraint,' thereby dovetailing with a neoliberal agenda. This is based on a Dahlian understanding of representative democracy, whereby it regulates competition for power, and there are 'weak publics' that form opinion but do not make decisions (Howell and Pearce, 2001). However, there may be advantages to this. Esman and Uphoff (1984, cited in Hadenius and Uggla, 1996, p. 1634), echoing Granoveter's (1973) work in a different context found that

Linkage to government agencies has a strong negative correlation with an organization's influence on claim-making and its ability to exert control over bureaucracy (average correlation: –0.36). They also show, however, that this correlation is non-linear. The obvious logic behind this finding is that total autonomy makes it impossible to maintain channels for demands and control. Instead, an intermediate position (a moderate connection to government agencies) proves the best.

There are methodological issues here and also issues around how interests are constructed, however. There are also concerns that

The notion of participation – an 'infinitely malleable concept'. . . has been transformed through its adoption by powerful development actors, and the nature of that transformation has resulted in a version of participation which is heavily weighted towards knowledge production, to the detriment of action and consciousness.

(Brock, 2002, p. 7)

We may think then of a form of 'guided participation' where the institutions, and consequently outcomes, are largely prescribed and the potential to engage in 'counter-research' (Illich, [1969] 1978) is very limited. 'Provided spaces' put in place at the behest of donors, may be quite different in terms of their politics than 'conquered spaces' resulting from successful civil society demands (Cornwall, 2004b).

Participation may thus serve to cloak the agency of development 'experts,' thereby hiding and illuminating different elements of the development process itself from public scrutiny/engagement. How can society criticize a development strategy which it itself has constructed? The key is then what issues are open for debate and policy change and which are not, and the mechanisms of societal interest representation. Participation as an end, in addition to being a means, suggests a 'transformation in power relations between donor and recipient, with the latter empowered and liberated from a clientelist relation with the former' (Parfitt, 2004, p. 539). Robert Chambers (1997, cited in Williams, 2004a), one of the foremost proponents of participatory approaches, sees this taking place through a change in the relationship between 'development uppers' (government, aid officials) and 'lowers.' In this formulation, power is to be given away by the development uppers in return for 'psycho-social rewards' such as those used by the Hunger Project (Chambers, 2006).

A narrow concept of participation is depoliticizing, thereby fitting with donors' discourse as they sometimes present themselves as apolitical, having no instrumental interests or goals (see Howell, 2000). However, as Howell and Pearce (2001, p. 16) note 'by assuming a neutrality that is taken for granted, however, international agencies leave unexplained the source of their authority to act as broker and reveal their relative power to decide the terms of their engagement.' Disembedded quotes from poor people can be used to support the organizational agenda of liberalization by the World Bank, for example, in its reports. However, as Nustad (2000) notes 'policy is the enactment of politics.'

A World Bank publication claims that PPAs

> Allow better technical diagnosis of the problem, as well as better design and implementation of the solution. [PPAs] have the potential to increase dialogue and negotiation at a policy level, and strengthen links between communities and policy-makers (that) . . . could challenge existing power relations in the long term.
>
> (Robb, 1999, cited in Rademacher and Patel, 2002, p. 172)

However, the power to be challenged is only that which is vested in the state, without recognizing that this itself is reflective of broader constellations of power in global society (Jessop, 2002).

PPAs also have methodological problems at the level of both scale and theory. As Fine notes, PPAs are how the World Bank allows the poor to define the key factors in their poverty (Fine, 2003). However he also notes that it is impossible for researchers not to bring analytical pre-conceptions to their interpretation.

> I suspect that none of the poor, in Tanzania or elsewhere, has ever identified their condition to be a consequence of inadequate social capital. Popular participation must conform to its presuppositions.
>
> (Fine, 2003, p. 140)

The extensive *Consultations with the Poor* for the World Bank *Voices of the Poor* Study had a wide-ranging remit. It asked participants to reflect on:

- Well-being and ill being, poor people's ideas of good and bad quality of life, degrees and categories of well-being and ill-being, and how relative numbers in these groups had changed.
- Problems and priorities, their relative importance, and how they had changed.
- Relationships with institutions of the state and of civil society, including institutions within communities, with rankings, and how these had changed.
- Gender relations, and how these had changed (Chambers, 2002, p. 141).

Robert Chambers (2002) notes that in the *Consultations with the Poor*, the fact that preset categories were presented meant you 'got out what you put in.' Knowledge production is political and the danger with PPAs is that it presents 'voices of the poor' as unmediated, when in fact this is not the case. The researchers use particular methodologies and quotes and experiences are often abstracted from their historico-geographic context. In the case of the *Voices of the Poor* study 'unhelpful questions were . . . suspended as researchers worked to read and interpret the data for a synthetic narrative that would bind localized parts of PPA narratives into a "global" whole' (Rademacher and Patel, 2002, p. 174). This leads Rademacher and Patel (2002, p. 176) to conclude that

> Until the Bank is open to hearing the criticisms of development and *its institutions* in what it invites from the voices of the poor, and until it is equipped to receive more contextualized, actual 'voices,' it is hard to refute the charge that narratives such as *Can Anyone Hear Us?* are simply the appearance of listening to remake a World Bank image while avoiding the real work of re-making the institutions (Lohmann, 1988). Is *Can Anyone Hear Us?* the institutions agenda made into local expression, or is it the other way around? A truly 'global' perspective

on poverty would include the institution itself in it problematic of global and local poverty.

The scalar problem with PPAs is that people will tend to identify local, rather than global, factors with which they are familiar as responsible for their poverty. However, as Rademacher and Patel (2002, p. 170) note:

> Often, social features we take as 'local' in fact have extra-local origins; limiting an inquiry to a bounded locality can sometimes obscure the important non-local origins of problems like poverty.

Particularly in a crisis situation, this may lead to an emphasis on palliative measures, rather than a deeper examination of the structural causes of the crisis (Wisner, 1993, cited in Rademacher and Patel, 2002). In policy terms, what this means is that there is emphasis on identifying 'poverty dynamics' through which people move into, stay or move out of poverty (see Shaffer, 2002). Many studies list '"determinants of poverty" (such as household size, level of education and region) but very little explanation of the pathways and mechanisms by which these "determinants" determine' (Shaffer, 2002, p. 50). Thus the 'second face of power'; to have things not discussed is in evidence as poverty is conceived as a 'lack' of money and services, individual characteristics, or even social capital, but not relational power.[8]

Some PPAs, such as the Studies in Social Deprivation project in Myanmar, have innovative theoretical frameworks; distinguishing between coping strategies of people living in poverty and enabling ones, which allow them to respond to opportunities (Shaffer, 2002). Others enabled people to identify why people move into poverty, for example, by selling assets during times of stress. This may conscientize people to try to hold on to assets (Yates and Okello, 2002).

One of the major benefits of the Ugandan PPA has been

> the power to communicate to and motivate a range of audiences by providing a vivid human picture of poverty that people can relate to, and by highlighting the terrible problems for real people of poor public-service provision, insecurity, geographical isolation, poor governance and discrimination against women.
>
> (Yates and Okello, p. 93)

Will 'development uppers' then redistribute their power? As noted in earlier chapters, the nature of this power in any event may be limited in its impact on poverty in relation to the power of the global market. In any event, PPAs appear to have limited policy impact. In Uganda's PPA powerlessness was defined as a key dimension of poverty (Yates and Okello, p. 93). However, when PPAs are scaled up into PRSPs, such as Uganda's

> power and control-centered conceptions of poverty are typically crowded out by the predominant money-metric and 'social-gap' approaches . . . Consistent with this conception, the implicit reme- dies involve filling this gap by specially targeted interventions to impact on the indicators.
>
> (Craig and Porter, 2002, p. 12)

There are also other problems with other participatory methods, such as the Abilene paradox, where individuals are reluctant to express their true preferences in (focus) groups. Furthermore people living in extreme poverty heavily discount the future (in an economic sense) rationally preferring daily survival; meaning that in terms of impact on policy, inter-temporal trade-offs, on investments that may have long gestation periods, may be given less attention than when using a longitudinal social rates of return approach.

One considered judgment is that

> Despite significant claims to the contrary, there is little evidence of the long-term effectiveness of participation in materially improving the conditions of the most vulnerable people or as a strategy for social change. While the evidence for efficiency receives some sup- port on a small scale, the evidence regarding empowerment and sus- tainability is more partial, tenuous and reliant on the assertions of the rightness of the approach and process, rather than convincing proof of outcomes.
>
> (Cleaver, 2004, p. 225)

However, the outcomes of participation are not predetermined. 'Participatory exercises must therefore be recognized as particular moments within ongoing struggles to re-present and re-organize the interests of clients and facilitators alike' (Williams *et al.*, 2003, p. 165).

One useful optic, raised earlier, through which to view and assess par- ticipation is the idea of 'policy spaces.'[9] These may be either 'invited spaces' opened up by relatively powerful actors, such as governments, or more autonomous ones where the less powerful organize, set agendas and then engage 'power holders.' The objective of participatory poverty research is to open up new, or reconfigure existing, policy spaces to make their governance more 'pro-poor.' In some cases there may be synergy between the two, with invited spaces creating the potential for the organization of more autonomous spaces (see Adan *et al.*, 2002). According to McGee (2002a, p. 201):

> Participatory research offers opportunities to shape and 'nest' emerging policy spaces, in such a way as to maximize the impact of what happens within them. Crucial to this is understanding the context and level of receptivity or rejection of civil society participation in policy research or policy processes themselves. Potential is maximized by treating poverty policy processes as having at least four entry strategies (the informational route; the stimulation of local-level action, including cooperation with others in pre-existing projects or programmers; the broadening of the policy community; and the experiential learning of decision-makers and researchers), and critically appraising the viability of each.

The politics of power, participation and poverty: Poverty Reduction Strategy Papers

In 1999, the World Bank and the IMF (the IFIs) announced that they are abandoning the language of 'structural adjustment' and that their loans or debt relief to poor countries would now be conditional on the development of Poverty Reduction Strategy Papers (PRSPs). This poverty rebranding of the IFIs was in response to the failure of the structural adjustment paradigm and subsequent crisis of legitimacy. The World Bank's chief economist at the time, Joseph Stiglitz, was particularly influential in bringing ideas about partnership and participation into the mainstream (Wade, 2001). The rebranding headed off criticism from both right and left. The Meltzer Report to the US Congress in 2000, for example, argued that the IMF had 'institutionalized economic stagnation' (Johnson, 2004, p. 275), by focusing on actual rather than structural budget deficits (the deficit which would exist if the economy was operating at full employment), for example (Stiglitz, 2002). In this way its policies have been excessively contractionary. The Commission also found the World Bank was irrelevant to its poverty reduction mission and that it should be closed down and turned into a grant-giving agency (Globalization Challenge Initiative, 2002).

PRSPs are designed by poor country governments and then presented to the boards of the IMF and World Bank for approval/funding. In part, this approval is dependent on the government in question putting forward its plans on how it will refocus expenditure and use debt relief monies to reduce poverty over the course of the program. PRSPs are meant to be designed using participatory (in practice consultative) mechanisms. The size of the assistance envelope is not open to negotiation in this, however. The international distribution of resources and power is taken as a given.

According to the World Bank and IMF, the PRSP process and approach is based on six foundational principles:

- Results-oriented, with targets for poverty reduction that are tangible and monitorable.
- Comprehensive, integrating macro-economic, structural, sectoral and social elements.
- Country-driven, representing a consensual view of what actions should be taken.
- Participatory, with all relevant stakeholders participating in formulation and implementation.
- Based on partnerships between government and other actors.
- Long-term, focusing on reforming institutions and building in capacity, as well as short-term goals. (Piron, with Evans, 2004, p. 3).

The three foundational pillars of PRSPs are 'Opportunity, Empowerment and Security' (Craig and Porter, 2006).

As noted earlier, PRSPs have their origins in the debt relief campaign and also the United Nations Summit on Social Development held in 1995. After that summit some governments, such as Uganda, Bolivia and Ireland, set about developing poverty mainstreaming plans and the UNDP launched its Poverty Strategies Initiatives Program (United Nations Development Program, 2003a) (on Ireland see P. Kirby, 2002). In Uganda, the Poverty Eradication Action Plan (PEAP) was formulated from 1995 to 1997 with inputs from a variety of national level actors, including employers, trade unions, NGOs and academics.

An explicit goal in the PEAP's formulation was to identify strategic areas in which increasing budget allocations would lead to poverty reduction, and since its inception the PEAP has been the major guide to the allocation of resources. . . . When the World Bank and the IMF announced in 1999 that eligibility for future debt relief under the

Highly Indebted Poor Countries (HIPC) II Initiative would depend on countries producing and implementing a national poverty reduction strategy, Uganda's revised PEAP (2000) was presented and accepted as its poverty reduction strategy paper.

(Yates and Okello, 2002, p. 71)

Some argue that the PEAP provided the template for the PRSP process, while INGOs such as Oxfam (1998, cited in Deacon, 2000, p. viii) pressed for the debt relief-poverty reduction expenditure linkage. Some argue that it was the national Uganda Debt Network which brought about PRSPs as its extensive partnerships enabled it to bridge the global–national divide (Callaghy, 2001, cited in Shaw *et al.*, 2003). The fact that the linkage between debt relief and poverty reduction expenditure was accepted may, in part, explain why Oxfam supported the World Bank's refunding in the US Congress.

The PRSP agenda shares similarities with the African populist one propounded by Jerry Rawlings in Ghana. Political ideologies are systems 'of beliefs that serve as a standard of evaluation and guide to action' (Young, 1982, cited in Chazan *et al.*, 1999, p. 160). According to Chazan *et al.* (1999, p. 166), 'the key element of the populist ideal in Africa is the need to restructure political institutions and dismantle the elite establishment that has dominated public affairs since independence. This goal would be achieved through mass participation in decision making [in Ghana, Committees for the Defense of the Revolution, PPAs in PRSPs], decentralization of economic control, and the creation of mechanisms for popular scrutiny of governmental affairs.'[10] Ghana also provided the World Bank with the first institutional innovation to popularize structural adjustment: PAMSCAD (the program of actions to mitigate the social costs of adjustment) in 1987, with World Bank and UNICEF support (Poku, 2001). This was mainstreamed in Bank programs through social funds and the 'Social Dimensions of Adjustment Program' worldwide for the next decade. The new PRSP development regime may be compatible with political parties 'a little to the left' and 'a little to the right,' such as those created by the Nigerian military dictatorship.

In Uganda, the budgetary process was opened up to participation in 1998-9, with sector working groups, with members from line ministries, donors, the private sector and NGOs, recommending priority spending areas for poverty reduction. The government also established the Poverty Action Fund to channel resources from debt relief to priority areas for poverty reduction. The perceived success of Uganda has led to a bandwagon effect, with aid accounting for 50 per cent of government expenditure or 10 per cent of GDP (Adam and Gunning, 2002). The PEAP also had political effects. According to a 'key stakeholder' in Uganda, PRSPs have created 'an environment in which CSOs can challenge government' (Yates and Okello, 2002, p. 83). However, there are strict limits to participation. The 2002 round of the PPA in Uganda had no mechanisms for feedback and there was no support for communities to help them work towards the resolution of the problems they identified (Hickey and Mohan, 2004a). Nonetheless lessons can be learnt from Uganda as in some instances senior civil servants allied with critical advocacy groups to extract greater policy leeway from donors.

(Gould and Ojanen, 2005)

There is also a scalar tension in the reforms. 'Decentralization and popular participation are seen as two aspects of a single process, the convergence of the state (decentralization) and civil society (participation)' (Veltmeyer and Tellez, 2001, p. 90). Decentralization is meant to bring 'good politics and good economics' together by 'enhancing political responsiveness and participation at the local level while simultaneously furthering economic objectives . . . by improving the allocative and operational efficiency of public expenditure' and strengthening accountability downward to clients and beneficiaries (World Bank, 2005b, cited in World Bank, 2002a, p. 9). While decentralization is meant to be a core part of the reform agenda, in part to build 'linking social capital,' under the PRSP in Uganda 85 percent of local government funding is earmarked for nationally determined priorities. In part this may be to prevent macro-economic control being compromised. Craig and Porter (2006, p. 178) refer to this scalar tension as 'telescoping' which 'happens frequently in Development, as one reform is laid down on top of another only half achieved one, resulting in mess and confusion.'

By regularizing state–society interactions, participation in PRSPs may facilitate stability and help define the 'rules of the political game' (Rothchild, 1994). However, this is a double edged sword.

In the new model of development assistance, 'civil society organizations' are expected to work in 'partnership' with governments through consensus building around SAPs or monitoring the government's implementation of its World Bank-approved poverty reduction strategy (PRS). The powerful influence of donor agencies on local organizations, combined with the application of civil society as idea to achieve their objectives of economic and political liberalization, may work towards stabilizing the [unjust] existing social and political order.

(Whitfield, 2003, p. 383)

'The Poor' also legitimate PRSPs. PRSP methodologies increasingly involve

Consultation processes, which bring together different stakeholders from government and civil society to discuss issues of poverty reduction . . . [and] research processes using participatory methodologies are often used as a vehicle to introduce the 'voices of the poor' into such processes and the policies they aim to inform.

(Adan *et al.*, 2002, p. 102)

Part of the agenda of PRSPs is to improve government systems to enable the phase out of previous 'by-pass [the state] strategies' (Booth, 2003a). They thus represent an attempt to rehabilitate the state through a quintuple movement to embed, constrain, legitimate, enable, and empower[11] it. Some argue that 'donors are once more dealing almost exclusively with governments' through the PRSP process (Ellis and Bahigwa, 2003, p. 997). However, this would seem to be an overstatement particularly given that 'civil society is the lynchpin . . . by fostering support among citizens for a government that maintains the inequality that undermines their lives' (Hearn, 2000).

Part of the logic of PRSP is that structural adjustment failed because it was not implemented.[12] Domestic ownership by civil society, and following on from that states, is meant to get around this issue (Bird, 2004). 'Civic involvement is expected to deepen commitment to macroeconomic reforms, with fewer policy reversals [achieving "lock in" or "irreversibility"] and more impact on poverty' (Brinkerhoff and Goldsmith, 2003, p. 685). Indeed some World Bank reports argue that 'ownership here means irreversibility of commitment to . . . reforms' (Abegaz, 2001, p. 199). Thus the shallow foreign interventionism of 'economic shock therapy' is replaced by the 'deep interventionism' of 'institutional shock therapy'(Cammack, 2004). In this way, social investment in PRSPs can be seen as a side payment to civil society. However, democratic participation is only compatible with a flexible conception of what 'good economic policy' might look like (Thirkell-White, 2004). Yet the World Bank and UN 'co-opt the language of progressive social movements, while structurally excluding feminist discourses and actions oriented to transformation, particularly those opposed to the notion that deregulation, liberalization and privatization are the best routes to democracy' (McLaughlin, 2004, p. 171).

In postcolonial Africa one of the problems was development was privately appropriated by state elites, so that development strategies were filtered through layers of self-interest to become strategies of survival, power and accumulation (Ake, 1996). PRSPs attempt to change the political opportunity structure.

In relation to PRSPs 'the basic idea is that if the different technical and social forces that are contesting or resisting reform policies are involved in their formulation, they will internalize them and cease to resist their implementation' (Kankwenda, 2004, p. 13). Consequently 'capacity building' has been extended from the state to the private sector and civil society. Thus PRSPs play an important role in social and economic regulation. While PRSPs approve spending for [primary] health and education, they do not for social insurance and universal welfare systems; thereby giving civil society a side payment, coincident with the interests of business. In some PRSPs, such as in Tanzania's, user charges for basic education have been scrapped.

PRSPs are an attempt to constitutionalize a type of politico-economic governance conducive to capitalist economic restructuring (Weber, 2004). They are an attempt to embed liberalism under the rubric of good governance, rather than a form of embedded liberalism.[13] As Held and McGrew (2002, p. 63) note:

> the growing emphasis on good governance [and] democracy . . . represents attempts to stabilize world order around the liberal-capitalist model. By comparison, effective global action to combat the accelerating gap between rich and poor through redistributive mechanisms, from official aid to technical assistance, remains negligible in relation to the scale of global poverty.

According to Øyen (2000a, p. 3), 'in this enterprise NGO's were the preferred partners rather than researchers or governments. New and original approaches were seen to be more interesting than those comprehensive strategies proven efficient in the welfare state.' However, the World Bank is striking roots in state and civil society. For example, in Zimbabwe an Enhanced Social Protection Programme, covering social protection, public works, targeted education subsidies and support for community childcare and public medical supply purchases, was developed by the government in collaboration with the World Bank and civil society (Kanyenze, 2003). However, it was only very partially implemented as World Bank funding was contingent on lapsed debt repayments being resumed, which did not happen.

The *2000/2001 World Development Report* (World Bank, 2000c, p. 10) advocates a 'modular [piecemeal] approach to helping poor people manage risk' in order not to 'undercut competitiveness.' Why? In part it may be to do with national resource constraints, but it is also because liberalization and privatization are about the deliberate enhancement of risk for segments of the population (Weber, 2004). Health and education will help people compete in the new 'risk society' (Beck, 1992). These public goods are meant to provide a facilitative environment for (transnational) capital development.

> PRSPs . . . are best seen as part of a 'Third Way' re-morphing of neo-liberal approaches, a new convergence in which governments and agencies of various stripes in both liberal OECD and developing countries focusing on optimizing economic, juridical and social governance in order to create ideal conditions for international finance and investment. . . . This primary orientation, combining global market integration with efficient disciplined governance and enhanced, activated human and social capital, is seen as the best hope for generating sustained growth, social and economic stability, and including the poor in emerging structures of opportunity (Callinicos, 2000). This ordering of priorities has a certain logic which is worth reiterating: global economic integration first, good governance second, poverty reduction following as a result, underpinned by limited safety nets and human capital development.
>
> (Craig and Porter, 2002, p. 53)

While rejecting a crude 'lump of poverty' thesis,[14] there is the issue of the 'fallacy of composition' in the structure of PRSPs. The class-structured nature of market economies means that people will not have equal incomes. While avoiding the determinism which says that if some people move up, others move down, there is, nonetheless, a trade-off. For example, investing in skills training or education may not in itself create employment unless there is latent or unmet demand in the labor market for the skills created (Terreblanche, 2002). Thus emphasis on the supply side (education) without looking at the demand side may be a misapplied version of Say's Law whereby supply creates its own demand.

For example, substantial primary educational investment in Zimbabwe in the 1980s did not create demand in the labor market (Narman, 2003). In fact, with economic liberalization in Zimbabwe in the 1990s, there were significantly 'declining returns to human and physical assets' (Alwang *et al.*, 2002, p. 47). While education obviously has its own internal worth, as a development strategy it may simply be playing musical (poverty) chairs, although in a context of globalization it is possible, though unlikely, to attract more foreign direct investment (FDI); at the expense of other locations.

As a report for the World Bank notes: 'one set of factors (for instance, poor economic performance) determines the overall level of poverty in a country, and another, such as lack of education determines which households are poor' (White and Killick, 2001, p. xvii). An extensive survey in Ethiopia found that 'in rural areas . . . education did not matter as much [as in urban areas as] . . . as agriculture using traditional methods does not seem to require formal education' (Bigsten *et al.*, 2005a, pp. 10–1). Indeed in cities having a secondary education increased the chances of being unemployed by 15–30 percent (Dercon *et al.*, 2005). Although it is only the relatively well-off who may be able to afford to be unemployed.[15]

Of course aside from the economics, it was cut-backs in health and education under SAPs which garnered the most international public attention and outcry. In part this was because they tended to worst affect those most vulnerable and dependent on public services; women, children and the elderly. Thus, the emphasis on renewed public provision of health and education serve a useful political purpose. Even the report of Tony Blair's Africa Commission is critical of cutbacks in health and education expenditure under SAPs, despite the fact that one of the commissioners was Michel Camdessus, who as director of the IMF presided over these (Commission for Africa, 2005).[16] There is now also meant to be a synergy between education and social capital, with one study in Burkina Faso finding that increased Parent Teacher Association attendance increasing the probability of children being sent to school (Grootaert *et al.*, 2002).

Part of the appeal of investment in the social sector is that it is amenable to sector wide approaches (SWAPs) (Maxwell, 2003), but 70 percent of African respondents in the *Voices of the Poor* identified 'self-employment and business' as the main factors allowing people to escape poverty, whereas under 5 percent mentioned education (Narayan *et al.*, 2000), suggesting much greater attention needs to be paid to the demand side of the economy (Jamal and Weeks, 1993).

The Commission for Africa noted that 'increased education can increase expectations of jobs and where economies are stagnant this can lead to further problems' (Commission for Africa, 2004, p. 24). While the provision of health and education are important developmental achievements in their own right (Arrighi, 2004), this suggests that educational planning needs to be integrated with active industrial policies so that there is a correspondence between supply and demand for labor (T. McKinley, 2003).

The emphasis on health and education in PRSPs is in part because these activities are meant to have high social rates of returns. However, others argue that these issues cannot be treated in isolation and that there is a need for a 'holistic health paradigm,' for example, which deals with issues such as social inequality which may be exacerbated by neoliberal economic policies that contribute to poor health (Tucker, 1997, cited in Nederveen Pieterse, 2001; Wilkinson, 1996).

There are also issues around the delivery of these services. Francis Owusu argues that 'one has to be skeptical of reform policies that ignore the survival concerns of employees as well as shock therapies that higher salaries alone could lead to higher productivity in the public sector' (Owusu, 2005, p. 174). What are needed are transparent reward systems and programs that aim to alter the culture of public institutions.

Others argue for a productionist reorientation of development assistance.

> Rather than concentrate on the social aspects of poverty, it would be better to provide infrastructure, cheap export finance, technological assistance and venture capital. 'If you have donor-led spending it is not sustainable . . . people need to make money.'
>
> (Kyerematon, cited in White, 2004, p. 17)

Debt relief expenditure is not sustainable, suggesting the need to develop the productive sectors of the economy and set up new mechanisms for international redistribution, as will be suggested later. The US administration has recently re-emphasized the importance of economic growth, although some would dispute that this forms part of a viable development strategy.

There are many other areas, outside of education, such as privatization, where the 'voices of the poor' are at odds with PRSPs (Mutume, 2003).[17] This suggests that deliberative democratic institutions, as in Porto Alegre, Brazil or Kerala, India may have greater poverty reduction potential, than mediated PPAs or NGO participation in PRSPs (Evans, 2004). The type of mediated participation currently being promulgated is reminiscent of the colonial mindset that the poor are not capable of representing themselves, 'they must be represented' (Gregory, 2004).

PRSPs are attempting to repair the tattered social contract, and build citizenship,[18] through better governance and service provision. They are a synthesis of development 'from above' and 'below,' of mainstream and alternative development, bearing in mind that this synthesis is ongoing (Nederveen Pieterse, 2001, p. 78). However, PRSPs main role and impact may not be reducing poverty, paradoxically.

We can think of PRSPs as a form of virtualism. Carrier and Miller (1998, cited in Leyshon and Lee, 2003, p. 10) define (neoliberal) virtualism as 'the conscious attempt to make the real world conform to the virtual image.' Fantu Cheru (1989) has characterized the old adjustment paradigm as 'do not adjust your theory, reality is not working.' In the past the less adjustment worked, the more rigorously it was enforced, as it was thought the lack of implementation was the problem, rather than the model itself. PRSPs represent a revision of that 'economic supply side' approach, and can be seen as synthesis of both logics (accumulation and legitimation) (Cammack, 2004) and scales (global and local [where poverty is experienced]), instantiated in the national. Former World Bank President, Jim Wolfensohn, and ex-chief economist Joseph Stiglitz talked about 'bringing together' the macroeconomic and social aspects of development (International Forum on Globalization, 2002). Instead of the world being interpreted as a perfect market, it is now interpreted as an imperfect one, replacing one virtualism with another (Fine, 2004). This is in contrast to pleas from within the World Bank as early as 1990 that 'economic theory must now give way to empirical application as a result of the wide variety of socio-economic conditions in the countries of Sub-Saharan Africa' (World Bank, 1990, p. 120).

Ravi Kanbur (2005) identifies two broad groups on socio-economic policy who he heuristically identifies as 'Finance Ministry'[19] and 'Civil Society' globally. In PRSPs, 'Finance Ministries' and the World Bank/IMF complex retain control of economic matters and 'Civil Society' 'gets' social policy. However, this is a dysfunctional division of labor because of the critical importance of macro-economic policy and its articulation with micro-economic policy in determining the nature and extent of poverty. The attempt to 'tack on' social services to the neoliberal accumulation regime represents part of a double movement; economic liberalization, combined with decommodification of primary social services, and as such is 'mildly Polanyian' (Craig and Porter, 2006).

As Bergeron (2003) notes, the World Bank is not interested in questioning the global free market, but only in releasing social and political constraints to its fuller development. Thus the goal is not to ameliorate, or regulate the unfettered market but to make it more competitive, particularly through increased labor supply (proletarianization) (Cammack, 2004). If early neoliberalism represented a sink or swim approach to the labor market, the renovated neoliberalism insists on swimming lessons until further notice (Craig and Porter, 2006). There is, however, some fluidity in processes of development planning and implementation. As Mosley *et al.* (1991) note, the World Bank is interested in negotiation over the shape of program implementation, not just economic models.

The fact that macroeconomics and privatization are off the agenda is presented as a government choice in the context of 'country-ownership' by the World Bank and the IMF (IMF/World Bank, 2002, cited in Craig and Porter, 2002). The extension of conditionality to governance is also significantly disempowering for national governments. According to one of the World Bank's vice presidents, 'we have abandoned the prescriptive character of the old policy statement, in which we essentially enshrined goals and methods' (J. W. Adams quoted in Mekay, 2004). Although according to an ActionAid official, Rick Rowden, this renationalization of poverty responsibility is 'a huge sham . . . a way of [the IFIs] relinquishing responsibility from their own accountability and saying, "oh, it's all on the borrowing government."' Thus the failure of PRSPs will be the fault of domestic states and civil societies, not the IFIs. Nonetheless PRSPs are populist by appealing to 'the poor' as a source of legitimation (Gould and Ojanen, 2003, p. 21). This serves to legitimate a particular form of donor–state relations, where resource allocation becomes based on 'partnership,' rather than democratic accountability. Thus, they share the broader problems of participatory development projects which

> Simply do not command *enough* power to transform radically the structural inequalities that reproduce poverty. To this extent, judgments of projects that see their problems merely as 'failures' *within the act of participation itself* are tilting at windmills.
>
> (Cornwall, 2004a, p. 98)

PRSPs increase the institutional power of the Bretton Woods Institutions (BWIs) by providing a 'framework for development assistance *beyond* the operations of the Fund and the Bank' (emphasis in original) (International Development Association and IMF, 2002, p. 3, cited in Weber, 2004, p. 197). For example, the European Union has decided to base it assistance to the African, Caribbean, Pacific (ACP) countries on the PRSP framework, although the continual dialectics of development are at play here too.

As a postindustrial economy, the EU is placing particular emphasis on the liberalization of service provision, such as water, and government procurement through 'economic partnership agreements' (EPAs) (Comhlámh, 2005). While the European Commission has indicated that it will not necessarily cut off budget support to countries which are 'off-track' with the IMF, on privatization conditions for example (Debt and Development Coalition Ireland, 2004, cited in Wood, 2005), EU aid is tied to liberalization in EPAs. This rescaling of conditionality to a bilateral level may be in response to global resistance, and be a new form of mercantilism, whereby the EU seeks preferential treatment in 'partner' countries to enable it to become 'the most competitive and dynamic knowledge-driven economy [in the world] by 2010' (European Commission, 2000), five years before the MDGs are meant to be achieved. The EU has also recently indicated it will distribute more of its aid directly, as it does not have the power that it thinks it should have in the World Bank.

Poverty mainstreaming is meant to be a new policy innovation, although the United Nations adopted the idea of 'unified socio-economic development planning' in the 1970s (Midgley, 1998). Indeed there are echoes of other 'developmental regimes' in PRSPs. It is worth quoting Midgley (1988, p. 55) at some length here.

Mass education helped the welfare departments to expand their activities into rural areas and to introduce programmes that were clearly developmental in character. Mass education was most enthusiastically adopted by colonial welfare administrators in West Africa and was regarded, as Peter Hodge (1973) noted, as an effective means for promoting development among rural people who were untouched by large-scale economic projects or the opportunities afforded by the urban environment. Hodge, who actually served as a colonial welfare officer in West Africa, reported that mass education emphasized self-help and self-determination as two critical concepts for mobilizing people's involvement.

The mass education programmes introduced in West Africa soon attracted the attention of the Colonial Office in London. Impressed with the West African innovations, the Colonial Office urged welfare departments in other colonies to adopt mass education as well and to use this approach to promote a developmental approach to social welfare. However, the term 'mass education' was not generally liked and, by the end of the Second World War, the term 'community development' had been adopted instead. This new term covered literacy education as well as women's activities, youth services, infrastructural development projects, health and sanitary services and similar programmers.

Indeed, Lord Lugard (1922, p. 194, cited in Craig and Porter, 2006, p. 40), the pioneer of the strategy of indirect rule, rejected a 'one size fits all' approach to governance. 'Principles do not change, but their mode of application should vary with the customs, traditions and prejudices of each [administrative] unit.' The rhetoric of partnership between Europeans and Africans was also used during the colonial period, with the Rhodesian Prime Minister Godfrey Huggins referring to it, this as equivalent to a partnership between a 'horse and its rider' (Meredith, 2005).

Thus 'inclusive liberalism can look much like classical liberalism in its "crumbs from the table" charity (aid, not trade access), its responsibilization, education, and policing of the poor, its keeping of questions of existing property and power distributions off the political agenda' (Craig and Porter, 2002, p. 3). As such PRSPs and partnerships can be conceived of as a form of indirect 'rule at a distance,' produced through coercion and consent (Cooke, 2004; Abrahamsen, 2004b). They form part of the strategic complexes of liberal governance (Duffield, 2001).

The African Development Bank (2003) argues that PRSPs represent a paradigm shift by virtue of the recognition of the benefits of comprehensive planning . However, it is only social spending which is planned to catalyze the unregulated market economy. Thus UNCTAD (2002) disagrees and mainly sees continuity with the previous structural adjustment policies, with their emphasis on lowering wages and welfare costs. Alan Whaites notes that adherence to traditional macroeconomic prescriptions is the definitive characteristic of PRSPs and a decisive issue in whether or not draft PRSPs are accepted by the World Bank and IMF (Whaites, 2002). Nonetheless PRSPs represent a partial restatization, with the World Bank belatedly recognizing that governments must make the running on improving social welfare (Deacon, 2000).

As Bjorn Beckman (1993) notes, the 'neo' in neoliberal results from the emphasis on state retraction; however, the dialectics of development mean that the role of the state is now necessarily, but incompletely, rehabilitated. The retraction of the state may have gone too far for it to serve the roles ascribed to it in the liberal worldview. However, after more than two decades of state retraction, without massive institution building, PRSPs may be courting failure and increased corruption (Whaites, 2002). The push toward the decommodification of primary health care and education,

which are not amenable to substantial private sector operational investment, is also accompanied by a push toward increasing privatization of
infrastructure, such as roads and water provision in particular. Thus
de and re-commodification proceed in tandem, dialectically.
However, the commodification of water under the auspices of the
World Bank is cloaked by the language of a 'human rights-based
approach' to allow tradable permits in water so that it can move 'from
lower to higher value uses,' thereby supposedly increasing allocative
efficiency (Bank/Netherlands Water Partnership Program, n.d., cited in
Cornwall and Nyamu-Musembi, 2004, p. 26).

PRSPs also represent a synthesis between the local and the national in
that 'second generation' PPAs have 'been marked by lengthier processes,
which have been carefully designed to maximize policy influence
through institutional embedding, and are linked to other consultative
processes within and outside national governments' (Brock, 2002, p. 4).
However, this may cloak current power relations. The problems are seen
as unequal power at local and national levels along the state–civil society axis, but not at global level. In part, this may be justified on pragmatic grounds that it is only at these levels that African governments
have significant power to influence change.[20]

PRSPs target poverty by attempting to generate 'pro-poor' growth,
facilitating empowerment by promoting good governance, enhancing
security through investment in health and education and social safety
nets. In this the disciplined inclusion of the poor is central. Thus the
governance of the poor is potentially achieved. This is not to suggest
that PRSPs are a conspiracy: rather they are a 'polymorphous crystal-
lizations' where a number of interests, within and without the state,
coalesce and find expression (Mann, 1986, cited in M. Shaw, 2003). It is
both a genuine attempt to promote good governance and reduce
poverty, respond to criticism of the IFIs and also an attempt to create a
new hegemony in the developing world; to co-opt resistance to the neoliberal world (dis)order (O'Brien *et al.*, 2000)[21] 'Poverty reduction' is
thus infused with power relations. This socialization of global capitalism can also be seen as a geopolitical pact between the neoliberal Anglo-
American regime and the more corporatist European ones, but not the
developmental statist one of Japan (Braathen, 2000).[22]

> [USAID] tend to act on the premise that associational life is inde-
> pendent of the state. The Europeans, in contrast, stress the intercon-
> nectedness between state, market and civil society, e.g. in the way
> that they see the role of governance in development.
>
> (Hyden *et al.*, 2003, p. 6)

European donors have historically given greater emphasis to the role of churches, trade unions and other organizations in struggling for state reform (Howell and Pearce, 2001, p. 51), and many have recent histories of 'social pacting' or concertation at national levels (see Fajertag and Pochet, 1997). In part this stems from a more 'radical' continental discussion of civil society which emphasizes 'the common good,' human emancipation and the 'conditions for inclusive rational-critical public debate' (Howell and Pearce, 2001, p. 51). The Swedish aid agency, SIDA views the state as the most important actor in dealing with Africa's economic crisis (Crawford, 1996). However, PRSPs do not countenance a social democratic role for the state, through comprehensive universal welfare and social service provision, and active labor market and industrial policies to generate the resources to pay for these.[23] In social democratic regimes, labor is substantially decommodified (Esping-Andersson, 1999). Thus the IMF (and the World Bank) remains poised between Locke and Montesquieu's conceptions of civil society, where civil society is autonomous through the market, versus playing a watchdog role on the state (Thirkell-White, 2004). In World Bank discourse, the type of corporatism being promoted is a micro, society-based, liberal one (Braathen, 2000), rather than the type of social pacting seen in Europe. Nonetheless the emerging development regime owes much to the EU policy of 'coordination, coherence and complimentarity' (Holland, 2002) or multilaterlization. While there are obvious advantages to this approach, it may stifle local and national level innovation, as may 'scaling up' (Garbutt and Pratt, 2003). Social capital is constitutive of the new social corporatism through the idea of a communitarian 'trickling up' to influence state policy (Braathen, 2000).

Donors are willing to tolerate 'virtual,' and actively promote choiceless (Joseph, 1999a; Mkandawire, 1999) democracy as long as (neoliberal) economic governance is maintained through accountability to civil society. Robinson characterizes this system as polyarchy; a system of rotating 'elite minority rule and socio-economic inequalities alongside formal political freedom and elections involving universal suffrage' (W. Robinson, 1996b, p. 356, cited in Hearn, 1999, p. 15; see also W. Robinson, 1996a). This could also be described as political empowerment with economic disempowerment (Tomasevski, 1997, cited in Deacon, 2000).

John Williamson, who coined the term 'Washington Consensus,' has argued that the emphasis on pragmatism, strengthening the state and targeting social spending constitutes a 'Santiago consensus' (cited in The Economist, 1996). The geographical relocation of consensus would appear to signal a number of things: economic liberalism combined with a strong state (as in Chile) (see Green, 1995b), and social spending by a democratic government.

Another moniker is the 'Post-Washington Consensus' (PWC) developed by Joseph Stiglitz. The fact that it is 'post' shows its origins in and affinities with the Washington Consensus. Its hallmark is to view the state and the market as strategic complements rather than alternatives.[24] The floating spatiality of the PWC, may speak to the power of global markets, although this may not do justice to the power relations in PRSPs. Given the synthesis between American and European regimes it might more accurately be called the 'Washington–Brussels' Consensus, where the role of the state is washed off and brushed up, via institutions and civil society. The agenda of donor harmonization is known as the Rome or Paris agenda and the UN is more deeply embedded in Europe, having its second largest 'duty office' in Geneva. This new consensus is a powerful one.

Craig and Porter (2002, p. 4) argue that 'the emerging convergence in policies for poverty reduction . . . represents an attempt to generate a level of global to local integration, discipline and technical management of marginal economies, governance and populations unprecedented since colonial times.' Thus 'the most significant consequences of the donor-imposed imperative for "consultation" and "civic participation" in public policy may not relate to poverty at all, but to the "new configurations of power and transboundary formations that it has helped to unleash"' (Callaghy, 2001, p. 144, cited in Gould and Ojanen, 2003). For Frances Stewart and Michael Wang (2003), the new governance structures 'enforce the power of international agencies by giving the appearance of ownership without the reality.' The claim that the logic of PRSP should infuse all aid is contrary to the idea of pluralism, national ownership and responsiveness to community initiatives (Cammack, 2004). Even the World Bank (2003a, cited in Bretton Woods Project, 2004) admits that the potential for PRSPs for fostering country ownership is 'undermined by its role as condition for access to concessional assistance from the Bank and Fund.' 'Partnership' and inclusivity are foisted on governments, undermining sovereign choice and sometimes giving rise to 'partnership backlash.' (Fowler, 2004c). Only by bringing in oppositional groups can processes be made more participatory (Kaldor, 2003). Nonetheless, while some have argued that there is a trade off between interior and exterior accountability (Leonard and Strauss, 2003), others argue that 'enhancing accountability to donors can be a first step towards building more democratic accountability'

(Piron, with Evans, 2004, p. 31). What seems clear is that the 'tax bargain' between citizens and state is central to accountability (Unsworth, 2006).

PRSPs are also a global pact between developed and developing countries to reduce debt in exchange for social development/regulation, further elaborated through the Millennium Development Goals and at the Monterrey Summit on Financing for Development.[25] It was at this that the term 'The Monterrey Consensus' was developed, which some in civil society see as 'an expansion of the Washington Consensus from the IMF, World Bank, WTO, and their political masters and multi-national corporations into UN processes, with the hope of the legitimization by civil society participation' (Gabriel, n. d., p. 2–3). South African Minister of Finance, Trevor Manuel (2003, p. 20) characterizes it, along with the MDGs, as a 'pragmatic adjustment to the Washington Consensus.'

Esteva and Prakesh (1998) note that power, in a globalizing context has been slipping away even from actors such as many TNCs and global finance, who are subject to cut-throat competition and whose actions consequently have 'force,' but are not powerful in the sense of having significant choice to do things differently. PRSPs national/global level of regulation is a compliment to transnational microregulation undertaken by corporations within their networks (Amin, 2004). However, there is an inherent contradiction between the economic and social elements of PRSPs as they 'first destroy existing social capital for the sake of achieving economic growth, and then by means of social policy seek to rebuild social tissue' (Nederveen Pieterse, 2001, p. 127).[26] A PPA in Benin noted that among vulnerable groups, *tontine* membership went down as much as 60 percent after the *Communauté financière d'Afrique* (CFA) franc devaluation of 1994, as nobody could afford to save (Narayan *et al.*, 2000). Thus the impact of economic crisis and (often contractionary) neoliberal economic reform has been dialectical; promoting incentives to build social capital as a survival strategy, while reducing the resources through which to do this, thereby rupturing social bonds. Where people are preoccupied with survival they do not have the time to engage in the public sphere (Mkandawire and Soludo, 1999), and active civil society may consequently stagnate, or at least not be representative of the marginalized.

Nonetheless PRSPs can be seen to have elements of both 'co-operative' and 'competitive' globalization (Arruda, 1996). They represent the merger of social and economic policy – a type of 'mainstreaming.'

Bob Deacon (2000) argues that

Despite the apparent shift from global neoliberalism to global social responsibility, four tendencies within the new global paradigm, if pursued will undermine equitable social progress and development – at a time when the resources exist to fund such advances. These tendencies are:

- The World Bank's belief that government's should provide only minimal levels of social protection.
- The concern of the OECD's Development Assistance Committee (DAC) to focus funding on only basic education and healthcare [allowing privatization and trade in other levels].
- The self-interest of international NGOs in substituting for government provision of services; and
- The moves being made within the WTO to open the global market in private healthcare, education and social insurance.

However, this is to misunderstand the nature of the new regime. The constraints which he identifies are foundational.

PRSPs also represent an attempted compromise between civil and social rights. As noted earlier, it is interesting that their focus is very much on health and education, and not on the development of welfare states, which would imply far greater citizenship rights. The gains from health and educational investment are individually appropriable, rather than being seen as entitlements. Individuals are poor because they do not have enough education is the logical conclusion that flows from this. This speaks to the fact that

> the internal logic of capitalism is . . . rooted in a conception of rights which is essentially individualistic. This is why under capitalism civil rights trump the others. There is then a form of citizenship which is itself wedded to a capitalist rationale, where it is the individual who has moral value and not the family, the community or the society. As a result social rights are non-existent because they cannot be ascribed to individual subjects and are thus not implementable.
>
> (Bustelo, 2001, p. 5)

However, it is only through the enjoyment of social and economic rights that people can be emancipated to participate in their civil and political rights. In this sense, social and economic rights should perhaps have preference. 'What difference would recognition of the right to property make to those who are poor if they possess nothing, or the right to vote if its exercise is ineffectual in changing the situation of social exclusion?' (Bustelo, 2001, p. 5). The UN Community accepts that poverty is the *denial of all human rights*. The United Nations Educational and Scientific and Cultural Organization (UNESCO) (2003) argues based on this that poverty is illegal. Orthodoxy justifies inequality using Rawlsian principles of justice, whereby it is permissible if it results in positive sum games. However, this has not been the case in Africa where increased inequality has gone hand-in-hand with absolute immiseration.

By not questioning the 'free' market as a co-ordination mechanism, but only social and political obstacles to its fuller development (Bergeron, 2003), PRSPs are not founded on a human rights framework. Indeed to be made acceptable in the IFIs, participation has been reconceptualized to 'connect it to the logic of free market access' (Cornwall and Brock, 2005, p. 8).

> While the World Bank and the IMF readily concede their impact on human rights, they have refused to hold themselves accountable to human rights standards. They have justified this policy on the basis of their constitutive charters, which arguably limit their mandate to the consideration of economic factors, distinguishing human rights concerns as political.
>
> (Jochnick, 2001, p. 167)

Thus part of the challenge may be the mainstreaming of socio-economic rights in the charters of these organizations. As specialized agencies of the UN's they are obliged to promote the UN's human rights mission. The principle that sovereignty can be over-ridden when there are serious violations of human rights is accepted in international law, however, this does not extend to telling countries how to organize their internal governance, accountability and representative structures. Ultimately African states must recapture the policy agenda (Mkandawire and Soludo, 1999). 'Development co-operation should be made unnecessary in the future, as institutionalizing it, would mean also institutionalizing global inequality' (Hakkarainen *et al.*, 2002, p. 14).

One of the central problematics of governance in Africa has been that overly centralized states have projected power to deflect weakness (Carmody, 2002). Posed in these terms the issue is how to increase, simultaneously, the power, legitimacy and accountability of African states. According to Midgley (1998, pp. 150–1), 'the institutional approach to social development requires that an organizational system be established and that overall responsibility for managing this system be entrusted to a government agency which is responsive to the interests of the diverse groups that are involved in social development.' Only empowered states will have the legitimacy to carry forward developmental programs which command popular support. However, the PRSP process represents the end of the development era – the target is amelioration of poverty, rather than structural transformation.

The market is now seen to be an instrument in achieving this goal, not an end in itself. However, in part this is because it has become unquestioned. World Bank reports talk of liberalization as a form of 'economic democracy' (World Bank, 2002a, p. 4). Rapid and unmediated global market integration has supplanted development strategy (Rodrik, 2000, cited in Amaïzo, 2004). That issue is now 'above politics' and not open to debate. It has been settled through the 'transnational politics of economism' (Teivainen, 2002). Hence now the focus is on poverty. By targeting an output of disarticulated development, rather than its causal drivers, the issue of power relations and structural inequities is elided. According to Deepa Narayan (2002, p. 77),

> Economic restructuring like civil service reform or the construction of large dams displaces large numbers of people . . . civil society organizations . . . can be valuable partners in understanding the political and economic context within which reform has to be shaped.

The neoliberal economic development strategy is focused on the development of micro and small- and medium-sized enterprises (SMEs), and skills and infrastructure upgrading.[27] However, in Africa 'traditional authority structures remain strong in many instances, and parallel economies are often thriving, undermining both state and civil society' (Rothchild and Lawson, 1994, p. 277). The 'free' market does little to resolve, and in fact promotes, this contradiction.

Howell and Pearce (2001, p. 89) argue that 'donor agencies vary enormously in their objectives, financial sources and strength, organizational structures, administrative procedures, geographical focus, and thematic breadth of programs and projects.' However, the international agenda around 'common pooling,' 'sector-wide approaches,' 'policy coherence' etc is substantially reducing these differences; hence one rationale for a new synthetic hegemonic discourse. This new discourse provides the cement around which a new transnational historic bloc is being shaped; including international and domestic NGOs, *and the poor* (Cox, 1987; Hardt and Negri, 2000).[28]

Large donor contracts have created incentives for the centralization, in the economic sense, through alliances and mergers of INGOS (Garbutt and Pratt, 2003). Their economies of scale, mean they can also squeeze local CSOs in terms of local fundraising. According to Concern's[29] Deputy Director in Mtwara in Tanzania, 'local NGOs don't reach the poor' (cited in Gould and Ojanen, 2003, p. 81). These organizations critiques of PRSPs tend to be more technical than political (see, for example, Sanchez and Cash, 2003).[30] This fits with the agenda of the World Bank and IMF where participation is meant to allow 'better technical diagnosis of problems' (Robb, 2002, p. 104). INGOs may also serve to 'disseminate the views of the policy elite through [their] grassroots networks – populist neoliberalism at its most concrete' (Gould and Ojanen, 2003, p. 81) and serve as surrogates for indigenous civil society. Gould and Ojanen (2005) in Tanzania found that transnational private aid agencies 'crowded out' indigenous civil society voices and exercised disciplinary power through 'capacity building' and 'empowerment.'

Concern in Tanzania funded a popularized version of the PRSP in Swahili. Another of these was produced with funding from the UK Department for International Development (DFID) and Africa's largest employer, Coca-Cola (Cammack, 2004). Indeed around 25 percent of Concern's spending has been shifted from service delivery to advocacy (Gould and Ojanen, 2005). However,

> Civil society does not lend itself to external manufacturing. It cannot be created via blueprints from offices in Washington or London. Civil societies in any context have a history and must develop in tune with their particular historical, cultural and political rhythms.
>
> (Howell and Pearce, 2001, p. 121)

Thus the sustainability of this conjuncture is open to question. We now turn briefly to a more detailed examination of the technical operation of PRSPs in general, and then to a specific case study.

Framing PRSPs (and civil society?): conditionality in PRSPs

PRSPs must substantially conform to the framing prescriptions of World Bank country assistance strategies (CAS) and the IMF Poverty Reduction and Growth Facility (PRGF).[31] PRGF negotiations are meant to be based on PRSPs but are often undertaken in advance in nonconsultative mode (Stewart and Wang, 2003). In its five year review of the PRSP approach, the IMF called on the World Bank to ensure much broader debate on macroeconomic issues (Eurodad, 2004). There is an interesting discursive political economy to this. Thandika Mkandawire

(1999) has noted the promotion of 'choiceless democracies' by donors. In this context calls for debate by the IMF can be seen not as democratic openness to alternatives, but as serving an instrumental function in delivering acquiescence to the neoliberal accumulation regime; negotiating the new hegemonic 'regime of truth' (Escobar, 1995).

Donor consultative group meetings continue to be nonparticipatory. The PRSP was also initially attached in conditionality to the Bank's Programmatic Structural Adjustment Credit (PSAC –1) (Mercer, 2003),[32] only renamed the Poverty Reduction Support Credit in 2001 (Wood, 2005). The World Bank has a *PRSP Sourcebook* which structures content and describes which groups should participate (including the private sector and the 'general public, particularly the poor and vulnerable') (World Bank, 2002b, p. 250, cited in Stewart and Wang, 2003, p. 8). Civil society groups who have questioned this circumscribed content have been excluded from the PRSP process (Malawi Economic Justice Network, 2001, p. 9, cited in Weber, 2004). Trade unions and parliamentarians have also been notable by their absence, or very limited engagement, in the process (Stewart and Wang, 2003), with Mozambique being an exception where a new law has been passed to allow Parliament to have a monitoring role in the PRSP (Coyle *et al.*, 2003). Often governments prepare or completely draft PRSPs before consultation. If they were substantially country-owned, there would be considerable variation between them. In fact there isn't and in a survey of seven countries Zaman found that in most cases civil society proposals were generally not incorporated (Zaman, 2002, cited in Stewart and Wang, 2003). This is so despite the fact that consultations were generally 'wide' in terms of CSO groups but 'shallow' in terms of content. Studies have found that civil society groups have had a negligible impact on policy outcomes (Robinson and Friedman, 2005).

Thirty-nine organizations and regional networks from across Africa argue that PRSPs are 'window-dressing' for the neoliberal model (Bretton Woods Project, 2001, cited in Stewart and Wang, 2003). Indeed the economic model underlying PRSPs excludes the possibility of poverty by assuming a single labor market and full employment (Fine, 2004). Very little research has been conducted by the IMF on the macro-economics of poverty reduction, in favor of other issues such as price stability (Agénor, 2005), favorable to international capital. In part, this may be strategic, as the circle between 'broad-based, pro-poor' growth and the economic models of the IMF which depend on deliberately increasing inequality to raise the profit share (Lensink, 1996), and thereby investment, is difficult to square.

Some argue that the new institutions of participatory governance, in the absence of other spaces which sustain countervailing power, may simply be captured by already empowered elites (Gaventa, 2004), although their power to alter program design may be limited in any event. According to an African Minister of Finance,

> We do not want to second guess the Fund. We prefer to pre-empt them by giving them what they want before they start lecturing us about this and that. By doing so, we send a clear message that we know what we are doing – i.e., we believe in structural adjustment.
>
> (Quoted in Cheru, 2001, cited in Stewart and Wang, 2003, p. 19)

Nowhere has PRSP been taken up by political leaders to offer an alternative vision of national development, to which donors must conform. (Booth, 2003b). Stewart and Wang (2003) argue that in fact the PRSP process, if it has empowered anyone, it has been the World Bank.

A poem about the World Bank has it that

> One proviso you must meet,
> You sit in the driver's seat
> But don't you ever dare reveal
> Whose hands you know are on the wheel.
>
> (Chambers, 2006, p. 50)

In these ways participatory development may be disempowering or at least stabilize inequitable social structures. As such 'participation' may be a technology for the surveillance and 'normalization' of civil society and the state, while playing an insignificant role in people's daily lives.[33] Its primary impact may be political and symbolic, rather than economic or social.[34] People living in poverty are reconstituted as authors of their own fate. They are reconceptualized as embedded in broader structures, from which they are nonetheless relatively autonomous.

PRSPs are marketed as a form of 'post-conditionality' assistance. However, upon closer inspection this turns out not to be the case. Rather it could be read as it's strengthening, as there is movement from ex-ante to ex-post conditionality, with aid being concentrated on 'strong reformers,' who have already implemented programs and demonstrated 'ownership.' As a donor mission to the World Bank and IMF noted, 'in its broadest sense, conditionality cannot be given up, and even though its form will change from ex-ante contracts to mutual commitments based on performance, the new form of conditionality will in some respects be more intrusive than the old form' (Utstein Group, 2001).[35] By 2002, governance featured in 72 percent of all conditionalities for Africa set down by the IFIs for financing (Craig and Porter, 2006). However, the effect of this technical presentation of governance as amenable to a donor applied 'quick fix' is to insulate politics from the domestic social classes which have historically been most concerned with accountability.

Financing of PRSPs is tied to the Poverty Reduction Support Credit (PRSC), which has quite an intricate architecture of conditionality, including prior, 'trigger' and 'benchmark' conditions. An important study of this for the Irish Debt and Development Coalition (Wood, 2005) found that while the number of binding conditions required by the World Bank has decreased, the number of 'benchmark' or indicative conditions has increased. Public finance management and 'good' governance conditions now account for 30 percent of total conditions in the 13 PRSCs examined. Also the fact that poverty is still conceived of in 'mopping up' terms is evidenced by the fact that Poverty and Social Impact Assessments (PSIAs) were conducted to see how the negative effects of the policies could be off-set, rather than questioning the policies themselves. The report found that both Parliaments *and civil societies* were excluded from the development and monitoring of PRSCs. Thus the 'World Bank continues to "buy reforms" with money only released after a range of "prior actions" have been met' (Wood, 2005, p. 3). Nonessential or 'trigger' conditions, around privatization for example, being met can increase the amount of money lent to governments from a 'base case' to a 'high case' scenario. Thus PRSPs cannot in any sense be said to be a form of postconditional assistance. In Ethiopia there are still more than 80 conditions attached to World Bank assistance, per year (Oxfam International, 2005). It is to an examination of that country that we now turn.

5
Remaking African Civil Societies and PRSP in Action: Ethiopia

> The political dynamics of a society are not easily 'read off' from a class register: civil society contains within it a diversity of organizations and forms of power which have their own particular 'stories'. . . . These can be collectively defined as political identities: ethnic, generational, religious, racial and gendered.
>
> (Harrison, 2002, p. 105)

African civil society

Whether European[1] conceptions of 'civil society' are an appropriate lens through which to view African societies is open to question. David Lewis argues for an 'adaptive' approach which sees the concept of civil society having value in non-Western contexts, but that it should not be applied too rigidly. In Africa high degrees of politicization with low opportunities for participation contribute to *political instability* (Whitfield, 2003). The 'development' of 'civil society' may contribute to this as some types of 'civil society in Africa [are] formed by all those who are able to manage and steer communal anger' (Monga [1995] 2000, p. 389). As John Sender (2002) notes 'participation' may be violent.

> Largely missing from the debate is the potential for the convergence of an expansive and highly mobilized civil society and a poorly institutionalized political system with an overburdened government coping not only with consolidating democracy but also with other demanding and politically sensitive tasks, such as decentralizing the

state and liberalizing the economy. This is an explosive prescription for political instability, societal disorder, and in a worst case scenario, democratic breakdown.

(Encarnación, 2000, p. 13)

In some cases NGOs are implicated in violence with the (American) Africa Rainforest and River Conservation group hiring mercenaries to attack poachers, for example, and paying for this through proceeds of diamond sales from 'its' area (Ferguson, 2006). There are other political contradictions in the liberal project in Africa. Particularly

> Scholars working in the liberal framework have effectively advocated the withdrawal of the popular movements from the political realm to the private and apolitical realm of civil society, where they should serve as interest groups or channels from community interests . . . Scholars working within this framework fail to recognize that, given the depolitized nature of civil society in the liberal account, a vibrant civil society is perfectly compatible with and authoritarian and bureaucratic state (Gibbon 1993; Neocosmos 1999). The liberal perspective fails to explain how the state will be held accountable if the people are once again removed from the public realm. In addition, by relegating the state to the role of regulating relations among voluntary organizations, capital and local government, this framework leaves open the possibility that the state will become the exclusive definer or guarantor of a general or national interest. Furthermore, given the fact that many of the strongest institutions in civil society are market-related, there is a danger that the people-driven approach which these authors see emanating from civil society may be overwhelmed by a market-driven approach to growth and development.
>
> (Johnson, 2002, p. 223–4)

This general insight has particular resonance in Ethiopia, as will be discussed later. Although the overwhelming of civil society by the market is not so much a problem, as an objective, in the liberal framework.

Functional classifications, such as networks, may be more appropriate analytical tool in Africa than thematic ones, such as civil society, particularly where the state is 'insufficiently [sic] structurally differentiated from society' (Chabal and Daloz, 1999). African societies tend to be polycephalous with multiple power and decision-making centers, which are products of different periods and have different meanings, rules and agents (Bierschenk *et al.*, 2000, cited in de Herdt and

Dastiaensen, 2004). Thus to assume a unified civil society engaged in a singular project of promoting democratic governance is myopic (McIlwaine, 1998b). Civil society organizations are not always organizing against the state and may pursue contradictory objectives, in some cases cooperating with oppressive states (Whitfield, 2003; Ndegwa, 1996). In Kenya, for example, relations with the state are collaborative on social development and conflictual when dealing with issues of democracy and governance (Hakkarainen *et al.*, 2002).

A significant part of the (capitalist) underdevelopment problematic in Africa is that the state has not been disciplined and made to serve the interests of domestic productive entrepreneurial classes (Samatar, 1999). The weakness of economies reduces the amount of resources for legitimate redistribution and undermines state legitimacy, and thereby fosters conditions conducive to authoritarianism and lack of accountability (poor governance). Given the weakness of the domestic bourgeoisie, some see pluralism in civil society as 'the cutting edge of the effort to build a viable democratic order' (Diamond, 1988, cited in Bratton, 1989a, p. 413). Whether or not this applies in Africa will be assessed below, however, before discussing this it is necessary to examine the nature and evolution of African civil societies.

There are a number of legacies of the colonial state in Africa, particularly on the political culture, which 'contained the notion that authoritarianism was an appropriate mode of rule and that political activity was merely a disguised form of self-interest, subversive of the public welfare' (Kasfir, 1983, cited in Chazan *et al.*, 1999, p. 43). Some argue that 'unilateral claims were a defining characteristic of the colonial state; they left only furtive, marginal space for a "civil" society' (Young, 1994, p. 38). However, it has also been noted that in parts of Africa the colonial state was partially constituted through the necessity to mediate struggles between international capital and local civil society, as the colonial state still needed to legitimate itself.[2] Indeed the colonial state can be seen to have created a civil society defined by rights in Africa.

The weakness of liberal African civil society, in part, stems from the 'bifurcated' nature of African states. Under colonialism, the state created (white) citizens in urban areas, but strengthened neotraditional, indirect ethnic rule in rural areas creating 'subjects' (Mamdani, 1996). In this perspective the 'original sin of civil society under colonialism was racism' (Mamdani, 2006, p. 268). Rural areas are marked by a 'colonially enforced customary order, which entailed the fusion "in a single person [of] all moments of power: judicial, legislative, executive and administrative"' (Mamdani, 1996, p. 23, cited in Engberg-Pedersen,

2002, p. 163). This in turn had implications for the development of rural civil society where many

> 'traditions' and associations contain structures of domination which oblige members of clans and ethnic groups to enact 'development' as part of their identity. It is on this understanding of 'participation as obligation' that many local initiatives are based rather than 'participation as a right' approach.
>
> (Hickey and Mohan, 2004b, pp. 14–5)

These structures of power are central to the intransitive articulation of capitalist and pre- or noncapitalist modes of production in Africa (Lonsdale, 1981). This also explains why 'unlike India, where poor people have established political parties that contest the elections, the African poor have little means of exercising their collective power' (White and Killick, 2001, p. 99). Civil society is weak because the structure of agrarian society did not encourage the emergence of 'vigorous accumulating classes,' which were independent of the state (Boone, 1994).

'Modern' civil society in Africa is a largely urban, donor-driven phenomenon, as the majority of people continue to live in rural areas.

> 'Simply put . . . autonomous agentic individual[s] freed from communal, ethnic and class loyalties [are] nowhere to be found in Africa. The conception of civil society to which that individual gives rise has little analytical value for the study of African politics. By privileging the imaginary "free, self-determining individuality" of a mythical citizen, it becomes an alien construct forced unto an "invented" Africa; an intellectual hallucination of a triumphalist liberal *fin de siecle*.' Thus if civil society is to be a useful heuristic tool in deciphering contemporary African history, it has to be conceptualized as the realm of collective solidarities generated by processes of class formation, ethnic 'inventions' and religious 'revelations.'
>
> (Fatton, 1995, cited in Howell and Pearce, 2001, p. 186)

It could be added that it is continuously molded and remolded by the state (Hutchful, 2002).

Africa has seen powerful cross-class social movements, particularly during the anticolonial struggles and during the 'second liberation' after the collapse of the Soviet bloc when multiparty democracy spread throughout the Continent (see Bratton and van de Walle, 1997). Some authors are leery of liberal civil society, but put more faith in social movements.

Wary of most Africanist scholars uncritical absorption of western perspectives on civil society and its relationship to the state, the second
approach – the popular democratic school – focuses on those organizations and movements in Africa that actually emerged during struggles
for democracy. . . .While both perspectives share the view that statism
is one of the primary obstacles to Africa's socio-economic development,
they propose different solutions to the problem. Whereas liberal analysts emphasize the need to reinforce the boundary between the state
and civil society, and strengthen civil society so as to provide a coun-
terweight to the state, popular-democratic scholars push for a reconceptualization of the very basis of state-society relations in order to
make it more democratic.

(Johnson, 2002, p. 223)

However, social movements have been deactivated by the (colonial)
structures of rural authority.

Precolonial elements of civil society, such as the recently revived dual
sex governance structures in Igbo areas of Nigeria, may also be anath-
ema to the Western conceptions of civil society (Mari Tripp, 2003). The
Igbo Women's Councils 'ensure moral behavior' which might be considered a violation of women's human rights. Indeed, some argue that
the purportedly universal human rights discourse serves as a form of
recolonization (Prakesh and Esteva, 1998). Although this can be countered with the argument that 'Western civilization' may be in fact a universal heritage with AfroAsiatic roots (Bernal, 1987, cited in Nederveen
Pieterse, 2001).

The absence of a developed middle class in Africa meant reduced
postindependence political competition, and that capital accumulation
remained tied to the state (Ravenhill, 1987). Thus in Africa it may be
more useful to think in terms of state, market, civil society complexes,
which are themselves liminal and transnationalizing systems,[3] rather
than discrete civil societies. Another older term which captures this idea
is 'social formations.' However, this term implies a degree of social cohesion and common purpose which is absent in many African countries
by virtue of fragmentation, particularly associated with socially constructed, sometimes invented, ethnicity and clientelist networks.

Traditionally civil society in Africa was viewed as a source of conflict
as it was fractured along ethnic lines, suggesting that the role of the
state was to regulate rather than reflect it (Barkan, 1994). However, there
is now research interest in 'how ties based on ethnicity, clan or another
ascriptive identities are gradually replaced by organizations that cut

across these affiliations and create linkages and networks that bring people together around larger causes' (Mari Tripp, 2003).

As noted earlier, the nature of the African state is central to the nature of civil society. In examining Africa, Chazan *et al.* (1999, p. 23) develop a 'political interaction approach' which examines 'the interaction of social forces, economic activities, formal institutions, and prevalent values, [through which] we may better grasp the meaning and direction of the diverse patterns that have evolved in Africa since independence.' In this framework politics are, therefore, perceived as a set of transactions, 'the manifestation of the exercise of choice by multiple actors within existing parameters' (Chazan *et al.*, 1999, p. 24).

Patterns of state–society interaction vary by regime type. In this context, political regimes refer to

> The rules, principles, norms and modes of interaction between social groups and state organs (Krasner, 1985). The concept of regime is, therefore, concerned with the form of rule. It deals with how political relations are carried out, with the procedures and mechanisms of political exchange. If the idea of the state is associated primarily with the organization of power, regimes focuses on how state power is exercised and legitimated.
>
> (Chazan *et al.*, 1999, p. 39)

The weakness of national identities and the virtual absence of nation states in Africa, as a result of the interaction between precolonial and colonial legacies, mean that associational life is primarily local and, to a more limited extent, transnational. Ethnicity is an important organizing principle because, like nationalism, it contains both instrumental and emotive elements. Chazan *et al.* (1999, p. 75) note, however, that most studies of African politics have emphasized the importance of class and ethnicity in the social roots of public institutions, but that 'African social and material life, however, revolves, in the first instance, around a medley of more compact organizations, networks, groupings, associations, and movements that have evolved over centuries in response to changing circumstances.' These may undermine the development of a shared public domain with universal values and discourse central to the idea of civil society (Lewis, 2002).

In sub-Saharan Africa, the main basis of political and socio-economic activity is 'the group, rather than the individual or broader social constellation. . . . These ties may be ones of blood, affinity, identity, utility or worship' (Chazan *et al.*, 1999, p. 76). In Africa group rights have traditionally superseded individual rights: e.g. through communal ownership of land (Sunmonu, 2004). This was reinforced under colonialism as group life allowed Africans to 'control fragments of daily existence' (Chazan *et al.*, 1999); and associational life has tended to follow inherited rather than voluntary patterns. This includes 'Islamic networks throughout western Sudan, trading alliances around domestic and transnational markets, craft guilds, women's associations at the interstices of local and state power, credit unions, and mafia-type bands' (ibid., p. 214). More recently people have sought refuge from the ravages of neoliberalism in millenarian cults and evangelical religions (Ferguson, 2006).

Chazan *et al.* (1999, p. 79) distinguish between different types of groups in Africa. Under 'primary groups' they consider 'indigenous institutions that have deep historical roots, such as clans, lineages, cultural associations, and village communities.' These geographically rooted communities are often times more developed than the 'communities-of-interest' of liberal civil society. The durability and importance of kinship is explained by the fragility and transformation of other institutions.

In urban areas, hometown associations (*associations des originaires*) are particularly important. In contrast to other 'primary groups,' language and cultural associations are twentieth-century constructions, perhaps partly related to increased urbanization. Group boundaries are often liminal, however. For example, 'Asantes in Ghana may see themselves as Akan in relation to Ewe (another broad linguistic group), as Asante in relation to the Fante (an Akan-speaking ethnic group) or as Mampong in relation to people from Offinsu (two political and geographical units)' (Chazan *et al.* 1999, p. 84). The 'fracturing' of African social complexes along ethno-linguistic, religious, kinship and other dimensions prevents the emergence of civil society conceived as a set of values or 'ideologique' (Bayart, 1986, cited in Azarya, 1994). It is arguably this value of (neo)liberal, 'good governance' which donors are trying to inculcate in African social formations. However there is a contradiction between 'imperialist liberalism – forcing men to be free (Young, 1993) and a set of culture in which the self is embedded in forms of community' (Harrison, 2002, p. 19).

The second type of grouping which Chazan *et al.* (1999, p. 85) identify are 'horizontal groupings developed around occupational concerns and include various associations of workers, farmers, teachers, lawyers, engineers, police, soldiers, entrepreneurs and traders.' These have often been forceful pressure groups, voices of dissent and in some cases instrumental in regime change. Women's associations are also prominent on the continent, particularly umbrella organizations, women's branches of trades unions, voluntary associations and transnational networks, such as the Association of African Women for Research and Development. Other African transnational groups are the Pan-Africa Civic Educators Network (PACE-NET), the NGOs of Southern Africa, and the African Debt and Development Network (AFRODAD). Religious organizations are also very prominent actors.

In contrast to some authors who see a prostrate civil society in Africa:

> State power is not unlimited. Although individuals and social groups cannot easily detach themselves from their national environments, governments, in turn, may not be able to skirt demands from well-organized social forces without losing access to the vital resources controlled by these associations. As the outlines of civil societies are emerging in many African countries, previous patterns of state–society relations may be undergoing change.
>
> (Chazan *et al.* 1999, p. 102)

Michael Bratton (1989a, cited in Barkan, 1994, p. 93) argues that civil society in Africa includes associational life beyond the purview of the state to include 'ethnic and village development associations, farmers associations, religious groups (Christian, Islamic and separatist), urban traders (market women), taxi drivers, urban welfare associations, labor unions and professional associations (educators, journalists, lawyers, physicians). He sees producers' unions of market women, taxi drivers and small farmers as playing a 'critical political role in key sectors of African economies' (Bratton, 1989a, p. 417).

The division between primary and horizontal groups is, of course, liminal with some associations appearing to 'view membership of "tribes" and/or parties as aiding the creation of conditions for their more effective role in society' (Monga, 1995, p. 393). 'Clientelism can lead to a pyramiding of client–patron ties, and, through the recruitment of new brokers, to an expansion of local or regional reciprocities on a more inclusive scale' (Lemarchand, 1972, cited in Chazan *et al.*, 1999, p. 131). However, it also leads to inter-network competition. The pre-scribed antidote of decentralization has merely enhanced the patronage power of local politicians and administrators (see Francis and James, 2003).[4] It has been noted that 'carefully drafted development plans whose implementation depends on existing social structures and institutions are, like these structures and institutions, impregnated with power and gender biases' (McGee, 2002b, p. 26).[5]

Rothchild and Lawson (1994, p. 256) make a distinction between horizontally organized interest groups, such as 'labor unions, bar associations, women's organizations, and farmers associations,' which add to the state's legitimacy by making demands on it, and vertically organized communal groups who 'weaken the authority of the state, and the public realm more generally, through clientelistic politics and other privatizing strategies.' As Patrick Molutsi (1999) notes, civil society can be disruptive and violent, particularly in a context of competition over limited resources where parochial social identities gain sway. Economic liberalization is associated with rising income inequality, which in Africa is often overlain by ethnicity. This may be implicated in the rise of 'popular' counter-mobilizations against 'market dominant minorities' as in Rwanda and Zimbabwe, for example (Chua, 2004). However, ethnic mobilization may also be positive if it promotes 'some notion of collective empowerment, rather than violence, chauvinism and revanchism' (Harrison, 2002, p. 143). An example, of this would be the Movement for the Survival of Ogoni People (MOSOP) in Nigeria, which was developed to contest environmental degradation and resource extraction from the Niger Delta. Ethnic (re)mobilization can also take place through the revival of traditional institutions of governance.

In Uganda

> The restoration of the Ganda kingship is politically significant despite its non-conformity with Western ideals of liberal participatory government. This restoration arguably promises a political order founded on co-existing clan-based organizations and royal rule, a more stable, responsive and representative institution than a national party system, and a long history of clans mediating between citizens and monarchy, checking excesses of power. The possibility for kinship to take on both a private and a public face in Uganda contradicts Western assumptions of civil society in which kinship relations are considered to be outside civil society norms: 'African sociocultural arrangements provide their own logic of sovereign accountability, their own public spheres, their own forms of nongovernmental organization and association.'
>
> (Lewis, 2002, p. 580, citing Karlstrom, 1999)

However, others argue that this is to romanticize African institutions, with the revival of kingship in Uganda, for example, being seen by some as a way through which the ruling party was able, for a time, to deflect donor demands for multiparty democracy, by appeals to an alternative 'authenticity.' It is not incommensurable that there is truth in both positions.

'Participatory' processes in PRSPs may also serve as a donor-accepted substitute for democracy. Indeed one study of Uganda found that the most important political factor in the success of the PRSP there was the effectiveness of the state which it attributed to 'the tight political structure around the President and the core of the Movement, the restriction on fully competitive politics, the penetration of the state down to the local level through the creation of the local councils, and the *cooptation of civil society organizations*' (emphasis added) (Piron and Norton, 2004). Over a 10-year period 22 percent of the population of Uganda were lifted over the $1 a day absolute poverty line (Asea, 2003). However, 'traditional' institutions have had their role severely restricted, and the PEAP has served to legitimate one party rule as it is seen 'as being broad-based and non-controversial even by political opponents' (Piron with Evans, 2004, p. 11), with donors accepting CSOs as 'acceptable proxies' for different political voices without multiparty politics. As governments are more reluctant to crackdown on 'human rights leagues' than opposition parties in Africa, some CSOs have become elements of *de facto* opposition movements (Monga [1995] 2000). However, in Uganda,

> Trade unions and NGOs too closely associated with the political opposition are not involved in the PEAP consultations or implementation processes. 'Consultation' has come to mean institutionalizing a specific kind of participation in policymaking with selected CSOs. These organizations cannot really be seen to represent alternative political views or developmental approaches. Should they become too vocal, they may no longer be invited to take part in policymaking.
>
> (Piron with Evans, 2004, p. 16)

Direct budget support also strengthens the center of government at the expense of mid-tier line ministries (Unwin, 2004). It also runs the risk of strengthening the power of African political elites, who some would argue, bear most of the responsibility for Africa's crisis (Porteous, 2005; see also Ake, 1996; Mbeki, 2005), while also allowing donors to 'turn the tap on and off' more easily than project aid (Abegaz, 2001). Some European donors have recently begun to reduce aid to Uganda as a result of the scrapping of presidential term limits (*Irish Times*, 2005a, p. 11). This has been offset, politically, however, by the legalization of multiparty politics. Thus Museveni has skillfully 'pulled in' the IFIs to consolidate territorial control and National Resistance Movement

(NRM) rule (Craig and Porter, 2006). The result has been to send 'Liberal modes of governance spiraling over distance into some very illiberal places' (Craig and Porter, 2006, p. 19), as will be discussed later in relation to Ethiopia. In the Ugandan case this has also been compatible with 'spectacular poverty reduction.'

The centralization of power in Africa has a logic to it, however. As Chazan *et al.* (1999, p. 137) put it, political 'leaders have had to devise strategies of legitimation and find appropriate means of maintaining social order while being beholden to particular groups, frequently without the benefit of viable domestic structures supported by widespread sentiments of national loyalty and without the ability to avert the influences of regional and global forces.' Thus, while Western donors may not like it, ethnicity may provide a partial foundation for state legitimacy.

Another example where state–civil society relations were accountable, without being democratic in the liberal sense of the term comes from Kenya where Barkan (1994, p. 97) notes that

> in Kenyatta's Kenya the combination of Harambee [state supported village self help associations], regular elections, and liberal patronage was used to establish a clientelist system that was both stable and accountable in terms of state responsiveness to rural civil society.[6]

However, there was also an opportunity cost to this.

> People are fed up and say, 'Now there is too much harambee [collective community work], we do not want any more' (Kenya 1996). The PPA estimates that there are over 300,000 groups in rural areas, mostly disconnected from any external technical or financial assistance. 'Hundreds of cases were recorded everywhere of the poor investing their resources in misguided harambee efforts related to water, farming, livestock, education, health, and a range of income generating activities. School buildings, without books, health clinics without drugs, chickens that die before they can be sold, and cotton that does not grow are of little use to anyone.'
>
> (Kenya 1996) (Narayan *et al.*, 2000, p. 151)

After independence, the rise of developmentalism and the 'overdeveloped' African socialist state reduced the space for civil society (Michael, 2004). However, the inability of the state to continue to deliver clientelist and public benefits as a result of economic crisis in the 1980s meant the withering/reconstitution of networks and withdrawal of society from the state (Reno, 1998). This created a vicious circle, with Chazan (1988, p. 239) arguing that in Africa 'the incapacity of the state is the end result of the disengagement of social forces from the public sphere.' It has also resulted in what Joshua Forrest (1998) calls the 'inverted state,' looking inward.

Changing state–society relations

According to Crawford Young (2004, p. 42),

> over time, the underlying contradiction between the 'integral' [where the state fully penetrates and transforms society] and 'patrimonial' states caused the demise of both and opened up new political space for civil society. The fundamental opposition between integral norm and patrimonial reality was not at first apparent; only over time did it take form.

Rothchild and Lawson (1994, p. 277) argue that 'the weakness of the state and civil society and the lack of mutual dependence between the state and society at large must be overcome in the search for effective governance.' Thus posed, the question is not perhaps how donors can directly 'embed' the state (something which only state and civil society actors can undertake), but to unravel the structural conditions which give rise to the poor relationship: in particular, the debt and current aid systems which promote external accountability, at the expense of internal accountability and developmental interactions (see Leonard and Strauss, 2003; Lockwood, 2005).

Reengagement as a response to changed political opportunity structures is seen as a form of state building as the state must look outward, and balance different societal interests (Mercer, 2002). However, whether this weakens or strengthens the state depends on definitional issues of strength and weakness. It may create incentives which strengthen state capacity, but reduce its autonomy for development planning and result in a proliferation of demands with negative implications for the economy (hence the rationale for keeping macro-economic policy insulated in the PRSP process). The growth of liberal civil society, in opposition to the state, has been supported in Africa by donors; however, the above analysis would suggest that this type of civil society is less politically influential than those with longer histories, which are more firmly embedded in the domestic environment.

While some, such as Basil Davidson (1993), argue that Africa's renewal will be dependent on the revival and reinvigoration of traditional institutions, others (e.g. Dia, 1996) take a more nuanced approach arguing that what is required is a 'straddling' strategy whereby traditional and modern institutions are reconciled and synergies achieved between them. There have been some concrete examples of this. In Rwanda existing indigenous participatory practices were used in designing the PRSP, for example (Stewart and Wang, 2003).

There may also need to be an end to the dissonance between ethnicity and state. Jenkins (2001) argues that ethnic organizations need to be integrated into competitive political systems, as in India, rather than dismissed as obstacles to modernity and good governance. As will be discussed later in relation to Ethiopia, however, ethnicity may be manipulated through a process of divide and rule to consolidate single party dominance. Others might also object that Tanzania's relative political stability rests on political parties based on ethnicity being outlawed (which has also perhaps helped the ruling Chama Cha Mapinduzi [CCM] to remain in power since independence). Nonetheless when political parties become detached from sectoral interests this may be dysfunctional to democracy.

While the World Bank may pay lip service respecting traditional African institutions, Williams and Young (1994, cited in Jenkins, 2001, pp. 250–1) argue that its enthusiastic support for civil society is

> nothing less than a backdoor attempt to transform African societies from the ground up by substituting a new understanding of political subjectivity – for it is only through such a novel basis for the 'self' that the accompanying features of an open political sphere and a 'neutral [pluralist] state' can perform the roles assigned to them in liberal political theory and neo-liberal economic policy.

Ironically, this project of atomization may undermine social capital. The project could be seen as one of dismantling actually existing civil society, to then reconstruct it in the image of the West (subject to political exigencies).

According to Hearn (1999, p. 4) 'donors are not funding the popular [rural] sectors of society, but are strengthening a new African elite committed to the promotion of a limited form of procedural democracy and structural-adjustment-type economic policies in partnership with the West.' The search by donors for 'true democrats' also violates the principles of neoclassical allocative efficiency; by attempting to 'pick winners,' they distort the 'political market' (Jenkins, 2001). It also risks 'adverse selection'[7] as more prominent civil society leaders, may be the most egotistically driven. USAID gave $145,000 over three years to Major Buyoya's Foundation for Unity, Peace and Democracy in Burundi. He subsequently staged a coup attempt (*The Observer*, 1996, cited in Jenkins, 2001). This suggests that civil society (Dr Jekyl) cannot be quarantined from political society (Mr. Hyde), as CSOs have their own, (selfish and selfless[8]) political interests. That such actions are unforeseen by USAID is ironic coming from an agency which has built its policy framework around rational choice theory.

In Africa the proliferation of NGOs and other CSOs is spurred by transformation of, resistance to and absence of, the state. Between a fifth and a half of all health and education services in sub-Saharan Africa may be provided by NGOs (Robinson, 1997, cited in van de Walle, 2003). This level of funding may also open up divisions between donors and states as each vie for 'influence, creating proxy organizations and shaping priorities through promises of funding' (Howell, 2000, p. 18).

In terms of the impacts of NGOs there is regional and country variation. 'The common perception of NGOs in Mali at the local level is that they contribute significantly to economic opportunities and overall well-being; moreover they function as important social safety nets' (Participatory Poverty Assessment Mali, 1993, cited in Narayan *et al.*, 2000, p. 135). However,

> a growing literature has challenged the earlier assumptions that took for granted the greater efficiency of NGOs in Africa and has shown them to be riven by corruption and their own clientelistic circuits built along ethnic and other lines . . . A few have even argued that were states to have access the large amounts of funding NGOs have at their disposal, they too might be able to provide services as cost-effectively and might be better able to ensure more even coverage nationwide.
>
> (Mari Tripp, 2003, p. 145)

Nonetheless local NGOs serve an important catalytic role with local-level development groups such as women's groups and credit associations in alleviating poverty (Michael, 2004).

A sentiment which is commonly voiced about NGOs is that there is little altruistic motivation in their foundation. In the context of substantial flows of aid to NGOs in very poor societies, what is to stop civil society being corrupted by donor priorities, to become coopted NGOs

(CONGOs) (Bond, 2001b) and economic accumulation, to become my-own NGOs (MONGOs). According to one newspaper, out of 3500 registered NGOs in Tanzania only 500 were operational, with the rest being 'briefcase NGOs' or COME'N Gos (*The Express*, 2001, cited in Mercer, 2003). In these ways civil society can be rent-seeking and clientelism may increase with aid-rent extraction (Gould and Ojanen, 2005). This calls forth government regulation, in the form of NGO codes of conduct, with the attendant risk, however, of CSOs becoming government run NGOs (GRINGOs). The World Bank even refers to Bank Organized NGOs (BONGOs) (Ferguson, 2006).

In parts of Africa civil society activists have been launched on to political careers. One of the most notable examples being Frederic Chiluba in Zambia, a former trade unionist, whose administration is commonly seen as being marked by greater venality than that of the out-going President Kenneth Kaunda – the attempt to disqualify Kaunda from running for the Presidency on the basis that he was 'Malawian' as a case in point. Chiluba is currently on trial. We now turn to a case study of the development of liberal civil society and its input and impacts on the PRSP process.

Making and marketing civil society: Ethiopia

Ethiopia is a large, multiethnic country. It has a population of roughly 65 million people. The two largest ethnic groups are the Amhara and Oromo; together accounting for about two thirds of the population. Roughly 60 percent of the population is Christian. Livelihood systems range from 'the settled upland teff cultures of the north; the enset-based farming systems of the south; and a variety of agro-pastoralist and nomadic systems along the margins of the Rift Valley' (World Bank, 2002a, p. 8). Food security is a perennial problem in the lowland areas, in particular. The country is divided up into nine (supposedly) ethnic regions, zones, *woreda* (of about 100,000 people) and *kebele* (of about 5,000 people).

About 85 percent of the population is directly dependent on agriculture for their livelihoods, which accounts for about 55 percent of GDP, and all land remains state owned. Industry accounts for about 14 percent of GDP. It is one of the poorest, if not the poorest country in the world. GDP was about US $6bn in 2002 (*Hutchinson Country Facts*, n.d.), and its per capita income is roughly $100 per annum (1999), less than a fifth of the sub-Saharan African average. Estimates vary from 45 and to 82 percent of its population living in absolute poverty (Muwonge *et al.*, 2002) and it ranks 169th out of 175 countries on the Human

Development Index (Gabriel, 2002; UNDP, 2003b). Working with the low figure, there is substantial inter-regional variation in poverty levels ranging from 26 percent in Harari to 61 percent in Tigray (Gabriel, 2002). Part of the explanation for the severity of poverty is the legacy of civil war during the 1980s, fuelled by $6bn of Soviet and Western arms supplies to the Horn of Africa (Abegaz, 2001). AIDS in an important problem, but does not appear to have breached the 5 percent 'epidemic level.'

Debt is also an important issue in Ethiopia. In 2001 its external debt was $9bn, with a debt service ratio of 20 percent. At the turn of the millennium, while half a million Ethiopian children were dying from diarrhea and other easily preventable diseases a year, the country was spending six times more on debt repayments than primary health care (Watkins, 1999, cited in Hanahoe, 2003). In late 2001 it qualified for $1.9bn debt relief under the HIPC initiative (OECD, n.d., cited in Doyle, 2004), and more recently for the 100 percent debt cancellation package.

The country is heavily aid dependent, accounting for 76 percent of capital accumulation and 25 percent of the recurrent budget of the government (Geda and Weeks, 2002). However,ODA averaged only $13 per capita in 2003, half the sub-Saharan African average (Ministry of Finance & Economic Development of the Federal Democratic Republic of Ethiopia and the United Nations Country Team, 2004). This also relates to other statistics. For example, Ethiopia has one of the lowest road densities in the world, with 'only 20 percent of its land area being within 10km of an all-weather road and 70 percent of its farms being more than a half day walk from an all-weather road' (Ministry of Finance & Economic Development of the Federal Democratic Republic of Ethiopia and the United Nations Country Team, 2004, p. 29).

After the overthrow of the military Derg regime in the early 1990s, the new government further liberalized the economy. Economic growth averaged over 5 percent for much of the 1990s, but the end of the decade saw this dramatically reduced as a result of a border war with Eritrea and a severe drought in 2000. The economy recovered strongly in 2000/2001 registering 7.9 percent growth. The agricultural dependence of the economy means it is subject to rapid, climatically induced swings. It registered growth of 11 percent in 2004 (Adow, 2005), leading the World Bank resident representative to posit that it was at the point of economic take-off.

It is estimated that absolute poverty declined by 2.9 percent between 1995/1996 and 1999/2000, although this is largely in rural areas, as there was an 11.1 percent increase in poverty in urban areas

(Gabriel, 2002). Increased urban poverty was concentrated in provincial towns such as Dire Dawa and Dessie, while it fell in the capital, Addis Ababa (Bigsten, Kebebe and Shimeles, 2003) which is increasingly plugged into transnational circuits of capital accumulation and remittances. As foreign exchange controls were relaxed remittances rose from 17 percent of total household income in Ethiopia in 1994 to 25 percent in 1997, with Addis Ababa benefiting disproportionately (Bigsten, Kronlid and Makonnen, 2005), contributing to making Ethiopia a 'virtual economy.'

Also the (gendered) distribution of income worsened in the 1990s counteracting, to some extent, the poverty reducing effects of growth (Bigsten, Kebebe and Shimeles, 2003). The Gini coefficient[9] rose from 0.39 to 0.54 from 1994 to 1995, largely because the consumption expenditure of the top rural decile of the population doubled during that year (Kebebe *et al.*, 2005). In urban areas the income of the lowest quintile declined by 7.7 percent from 1994 to 1997, whereas it rose by over a tenth for the top quintile (Bigsten, Kronlid and Makonnen, 2005). Women's private sector monthly wages fell by 8 percent, during this time, whereas they rose for men by 9 percent (Dercon *et al.*, 2005).

Ethiopia has a history of centralized political control under the empire of Haile Selaisse, through the Marxist military Derg (Amharic for Committee) and the current regime.[10] 'This long authoritarian tradition has given rise to a zero-sum approach to attaining, and maintaining, political power in Ethiopia' (DCI, 2004, p. 9). The current ruling Ethiopian Peoples Revolutionary Democratic Front (EPRDF), a coalition of 24 political parties and, in power since 1991, has a vision of 'revolutionary democracy' involving collective participation and representation by consensus.[11] The leadership of the EPRDF is mainly drawn from the minority Tigrayan ethnicity and the ranks of the Tigrayan People's Liberation Front (TPLF). This system has echoes of 'one party' or 'no party democracy' elsewhere on the continent.

The EPRDF party has had a three-track strategy to remain in power; local, national and business. The public sector accounts for more than 40 percent of total employment in urban Ethiopia, giving the government substantial leverage (Dercon *et al.*, 2005). Also the establishment of a consociational ethnically federal structure in the country[12] has facilitated a modified strategy of divide and rule; a kind of 'multi-Mobutuism' (Aspen, 2002).[13] There are 68, mostly ethnically based political parties in Ethiopia, but 98 percent of seats during the last Parliament were held by the EPRDF (Confidential interview, September 2004). Both the 1995 and

2000 elections were uncontested in many constituencies (DCI, 2004), but ethnicity has become more polarized and is associated with pronounced political instability in some regions of the country, particularly Oromia (Mengisteab, 2002). The real power brokers in the regions are often Tigrayan 'advisors' to regional governments of EPRDF affiliates (Aalen, 2002, cited in Pausewang *et al.*, 2002a). In a detailed case study of the Somali region, Abdi Samatar found that current and previous regional presidents there serve at the pleasure of the authorities in Addis (Samatar, 2005). No fewer than five of the past seven regional presidents have served prison terms after they were 'deposed.'

Nonetheless some argue that 'ethnic contract of the Tigrayan political entrepreneurs, a relatively preferable option' (Abbay, 2004, p. 614) when compared to Ethiopia's past or other possible alternatives, as it allows for relative political stability and lack of discrimination. However, there is evidence that discrimination exists. For example, Agarfa *woreda* in Bale zone got a transfer of 47.4 Ethiopian birr per person from the central government in 1998/9 versus 8.9 for Liben *woreda* in Borena zone. While the government takes some account of other resources, such as those provided by INGOs, this would not explain differences of this magnitude. While both regions are in Oromiya, the Borena zone has been marked by substantial ethnic conflict, and had the lowest turnout in the 2005 election. Nonetheless the opposition won five of the six seats on offer with the sixth disputed (*Ethiopian News and Views*, 2005). 'The serious ethnic conflicts that broke out in Sodo Zuria and more generally in North Omo Zone in late 1999 and early 2000 were in part fuelled by perceptions that certain groups had received preferential treatment from the Government' (World Bank, 2002a, p. 44).

A study for the World Bank (2002a, p. 2) found the new system to be one of 'administrative deconcentration, not the devolution of powers' with the government continuing to exercise control through local government. This is evidenced by the fact that while in theory the Federal Constitution devolved authority

> technical line agencies in Awabel in 1998–9 delivered products that conformed closely to the types of service evident throughout the highland areas of the country: thus, for example, the agricultural development agents in the woreda were intent on promoting fertilizer, packages of seed, and credit on half-hectare teff demonstration plots in a manner identical to what could simultaneously be observed in teff-producing areas of Oromiya or Southern Nations region.
>
> (World Bank, 2002a, p. 19)

This study found that community input and elected official input was subordinated to top-down planning, with woreda plans ghost written by zonal technical bureaux. 'Apart from articulating their needs (without much prospect of satisfaction), the major role of the community is to discuss suggestions from a capital menu, [e.g. roads, schools] the scale of which is severely limited and the final design of which will be referenced to pre-existing sector plans' (World Bank, 2002a, p. 36). This type of deconcentration would appear to accord well with PRSPs, where spending priorities are largely centrally determined, and with the IFI-sponsored experience of decentralization on the continent which 'risk[s] reproducing old patterns of indirect: administratively driven local authorities managing people in the name of self-determination' (Ribot and Oyono, 2006, p. 206).

The form of decentralization in Ethiopia has been characterized as deconcentration or administrative decentralization, without devolution of power to elected bodies as prescribed in the Federal and regional constitutions. Paradoxically this is a form of centralization as

> When deconcentration occurs in isolation, or when it occurs with fiscal decentralization but without simultaneous democratization – that is, when agents of higher levels of government move into lower level arenas but remain accountable only to persons higher up in the system – it enables central authority to penetrate more effectively into those areas without increasing the influence of organized interests at those levels. The central government is not giving up any authority. It is simply relocating its officers at different levels or points in the national territory. In such circumstances, it tends in practice to constitute centralization, since it enhances the leverage of those at the apex of the system.
>
> (Manor, 1999, cited in World Bank, 2002a, p. 78)

There are parallels with the PRSP here as a form of governance, as both the Ethiopian constitution and PRSP represent a form of centralized decentralization. Whereas SAPs have been described as central planning or 'command and control' from Washington (Abugre, 2000), PRSPs are decentralized planning from Washington. Nonetheless, communities in Ethiopia are able to by-pass the state as 'regardless of the Woreda resource allocation decisions, communities achieved the successful completion of their top priority interventions. . . . Sometimes the community went elsewhere (Church, NGO) other times they presumably mobilized community resources to achieve their aims' (INTRAC, 2004, p. 5).

Given the poverty of the country, institutions of community support are strong in Ethiopia and there is very little social exclusion (World Bank, 2002a). One survey found that *idir* (burial society) membership ranged from 100 percent to 48 percent, 'but tended towards the higher level' (Muir, 2004, p. 6). There are two types: *idir* and multipurpose *idir*, which may offer loans for contingencies outside of death. In one kebele in Addis Ababa the *idir* are forming a union to deal with HIV/AIDS and other social issues. Some talk of 'development *idirs*.' The Kaffa Development Association started as an *idir* in 1958, and there have been others associated with forest protection. There are also umbrella groups for *idir* called *modi*. *Equbs* (savings clubs) are common in some kebele but not in others. In Addis Ketema only 3 percent were members, versus 12 percent who were in formal credit associations (Muir, 2004). Pastoralists use their livestock as 'banks.'

However, the state is also deeply imbricated in CBOs. Membership in *kebeles* in mandatory, and *idir* are commonly used as access points to the community by *kebele* cabinets, as people respond more favorably to calls for labor through this channel. This institutional arrangement seems to serve a buffer function, whereby the coordination demands of the state can be transmitted, thereby bypassing coercion and reducing enforcement costs, but communities retain a certain level of autonomy.

> In Jinka 02 the Kebele Cabinet 'often uses the iddir to make such announcements and requests. They were wary, however, of government interference in their affairs. The iddir was free from Government interference at the moment, but the possibility of this was felt to be always present, especially if they were to obtain significant funds for development – from an NGO for example. Their view was that projects initiated by government or NGOs are unlikely to be 'owned' by the people – 'government and NGOs simply tell you what they are going to do and go about it their own way, without reference to the affected population.'
>
> (D. Turton, cited in Muir, 2004, p. 28)

Agricultural mutual assistance groups are ubiquitous in rural areas, where they sometimes overlap with *mahaber* (social religious groups). Unpaid community labor in the development of infrastructure in particularly important in Amhara region through the *mengistawi buden* ('governmental team') networks, indicating that there is no clear separation between 'community' and local government. This community labor is thought to exceed official capital transfers in Amhara region. 'Voluntary' labor is linked to the ability to access employment generation scheme work, with 30 days free labor generally required to access the scheme in Amhara region. The counterparts of rural mutual assistance groups in urban areas are business/trader groups; the development of which government assistance has been the driving force in (Muir, 2004). Other informal support networks include clan, subclan, age groups and women's and youth organizations. Almost all groups, barring women's groups, tend to be led by men.

Community engagement and participation in, as opposed to receiving directives from, local government is generally thought to be low (Muir, 2004). 'Local authorities tend to act more as though they are representatives of the state and the ruling party, rather than working in the service of their electorate/citizens' (INTRAC, 2004, p. 5). In Oromiya, which has an active secessionist movement, rural militias (a part of 'civil society') have reportedly exercised undue influence on elected *kebele* council officials (World Bank, 2002a).

Party-controlled business conglomerates, along with the business empire of billionaire Sheikh Al Amoudi, dominate the economy and enjoy a 'virtual monopoly of rural services, transport and trade of essential goods' (Pausewang *et al.*, 2002b, pp. 231–2).[14] 'A large number of enterprises wholly or partially owned by EPRDF are being organized into interlocking financial and industrial groups (FIGs)' (Abegaz, 2001, p. 207), often registered in the name of NGOs. Given the previous Marxist ideology of the EPRDF, the indigenous private sector tends to be regarded as exploitative and 'the spread of rural entrepreneurship envisaged under the ADLI [Agriculture Development Led Industrialization strategy] has faltered' (World Bank, 2002a, p. 5). Privatized industries were often bought by EPRDF affiliated parties, providing an important source of funds and political control.

In Gojjam, for example, the primary non-government purveyor of fertilizer is the Anbassel Trading House Private Limited, owned by the EPRDF-affialted ANDM [Amhara National Democratic Movement]. Though small traders in theory may distribute fertilizer, they have not been able to do so since 80 percent of all fertilizer in Ethiopia is financed through government credit, a method of payment that private traders cannot afford.

(Degefe and Nega, 2000, p. 191, cited in McCann, 2002)

Access to fertilizer is in turn dependent on support for the ruling party. Land reform has also been used as a mechanism through which the state can 'capture' the peasantry, as has the adoption of a peasant cadre system (see Ege, 2002; Aspen, 2002). Given its historic basis in rural areas, however, the current government is widely credited with delivering infrastructure to rural areas over the last decade (Adow, 2005).[15]

One of the side benefits of this system, where the state penetrates and dominates the 'private' and to some extent, as will be discussed later, the 'voluntary' sectors is the relative absence of corruption.[16] The relative lack of corruption and efficiency of state services may also be to do with the long history of statehood in Ethiopia (J. Grindle, personal communication, October 2004). It may also relate to the fact that Ethiopia was never colonized and consequently the types of patronage networks associated with indirect rule, or the 'rhizome state,' were never established (Bayart, 1993). Furthermore the EPRDF originated as a military movement, with strict discipline and this has been transferred into government, with malfeasance rare, and corruption punished (World Bank, 2002a). A strong state and a 'hierarchical approach has permitted a strong budgetary emphasis on key ADLI priorities, in particular universal primary education and increased agricultural production, with impressive results through the mid-1990s. The civil service remains well disciplined, and fraud and absenteeism are rare by any standards' (World Bank, 2002a, p. 4). Almost two million farmers had access to government seed and fertilizer packages in 2000 (World Bank, 2002a).

Some civil society groups, such as the Ethiopian Economics Association, have been quite critical of government economic policy, and Ethiopia's marginalization in the global economy, suggesting the adoption of strategic trade and industrial policies, such as those adopted in East Asian 'developmental states' (EEA, 2004). The government itself is, in theory, quite receptive to such a perspective, with Nobel Laureate Joseph Stiglitz advising the government on how to block IMF demands for full capital account liberalization. However, in practice given the party's vested interest in much 'private' business, the state is hostile to local capital and tends to favor multinationals (Rahmato, 2002). Although there has also been some conflict with them as in 2002, a famine year, when Nestle sued the government for millions of dollars in losses, for the privatization of its coffee operations under the Derg (Denny, 2002). Ironically the Derg promoted micro and small businesses, but, contrary to expressed World Bank preferences, 'there is less support now, forcing small and business cooperatives into stronger competition with larger private sector companies' (Muir, 2004, p. 25).

Private businesses often suffer from arbitrary and discriminatory practices, in relation to tariffs for example.[17] Also party businesses receive special privileges such as tax breaks and low interest rate loans at 2 percent, rather than the market rate of 10 percent (Confidential interview, Addis Ababa, September 2004).

EPRDF rule has been marked by serious human rights abuses, including summary executions (Pausewang *et al.*, 2002b; European Commission, 2001). 'At the heart of the problem of the Ethiopian state lies the fact that it does not function as a democracy, does not serve free citizens, and does not safeguard human rights' (Pausewang *et al.*, 2002b, p. 243). Freedom House ranks Ethiopia as having a score for 5 for both civil and political rights on a scale of 1 to 7, where 1 is the 'most free' (*Electionworld*, 2005). However, there has also been an attempt to legitimate EPRDF rule through gradual liberalization of the political system, which has seen the opposition parties making important gains, particularly in Addis Ababa, where they took all of the seats in the recent national election (*The Economist*, May 2005a). Prior to the 2005 election some argued that suppression of dissent could impact negatively on political order (Interview with development assistance official, Addis Ababa, September 17, 2004) and 'freedom of the press and organization are, for example, now more respected in the country than ever before' (Mengisteab, 2002, p. 184). However, political liberalization may be a continuation of a 'stage play' largely confined to Addis for the benefit of the donor community, while firm control is maintained in rural areas (Pausewang *et al.*, 2002a).[18] Indeed some argue that the partnership approach of transnational private aid agencies 'indirectly contribute to the consolidation of a "parasitic" class alliance at the core of state power that has a strong symbiosis with quasi-feudal political configuration at the base' (Gould and Ojanen, 2005, p. 51). For one INGO official in Ethiopia, however, 'it is not all Machiavellian. There is a genuine fear on the part of the government of what would happen if they let go too much' (Interview, Addis Ababa, September 17, 2004).

The 2005 elections were arguably the most free in Ethiopian history, marking a breakthrough for the opposition in urban areas in particular (Adow, 2005). However there are tensions in this as pressure for political liberalization led to unrest, as in other contexts (see, for example, Longman, 1998). When the opposition disputed numerous results, the government banned demonstrations. Protest took the form of a strike by taxi drivers in the capital, and when the ban on demonstrations was not observed around 40 people were shot dead in the capital, and thousands were detained until most were released under donor pressure (BBC News, 2005d). The President characterized the protests as a coup attempt (Bolderson, 2005). According to the Information Minister these actions were necessary because 'the alternative was strife between the different nationalities of Ethiopia which might have made the Rwandan genocide look like child's play' (Bereket Simon, quoted in Plaut, 2005).[19] However, the protests were led by students. When an EU report on the elections was critical, the Ethiopian Prime Minister accused it of colonialism and not being willing to accept the 'natives' decision. There are remarkable similarities with the 'anti-imperialist' discourse of Robert Mugabe here, discussed later.

More people were shot dead subsequently and most of the opposition Coalition for Unity and Democracy (CUD) leadership are being tried for inciting 'genocide' or 'treason,' which carries the death penalty. Attempts to displace domestic tensions in Ethiopia have also resulted in 'saber rattling' along the Ethio-Eritrean border.

According to Pausewang *et al.* (2002a, p. 28), one of the main social forces opposed to an ethnically oriented renewal was

> the urban middle class, which speaks Amharic, is ethnically mixed, and feels more Ethiopian than Amhara, Oromo or otherwise. The majority of this group were middle-class Amhara who [fear] victimization for their erstwhile positions in the Derg regime and their relatively privileged access to positions and influence.

Part of the EPRDF's suspicion of civil society may be that many of its members are associated with the former Derg regime, as they have been excluded from state positions (Confidential interview, Addis Ababa, September 2004). However, it may relate to Amhara dominance in the NGO sector, rather than previous association with the Derg (B. Pratt, personal communication, June 2005).

The geopolitical context is also an important one to understand the nature of state–society relations in Ethiopia. 'The US is by far the largest donor in all categories of assistance' (Rahmato and Ayenew, 2004, p. 102), followed by the International Development Association of the World Bank and the European Commission (OECD and World Bank, n.d., cited in Ford, 2005). Ethiopia is a key strategic ally for the United States in the region given its proximity to the 'rogue' and failed states of Sudan and Somalia. The Ethiopian secret services cooperate closely with the US in tracking al-Qaeda operatives in Somalia, and the Ethiopian army is training the forces of the transitional government army there;

although this created resentment in segments of the local population given the history of conflict between Somalia and Ethiopia.

The desire for stability in the Horn has made the US 'overlook severe violations of human rights and excuse outright manipulations of elections and democratic processes and a constant reinforcement of the political, economic and military domination of the TPLF' (Pausewang *et al.*, 2002a, p. 43). The US policy would appear to be one of continuing to promote 'illiberal democracies' in the Horn where there are regular elections, but the daily practices of the state are marked by continued abuses (Zakaria, 1997, cited in van de Walle, 2001). Thus there is an essential continuity of 'political structures [that] have remained rooted in its legacy of autocratic and bureaucratic rule that concentrated power in state authority at the expense of individual economic and political rights and an open process of rule making' (McCann, 2002, p. 63). Ethiopia would thus appear to be a 'virtual democracy'[20] with the trappings of democratic practice, but a party structure which maintains tight control at all levels to ensure that democratic institutions cannot be used to challenge its power (Pausewang *et al.*, 2002b). According to one peasant farmer 'under Mengistu [of the former Derg regime], the enemies of the state were "anti-revolutionary." Today they are "anti-democratic"' (quoted in Aspen, 2002, p. 67). The consociational constitution is reminiscent of the old Soviet system, whereby republics could technically secede it they wanted to. The current prime minister's thinking on ethnic federalism may have been influenced by Stalin's theory of the 'national question' (Clapham, 2004). Thus the brutal repression of dissent after the 2005 election in Ethiopia represented 'business as usual' (Abbink, 2006).

The evolution and growth of civil society in Ethiopia

Depending on one's definition there are different types of interlinked and at time overlapping civil societies in Ethiopia. Within the NGO sector in Ethiopia, civil society is taken to mean 'formal and informal groups and associations that are not of the public and business sectors' (Rahmato, 2002, p. 104). Outside of more traditional *idirs* and *equbs* which have widespread membership,[21] and their confederations and churches, civil society, in the sense of organizations whose primary target is state reform, is of relatively recent vintage. Civil society has tended to be fragmented and to operate at local and regional, rather than national level, because of ethnic and linguistic diversity (European Commission, 2001).

Hyden and Hailemariam (2002) note that Ethiopia was unusual in Africa in that it had caste like stratification as a result of the prohibition of marriage across kinship lines. At a higher level, however, the emperor encouraged the marriage of royals to members of other ethnic groups (B. Pratt, personal communication, June 2005) – a kind of 'co-opt and rule' strategy.

The last few decades of imperial rule saw the emergence of professional and commercial associations, such as those by students and lawyers, and also farmer's co-ops and local development associations. There were also ethnic development associations, such as the Mecha-Tuluma Self-Help Association, although the imperial regime viewed this as a threat and executed or imprisoned its leadership (Zewde, 2002). Sometimes regional development associations sought the patronage of the emperor, or other royal, to demonstrate their fealty to the regime.

Trade unions in Ethiopia originated among railway workers in the mid-1940s, whereas the earliest business association is the Addis Ababa Chamber of Commerce, which dates from the 1960s (Clapham, 2004). There are also many faith-based organizations involved in relief, service delivery and advocacy.

After the fall of the Empire in 1974, according to Pausewang *et al.* (2002a, p. 5), 'the Ethiopian peasant associations, as they were established in 1975 to administer the land reform, provide another example of an Ethiopian attempt to establish indigenous democracy,' at least before they were recaptured by the Derg. Under the Derg in the rural areas every adult male had to belong to a local peasant association. 'In the urban areas, the equivalence [sic] was the *kebele*, a quasi-civic entity used both for political mobilization and civil administration. Voluntarism was abandoned and civil society lost its meaning' (Harbeson, 1988, cited in Hyden and Hailemariam, 2002, p. 219). Membership in both urban and rural *kebeles* is still mandatory. Under the Derg these provided a mechanism for both service delivery and the exercise of political control. The EPRDF inherited this system and has put it to use (World Bank, 2002a, p. 2). Producer cooperatives involving millions of peasants were also formed under the Derg, but most quickly dissolved following its overthrow in 1991 (Rahmato, 2002). Those that remain are tied to the current governing party.

During the 1970s and 1980s two events contributed to the growth of NGOs in Ethiopia: famine and war. During the civil war voluntary groups associated with opposition political fronts, such as the Relief Society of Tigray (REST – tied to the TPLF) and the Oromo Relief Association (associated with the Oromo Liberation Front), were established. According to a development assistance official in Ethiopia 'the most important NGOs have their roots in conflict' (Interview with development assistance official, Addis Ababa, September 17, 2004) and were a central part of the EPRDF to overthrow the Derg (Duffield and Prendergaast, 1994, cited by INGO official in interview, Addis Ababa, September 17, 2004). According to the same official, REST is 'huge in Tigray,' and funded by INGOs because they 'have the scale to deliver.'

From the 1970s to 1990 the number of NGOs operating in the country grew from 30 to over 100, largely in response to the famines of the 1970s and 1980s (CRDA, 1998, cited in Berhanu, 2002). The Christian Relief and Development Association (CRDA), the umbrella group for relief organizations, was founded in response to the famine of 1973. NGOs have been very effective in famine relief, but less so in development, perhaps partly because they are not rooted in the communities which they serve (Rahmato, 2002). CRDA's apolitical nature has allowed it to have good relations with the government. It 'doesn't do human rights,' but is often criticized as presenting itself as the voice of civil society in Ethiopia (Interview with development assistance official, Addis Ababa, September 14, 2004). Because of their origins in famine relief, 'very few CSOs have a rights based advocacy mandate or policy orientation as the primary mission of their organizations' (DAG, 2002, p. 3).

Hyden and Hailemariam (2002) argue that when the EPRDF regime came to power it maintained the administrative structures from the Derg era, with only minor modifications and that consequently associational life remains 'feeble;' a limited opening to voluntary organizations under donor pressure notwithstanding. This opening is state-guided, however. 'The government has created mass organizations for youth and women at regional level' (Interview with development assistance official, Addis Ababa, September 14, 2004). The Women's Network, has been successful, perhaps because it is politically connected (Interview with development assistance official, Addis Ababa, September 14, 2004). In 1994, 72 percent of all NGOs operating in Ethiopia were engaged in welfare programmers through subsidized service delivery. By 1997, there were 220 NGOs, and a year later 270 (CRDA, 1998, cited in Berhanu, 2002).

'The past ten years have witnessed the growth of a third generation of associations that are cautiously addressing the country's development needs without necessarily challenging the political establishment' (Hyden and Hailemariam, 2002, p. 220). There has recently been an explosion in NGO numbers and by 2002 there were 1120 registered

NGOs in the country. Four hundred and nineteen of these were registered with the Disaster Prevention and Preparedness Commission
(DPCC) – 291 were local and 128 INGOs. According to the CRDA (2002,
cited in Hyden and Hailemariam, 2002), these NGOs reached 15 percent
of the total population and provided services to the value of about 1bn.
birr (US $120m approx).[22] One survey found that 'NGOs (foreign and
international) were found in all the woredas, with association ranging
from almost 100 percent in Shinile (relief) . . . to 70 percent in Tikur
Inchini (development programs) to about 3 percent in Mekit (where an
NGO has handed over activities to local community-based organizations,' including the Mekit Micro Finance Institute (Muir, 2004). Local
NGOs are relatively rare, but can be innovative, such as Hundee in
Oromia, which develops cereal banks (INTRAC, 2004). The growth of
civil society should be facilitated by the new NGO law which will allow
the right to undertake income-generating activities (Ministry of
Capacity Building, 2004).

The political opportunity structure for CSOs is currently ambiguous.
According to one development assistance official, 'NGOs can be closed
down for the smallest things, like administrative mistakes' (Interview
with development assistance official, Addis Ababa, September 14, 2004).
Most NGOs are heavily donor dependent and have 'kept their heads
down' to avoid confrontation with the government and ensure their
own survival (Berhanu, 2002). As of 1999 there were about a dozen
rights-based advocacy organizations in the country, but most were small
scale, with little experience and hence organizationally vulnerable
(Rahmato, 2002). They tend to confine themselves to 'safe' (i.e. relatively
uncontentious) issues such as children and women's rights and respect
for the rule of law. As such they have had a limited impact on policy
change to enhance the well-being of 'target groups' (Berhanu, 2002). The
experience of repression during the Derg contributes to this atmosphere
of quiescence.

In general, independent groups, such as the Women's Lawyers
Association, and the Ethiopian Human Rights Council have been
allowed to operate, probably to protect the international reputation of
the regime. Recently the Women's Lawyers Association was suspended,
despite financial probity, however. It may have been 'too successful' as
it was able to lobby for, and influence the provisions of a new family law
(Pausewang *et al.*, 2002b).

The Human Rights Council has also been harassed, with the state-
owned Commercial Bank blocking its account, for example, in 1996
(Rahmato, 2002).

Many of the major diplomatic missions, including the U.S., were expressly unhappy with the EHRCO. It is quite telling that Western donor agencies which placed so much emphasis on civil society as the best hope for fostering democratization in Africa felt it prudent to kowtow to the government when it decided to take punitive measures against the one and only human rights organization in the country.

(Rahmato, 2002, pp. 110–1)

This suggests that *realpolitik* is more important than normative ideals as a driver of policy, at least among major donors with geo-strategic objectives. Trade unions have also been the subject of government manipulation with the government encouraging splits and then supporting leaders favorable to it. In some cases independent leaders have been harassed, jailed or forced into exile (Rahmato, 2002).

Different donors have different objectives. In Ethiopia, as well as Mozambique and Rwanda, DFID had memoranda of understanding with the governments – a contractual form of partnership (Piron with Evans, 2004). However, Britain did suspend an increase of £24m in aid after the postelection shootings of demonstrators (Plaut, 2005), and subsequently it suspended all budget support.

The World Bank has been praiseful of Ethiopia for the high priority it attaches to basic education and healthcare (Abraham, 2001).[23] According to the World Bank, it is the major partner with the government and is undertaking a major civil society capacity building project there (Interview with World Bank official, Addis Ababa, September 14, 2004). However, the 'World Bank is not very concerned with governance, but more concerned with the economic side – it is not really interested in human rights. The government tends to side with the World Bank because it is less demanding on this' (Interview with development assistance official, Addis Ababa, September 9, 2004). According to another development assistance official (Interview, September 14, 2004) 'sometimes it seems like they [the World Bank] are the only donor the government listens to.'

The general suspicion of CSOs on the part of the government has extended to INGOs. In some areas, such as Debre Berhan, INGOs have withdrawn under government pressure. As McCann (2002, p. 76) explains

The EPRDF imposed much tighter restrictions on international NGOs than the previous government, which had granted them virtual extraterritorial status as they went about their business. Relief and rehabilitation activities now took place through a government-organized non-government organization (GONGO), the Amhara Development Association and a state food security agency.

– thereby reinforcing patronage ties.

This less liberal attitude toward INGOs is likely a function of donor pressure for liberalization at national political level. Under the Derg, given the extremely illiberal nature of national level politics, INGOs were not perceived as a threat. 'The Derg could only tolerate INGOs' (Interview with social researcher, Addis Ababa, September 13, 2004). This would appear not to be the case under the ERPDF. 'The continued association of international NGOs with disaster and disaster relief ha[s] . . . tarnished their image and left a residue of resentment in government circles and sections of the informed public' (Rahmato, 2002, p. 106). They are a reminder of diminished sovereignty and state weakness in service delivery. Although 'the government is more cautious with INGOs because they have some power' (Interview with development assistance official, Addis Ababa, September 9, 2004). However, there is regional variation. Given the level of political dissent, it is very difficult for 'native organizations,' unlike INGOs, to work in Oromia (Interview with development assistance official, Addis Ababa, September 14, 2004).

This suggests a 'balloon problem': that is that pressure applied by donors to liberalize at national level, may simply result in illiberal pressure building up regionally. Of course there are also counter-tendencies in such a scenario. When the state takes greater responsibility for service provision as this may strengthen the social compact between citizens and state, thereby strengthening accountability (Wood, 1997). However, where service delivery is undertaken by 'shadow state' organizations, concerned more with patronage, this may not be the case. For McCann (2002), the conclusion to flow from this is that further economic liberalization would appear to be a prerequisite for political democratization. However, the channels of social change are not as straightforward as this would suggest. The privatization of agricultural marketing and input supply may result in private monopsonies, which even the World Bank admits may further impoverish peasants; militating against democratization.[24] In Ethiopia the state is overextended in the sense that many posts in basic rural administration, extension, health and education are unfilled, because of resource constraints (B. Pratt, personal communication, June 2005). Thus synergy is not achieved between private and public sectors.

The fact that CSOs were required to renew their registration every year, under the Internal Security Act, gave the government immense power over the voluntary sector. NGOs are legally restricted to famine relief and development (Zewde, 2002), and The Ethiopian Free Journalist Association recently experienced suspension (Rahmato and Ayenew, 2004). Legally, NGOs are not allowed to raise funds domestically or form networks (Interview with development assistance officials, Addis Ababa, September 9 and 14, 2004), although this is set to change with the new NGO law. Some networks have recently been developed and licensed.[25]

In 2002 the Ethiopian Association of Voluntary Services (EAVOS) was established, bringing together 28 voluntary organizations, mostly in health and education who had worked with Oxfam-Canada (Hyden and Hailemariam, 2002). 'Soft' dialogue, rather than open confrontation with the authorities has allowed the association to advance its agenda. The Poverty Action Network-Ethiopia (PANE) was formed in March 2004. It grew out of the NGO PRSP Task Force, which was formed by the Christian Relief and Development Association (Interview with NGO activist, September 21, 2004).

The push to establish PANE was donor driven, particularly by the UNDP in the donor coordination Development Assistance Group (DAG) (Interview with development assistance official, September 15, 2004; DAG, 2002). 'PANE is composed of well established NGOs, but may not represent the majority of CSOs. . . . There need to be standards for representation' (Interview with development assistance official, September 22, 2004).

There have been substantial and significant increases in voice among NGOs in recent years. Prior to the recent election, the CRDA issued a very critical response to the ruling of the National Election Board on which organizations could participate in election monitoring (see http://www.crdaethiopia.org). Nonetheless, Ethiopia is some distance away from conditions of 'ideal speech' where people can express their opinions without fear of reprisal (Habermas, 1990, cited in Parfitt, 2002).

There is an operational/representational bifurcation within civil society in Ethiopia which is instantiated spatially in the division between Addis Ababa and the rural areas. Civil society in Ethiopia is 'dominated by the Addis elite' (Interview with development assistance officials, Addis Ababa, September 17, 2004). Some go so far as to argue that 'advocacy has been hijacked by people in the city' (Interview with development consultant, Addis Ababa, September 20, 2004), and that some NGOs are a personal accumulation strategy for some people.

Most [NGOs have] simply extended their ad hoc interventions of the famine years without further ado. Their leaders and staff are mainly taken from the cosmopolitan elite, whom target groups and communities tend to view as outsiders and external benefactors. They lack the necessary constituency of support which renders their position increasingly vulnerable to pressures from power centers.

(Berhanu, 2002, p. 128)

Some might consider this rural–urban division problematic given that regional market towns were the historical birthplaces of civil society in 'the West' as they integrated 'rural producers, mercantile interests and service sector populations' (McCann, 2002). However, Ethiopia may simply lack the social contradictions which gave rise to the development of civil society and nation building in Europe (Hyden and Hailemariam, 2002). 'It has historically been extremely difficult, in highland Ethiopian society, to express open dissent from the actions and opinions of one's social superiors and especially one's rulers' (Clapham, 2004, p. 25).

According to McCann (2002), those areas, such as Addis, which have experienced economic growth will move more quickly toward democratization and supporting civil structures. Thus increased uneven development, associated with globalization, as the country's capital is plugged into transnational circuits of accumulation, remittances and aid may exacerbate centrifugal tendencies in civil society. However, the rural-urban boundary is liminal and porous in Ethiopia, as elsewhere in Africa (Andersson, 2001).

Many civil society associations are based in Addis, but support development in their 'home' regions. An example of this would be the Burie-Womberma Anti-Malarial Association, founded in Addis (McCann, 2002). Thus the forces of uneven development may be countervailed by collective action, to some extent. In some cases relations between these associations, such as the Guarage People Self-help Development Organization, and the government are conflictual as the government claims think them to have their own political agendas (INTRAC, 2004).

Civil society organizations in Ethiopia face both external (policy environment) and internal (managerial and resource constraint) obstacles to their growth (Rahmato, 2002). The recent and limited *appertura* is partly the result of government's attempts to woo the voluntary sector in the wake of the Ethio-Eritrean war in 1998.

Under present circumstances, civil society institutions can do no more than promote public awareness and stimulate public discussion about democratic rights and responsible governance. . . . To be able to have a meaningful impact on the democratization process or to promote good governance, Ethiopian civic organizations would have to transform themselves into civic movements. . . . As it is at present [the state is] the only active force in society.

(Rahmato, 2002, pp. 118–9)

Rahmato and Ayenew (2004, p. 99) conclude, however, that there are now grounds for cautious optimism. Donor financial support has been instrumental in the growth of the voluntary sector. 'Without such support . . . its achievements in the areas of human rights monitoring, training and advocacy would have been far more limited.' Nonetheless they argue that such successes as there have been in establishing a more open and accountable political environment have been largely the result of local initiative, organizations and struggles. They express concern that the shift to DBS by many donors may strengthen the ruling party and external, rather than internal accountability. DBS has also taken funds away from NGOs (Bevan, 2000). The Ethiopian government 'tends to only want to be accountable to donors and even then not really' (Interview with development assistance official, Addis Ababa, September 17, 2004). However, others argue that CSOs' quietism has been undermined by the PRSP process, although not necessarily with positive results as 'the strategy followed by some CSOs and NGOs for participation, which was confrontational, might have had a negative effect on national ownership' (Geda and Weeks, 2002, p. 10).

Influence of civil society on the PRSP

Most donor coordination and donor-government policy groups, such as the MDG task force in Ethiopia, exclude NGOs; the exception being the Sector Development Group. However, the EU has embarked on a major funding program for civil society development (British Council, 2004), as has the World Bank. Thus there would appear to be a logical or functional inconsistency in some donors' positions, as CSOs are excluded from arenas where donors might have to share power or be accountable, but urged to be included in government ones.

The interim-PRSP (I-PRSP) was prepared by government alone. In order to voice their concerns over the I-PRSP and the process through which it was constructed, an NGO workshop was conducted on it, under the auspices of CRDA. The Task Force which arose from this workshop had 20 members and met biweekly. The World Bank and the IMF felt the I-PRSP had analytical weaknesses and that it was not clear what role civil society would play in its monitoring.

Participation is meant to be a key component of PRSPs. In Ethiopia the influence of CSOs on their design, as in much of the rest of the continent has been limited. Consultations were only held after the I-PRSP was published. 'The I-PRSP was not participatory and civil society was not sufficiently organized to participate in the PRSP process' (Interview with CSO activist, Addis Ababa, September 21, 2004). Some CSOs ran their own consultations around the process, such as the Forum for Social Studies Poverty Dialogue Series (Gabriel, 2002). The Inter-Africa Group produced colored flyers and education kits on the PRSP, as the 'primary stakeholders' (those in poverty) are mostly illiterate. This meant that 'people had questions when the consultation came' (Interview with CSO activist, Addis Ababa, September 21, 2004). In the Inter-Africa Group, consultations on the PRSPs 'poor people were critical of the government and NGOs.' However, the NGOs suppressed publication of the report of the consultations (Confidential interview, Addis Ababa, September 2004), raising questions about the role of NGOs as providing voice for the poor.

Most CSOs lacked the technical capacities to fully engage with the process.[26] Indeed 'a striking feature of the landscape of reform in Ethiopia is the absence of an institutionalized mechanism for subjecting economic policy proposals to discussion or debate between the government and the various business and civic organizations' (Abegaz, 2001, p. 194). 'PRSP consultations were largely based on government structures with varying levels and quality of civic participation' (Inter-Africa Group, 2001, p. 7), despite the production of CSO briefing papers on how to facilitate engagement and input and 'ardent lobbying' (Mebrahtu, 2004).[27] Initially the Ethiopian government thought civil society engagement in the design of PRSPs was '"for the birds," but quickly came on board after they were told that this was the way the World Bank would be doing business from now on' (Interview with World Bank official, Addis Ababa, September 14, 2004). According to the joint staff assessment of the IMF and the International Development Association of the World Bank (IMF and IDA, 2004, p. 1), 'the PRSP process has taken root in Ethiopia quite significantly in the past year' and is 'increasingly seen by government as the organizing framework for policy and programs.' Ownership in this context means something quite different from its usual meaning, as discussed earlier, approximating self-disciplining.

Lack of capacity among CSOs to engage in the process 'had to be corrected by forging a strong coalition of institutions of civil society and the donor community to be actively engaged in the consultative process to design the PRSP' (Gabriel, 2002, pp. 6–7). According to the DAG of donors in Ethiopia

> The development constraint for present civic engagement partially derives its roots from Ethiopia's past political apparatus, where civil society was not encouraged to provide alternative voices to Government policies and decisions. Therefore, the nascent state of systematic policy dialogue between the Government and CSOs must continually be nurtured, strengthened and institutionalized over the long term.
>
> (DAG, 2002, p. 2)

Another way of putting this is that donors imposed a PRSP process on the government and then encouraged and provided resources for CSOs to engage with this process. Some might call this a synthesis of attempted social control from above and below. Donors tend to view themselves as neutral mediators/catalysts, for example as 'there is a tension in Ethiopia between UNDP maintaining close relations with the government and civil society' (Geda and Weeks, 2002, p. 10). The DAG (2002, p. 3) also bemoans the

> Predominance of the modern, well-established NGO sector in the on-going policy dialogue of the SDPRP [Sustainable Development and Poverty Reduction Program – the name of the PRSP in Ethiopia] [which] has isolated smaller, yet equally important, CSOs. Albeit their numbers are few, this has resulted in the displacement of other constituencies of civil society such as the demand driven traditional institutions, trade unions, farmer co-operatives and faith-based institutions from directly participating in the on-going policy dialogue.

The political economy of inclusion/exclusion remains unexplored, however. The CSO consultation processes around the PRSP were also criticized for 'limited linkages with grassroots CSOs at the *woreda* [district] level leading to scarce participation by the direct representatives of the poor themselves' (DAG, 2002, p. 4). In any event, 'civil society stakeholders have complained that issues brought up during the consultative process were not fully realized in the final SDPRP document therefore demoralizing future participation' (DAG, 2002, p. 4). However, the imperative to penetrate and change the values of grassroots CSOs and society at large is reflected in the recommendation in a report for the UNDP to translate a simplified version of the PRSP into local languages, identify '"grass-root" communication channels and associations with a view to enhancing upward linkages' and commission studies to promote 'social/cultural acceptance and valuing by the population at large of private initiatives to deal with public issues and promote socially responsible profit seeking behavior' (DAG, 2002, p. 6).

In Ethiopia 100 districts were targeted for consultation over three days for the PRSP (Muwonge *et al.*, 2002). The government consultations on the PRSP only lasted from March 27–30, 2002 in 117 woredas (districts), with about 6000 participants. (Gabriel, 2002). After that there was a drop off in CSO's engagement in the process, partly because of the major humanitarian crisis which gripped the country (Interview with development assistance official, Addis Ababa, September 15, 2004). 'It was widely believed that at woreda level, the consultations were quite effective and participatory. At regional and federal levels, government intervention to steer the direction of the discussion was strong, with a negative impact on the outcome' (Geda and Weeks, 2002, p. 12).

Donors are involved with the monitoring and evaluation of the PRSP, but there is a 'closed door' to civil society. This continued a previous pattern, as the NGO Task Force on the PRSP were not allowed to be represented on PRSP technical committees or on the MDG Task Force (Geda and Weeks, 2002, p. 12; Ministry of Finance & Economic Development and UN Country Team, 2004), as noted earlier. Nonetheless the PRSP was widely seen as having improved the CSO–government relations by opening up space for dialogue. The impacts of CSOs on content of the PRSP were limited, except in the area of 'alternative' (e.g. adult) education (Interview with development consultant, September 20, 2004).

The newly formed PANE ran five regional consultations on the review of the PRSP 'in partnership with the government,' four of which were successful. Regional governments were very open to the process (Interview with CSO activist, September 21, 2004). The PANE conducted these workshops 'to broaden knowledge of the SDPRP as a first step to greater community engagement' (Ethiopian Civil Society Organizations, n.d., p. 2). On the other hand, 'INGOs have not engaged with the PRSP process because they are still focused on project management . . . NGOs are doing good work, but are not agents for change' (Interview with development assistance official, Addis Ababa, September 17, 2004). Perhaps this is part of their appeal. According to the PANE, *'civil society* (emphasis added) recognizes the importance of the SDPRP process in Ethiopia and seeks to contribute at all stages' (Ethiopian Civil Society Organizations, n.d.).

In order to facilitate CSO participation, the Ethiopian government has set up a capacity building program through the Ministry of Capacity Building. The design of the program was paid for by DFID. The sheer scale of capacity needs and number of organizations make 'building civil society' and rolling the program out across the country a daunting task. (T. Silken, personal communication, cited in Muir, 2004). However, some argue that this may not be a problem as the real goal is to control, not build, civil society (Confidential Interview, Addis Ababa, September 2004). On the advisory group for the capacity building program, the civil society representatives 'didn't say a word' (Interview with development assistance official, Addis Ababa, September 22, 2004). According to this development assistance official, there was a need to balance representativeness on committees with 'people who make a difference; change agents, which are about 20–30 people in Ethiopia who sit on all the committees.' However, there is an opportunity cost involved in this as these people don't get the time to run their own NGOs. This official suggested that this is where the role of capacity building came in. 'Civil society is so busy asking for voice that they don't know what to do when they are there.' An alternative interpretation is that there still might be fear of government reprisal.

One CSO activist felt that in Ethiopia 'at a macro level there is very good political will' (Interview, Addis Ababa, September 21, 2004). At a workshop held in Addis on the introduction of 'citizen report cards' on services, it was noted that the government was receptive to the idea. According to one government official 'the Ethiopian government is convinced that without civil society there can be no development, no good governance' (Interview with ministry official, Addis Ababa, September 16, 2004). However, he also noted that there were problems with accountability and transparency with one study finding that 80 percent of the cost of NGO projects was overhead, hence there was a need for regulation. 'NGOs are only there for a certain period of time and then will hand over the project to the government who will sustain it.' He also noted that 'some CSOs have gone beyond the limit and are working like opposition parties.' According to this official INGOs were responsible for local NGOs being labeled pro or anti-government and 'most of the problems of civil society are donor created.' Some also see a tension between the growth of CSOs and parliaments. According to some 'it is pure laziness on the part of donors, as it is easier to give money to CSOs than to build up governance structures' (Confidential interview, Addis Ababa, September 2004). However, this preference may also relate to the fact that there are substantial gaps between aid allocations to government and actual disbursements, for capacity or ideological reasons.

The findings of a survey in Ethiopia lent 'weight to a causal formula whereby increased participation leads to increased representation and thereby increased empowerment, which leads to benefits for all and reduced poverty,' particularly in relation to *idirs* and *equbs* (Muir, 2004, p. 9). While participation may bring some of these benefits at local level, the channels through which this might operate at national level are obscure as noted earlier, but truncated, in any event, by curtailed participation. There is a need both for better specification of what these channels might be and how greater participation might catalyze these.

The Ethiopian PRSP (SDPRP) was launched in July 2002. It is built around four key areas:

- The government's strategy of ADLI.
- Judicial and civil service reform
- Decentralization and empowerment
- Capacity building

The main sector development policies that are identified as poverty related are 'agriculture, food security, roads, water resources development, education and health' (Gabriel, 2002, p. 11). In particular it identifies health and education as key areas for investment to generate a 'pro-poor' growth pattern, as they can enhance the productivity of (rural) labor. For urban areas,

The element of 'strengthening employment opportunities' revolves around design and implementation of public work programs, skill development for self-employment, expansion of pro-poor microcredit facilities, etc. It doesn't seem to be strongly and explicitly linked with 'private sector' development. Hence in this respect, the link between major development policy and poverty reduction doesn't seem to be direct.

(Gabriel, 2002, p. 15)

This is interesting for a number of reasons. First, it may speak to the government's unwillingness to develop the private sector as an alternative power source. Second, it may be a reflection of the government's 'rural bias,' as this is where the vast majority of the population lives, and which provided political support for the rebellion against the Derg. As such, some see the PRSP not so much as a new policy direction, but as a restatement of previous government policy of ADLI. It may also speak to the palliative, rather than the transformative agenda of PRSPs more generally. The key macro-economic goals were to raise real GDP growth to about 7 percent and to reduce the budget deficit from 6.1 percent of GDP in 2002/3 to 5.2 percent by the end of 2004/5. The tax yield in Ethiopia is only 14 percent of GDP, but the share of 'poverty related expenditure' was to increase from 46 percent in 2001/2 to 56 percent for the next three years (Gabriel, 2002). These were expected to be financed 'largely from budgetary adjustments including savings on budgetary *cuts in administrative and government service delivery*' (emphasis added) (Gabriel, 2002, p. 18). Some of the funding would also come from increased aid levels which according to the UNDP rose from $605m in 1997 to $1.937bn in 2003, the majority of which was in grant form (WAAG Communications, 2004b).

Civil society is to be incorporated into the SDPRP not only through consultation around design and monitoring, but also through the Ministry of Capacity Building's (2004, p. 14) program

> CSOs will be able to gain access to public funds for development programmes that lie clearly within the framework of SDPRP-related programmes and activities, such as sector development programmers. This implies a form of 'sub-contracting' by government agencies of CSOs to meet sector and other programme objectives.

'In Ethiopia . . . PRS [poverty reduction strategy] provides donors with a selection of indicators that can be used for performance assessment purposes, although it is not yet clear whether donors will use these indicators' (Coyle *et al.*, 2003, p. 3). There is a small unit in the Ministry of Finance which monitors the PRSP and produces an annual progress report. It was the Ministry of Finance which chose the core indicators for the PRSP, although the World Bank/IMF Joint Staff Assessment found that priority areas of private investment, food security and employment were not well represented in the indicators.

Monitoring proceeds by identifying:

> A starting point for the intervention and . . . identify[ing] the target group. What was the situation of the group before the intervention,

both in general and in terms of those specific circumstances that the intervention is designed to change? What is the problem and how can the living conditions of the target group be described? Can certain indicators of the problem be identified and can they be monitored and followed through out the intervention?

(Øyen, 2001, p. 3)

'In Ethiopia and Zambia, the emphasis if firmly on large scale surveys with no indication that lighter instruments were considered' (Coyle *et al.*, 2003, p. 10). Also in Ethiopia, as in a number of other countries there is little institutionalization of participatory monitoring of the PRSP. Rather it is simply stated that civil society is important and that organizations can develop their own impact assessments. For Craig and Porter Ethiopia's PRSP is close to the norm in that 'before the PRSP ink was barely dry, key policy decisions, for resettlement, education, water sector reforms, all differed from the PRSP commitments' (Craig and Porter, 2006, p. 88). This again suggests that the main impact of the PRSP has perhaps been political, rather than economic.

Civil society, economic structure and poverty

A progress report on the MDGs in Ethiopia found that poverty is mostly responsive to economic growth, with an elasticity of –2.3, meaning that priority should be assigned to the rate of investment. Also, 'preliminary estimates have shown that expenditure on education, water and sanitation development and natural resources tend to be associated strongly with the state of poverty,' and that resources should perhaps be concentrated in those areas (Ministry of Finance and Economic Development and United Nations Country Team, 2004, p. x) rather than primary health care, for example. The country would appear to be 'on-track' to achieve universal primary education (enrolment) by 2015. It is also interesting that debt relief expenditure under heavily indebted poor country (HIPC) would only account for less than 7 percent of planned poverty-oriented expenditure from 2001/2 to 2003/4 (Ministry of Finance and Economic Development and United Nations Country Team, 2004).

The key issue for poverty in Ethiopia is the structure of its economy, with its emphasis on subsistence farming and low-value cash crop exports, creating a mixture of independent and dependent poverty. The introduction of the nontraditional export crop chat, a chewable mild narcotic, raised incomes for some farming households recently (Bigsten, Kebebe and Shimeles, 2003). However, as was noted by *African Development* in 1971 (p. 9)

Ethiopia's heavy dependence on coffee, with its erratic price on the world market, have caused recurrent balance of payments crises. Foreign exchange reserves have come under increasingly severe pressure. There is an urgent need to expand and diversify exports.

The collapse of the International Coffee Agreement in 1989, and consequent price falls, contributed further to this dependence (Chossudovsky, 1997). This is reflective of broader trends in Africa.

In Ethiopia coffee accounts for about 60 percent of exports and about 10 percent of GDP, but prices fell from 79 cents a pound in 2000 to just 24 cents in 2002 (Fairtrade, 2002; AGOA, 2003). The result was that farmers pulled up coffee trees and their children out of school. Ethiopia's export earnings from coffee fell from US $420m in 1998 to just $187m in 2001, while its oil import bill rose from $143m to $275m (IMF, 2002, cited in World Bank, 2002a). The loss implicit in these figures for 2001, versus 1998, is equivalent to 6 percent of GDP. It also affected government revenues, needed for social and infrastructural investment, particularly as the government scrapped its 6 percent *ad valoreum* export tax, in order to bring relief to the farmers (Bigsten, Kebebe and Shimeles, 2005b). This scenario may create, in the absence of external financing, a vicious circle where public and private investment decline in tandem. Bigsten, Shimeles and Kebebe (2005) estimate that to attain an 8 percent rate of economic growth Ethiopia would need to invest 48 percent of GDP a year, versus the current 14 percent.

Kebebe, Shimeles and Taddessee (2005, p. 53) have argued that 'poverty in Ethiopia is largely caused by structural factors, deeply entrenched in the economy, so that nothing short of structural transformation is likely to overcome the enormity of the problem.' As noted earlier, the Ethiopian state has shown interest in the East Asian model of development (a 'state-led market economy') and the capital account remains strictly regulated (WAAG Communications, 2004a), contrary to the advice of the IMF. The financial sector, vital for channeling preferential capital to productive industry in the East Asian model, remains largely state-owned in Ethiopia. The state-owned Commercial Bank of Ethiopia holds 80 percent of total deposits and 60 percent of formal loans (Abraham, 2002, cited in Doyle, 2004). Corruption has been blamed for the extent of its nonperforming loans, however, estimated at 40 percent of its portfolio.

While a report for the World Bank argues that 'the residual dirigisme of the ruling party . . . appears to frustrate the enactment of important second-generation reforms' (Abegaz, 2001, p. 170), state strength may be responsible for the relatively effective implementation of economic reform. Although it should be noted that the economic growth rate during the 'Marxist 1980s,' when there was a civil war in progress, was 5.5 percent versus 6.2 percent during the 'liberalized 1990s.' This was partly attributable to higher coffee prices during some of that time (Abegaz, 2001). Another report for the Bank by the International *Non-Governmental* Training and Research Center (INTRAC, 2004, p. 6) (emphasis added) notes that 'there is still much to be done to break down the belief that the central state will be the engine of economic and social development.' The political economy of this is obscure, however, as it is put down to the state to 'work with its employees across the country, to move away from the assumption that the state exists to control, own and tax, rather than to serve, facilitate and support the actions of its citizens' (INTRAC, 2004, p. 6).

Despite state strength, however, perhaps partly out of lack of resources and partly out of fear of social disruption, there is not currently 'a comprehensive and integrated approach to rehabilitation and development of the country's agrarian economy, shifting it away from the subsistence focus that is a large part of the problem' (Inter-Africa Group, 2001, p. 18) While the World Bank presses for land privatization, 'a possible reason for the relatively low level of rural poverty is the land-tenure system' (Bigsten, Kebebe and Shimeles, 2003, p. 92). Land privatization would likely result in concentration of ownership, perhaps through force as in other parts of the world, and increased emphasis on cash cropping. While this 'primary accumulation' might help increase exports, it would be unlikely to substantially reduce poverty, and might increase destitution through landlessness. What is needed is a comprehensive, but flexible, strategy for structural transformation.

Other than through the promotion of popular and, to some extent, export-oriented popular economic organizations, it is difficult to see how civil society can contribute substantially to economic diversification. This type of engagement has already happened in Ethiopia to some extent where there are coffee co-ops who have cut out 'middle men.' For example, the Oromiya Coffee Farmers' Union is a major exporter of coffee (Muir, 2004). How has neoliberalism affected state–society relations in other African countries? We now move on to a consideration of how neoliberalism has affected this and human security in what were formerly sub-Saharan Africa's two most developed economies, Zimbabwe and South Africa, and examine the impacts of the latest neoliberal partnership on the continent: the New Partnership for African Development.

6
The Making of a Zimbabwean Rogue (State): Robert Mugabe, Neoliberalism, Civil Society and NEPAD

> The future of Zimbabwe is absolutely vital to the future of capitalism in Africa.
>
> (Iliffe, 1983, p. 43)

> Weak, patronage-based 'quasi-state' regimes face geopolitical pressures and opportunities that compel rulers to experiment with administrative innovations, including war, to consolidate their power, control markets and manage rivals.
>
> (Reno, 2002, p. 416)

> The political 'game' in most African states is not yet governed by regulations that effectively prevent the unsanctioned use of coercion and violence.
>
> (Jackson and Rosberg, 1982, p. 1)

> I have many degrees in violence.
>
> (Robert Mugabe, 1998, quoted Blair, 2002)

Neoliberal personal rule: Robert Mugabe and structural adjustment

As noted previously, neoliberalism is in some cases associated with state strengthening, as in Ethiopia; in others with state collapse depending on preexisting conditions, policy choices, institutions and resource inflows (Bauer and Taylor, 2005). There is an extensive literature on the political economy of reform in Africa. In the theory of the World Bank, markets are meant to counter corruption by substituting for the state as a social coordination mechanism. Market efficiency, through privatization is meant to be the antidote to the soft budget constraints of public enterprises and the potential for corruption evident in administrative allocation. However, as even the World Bank now recognizes African elites have shown themselves to be very inventive in the reconfiguration of what Bayart (2000) calls 'the strategy of extraversion.' Graham Harrison (2005) has argued that clientelism and neoliberalism are mutually compatible in sub-Saharan Africa. By giving access to policy rents it can even bolster clientelistic regimes (van de Walle, 2001). However, how neoliberal reform plays out is contextually dependent.

Zimbabwe began its reform process with a diversified economy and stable political economy. Up until 2000 Zimbabwe was widely hailed as an 'African success story' which had overcome its legacy of racial division and extended social services to the majority of the population after its transition to nonracial government in 1980. However, the economy contracted by 35 percent between 2000 and 2005 (Masland, 2005). Inflation has skyrocketed, to 1200 percent in 2006 (Rogers, 2006), and social indicators are deteriorating. Unemployment is 85 percent (Corcoran, 2005a). Zimbabwean society has become increasingly wracked with instability, authoritarianism and brutality. Rape has been deployed as a weapon against opponents of the regime (Akeroyd, 2004). These trends were particularly acute during the run-up to the March 2002 Presidential elections, and after the 2005 Parliamentary elections.[1] Up to three million Zimbabweans, out of a total population of 14 million have emigrated to South Africa, or other countries (*The Economist*, 2004f). How has this situation come about, in what was, until recently, one of Africa's most stable and prosperous societies?[2]

Zimbabwe burst onto the international media stage in 2000 with state-sponsored land invasions of large-scale, white-owned commercial farms. The different political and economic dimensions of these land invasions have been discussed elsewhere. The purpose of this chapter is somewhat different. It is to examine the way in which neoliberalism changed state–civil society relations in Zimbabwe away from the initial postindependence settlement and how this has resulted initially in exterior, and subsequently interior rounds of violence and increased authoritarianism in Zimbabwe. This will be traced through a focus on the persona of Robert Mugabe.

Robert Mugabe is now one of Africa's longest serving leaders, along with Omar Bonga of Gabon. He is both a highly educated and skilled politician who has survived the viscidities of power and popular discontent for almost three decades. He was already well into middle age when he ascended to power, and is now over 80, with no retirement date set, construction of a multimillion-dollar retirement home, partly funded by the Chinese government, notwithstanding. The Economist Intelligence Unit predicts that he *may* retire after this term expires in 2008, when he will be 84 (Economist Intelligence Unit, 2005a).[3] Jackson and Rosberg (1982) more than 20 years ago argued that 'personal rule, not constitutional rule, is the prevailing form of government in Black Africa and most of Africa's personal rulers are more like Princes in their characteristics and methods of rule.' Chris Allen (1995) refers to this mode of rule as 'presidentialism.'

Robert Mugabe is an exemplar of this tendency which reflects both the authoritarian legacy of the colonial state, the underdeveloped nature of civil society, in part resulting from colonialism, and current economic restructuring. Even supposedly reformist leaders, such as Meles in Ethiopia and Museveni in Uganda, have displayed this 'big man' tendency, determined to cling to power at all costs, including violence and bloodshed.[4] This desire to hang on to power is perhaps a natural human impulse in the absence of countervailing social pressure and institutionalization. However, it becomes particularly acute in African contexts where the state is often the primary locus of accumulation, given underdeveloped economies, and ethnicity is often politicized. Thus Robert Mugabe is far from being exceptional, despite the scale of the atrocities, which he is responsible for.[5]

Mugabe has been central to the political economy of Zimbabwe for three decades not only because of his agency ('its amazing how one person can wreck a country'), but also because he has acted as a lightning rod for structural forces. As David Moore (2001) argues, the collision of the personal and political on his head can be seen as a form of what Marx termed Bonapartism or what others have called Caesarism, where a 'strong leader' emerges in a time of societal crisis.

Mugabe has undergone a number of ideological conversions from 'scientific socialism,' to neoliberalism, to patriotic 'anti-imperialist' and authoritarian nationalist; each time reinventing himself to enable his continued hold on power. His political and ideological journey then tells us much about the nature of state–society relations in Zimbabwe and the way in which neoliberalism reconfigured these.

Robert Mugabe came to power in 1980 as prime minister of Zimbabwe. He had led one of two guerrilla movements against minority white rule in the country that fought in a brutal civil war, with a power base in the numerically dominant Shona-speaking community. During the course of the civil war Mugabe had been backed by the Chinese, a relationship which was to be reinvented in the early years of the twenty-first century.

On coming to power, Mugabe claimed to be an adherent of Marxist-Leninist scientific socialism. However, this ideological predisposition was tinged with pragmatism, partly on the advice of the Mozambiquan President Samora Machel who had seen first-hand the destructive effects of European (capital) flight after independence. Consequently, the first decade of independence in Zimbabwe from 1980 to 1990 was characterized by reformism; maintenance of the existing racialized economic structure, combined with the extension of social services to the majority of the population, hitherto excluded. Prior to economic liberalization, an estimated 3 percent of the population controlled two-thirds of gross national income (Stoneman and Cliffe, 1989, cited in Kanyenze, 2003) and income inequality was to worsen after that (Bond and Manyanya, 2002).

The new government was also constrained by the negotiated nature of the settlement through which it came to power; the Lancaster House Agreement, which provided that land redistribution would only take place on a 'willing seller–willing buyer basis' for the first 10 years. However, when the agreement expired, it was not a radical redistributionist programme that was put in place, but a shift to neoliberalism through the adoption of the economic structural adjustment programme (ESAP) (1991–1995). It was a precursor to PRSPs in as much as it was meant to be 'homegrown' and was preceded by other liberalizing policy statements committing the government to extensive consultation and a 'stakeholder approach' to economic management (Government of Zimbabwe, 1990, cited in Dansereau, 2005).

In Zimbabwe, the state and society were, to a significant extent, structurally differentiated (Chabal and Daloz, 1999), given the relative level of the development of the productive forces. This encouraged the development of influential civil society groups, such as the Confederation of Zimbabwe Industry (CZI), the Commercial Farmers Union (CFU) and the Zimbabwe Congress of Trade Unions (ZCTU), and institutionalization. The state exhibited substantial capacity across a range of areas in the 1980s.[6]

The CZI and CFU were influential in having the ESAP adopted, whereas the ZCTU reached an uneasy accommodation with it, describing economic liberalization as a 'necessary but not sufficient' condition for development in 1996 (see ZCTU, 1996). Others argued that the adoption of the structural adjustment program was less to do with the structural or direct power of national capital, but with the embourgeoisment of the state elite and the development of their interests in commercial farming, one of the main beneficiaries of adjustment (Dashwood, 1996 and 2000). There is merit in both positions. What has received less attention, surprisingly, is Mugabe's change in ideological orientation and the reasons behind this. This is surprising because the adoption of ESAP was ultimately sanctioned and dependent on him.

In the immediate postindependence period after 1980, socialism was popular with the electorate, given the legacy of brutal and racialized Rhodesian capitalism. However, the political opportunity structure confronting Robert Mugabe changed as the decade wore on, both internally and externally. Externally, the collapse of the Soviet bloc made neoliberal strategies appear more attractive. Internally, the postindependence economic model had failed to generate employment, with only one out of every ten school-leavers finding employment (Government of Zimbabwe, 1991). Rising youth unemployment portended unrest later in the following decades.

Mugabe was never naturally a neoliberal, preferring a strong directive role for the state. For example, in 1986 he argued that the solution to the country's balance of payments problems was that the manufacturing sector should be restructured to lessen dependence on foreign inputs (quoted in Skålnes, 1995). Thus in the first decade of independence less emphasis was placed on 'legitimized private accumulation than on the extended reach and interventionism of the state' (Raftopolous, 2004, p. xi).

Mugabe's minister of finance in the 1980s, Bernard Chidzero, who chaired IMF/World Bank committees and was at one time a favorite to become UN Secretary General, undoubtedly played an important role in his conversion. According to Patrick Bond (1998), Chidzero as the Finance Minister 'played a schizophrenic game,' arguing for market rationality while parroting 'Marxism-Leninism.' Support for the adoption of ESAP was less than a quarter of the cabinet, but it was 'the Minister of Finance, just using his clout and his ability to access the President' who drove it through (Interview with G. Mhone, cited in Andreasson, 2003, p. 401). Particularly as the idea of a one party state was now abandoned, there was a political imperative to develop an indigenous business class. The previous system of foreign exchange rationing and allocation had favored the status quo, i.e. white capital (Davies, 2004).

The adoption of ESAP in Zimbabwe was associated with deindustrialization and increased accumulation through trading and financial circuits and large-scale agriculture. According to Bayart (1993), Mugabe's party, the Zimbabwe African National Union –Patriotic Front (ZANU-PF) and white capital formed one of the few consolidated historic blocs in postcolonial sub-Saharan Africa. However, deindustrialization and increased racialized inequality in the agricultural sector in Zimbabwe meant this bloc began to erode by the mid-1990s. The generalized erosion of the possibilities for productive accumulation had the effect of reinforcing the importance of the state as a site of potential accumulation; what we might think of in the Zimbabwean context as neoliberal personal rule. According to Sara Rich Dorman (2001, p. 168), NGOs were complicit in this as 'despite the impact of ESAP on many Zimbabweans, NGOs paid relatively little attention to the policy-level of government, contenting themselves with trying to alleviate the impacts of ESAP.' Although MacLean *et al.* (1997) argued that by the late 1990s there were 'vibrant pockets' of antigovernment and anti-ESAP resistance within the NGO community. The ZANU-PF 'party-state' was to turn against the previously most influential CSOs. Indeed there has been a concerted attempt to merge civil society with the state, creating a State-society, which will be discussed later.

The year 1990 is interesting for other reasons as well. Economic liberalization also coincided with a limited political *appertura* as the idea of a one party state was finally abandoned (Dashwood, 2000). It was only in 1990, for example, that the state of emergency was lifted in Matabeleland, in the context of a settlement in South Africa taking shape (Interview with firm manager, Bulawayo, 1996). While at this time there had not been any viable opposition to ZANU-PF, in part because Ndebele dissent had been viciously suppressed during the *Gurkurahundi*[7] of the 1980s, in 1990 the ruling party also agreed to the formation of a war veterans association, as long as it was under party patronage (Kriger, 2003b). In part this may have been to prevent the veterans being recruited to the opposition Zimbabwe Unity Movement (Kriger, 2001, cited in Dorman, 2001). However prior to this, war veterans did exercise substantial power through works committees in factories, for example, with one African manager in National Breweries claiming that they were virtually a wing of the Central Intelligence Organization (quoted in Kriger, 2003b, p. 107).

Civil society in revolt 1: the war veterans

The economic adjustment program was associated with rising unemployment and a take-off in consumer price inflation (Carmody, 2001). The authors of a recent report for the World Bank are perplexed at the coincidence of 'improved macroeconomic policy and increased poverty' in Zimbabwe from 1991 to 1996 (Christiaensen *et al.*, 2002, p. 24). There were also meant to be micro-economic achievements with 'the reform of the Cotton Board (first downsized and then privatized) . . . the only successful reform of a cotton board in Africa' (World Bank, 2004c, p. 22).[8] However, another report 'calls into question the efficacy of the Economic Structural Adjustment Program' (Alwang *et al.*, 2002, p. ix), despite the fact that it was implemented with 'determination and persistence' (World Bank, 1997a, cited in Zamponi, 2005). These World Bank researchers acknowledge that 'poverty in Zimbabwe increased significantly during the 1990s' and that this was 'closely tied to the poor performance of the economy and economic restructuring that characterized the 1990s' (Alwang *et al.*, 2002, p. 46). In other reports, however, the problem is blamed on too little ownership and the World Bank being too trusting in 'commitments with technocrats in ministries,' rather than politicians who 'did not believe in the efficacy of the market in redistributing wealth' (World Bank, 2004c, p. 28).[9] This perhaps suggests the importance of a reduction in social capital between government and World Bank technocrats, and the importance of politics? As a result of macro-economic targets being missed, the IMF and World Bank suspended disbursement of structural adjustment credits in 1995. Not surprisingly the government hadn't wanted to 'own' failure.

Whereas the ideology of socialism had served to contain private accumulation among state elites during the 1980s (Robinson, 2001), by the 1990s, to become rich was 'glorious.' This even extended to pillaging and defrauding the war veterans compensation fund. Against a background of rising unemployment and inflation, the suspension of pension payments and pending investigations led the veterans to take party/government leaders hostage in 1997.

Mugabe was confronted in his official residence by war veterans, who had been admitted to the inner sanctum with the collusion of the army (Moore, 2001). He undoubtedly saw that his political future was limited unless he could reach an accommodation with/co-opt this newly 'vocal' civil society group. The massive unbudgeted pensions payout which he agreed for the veterans resulted in the macro-economy spiraling out of control and ultimately the abandonment of economic liberalization. The Zimbabwe dollar fell by 74 percent in a single day in late 1997. The World Bank remained oblivious to the gathering storm. According to one of its own reports (2004c, p. 27) 'until 1998, the [World] Bank was under the impression that poverty was not high and was debating whether poverty had or had not increased during 1991–96.'

For E.A. Brett (2005), the pensions payout represented a political choice, rather than being an impact of neoliberal policies, as the economy was rebounding strongly in 1997, on the back of improved agricultural output. However, neoliberalism was complicit in unleashing societal discontent, of which this can be seen as a culmination, particularly as a result of dramatic distributional shifts. The World Bank (2004c, p. 4) has noted that 'the ESAP . . . entailed a massive redistribution of income from formal sector [mostly urban] wage earners to commercial agriculture.' Indeed reduced urban remittances was one of the reasons for rising rural poverty during the 1990s (World Bank, 2004c). The ballooning budget deficit, which rose from 8 to 20 percent of GDP from 1998 to 2000 (Rotberg, 2000), can thus be seen as a government attempt to redress maldistribution driven by economic processes. However such budgetary indiscipline ultimately undermines progressive redistribution by stoking inflation, which affects those on lower incomes more severely.

Sam Moyo (2000, p. 164) notes in relation to the land issue in Zimbabwe under ESAP that the 'emergence of a multiplicity of state, private, farmer, NGO and community organizations lobbying for various specific policy changes, while on the surface introducing a form of pluralism in Zimbabwe's struggles . . . did not change the substantive ideological and material lines of cleavage in the society.' Nonetheless the World Bank (2005d, p. 163) persists with its apolitical approach noting recently that in 'Zimbabwe postindependence [land] reforms were quite effective but short lived for political reasons.'

Where state hegemony is compromised, there is often reliance on force to ensure societal compliance with state diktats or at least rule: that is authoritarianism. Authoritarianism is the logical outgrowth/accompaniment of peripheral economic structures. Ultimate power rests with those who have control over 'the means of violence': the military. The war veterans had substantial popular support for their cause and also links with ex-combatants in the military and police.

The pensions payouts were to be funded by increased taxes on workers. Thus Mugabe attempted to pit two different civil society groups against each other in terms of distributional politics. However, this was rejected by both the Parliament and ZANU-PF. The ZCTU called a general strike in 1997, nonetheless, to protest the introduction of other new taxes.

These developments marked a shift from consent to coercion within the broader social formation. The strategy through which Mugabe had come to power – 'through the barrel of a gun' – was now to be resurrected, although this time it was to be deployed against a somewhat different set of 'enemies' in order to retain power. This also marked a decisive shift from productivist economic concerns to spoils politics. The fusion of civil society (war veterans) and arms of state (military and police) had already begun, driven by Zimbabwe's historical legacy and market processes. The challenge for Mugabe was how to deepen and direct this social phenomenon to his own advantage. The most immediate task at hand was to placate the military, and particularly the 'top brass' who might form a lightening rod for societal discontent and topple him. Indeed before the 2002 election the top military commander declared that the army would be the ultimate arbiter of who governed Zimbabwe (Carmody and Taylor, 2003). In Zimbabwe, as in other postcolonial countries, the strength of the military is part of the colonial legacy (Barkawi, 2006).

The man who forced Mugabe's hand into making the payments to the war veterans was medical doctor Chenjerai 'Hitler' Hunzvi, who had become leader of the Zimbabwe National Liberation War Veterans Association (ZNLWVA) in 1997. He had a conflicted relationship with Mugabe; actively criticizing and organizing protests against him, until Mugabe came 'onside' with the lump sum and pension payments of 1997. Mugabe was acutely aware that Hunzvi posed a continued political threat to his rule; prompting both cooperation and attempts to undermine him.

Ironically while Hunzvi rose to power on the back of allegations of elite looting of the war veterans fund, he himself had been complicit in this, signing medical disability certificates for leading ruling party claimants without medical exams (Kriger, 2003b), and also submitting claims himself that would have made him 115 percent disabled. This fraudulent claim ended him temporarily in jail in 1999, being fined and his being voted out as leader of the 'war vets' in 2000. This resulted in a loss of credibility and influence for the movement. Indeed after their initial success,

> Mr. Hunzvi and his organization remained on the brink of political oblivion until the government's shock defeat in February (2000) in a referendum on a proposed new constitution. Alarmed by the prospect of a similar result in the forthcoming elections, the ruling party immediately invited the War Veterans to join its campaign strategy.
>
> (Smith, 2000)

Nonetheless, discontent in the military still posed a potential threat to Mugabe in the 1990s, which had to be addressed.

Violence as accumulation 1[10]: war in the Democratic Republic of the Congo

The civil and inter-state (cinter–state) war in the Democratic Republic of the Congo (DRC) which has now largely ended, but at its height brought in eight foreign militaries, was a complex phenomenon. It was initially unleashed by the Rwandan genocide in 1994 which prompted mass migration and subsequent regional tensions, and Zaire's dictator, Mobutu, being forced from office.[11] The merger of domestic and inter-state conflict can be seen as a outcome of continuing globalization and 'new regionalism.' The regional instantiation of this type of conflict is a function of both incomplete nation building and the broader development of transnational networks associated with globalization conceived of as taking place over centuries rather than decades (Cramer, 2006).

There are a variety of explanations for Zimbabwe's involvement in the conflict. In 1998, Robert Mugabe headed the security organ of the Southern African Development Community (SADC) and was appealed to to help repel invasions by the Rwandan and Ugandan armies who had previously brought Laurent Kabila to power in the DRC (Campbell, 2003).[12] After a SADC fact-finding mission, Angola and Zimbabwe entered the war on Kabila's side. Mugabe had previously given Kabila US $5m to finance his rebellion against Mobutu. Lucrative deals were subsequently negotiated when Kabila assumed power (Helen Suzman Foundation, n.d.). The fact that the DRC government then owed US $145m to Zimbabwe provided an incentive to keep it in power (Nest, 2001). These loans could be seen as down payments, as some were repaid with diamond mining contracts, for example (Nest *et al.*, 2006).

Some have also speculated that the Zimbabwean military intervention also represented an attempt by Mugabe to reassert regional leadership in the face of a resurgent regional hegemon in the shape of South Africa, led by Nelson Mandela (Meredith, 2002). For Horace Campbell (2003, p. 134), 'the intervention in the Congo offered a last-ditch opportunity for the concepts of manhood, masculinity, and valor to be resuscitated and orchestrated to mobilize the population to support the territorial integrity and sovereignty of the DRC' and also to protect the Inga dam which supplies Zimbabwe with a third of its electricity. Thus it could be read as a jingoistic, 'wag-the-dog' 'patriotic' war to distract attention from troubles at home, while also opening up new economic opportunities. Undoubtedly there are elements of truth in these explanations. However one of the most compelling explanations is that the DRC served to deflect both the rank-and-file military and the top brass, from plotting Mugabe's over-throw domestically (MacLean, 2002). It opened up massive opportunities for both 'legitimate' trade and plunder for military connected companies such as Zimbabwe Defense Industries and Operation Sovereign Legitimacy (named for the military intervention in the Congo). The DRC government leased aircraft from Zimbabwean companies to bomb rebels (Campbell, 2003). Indeed it was probably the potential loss of previously concluded, and impending, lucrative mining and timber deals involving Zimbabwean top brass that ultimately motivated the intervention (Klare, 2001). Mugabe must have been aware that 'regime change' in the DRC could lead to contract cancellation.[13] Had these been lost, Mugabe's domestic position would have become very tenuous indeed. As international sanctions on the regime began to bite in 2000, diamond concessions in the DRC ensured a continued flow of forex to its members (Zeilig, 2004).

Payment to Zimbabwean firms owned by 'top brass' and chefs, initially in dollars, later took the form of mining, forestry and agricultural concessions in the DRC. In 2000 the Minister of Defense claimed the Zimbabwean military was involved in business in the DRC in order to generate revenue to sustain the military operation there (*BBC News*, 2000, cited in Addison and Laakso, 2003). Mugabe sent his Minister for Justice Emmerson Mnangagwa to the Congo to oversee business deals, where he became so heavily involved that he received a cut on his hand fighting at the war front (Helen Suzman Foundation, n.d.). Violence as a mode of accumulation was later to be brought back home to Zimbabwe (Reno, 2002).

During the DRC intervention an official of the trade development organization, Zimtrade, noted that 'within Zimbabwe the small to medium guys [often indigenous firms] are being squeezed out. Thus they are being forced to look outwards' (quoted in Nest, 2001, p. 476). Indeed 'independently of their military campaigns, regional economic expansion had been an element of the Zimbabwean and Ugandan government's economic strategies since the early 1990s' (Nest *et al.*, 2006, p. 41), as SAPs were intentionally deflationary of the domestic market.

Politically for Mugabe, the DRC intervention killed two birds with one stone, distracting and rewarding the military. Zimbabwe sent 15,000 troops to the DRC, out of a total army of 25,000. It is estimated that this cost around $1m a day to pay and provision them – a substantial drain on the exchequer in the context of a collapsing economy. The daily hard currency allowance of US $12 for Zimbabwean soldiers serving in the DRC was 'worth its weight in gold' (Johwa, n.d.). So many soldiers bought houses in Harare with these allowances that one area became known informally as 'DRC.'

Some estimates put the total cost of the war to Zimbabwe as high as US $5bn (Hill, 2005). As Ian Taylor (2005b, p. 103) notes the resources spent on 'facilitating the personal enrichment of top Zimbabweans in the DRC could have been spent on helping to resolve the land issue. Yet Mugabe chose otherwise' as he knew which side his bread was buttered on. Nonetheless there was discontent in the rank-and-file over the hardships of war. A report of an attempted army coup being foiled led to the illegal detention and torture of journalists by the army in 1999 (Dorman, 2001). The rank-and-file military and militia are periodically bought off with huge pay increases, such as the 1,400 percent pay increase for the militia in 2005 (*NewZimbabwe.com*, 2006). Soldiers returning from the DRC in 2002 were told that there was also still a lot of land to parcel out (*Zwnews*, 2002, cited in Scarnecchia, 2006). Also after the Zimbabwean military withdrew from the Congo, Zimbabwean generals created private security companies to guard their diamond concessions there (Nest *et al.*, 2006). The part Zimbabwean owned Segamines routinely shot local people who attempted to dig up arable diamonds on its concession (Amnesty International, 2002, cited in Ferguson, 2006).

Michael Nest (2001) and Horace Campbell (2003) have well described the economic dimensions of Zimbabwe's involvement in the DRC. For John Makumbe of the University of Zimbabwe, it was the first time one African country had colonized another. As such it represented a form of strategic and clientelistic accumulation. One of the strangest elements of it was the handing over of the management of Gecamines, the Congolese mining conglomerate, to Rhodesian era sanctions buster Billy Rautenbach. In another case a joint venture company between the Zimbabwean and the Congolese militaries and an Omani investment company, which was to mine diamonds under military protection, had to withdraw a flotation on the London stock exchange.

The military intervention was economically dysfunctional for the Zimbabwean economy and indeed many of the ZANU-PF business ventures in the DRC were not as profitable as had been hoped as 'inexperienced military owners clearly underestimated the technical and financial problems of turning decrepit mining operations around in the middle of a civil war' (Paes, 2003, p. 88). Laurent Kabila attempted to compensate Mugabe and cronies for this lack of profitability through the largest logging contract in the world in an area of the Congo, one-and-a-half times the size of the U.K. (Masunda, 2001). Zimbabwe may also have been able to export the Congo's American built nuclear reactor (*The Zimbabwean*, 2005c), which could be used to process newly discovered uranium deposits in Zimbabwe. Whatever the overall profitability, the DRC invasion bought quiescence from military leaders and provided Mugabe with time to bring the war veterans to heel domestically and reinvent himself ideologically, a third time.

Civil society in revolt 2: trade unions, the National Constitutional Assembly and the Movement for Democratic Change

In 1997, a new civil society grouping called the National Constitutional Assembly (NCA) was founded. It consisted of 96 CSOs including trade unions, academics, lawyers and human rights groups (Bauer and Taylor, 2005). Its *raison d'être* was to promote a new constitution to promote individual rights and do away with the last vestiges of colonial-era provisions. The impetus for the NCA came from the Zimbabwe Council of Churches, who subsequently withdrew when it became 'too political' (Dorman, 2002), particularly as the ZCTU moved toward forming a political party. The emphasis of some Pentecostal religions on individual responsibility had previously served to distract attention from structural issues (Maxwell, 1998).

The main political opposition to the ruling party emerged from within the trade union movement and other civil society groupings in the NCA. The Movement for Democratic Change (MDC) was founded in 1999 under the leadership of the secretary general of the ZCTU, Morgan Tsvangari. It was given impetus by the parlous state of the economy, accentuated by the war in the DRC.

The foundation of a potentially viable opposition movement capable of mobilizing popular support and financial backing from the wealthy white business community was a milestone in Zimbabwe's political economy. Initially, political stirrings in the ZCTU focused around opposition to the neoliberal nature of the Zimbabwean state, and rising inflation and unemployment. However, the evident corruption and catastrophic economic management from 1997 created the conditions for the emergence of the MDC as a cross-class movement focused on opposition to the state and its elites, rather than to a particular model of economic management *per se*. The contradictions which this entailed have been explored elsewhere (Carmody and Taylor, 2003). What is interesting for our purposes is that the MDC reflected a class alliance and merger of civil society interests around the erosion of the quality of, and ultimately, market relations themselves in Zimbabwe by an increasingly predatory state. This contest was to be played out in political society. For Bauer and Taylor (2005, p. 192), 'civil societies awakening was both consequence and cause of ZANU-PF's declining hegemony.' The government had previously shown authoritarian tendencies, such as jailing journalists in 1996 and 1997 for stories deemed to be hostile to the national political leadership (Makumbe, 1998). In repressing opposition, Mugabe later favored comparison to Hitler (Meredith, 2005). He had learnt from the war vets; force works.

The watershed in Zimbabwe's political economy came in 2000 when for the first time since coming to power in 1980 ZANU-PF lost a popular vote. The referendum was on a new constitution promulgated by ZANU which would have strengthened presidential powers and allowed the confiscation of white-owned commercial farms without compensation. The NCA and MDC had organized the 'No' campaign. Mugabe immediately deferred up-coming elections and looked for a new strategy to maintain power.

Violence as accumulation 2: land as economy and neofeudalism in Zimbabwe

Zimbabwe inherited a grossly unequal land distribution at independence, with about 4000 white commercial-farming families owning about a third of all agricultural land. Some commercial farms in Zimbabwe were larger than the English county of Berkshire (Weiner, 1988, cited in Thomas, 2003). While most Zimbabweans were more concerned with access to jobs than land, 'the largely spontaneous land occupations of Svosve, Mashonaland East in 1998, brought to the fore the growing pressures of rural poverty' (Raftopolous and Phimister, 2004, p. 362).

In order to punish white farmers for their support of the MDC and deflect increasing (urban) discontent about the deteriorating economic conditions, the Mugabe government launched its land invasions in 2000. This represented an attempt to instrumentalize and normalize state-sponsored violence (Chabal and Daloz, 1999). It had an important 'demonstration effect,' that the regime was willing to use violence to remain in power and put down opposition prior to the election.

The land-invasions led to the development of new forms of semi or uncivil society in the form of the 'green bomber' youth militias, who were used, along with the war vets to spearhead the land invasions. The employment and deployment of previously unemployed youth served the political purpose of displacing an important source of urban discontent to the rural areas (Carmody and Taylor, 2003). The 'war vets' were already an element of uncivil society, by virtue of their willingness to use force to challenge the state's monopoly on the 'legitimate' use of violence. Now they were co-opted as an element of semicivil society as they were incorporated, *de facto*, into state structures. In the land invasions, hundreds of people were killed and hundreds of thousands of commercial farm workers lost their jobs and were displaced. Land and property confiscations amounted to US $18bn, more than the entire continent of Africa receives in a year from foreign aid (Cross, n.d).

Several subsequent elections were stolen and Mugabe has proven very adept at disrupting and repressing opposition. However, after the 2000 election Mugabe also sought to manage the economic crisis, appointing a technocratic cabinet, with 11 of its ministers having doctoral degrees (Laakso, 2003).

The 2000 elections were run under the ZANU-PF slogan that 'Land is the Economy, the Economy is Land.' This is interesting for our purposes because under feudal systems 'the regulation of peasant labor with access to land was the task of the "state." There was no economy or civil society separate from the state: the state was the economy' (Kiely, 2005, p. 35). Ownership of much requisitioned land in Zimbabwe is now vested in the state. David Moore (2003b) argues that Zimbabwe is 'approaching a feudal mode of political rule – in which problems of leadership succession have society-wide consequences.' This could, however, been seen as a continuation of the postcolonial project, where the priority put on nation building and 'unity' served as a cover for ZANU dominance (Dorman, 2001).

There were also factory invasions in the early 2000s (McGregor, 2002), and a highly repressive NGO bill was introduced in 2004. The only independent human rights group in the country, Zimrights, collapsed in 2001 under a state onslaught, including harassment by the Central Intelligence Organization, although its chair had been supportive of the intervention in the Congo (Dorman, 2001). It also became illegal to have a meeting with more than two other people. State control of the media has been reinforced since 2002 by the government strategy, borrowed from intelligence services of apartheid South Africa and modern Angola, of taking majority shareholdings in most of the country's 'independent newspapers.' ZANU also has an extensive business empire in the form of M and S Holdings and Zidco.[14] For Brian Raftopoulos and Ian Phimister, the land invasions form part of a more general strategy by the ruling elite to control other sectors of the economy, given their dependence on agricultural inputs, with 45 out of 77 companies listed on the Zimbabwe Stock Exchange now controlled by indigenous investors (*Financial Gazette*, 2003, cited in Raftopolous and Phimister, 2004). The land invasions could also, ironically, be seen as a form of mainstreaming; combining both accumulation and legitimation.

Violence as a mode of accumulation and attempts to merge civil society, economy and state were not limited to the land invasions of 2000. In 2005, the government launched an abominable Operation *Murambatsvina* ('drive out trash') which made at least 700,000 people in informal settlements homeless and contributed to further economic decline. This was driven by the fact that the real, 'informal,' economy had escaped government control (Bracking, 2005). The governor of the Reserve Bank estimates that only 12.5 percent of Zimbabwe's money passes through the banking system, with the rest in the informal economy (cited in *Irish Times*, 2006).

The operation was also pursued, arguably to punish voters in urban areas for their support of the opposition in the 2005 election. This then represents a neo-feudal mode of rule, in which citizenship becomes reserved to the political class and others become subjects – a medieval 'chain of being' where sovereignty is ultimately vested in one person. For some this is tied to legacies of precolonial state culture (Maundeni, 2004). Indeed at the most recent opening of the Parliament, Mugabe was draped in a leopard skin, a traditional sign of royalty in Zimbabwe (*Zwnews*, 2006). Further attempts to recapture the economy include the 1000 percent devaluation of the currency announced in 2006, and the limits on how much cash can be exchanged, which will affect many ZANU-PF notables engaged in the informal economy (UN-IRIN, 2006a). The ability to access hard currency and trade it on the black market had been a source of profit for some members of the ZANU elite (Corporate Watch, 2003); making the economic crisis functional for them.

The social revolution, which has been promoted, is one in which unquestioned loyalty to the material prospects of political power holders becomes a precondition for survival, such as access to food aid. Life then, for most, in Zimbabwe has become bare life, rather than politically qualified life, which has rights attached to it (Agamben, 1998, cited in Sylvester, 2006).

The recent demolitions of informal settlement was not just confined to urban areas, but extended to ZANU-PF supporters on former commercial-farming lands. The demolitions thus have had the possible side-benefit of further marginalizing the war veterans as an independent source of politico-economic power (Winter, 2005). However, according to some observers the shanty demolition program will worsen the economic crisis as 'even on the most conservative estimate the campaign could cost 7 per cent of GDP, compared with the 5 per cent government promises to spend on reconstruction – in a year in which the IMF team that visited Zimbabwe this month believes GDP could fall by as much as 7 per cent' (T. Hawkins, quoted in Mberi, 2005). Survival for many is dependent on overseas remittances, with many people living a '001 lifestyle' – zero breakfast, zero lunch and one dinner. (Respondent quoted in Bracking and Sachikonye, 2006). Driven by inflation, urban dwellers are seeking out new lives in the countryside (UN-IRIN, 2006c).

Hegemony undone: populism, repression, clientelism

In Zimbabwe the failure of the 'free' market resulted in a crisis of legitimacy for the neoliberal state and the Presidency of Robert Mugabe. It unleashed a market backlash (Chua, 2004), politically directed to serve the interests of the ruling political elite, drawing on previous registers of national liberation struggles. Zimbabwe now has a failing state and contracting markets: the worst of both worlds.

> Clientelism is not a complete substitute for institutionalized politics, but neither is it merely a type of praetorianism. It is a structure between 'civil society' and the (Hobbesian) 'state of nature.'
> (Jackson and Rosberg, 1982, p. 40)

The market backlash which resulted from economic decline has meant that the Zimbabwean state under the leadership of Mugabe has pursued a three-fold strategy: of clientelism for those within the political circuits, and repression for those without, combined with a populist rhetoric.

'For the government of Zimbabwe, economic development in the decades following majority rule has been an exercise in balancing three interrelated needs – those of social justice, capital generation, and regime survival' (Logan and Tevera, 2001, p. 103). Government policy since 2000 has been to mainstream regime survival.

After the ESAP era, business opportunities largely played as rewards for political loyalty to Mugabe and this was one of the factors in the emergence of 'political businessmen,' such as the notorious rogue banker Roger Boka. Another declared 'I am rich because I am in ZANU-PF' (quoted in Meredith, 2005). One of President Mugabe's nephews recently purchased a twin-turbo Mercedes Benz S600 for US $130,000; the first of its kind in Africa (UN-IRIN, 2006a). 'As long as Mugabe can keep ZANU (PF) united—not as a political organization but as a clientele and a kind of crime syndicate—so he believes, nobody will kick him out of office or force him to accept major reforms to curb his extensive powers' (Raftopolous and Compagnon, 2003, p. 25). William Reno (1998) refers to such a structure as a 'shadow state,' where the public interest is given scant regard. However, there are limits to this as the imperatives of legitimation and broader accumulation still register. For example, there is continuing legitimation expenditure by the government, which continues to fund education fees for deprived children (World Bank, 2004c), and also attempts to stabilize and revive the economy. This even extended to paying US $2m in 2005 to host Miss Tourism World in an effort to revive the industry there, previously one of the country's main foreign exchange earners (IWPR, 2005). Previously, there was an outcry from the indigenization lobby over a preferential deal which a Malaysian company received for power generation, rather than opening it up to them (Raftopolous and Compagnon, 2003),[15] perhaps bespeaking continuing economic rationality on the part of the government, given limited technical capabilities among the indigenous business class. Alternatively the government may simply have wanted the forex.

Prior to the 2005 elections Gideon Gono, Governor of the Reserve Bank, launched an anticorruption drive and tightened monetary policy. Some politically connected asset management companies, which had thrived on loose monetary and fiscal policy collapsed. Eddie Cross of the MDC (quoted in *Africa Today*, 2004) explained how 'we watched astonished as the State hauled previous "untouchables" in front of magistrates and the Police ran around collecting luxury vehicles from the homes of prominent Zanu PF businessmen.' However, as entire 'edifice of ZANU-PF sponsored business teetered on the edge of collapse,' Gono relented and made 'unlimited credit' available to the banking sector at a 30 percent interest rate (*Africa Today*, 2004).

So far this has shown itself to be a stable political configuration, even as the economy falls ever deeper into decline, as Mugabe represents the 'devil you know' for ZANU elites. Mugabe has skillfully manipulated his position, selectively disciplining or expelling those who dare to ponder the succession such as former Minister for Information, Jonathon Moyo.

The end game is now approaching for Robert Mugabe in Zimbabwe, probably as a result of voluntary retirement. Recently 12 new fighter jets and 100 military vehicles were bought from China, perhaps partly to compensate the military for the $200m in military equipment lost in the war in the DRC (*BBC News*, 2004; Chimakikire, 2003). President Mugabe had previously bought 16 new armored limousines (Rotberg, 2002), and built a new US $10m mansion with 25 bedrooms for his wife (Baker, 2004). A cabinet reshuffle in 2004 appointed military officers to key political posts, and to posts in the parastatal sector, including in the National Oil Company and the Grain Marketing Board (Dansereau, 2005). In 2004 US $1.8m was spent to buy new cars for generals, brigadiers and air chiefs (Hill, 2005). War veterans have been integrated into the army reserves and their new leader Jabulani Sibanda was disciplined by Mugabe (Winter, 2005). Prior to this 'Mugabe's decision to take over the chairmanship of the ZNLWVA suggests that he would like to rein in and control the war veterans' (Kriger, 2003a). Sibanda was suspended from ZANU-PF for four years, and a new war veteran's leader appointed. This was in punishment for Sibanda being in a succession plot (Phiri and Dube, 2004). Also, perhaps mindful of Asian precedents, where wives have sometime succeeded their husbands as leaders, the wife of late ZAPU leader, Joshua Nkomo, was reportedly poisoned in 2004 (*NewZimbabwe.com*, 2005).

While efforts to stabilize the regime have so far been successful, powerful cleavages and fracturing is in evidence in ZANU-PF, and the ineluctable logic of economic decline means that change will eventually come of necessity. Jonathon Moyo, Mugabe's notorious information minister was sacked for allegedly plotting to position Emmerson Mnangagwa to replace Mugabe as leader of ZANU-PF prior to the 2005 parliamentary elections (Masland, 2005). Moyo, who was alleged to be a multiple farm owner had previously used the state media to attack the government's 'one person, one farm' policy (Kamete, 2005). After his expulsion, Moyo was subsequently elected as the only independent MP in the new Parliament. However, the patronage base is shrinking further and becoming more ethnically narrow and defined, with all but two parliamentarians from Mashonaland East being appointed to ministerial or deputy ministerial posts.[16]

Moyo has now turned his invective against Mugabe arguing (in Masland, 2005, p. 24) that 'there cannot be a more sinister and dangerous internal enemy than the tribal [Zezuru] clique that wants to monopolize State power.' He argues that Mugabe listens 'much more to security than political people' (Interview on *Hard Talk*, 2006). The potential for a split was also evidenced by the resignation of the former director of the secret police, the Central Intelligence Organization, over Operation *Murambatsvina* (*BBC News*, 2005c). However, increasing numbers of

Zimbabweans acquiesce to one-party rule as party competition is seen to lead to social conflict (Chikwanha *et al.*, 2004). Also Mugabe exhibits consummate political skill in managing these contradictions, expanding his cabinet by eight ministers in 2005 and reappointing Mnangagwa to the cabinet as Minster for Rural Housing (*Economist Intelligence Unit*, 2005b). Three of Mugabe's family members were also elected to the Parliament in 2005 and his newly favored successor and Vice-President Joyce 'Spillblood' Mujuru[17] is unlikely to challenge him for the leadership. Her husband, former army commander Solomon Mujuru, is now thought to be the biggest landowner in the country with between 6 and 16 farms (Moore, 2001). The Mujuru's live on a 3,500 acre requisitioned farm south of Harare. Ownership of some prime farms has now changed from a white to black elite. Thus these policies could be seen as a continuation of a particular model of 'black economic empowerment' promoted under ESAP.[18] However, it must also be noted that 66 percent of the land redistributed from 2000 went to small farmers and that 87 percent were drawn from the ranks of the rural poor (Government of Zimbabwe, 2003 and Moyo, unpublished, cited in Freeman, 2005a).

Following parliamentary elections in 2005, MDC now holds 41 (down from 56 in 2000) seats in the Parliament and still represented a credible political force, although the party's success and influence is constrained by an electoral system that overwhelming favors the ruling party. However, in 2005 the MDC split on whether or not to participate in a new Senate structure set up by Mugabe. Indeed tensions were already in evidence in 2002 with the expulsion of the 'workerist' member of parliament (MP) for Highfield, Munyaradzi Gwisai, who blames the MDC's repeated defeats on detachment from its base and failure to confront the regime.[19] The break up of large-scale commercial farms also undermined the party's economic base. Other commentators agree 'the MDC must be constructive or remain on the sidelines, looking uncomfortably like a front for Ndebeles and white people' (*Africa Confidential*, 2005c, p. 3).

Mugabe has also been successful in dividing churches in Zimbabwe as a new alliance of church leaders backing him, whereas a rival group does not. He is quoted as saying that he welcomes constructive criticism from the church; but in a reference to his critic Archbishop Pius Ncube, he says that 'when the church leaders start being political we regard them as political creatures and we are vicious in that area' (UN-IRIN, 2005e).

Nonetheless ZANU-PF is now hedging its bets by re-engaging with the IFIs, perhaps in preparation for the succession. In 2004 partial repayments to the IMF began again (*Business Day*, 2004, cited in Dansereau, 2005).

If payments were stepped up, the IMF representative indicated that a 'comprehensive policy package supported by external financing' might be available (A. Bio-Tchané, quoted in *afrolNews*, 2005b). The World Bank is also keen to re-engage, pursuant on reform (World Bank, 2004c). A further payment of $120m was made in 2005.

Prior to an IMF mission to assess whether Zimbabwe should be expelled from the organization, there were reports that the government was preparing to sell back 99-year leases to white farmers (*Africa Confidential*, 2005d). The Associated Bank of South Africa, recently bought by Barclays has signed a $25m-loan agreement with the Zimbabwe Allied Banking Group to revive the tobacco industry (*Africa Confidential*, 2005d). However, a program to evict the last remaining white commercial farmers was undertaken in September, 2005. Thus talk of re-establishing private property rights may represent a 'stage play,' in which the IFIs are also actors.

'In keeping with the governance approach [the IMF] indicated the need to restart tripartite discussions and involve all social partners in discussions over ways to improve the economy' (IMF, 2004, cited in Dansereau, 2005, p. 24). This is again an interesting interpretation of the word 'governance.' In the IMF's view consensus between the legitimate triad (state, business, civil society) is still possible on how to achieve economic development and poverty reduction, in a context in which the state has destroyed the rule of law, torture and intimidation are widespread and elections have been repeatedly stolen. This belies the IMF's economistic interest in, and definition of the term. This apolitical language is similar to that used by the World Bank prior to the Rwandan genocide (Storey, 2001), which some church leaders have argued Zimbabwe is on the brink of. One of President Mugabe's ministers (quoted in Meredith, 2005) has expressed the opinion that Zimbabwe would be better off with only six million people who believed in 'the revolution.' This language of partnership is also used by the governor of the Zimbabwean Reserve Bank who has talked recently about the need for 'labor, Government, business and civil society to recommit themselves to a progressive social contract which would anchor a balanced incomes and pricing framework' (Dr. Gideon Gono, quoted in Ruzvidzo and Benza, 2005).

The government had promised there would be a 2.4m ton grain harvest in 2005, versus the 600,000 to 750,000 tons actually brought in. In part, this is because of a severe drought that the government-run *Herald* newspaper has recently blamed on chemical weapons deployed by the UK and US to alter the climate of the region (*BBC News*, 2005g).[20] This meant that at least $420m would be needed for food imports. While the government had imported 150,000 tons from South Africa, UNICEF estimated that 5.5m people faced starvation if the government continued to prohibit international food agencies operating in the country, thereby using food as a weapon to punish/control opposition, making outright repression less necessary in the 2005 election campaign. The government had previously introduced new SADC sponsored election guidelines and regional electoral observers, including from South Africa, and friendly states, such as Russia and Iran, have continued to declare the elections free and fair (*BBC News*, 2005e; Leithead, 2005).

African countries from Zambia to Nigeria have welcomed 'white' African farmers from Zimbabwe because of their skills and capital. While Zimbabwe was at one point the third largest tobacco exporter in the world in the 1990s, the crop yield is now only a quarter of its former level. Food production was less than 50 percent of a normal year in 2003 (Economist Intelligence Unit, 2003, cited in Brett, 2005) and this decline has continued. Since 2001, when payments to the IMF stopped (*afrolNews*, 2005b), President Mugabe has advocated 'a command economy.' Economic policy is now Stalinist, with the army now forcing peasants to grow maize (Pepper, 2006). The use of the military on farms is 'an idea which Mugabe got from China, where the army is used in agriculture and industry' (J. Robertson, quoted in Lloyd Roberts, 2005).

The Zimbabwean economy has now contracted to 1953 levels (Center for Global Development quoted in UN-IRIN, 2005b). Women have been particularly affected by the economic crisis, with an acute shortage of sanitary products, for example. A packet of 10 sanitary pads can cost up to 12 percent of a textile worker's monthly salary (Madziwa, 2006).

Given the extent of economic contraction, it is clear that international constraints cannot be ignored indefinitely. However, the expectations of some observers that a standard IMF program would be adopted have, so far, proved false.[21] Indeed, rather than the West, Mugabe's regime deepened its relations – and reliance – on states like Libya and China (Bond, 2002c). However, as Zimbabwe became unable to deliver the agricultural products, it traded with Libya in return for 70 percent of its oil supplies, the economic agreement between them broke down (*afrolNews*, 2005a). On the other hand, there remains greater complimentarity between China and Zimbabwe's economies, as the Chinese remain eager to gain access to precious minerals to fuel their industrial growth. Zimbabwe and South Africa contain 90 percent of the world's chrome reserves (Mbendi Information Services, n.d.), for example, and Zimbabwe and China signed an economic cooperation agreement in

July 2005, despite reports of Mugabe's plane being delayed in Zimbabwe by a fuel shortage (*Irish Times*, 2005c).[22] The Chinese have encouraged Zimbabwe in pursuit of its siege economy, arguing that this is similar to the boycott the West imposed on Chinese communism (Economist Intelligence Unit, 2005b). The Chinese reportedly sent jamming equipment to prevent independent radio stations broadcasting during the most recent election there (Mark, 2006). This strategy may have the additional benefit of reducing Western consumption of Zimbabwean resources and reserving them for China. The Chinese are 'all weather friends' (Taylor, 2004), given the brutal suppression of civil society in China itself.

The 'Look East' strategy, named after Mugabe's friend Mohamed Mahathir's policy in Malaysia, may temporarily stave off collapse.[23] The agreement with China included a grant of US $6m for maize imports and other loans to the Zimbabwe Electricity Supply Authority (ZESA), for the Hwange power plant among other things, and a variety of commercial projects (UN-IRIN, 2005c). Chinese retailers now supply much of Harare's consumer goods and are apparently doing brisk business since Operation *Murambatsvina*. Using the term 'zhing zhong,' which refers to the poor quality of Chinese goods is now a criminal offence. The new system, however, has its contradictions as it is characterized by clientelistic involution. As the economy continues to contract the resources for redistribution become more limited. To some extent this has been staved off by Chinese economic support, with energy and mining deals worth $700m signed in 2006 (Meldrum and Watts, 2006). Zimbabwe has also received a loan from Iran for the expansion of the Kariba South Power plant. However, the 'Look East' policy has been accompanied by an undeclared 'Look South' policy.

Zimbabwe and NEPAD: explaining the contradictions

As will be discussed later, the New Partnership for African Development (NEPAD) is meant to be based on a bargain between the developed world and Africa, whereby African governments will govern themselves better in exchange for more aid, reductions in trade barriers etc. Zimbabwe is often cited as a test case for NEPAD, however, it is not part of the initiative. Countries join NEPAD by signing up the Democracy and Political Governance Initiative (peer-review mechanism). However, Zimbabwe has not signed up. In any event, peer review does not contain any (direct) incentives or sanction, but merely serves as a guide to foreign investors and donors. However, the way in which South Africa deals with Zimbabwe and the impacts of neoliberalism there tell us much about the nature and prospects of NEPAD.

International pressure – which mounted after the March 2002 presidential elections and the accelerated removals of white farmers that followed – has been largely ignored by the government. Indeed the neoimperialist rhetoric of neoconservatives and fellow travelers in the US and the UK has been skillfully manipulated by Mugabe (Phimister and Raftopolous, 2004). However, regionally, South Africa could still 'turn off the lights' (electricity supply) as it could have for the Rhodesian regime.[24]

In 2005 the financing gap for imports of food and fuel was to be filled by a $1bn loan from South Africa, which the head of South Africa's Government Communication and Information Services said would be dependent on 'economic recovery' and 'political normalization' (J. Netshitenzhe, quoted in UN-IRIN, 2005c). South Africa was also considering taking on a portion of Zimbabwe's $4.5bn debt (T. Mbeki, cited in *Irish Times*, 2005b). South African ministers have spoken of the 'catastrophe' of shanty demolitions in Zimbabwe, and are 'determined that it will not happen again in Africa.' However, because of over-rapid urbanization, unsupported by the necessary infrastructure, according to the South African Minister of Housing it was 'a catastrophe waiting to happen' (L. Sisulu, 2005). However, the offer of the loan was initially rejected as Mugabe 'scrounged $135m in hard currency from internal sources – by depriving most Zimbabweans of gasoline and food imports – so as to make a down payment on the arrears' to the IMF (Bond and Saunders, 2005). Operation *Murambatsvina* had forced some trade back into formal channels and captured foreign currency held in the informal economy (Corcoran, 2005b).

It is estimated that between 2000 and 2002 alone Zimbabwe's crisis cost the region, US $2.6bn. Most of this loss was to South Africa because of cancelled exports to Zimbabwe and failures to pay for exports, such as electricity (M. Schussler, interviewed in *The Economist*, 2004b). NEPAD has perhaps been 'quarantined' from Zimbabwe[25] already with the South African Minister of Trade and Industry (quoted in Taylor, 2002, p. 1) noting that the West 'should not hold the NEPAD hostage because of mistakes in Zimbabwe. If NEPAD is not owned and implemented by Africa it will fail and we cannot be held hostage to the political whims of the G8 or any other group.' At the Monterrey Conference in 2002, 'contrary to local [South African] consternation that Mbeki's Zimbabwe position will derail the NEPAD express, [it] was given a very high profile . . . with most industrialized countries and the G77 [Group of 77 developing countries] declaring their commitment to ensuring [its] success' (Gabriel, n.d., pp. 2–3). However this does not explain why South Africa is willing to actively bail out Zimbabwe, despite the fact that Mugabe obviously has little respect for Mbeki.[26] As noted earlier, there may be fears of regional contagion from a complete collapse and President Mbeki has argued that the slow pace of previous land reform there perhaps made a 'forcible process' inevitable (*Africa Today*, 2004).

A report from President Mbeki's investment council noted:

The centrality of the agrarian question in the Zimbabwean body politic was recognized. While the 1979–80 political settlement acknowledged the critical need for land reform and whilst various efforts were put in place over the past 20 years, including interaction with the donor community, the reality is that these were woefully inadequate to address the issue of equitable land distribution.

The active participation of SA and the President since 1998 to facilitate interaction between Zimbabwe, the UK and the donor community in order to secure the resources for the land redistribution programme entailing fair compensation and fairness, was appreciated.

Given this socio-political background, the approach of the SA government to seek the kind of engagement that brings about concrete results is the only viable one under the circumstances.

(Government of South Africa, 2000, p. 2)

In part, the South Africa's engagement may be tactical. Welshman Ncube secretary general of the MDC quoted an unnamed African head of state:

Trying to deal with Mugabe in the way the EU and America are doing is like putting your dog in a room and closing all the doors and then telling it to get out. The result is that it might bite you. What is the best way? No, not to open the gate – feed it! You feed it until it is so happy, it is so satisfied that it is a dog among dogs, and then, of its own volition, happy and satisfied, it will walk out.

(Quoted in *Africa Today*, 2004)

However Mugabe maintains regional support. Former Zambian President Kaunda has declared that 'Blair is more of a Devil than Mugabe' in relation to the land question, given the (disputed) lack of fulfillment of British promises to pay for redistribution (Africa News

Archives, 2005). President Mbeki has also bemoaned the extent of media coverage in the West where perhaps 200 Zimbabweans (some of which were 'white') have been killed compared to the war in the DRC, where several millions have been killed (cited in *BBC News*, 2005f). Some have argued that the mass evictions and removals in Zimbabwe might have tested South Africa's patience, but South Africa itself is using what some claim are apartheid-era laws to enforce mass evictions in central Johannesburg of 'unsafe buildings' (UN-IRIN, 2005b).[27] Also the conditions in the detention camps for Zimbabweans in South Africa are by all accounts horrific, where there have been numerous deaths from infectious diseases (*The Zimbabwean*, 2005b). However, the reasons for South Africa's support appear to be more geo-economic and political.

By putting forward an independent position on Zimbabwe more in line with the rest of Africa, South Africa can show it is not simply a 'stooge' of the West, thereby increasing its legitimacy in other African countries and paradoxically, and indirectly the legitimacy of NEPAD. Support for Zimbabwe enables it to enhance its leadership role in the continent, given the suspicion which has attached to it and its politico-economic-military dominance of the region since the era of apartheid. This enables it to cement an emerging African elite consensus on, as Thabo Mbeki (1999, cited in Taylor, 2001, p. 164) puts it, 'the *objective process* of globalization and its positive and negative features (emphasis added),' with South Africa playing the lead role in this process regionally. This more materialist analysis also has another dimension.

In the mid-1980s South African companies owned around a quarter of private capital in Zimbabwe (Southern African Development Co-operation Conference, 1986, cited in Poku, 2001). During that decade the government bought out some South African investment at about 30 percent of its market value (Dailami and Walton, 1989). South African companies accepted this as their profit repatriation was blocked during that time and it afforded them an exit option. However, the crisis in Zimbabwe has changed this. As *The Zimbabwean* (2005a) puts it:

> The good-natured, neighborly 'rescue' operations have been carried out in line with accepted good business practice all over the world. But the result has been, nonetheless, a transfer of ownership of the lion's share of a once vibrant, resilient and diverse manufacturing industry to South African business interests. . . . In the past five years, Zimbabwe's economy has been in an ever-increasing tailspin, which has rendered it wide open to predatory cherry-picking.

For Dale McKinley (2003), this is the key to understanding South Africa's Zimbabwe policy. He argues that repeated South African economic bailouts over the last number of years have had the effect of institutionalizing Zimbabwe's political and economic crisis. He argues that the privatization and corporatization of parastatals in South Africa has largely benefited the emergent and politically connected 'black' bourgeoisie in South Africa.

One investment, in a platinum mine, in the mid-1990s in Zimbabwe exceeded the total FDI in since independence several times over (Gibbon, 1996). This mine cost US $200–250m to build, but the Australian miner BHP shut it down in 1999 because of difficulties with equipment, manpower and unstable geological conditions (Economist Intelligence Unit, 2005). It was subsequently sold to Zimplats in 2000 for a 'nominal amount' (Zimplats, n.d.). Zimplats is 83 percent owned by the South African Impala holdings – the holding company for the South African Impala Platinum (Implats) Ltd. Some members of the board of directors of Implats, such as Khotso Mokhele and Thandi Orleyn, 'straddle' both public and private sectors, being President of the South African National Research Foundation and a member of the board of the South African Reserve Bank, respectively. However, most of the board are 'white.' South African investment in Zimbabwe rose in 2001 (Palloti, 2004).[28] Thus Zimbabwe's crisis may be very profitable for South African capital in the medium to long-term, with it getting substantial assets like this for free. Zimplats made an operating profit of US $25.4m in the quarter to June 30, 2006 and is planning to invest US $2.5bn in Zimbabwe in the next 10 years (*The Herald*, 2006).

It is the black bourgeoisie in South Africa which McKinley says is establishing its ownership of the Zimbabwean economy, through both private and state mechanisms, he argues. This may be a more secure basis for the development of this class than domestic unbundling of conglomerate assets in South Africa. The development of this class then bolsters the ANC, making Zimbabwe South Africa's DRC. Reportedly some of Zimbabwe's debts have been settled in gold bars and ivory (*The Zimbabwean*, 2005a). When the end game does come for Mugabe in Zimbabwe, South African companies, both state and private, will be firmly in control of the economy. This is consistent with broader changes in the regional geo-economy (Pedersen, 2004).

An alternative and somewhat more nuanced approach is provided by Chris Alden (2002). He argues that the South African response to the Zimbabwe's crisis must be set in the context of both South African experience with negotiated settlement, its own land issue, the desire to avoid an implosion, and its continental aspirations. According to Alden, the South African government believed it had sufficient leverage to bring about a peaceful resolution to the crisis in Zimbabwe. The African Renaissance and NEPAD allow for the rehabilitation of South Africa's regionally dominant role, in more benign form than under apartheid. However, South African dominance is dependent on consent.

Under Mandela, South Africa was unique on the continent for condemning the human rights abuses of Sani Abacha's regime in Nigeria. Mbeki is keen not to repeat the experience of South African isolation which resulted from this, but to reinforce its leadership, particularly in economic affairs. Thus, the non-application of NEPAD principles in Zimbabwe is to enable the initiative to progress on the continent. As Linda Freeman (2005b, p. 143) puts it: 'The delicate balancing act has been to accentuate the differences between South Africa and Zimbabwe for foreign investors without alienating African opinion.' After all SADC leaders had 'congratulated' Mugabe for the way he conducted the 2000 parliamentary elections (Taylor, 2005c). This type of realpolitik was also in evidence in Tony Blair's Commission for Africa, which side-stepped the issue of Zimbabwe for the sake of consensus (Mbiba, 2006).

South Africa's position has also helped assuage continental suspicions that the ANC government is dominated by white interests. However, how successful this balancing act in relation to NEPAD has been is open to question as the political and economic investment climate in much of Africa meant that 'in three years not a single company has invested in the plan's 20 high-profile infrastructure development projects [roads, energy, water telecommunications and ports]' (*Business Day*, 2004, cited in Bond, 2004b, p. 611).

In the wake of the recent shantytown demolition program, President Mbeki has privately conceded the failure of 'quiet diplomacy,' something long known by senior South African civil servants. However, according to the South African Ambassador to Ireland 'South Africa cannot act as a single country, as it belongs to the AU (African Union), and it is up to the AU to take a stand against Zimbabwe' (D. Jana, quoted in Corcoran, 2005a). Recently, however, the South African phone company *Telkom*, suspended phone services from Zimbabwe for nonpayment, and supplies of electricity and petrol from South Africa were cut off in February 2006 (*African Business*, 2006b). President Mbeki (quoted in *African Business*, 2006b) has recently washed his hands saying 'we are now inclined to leave the Zimbabweans to sort things out for themselves before we can move along.'

Neoliberalism in Zimbabwe contributed to the undermining of political order through an illiberal backlash. Political opposition and elements of civil society were repressed. This has been tolerated by the South African government and perhaps fits with the nonconsultative way in which NEPAD was designed, with President Mbeki, for example, saying civil society was ill-informed and that they should 'ask what they can do' rather than criticizing (quoted in Stoppard, 2002, cited in Mathews, 2004). This is also in keeping with the top-down implementation of the initiative, and the inclusion of some of Africa's most notorious despots on the NEPAD heads of state implementing committee (Taylor, 2005b), representing business as usual. Indeed, Mugabe was elected as one of the African Union's vice-chairpeople, of which NEPAD is an official program, in 2003 (Sefera, 2003).

If a liberal trade and capital regime are accepted as givens, experience has shown that in Africa, in countries working off a very low base, it is possible to grow the economy (distribution is another matter). NEPAD seeks to modify and stabilize the current growth regime, not transform it. However, as the previous chapters have demonstrated this will not result in the structural transformation of African economies. Far deeper local, national, regional and global changes are required for that. Some of these may be in the offing as Africa has now moved center stage in global oil and security politics.

7
Regionalizing Neoliberalism: The New Partnership for African Development and the Political Economy of Restructuring in South Africa

> Is it an illusion to desire poverty eradication while wishing fully to participate in the system that is known to increase poverty and inequalities?
>
> (Muchie, 2003, p. 6)

> While 60 per cent of the population remains landless, almost all agricultural land is owned by 60,000 white farmers. Post-apartheid, the income of the 40 per cent of the poorest black families has diminished by about 20 per cent. Two million have been evicted from their homes. Six hundred die of AIDS every day. Forty per cent of the population is unemployed and that number is rising sharply. The corporatization of basic services has meant that millions have been disconnected from water and electricity.
>
> (Roy, 2003, quoted in Saul, 2004, p. 80)

Despite its problems, neoliberalism has undergone multiscalar institutional embedding in Africa. PRSPs are also linked to other policy frameworks. According to Ronald Kempe Hope (2001, cited in Simon, 2003, p. 71), 'the PRSP process is . . . recognized in the NEPAD framework document as the principal vehicle for building continent-wide priorities into national poverty reduction programmers and co-coordinating international support.' NEPAD was launched in 2001 and later adopted by the African Union as an official program. Western leaders were consulted on NEPAD by Thabo Mbeki prior to the African National Congress, but African civil societies were not consulted (Anon., 2004a). NEPAD has consequently been dismissed by some analysts as a 'western wolf in

191

African sheepskin,' suggesting continued subservience to western power and values (Adebayo, 2003c, cited in Abrahamsen, 2004b). In particular its emphasis on regional integration and infrastructural development will facilitate continued extraction of Africa's resources (Toulmin and Wisner, 2006).

NEPAD has four initiatives around: (1) Peace and Security, (2) Democracy and Political Governance, (3) Economic Governance and (4) Sub-Regional and Regional Approaches to Development (de Waal, 2002, cited in Abrahamsen, 2004b). The central premise or bargain in NEPAD is that developed countries will help Africa through fairer trade and better market access, more aid and foreign investment, while in return Africans will govern themselves better, thereby reducing negative externalities for the international system (Government of South Africa, 2001).[1]

According to Simon Maxwell (2003), there are a number of ways to counteract 'asymmetric accountability' between donors and aid 'recipients.' These are for partnerships to be contractual or, in a weaker approach, through peer review, which has long been used in the Development Assistance Committee of the OECD and has now been adopted in NEPAD. In NEPAD 'the rationale of the PRM [peer review mechanism] is to make donor-imposed conditionalities superfluous, hoping that donors will eventually abandon their own monitoring processes and accept the outcomes of the African peer review' (de Waal, 2002, p. 471). Its top-down nature is evinced by the fact that it was not designed with grassroots civil society input, but was first presented to the World Economic Forum (Bond, 2006).

NEPAD is premised on deeper and unmediated integration into the global market system and driven by the leaders of some of the principal recipients of foreign direct investment (FDI) in Africa; Nigeria, South Africa and Algeria (Taylor and Nel, 2002). In terms of its economics, it draws on older theories of 'resource gaps' and new growth theory which focuses on the importance of institutional quality (Luiz, 2006).

South Africa is also a major sender of FDI, and continental integration opens up the possibility for the expansion of South African capital. To ensure acceptability, some argue, this required 'placing the neoliberal message within a broader transformational agenda' (Tieku, 2004, p. 255). This is not without contradictions, however, with South African President Mbeki sometimes telling people to 'just call me a Thatcherite,' while at other times imploring South Africans to challenge 'the notion of "the market" as a modern God' (Mbeki, 1998, cited in Saul, 2002, p. 45). While Mbeki may tailor his remarks to his audience, to avoid upsetting either business or the ANC's left wing allies (Barrell, 2000a, cited in

Saul, 2002), it is not necessarily duplicity, but reflective of his role as an organic intellectual struggling to bridge the cognitive dissonance between the real and ideal, and the inclusionary/exclusionary dialectic of globalization.

NEPAD claims that it does not want to further entrench aid dependency, but requires another $64bn a year in foreign assistance. In 2002, the G8 pledged $12bn a year by 2006. Nonetheless this led South African President Mbeki to claim that this 'signifies the end of the epoch of colonialism and neo-colonialism' (T. Mbeki, 2002, quoted in Bond, 2003). Trevor Manuel (2003), the South African Minister of Finance argues that NEPAD will fundamentally re-orient the aid relationship from welfare to 'partnership.'

Much has been written about NEPAD, some of it celebratory, some highly critical (see for example, Taylor and Nel, 2002; Ronald Kempe Hope, Sr., 2002; and F. Owusu, 2003). The approach taken here is different. It is to examine the likelihood of success of NEPAD by looking at neoliberal principles in action in the most developed economy of sub-Saharan Africa and principal promoter of NEPAD: South Africa. South Africa has won plaudits from international economic and political commentators for sound macroeconomic management and good governance, with the South African President recently sacking his deputy for being tainted with corruption. South Africa would thus appear to be a normative case of neoliberal 'good governance.' What has the experience been?

The globalization context in Southern Africa

When South Africa achieved its transition to nonracial government in 1994, a debate took place about the future direction of economic restructuring.[2] Two years later the Government of South Africa (1996) changed its development strategy by adopting an orthodox economic reform program. The South African economy is now rapidly globalizing, but the nature of that globalization differs significantly from that experienced by the rest of the region. While most of Southern Africa has experienced globalization as something externally imposed in the form of World Bank/IMF SAPs/PRSPs, in South Africa globalization has been largely internally generated. The two sets of actors that have most promoted globalization from within are the state and the country's major conglomerates. How this politico-economic project evolves has important implications for globalization theory, the popular classes of South and Southern Africa, and their resistance to it.

The Southern African region accounts for only 0.5 percent of global economic output (Davies, 1996, cited in Mittelman, 2000). However, elements of the South African economy are highly developed – it contains the highest number of Internet servers of any non-OECD country, for example (*Internet Wizards*, n.d., cited in Castells, 1996)[3] – and its economy dominates the region, accounting for 77 percent of the regional economic output (Economist Intelligence Unit, 1997, cited in Jordan, 2001). As such, with the end of apartheid, it was meant to be well placed to act as an 'engine of growth' for surrounding countries; a role which the American ambassador to South Africa in 2004 claimed it was fulfilling (Hume, 2004).

In order to try and overcome the legacy of the regionalized apartheid space economy, and attract FDI, the South African government, beginning in 1995, has also promoted the development of 'Spatial Development Initiatives' (SDI) (Hentz, 2005). Development 'corridors' are a key motif in these. Timothy Shaw (2000) notes that these corridors are subject to trilateral governance in varying degrees by state, market and civil society, however, at least in terms of their initiation they are state-led.

Rather than countries surrounding South Africa simply acting as a labor reserves, the aim is to encourage productive investment in these countries. This can serve a number of functions. In the first instance, it can potentially help in the regeneration of the regional political economy, which is a prerequisite for South African stability in the long-term. Secondly, if these initiatives create substantial employment they may alleviate the pressure of increased migration to South Africa, in a context in which its own economy is sluggish. Thirdly, the rehabilitation of the regional infrastructure, through the Maputo Development Corridor, for example, may help off-set the fact that South Africa's industrial heartland Gauteng is 'in the wrong place,'[4] in the interior of the country, in terms of getting access to overseas markets.

Shaun Breslin (2000) draws a useful distinction between regionalization which is private sector led, and regionalism which results from inter-state cooperation. In East Asia, regionalization has taken the form of 'growth triangles' where there are synergies between different factors of production in different territories. In the case of 'triangle manufacturing,' finance may originate or be channeled through a regional center such as Singapore. Production of the lowest quality garments, for example, may then be 'relayed by NIC [newly industrialized country] proprietors to increasingly low-income countries' (Gibbon, 2001b, p. 348). In this instance, the impetus for micro-regionalization comes from asymmetric levels of development. In Southern Africa, such synergies do not appear to exist. The history of state subsidization of industrial decentralization has not been successful in South Africa (Hart and Todes, 1997; see also Hart, n.d.). The response to SDIs has so far been weak. In order for subsidized investment to benefit the economy it must have external benefits. So far much investment in SDIs has been in enclave types of activities which are unlikely to bring these.

Despite the elimination of international sanctions, from 1996, when neoliberal economic reforms were introduced in South Africa, to 2000 more than a half a million jobs were lost, in contrast to the 600,000 that were meant to be created (Department of Finance, 1996; Economist Intelligence Unit, 2000). Total private nonagricultural employment fell almost 6 percent from 1997 to 1998 alone, and employment declines have continued largely unabated since then (SARB, 1999, 2001).[5] In total since 1994 more than a million formal sector jobs have been lost, amounting to a fifth of the formal sector labor force, and 260,000 redundancies were announced in the first quarter of 2002 (Bond, 2002b). Only 13 percent of the ['black'] African population are now employed in the formal sector of the economy, versus 34 percent in 1970 (Terreblanche, 2002). The unemployment rate for people under 30 is now reported to be over 60 percent (Seidman Makgetla, 2004), although there is also some debate about employment statistics (Simkins, 2004).

This deepening jobs crisis could be read as a working through of the previous economic crisis (see Gelb, 1991), and an adjustment to globalization, which will bring renewed growth and job creation in its wake: the position espoused by ministers in the South African government (Zuma, cited in Mnyanda, 1999, p. 11). Alternatively, the interaction between internal economic conditions, external competition and capital flows may indicate deepening economic dualism and marginalization. Which of these outcomes results depends importantly on the actions and strategies of the major companies which dominate the South African economy, and on state policies which frame the context in which these strategies are adopted.

The South African economy is dominated by a group of conglomerates, the four largest of which controlled 83 percent of the companies listed on the Johannesburg Stock Exchange (JSE) prior to the end of apartheid (Jones, 1992, cited in Iliffe, 1999).[6] The investment strategies of these conglomerates are important not only in their own right, but also because the success of small businesses, and hence the potential for substantial job creation, is intimately bound up with them through their control of financing, linkage and demand effects, and technological spillovers (Fine, 1997; Kaplinsky and Manning, 1998). The context for conglomerate strategies is framed largely by state policies, and the context in which they, in turn, are embedded. While much of the recent literature has focused on the role of the country's major conglomerates in promoting globalization from within, in South Africa the state has also been a critically important promoter of globalization.

The state and globalization in South Africa

Under globalization, capital is deregulated through the international regulation of states. While the policy formulation of most developing countries is highly circumscribed, the new postapartheid South African state seemed to have more freedom to pursue a heterodox development strategy given its relatively low level of external debt (Marais, 1998). Nonetheless, the South African government adopted an orthodox economic reform program, Growth, Employment and Redistribution (GEAR) in 1996 which made the extent of reconstruction and development largely contingent on profitability (Lesufi, 2005).

There has been a sustained debate about the reasons behind the rightward shift in economic policy, and the effective abandonment of the social democratic Reconstruction and Development Programmed (RDP) in favor of GEAR (see, for example, Adelzadeh, 1996; Padayachee and Michie, 1998; Hanson and Hentz, 1999; Williams and Taylor, 2000). For some, the government's conservatism was related to the externalized nature of the liberation struggle, and the 'petit bourgeois' nature of the African National Congress (ANC) leadership (McKinley, 1997). For others it was an outgrowth of domestically embedded structures of economic power, 'élite pacting,' the influence of neoliberal discourse of the 'transnational managerial class' and the 'governmentalizing' of the RDP (Marais, 1998; Swatuk, 1999; Bond, 2000; Kunnie, 2000; Götz, 2000). For Alan Hirsch, the chief economic advisor to President Mbeki, 'the shrinking economy [of the late apartheid era] imposed a terrifying parameter on the new government' (Hirsch, 2005, p. 2), suggesting the primacy of reviving economic growth.

Apartheid was a heavily statist system. Under apartheid a quarter of the 'white' labor force was in the civil service, and half were employed in parastatals (GATT, 1993, cited in Hentz, 2005). In the minds of many members of the new government, the economic stagnation of late-apartheid was associated with protectionism (Bond, 2000), or what James Hentz (2005) has called the 'laager economy.' Also, soon after the exchange rate was liberalized in 1996, the rand depreciated rapidly (Pillay, 1997). The government adopted GEAR in an attempt to reassure international investors of its economic orthodoxy.

While the proximate causes of the 'run' on the rand were a Union Bank of Switzerland report which assessed it to be over-valued, and rumors about President Mandela's health, it reflected the unwinding of a speculative bubble which had developed as a result of tight Reserve Bank monetary policy, and financial liberalization which encouraged inflows of speculative portfolio capital (Roberts, 1997; Bond, 2001a). Financial liberalization had begun under late-apartheid, and Reserve Bank 'independence' had been enshrined as part of the new political dispensation; largely because this was seen as important in renewing access to private international capital markets (Kelly, 1993; Bond, 2000).[7] Thus 'insulation' of monetary policy from democratic politics was one of the structural factors which led to the adoption of more far reaching neoliberal economic reforms.

The South African state's attitude toward globalization has been a seemingly contradictory one. On the one hand, it has been 'hyper-liberal' (Cox, 1987), pursuing an extremely tight fiscal policy, exceeding that proposed in GEAR,[8] and cutting tariffs more deeply than required by the WTO (Economist Intelligence Unit, 2000). Incredibly, 60 percent of imports faced a zero tariff into South Africa in 2001 (Gelb and Black, 2004). On the other hand, it initially introduced stricter labor market regulation in the form of the Labor Relations Act (Adler and Webster, 2000).

President Mbeki (quoted in van Audenhove, 1999, p. 5) has argued that 'globalization, liberalization, deregulation and the information society . . . all originate from the developed countries of the North [and as such] reflect the imperatives of the economies and levels of development of these countries and therefore . . . serve the purposes of our rich global neighbors.' However, he qualified this by stating that under globalization, development cannot be achieved 'under conditions of autarky or self-contained development within our national boundaries or regions.' Hence the South African state is trying to negotiate globalization;[9] the approach later adopted in NEPAD.

Several explanations of the government's highly neoliberal trade, investment and fiscal strategies have been put forward. The World Bank (n.d., p. 13) argued that trade liberalization would facilitate the development of indigenous-owned small- and medium-sized enterprises in 'intensive–intensive, light manufacturing industries.' However, within the South African government there is a recognition that 'trade liberalization overseen by the WTO is benefiting only a few countries' (Department of Trade and Industry, 1999, p. 7).[10] Nonetheless foreign portfolio investors favored deep tariff cuts, and particularly after the depreciation of the rand in 1996, it was argued that there was no alternative to adapting to the 'dictates of the global economy' (IDC and Department of Trade and Industry, 1998, p. 1).[11] Pressure from large domestically based conglomerates was also important, as big business saw trade liberalization as a way of ensuring continued supplies of imported inputs and disciplining labor. The Congress of South African Trade Unions had also previously endorsed limited trade liberalization as a way of raising the real wage, by reducing the price of consumer goods (Bell, 1997). Once implemented the logic of trade liberalization was self-reinforcing as reduced revenues from tariffs were partly offset by the elimination of export subsidies (Jenkins and Siwisa, 1997).

The strategy of trade liberalization was also presented as a proactive one. Cutting tariffs more deeply than required arguably gave the government more flexibility should they need to be raised again in the future (Hirsch and Hanival, 1998). Thus tariff reductions were motivated, in part, by the state's desire to get ahead of globalization; to try to force industry to restructure to become internationally competitive ahead of the next round of global trade liberalization, and to create space for some (constrained) autonomy in policy making.

The South African government has also pursued a free trade area with the European Union, despite economists in the Department of Trade and Industry warning that this would be deleterious to South Africa's economy (Teljeur, 1998). The adoption of the free trade agreement was partly related to South Africa's extra-regional trade orientation, with only 4 percent of exports going to the rest of Africa prior to the end of apartheid (Belli *et al.*, 1993), and was also an attempt to try to establish South Africa as an export platform to Europe. The asymmetrical nature of the negotiations is evidenced in a quote from the South African government that during the negotiations with the EU 'we learned that rules of origin are not only about customs control, but more importantly, about economic development, jobs and investment' (Smalberger, 2003, cited in Palloti, 2004, p. 517).

Trade liberalization is meant to attract FDI by enabling inputs to be easily sourced abroad and by improving incentives to export. Tight fiscal policy enables the continuing reduction of corporate taxes on FDI profits (Schoeman *et al.*, 2000). FDI, in turn, is meant to diversify the economy, bring new technology and create employment.

In 1996, the IMF argued that the end of apartheid and sanctions 'created the opportunity for external capital flows to return to the role they played in the quarter century before the mid-1980s, when foreign saving averaged more than 5.5 per cent of GDP' (IMF, 1996, p. 84). In a similar vein, tripartite alliance[12] press statements (*anclist*, 1999) argue, 'much still need(s) to be done for South Africa to become part of the capital flow process.' Given South Africa's historic dependence on primary exports, in order to diversify the country's export basket, the government has paid particular attention to attracting FDI in manufacturing, (Hesse, 2000) although outside of car assembly, and disturbingly much of this is domestic market oriented rather than integrated into global production networks (Gelb and Black, 2004; see also Gibbon and Ponte, 2005). However, the government's emphasis on foreign investment can be explained, not only by the changing nature of the global economy, but also by the political economy of transition in South Africa.

While Derrick Cogburn (1998) argues that the South African state is characterized by substantial autonomy in its policy making, he does not sufficiently specify in relation to which actors or along what dimensions. Alternatively, Adrian Leftwich (2000) identifies South Africa as a 'class-compromise non-developmental democracy.' Given that capitalist development often requires nonconsensual measures to mobilize resources to promote capital accumulation, it is in tension with liberal democracy. In South Africa, the negotiated nature of the settlement meant the basic maintenance of the previous economic system, including respect for private property 'rights.' Thus rather than enforcing redistribution and resource mobilization internally, 'industrialization by invitation' – drawing capital from overseas – became an attractive strategy for the South African state.

Given the low rate of private saving in South Africa, fiscal deficit reduction was seen as important by the government in order not to 'crowd out' private sector investment. It also enables corporate tax rates to be cut, thereby offsetting firms' workforce costs of the AIDS/HIV pandemic. These are substantial as it was estimated that already by 2003–2004 that 3–4 percent of the workforce would die each year from AIDS after, and that this will cost companies between 3.5 and 6.3 percent of their salary bill in benefits, absenteeism, retraining and other costs (Simon *et al.*, 2001). About one in five adult South Africans is currently infected with the disease (Campbell, 2003).

Neoliberal reforms have also enabled the South African government to achieve investment grade on its bonds, and thereby reduce its borrowing costs and free up money for other expenditure (Swarns, 2000).[13] Deficit reduction means that the state is less exposed to volatility in financial markets, again giving it some more policy autonomy.

The government's extreme neoliberalism in trade, fiscal and investment policy has not been reflected in other elements of policy, however. By going beyond orthodox macroeconomic practice the government may have hoped to gain more 'running room' from foreign investors for its more interventionist labor market and 'supply side' industrial policies.[14]

The political economy of South Africa precludes a development strategy predicated on lowering wages, as the African National Congress remains dependent on the votes of the working class. Even World Bank reports implicitly recognized this by arguing the government should 'encourage the positive aspects of trade unions' (Fallon and Lucas, 1998). Also given the country's history of brutal labor exploitation under apartheid, the government has opted for 'regulated flexibility' in the labor market — that is minimum wages, combined with a recognition of a two-tier labor market of permanent protected and temporary less protected workers (Standing *et al.*, 1996). The solution that has been adopted has been to raise wages, while at the same time trying to raise productivity through supply-side industrial policy based on training. Nattrass (2001) has characterized this as a 'High Productivity Now' strategy and questions its applicability in South Africa, given that many other middle-income countries are adopting similar strategies.[15] However, many low-income countries have adopted the strategy of competitive bidding down of wages, and competition is arguably more intense in that segment of the global market. The strategy of labor upgrading cannot be effective when the institutional structures of South African corporate capital are predisposed to cost-cutting strategies. Also their size and increasing economic liberalization means that they are able to rescale their operations to do this.

While unemployment has increased since 1994, so too have real wages for those in employment,[16] sustained by increased productivity. And while there are now moves toward further 'liberalization' and casualization, to try to attract more FDI and perhaps reduce firms' AIDS related costs, this more cautious strategy toward the labor market, was adopted not to alienate the government's traditional support base in the labor movement (Hentz, 2000).

Thus the South African government is attempting a compromise between globalization and social democracy (Koeble, 1998; Padayachee, 2000). However, this is being undermined as the state is increasingly characterized by embedded dependence on global forces.[17] In South Africa, this has gone as far as the President setting up an advisory International Investment Council made up of 'international business leaders' (Government of South Africa, 2000).[18] This dependence is manifest in 'negative autonomy' from domestic social forces, or a shift to what Habib and Padayachee (2000) identify as 'delegative democracy.' Negative autonomy is where the state appears autonomous from domestic social forces, but that autonomy is the obverse of dependence on global forces, and therefore reflective of their priorities. Thus, the state liberalizes the economy to maintain the 'confidence' of international investors and uses the global market to discipline productive capital and labor, rather than being able to discipline them on its own to achieve developmental goals.[19] In this way, the state uses its power to constrain its power.[20] As the state globalizes, the success of the government's development strategy increasingly depends on private sector actions and investment.[21]

The globalization and regionalization of South African conglomerates

The large-scale capital requirements for deep-level mining gave rise to conglomerates in South Africa (Levy, 1996). In the wake of the Sharpeville massacre of 1960 and subsequent capital flight, overseas investment opportunities were restricted for South African conglomerates by domestic exchange controls, and later by international sanctions (Pillay, 1997). Consequently, South African conglomerates diversified further from mining into manufacturing and financial and other services. The biggest of these conglomerates, Anglo-American Corporation, is the world's largest natural resource company, with an annual turnover of over $20bn. In the mid-1990s, it had 100 subsidiaries in South Africa, and manufacturing accounts for about 30 percent of its revenues (*The Economist*, 1995b; *Wrights Investor Service*, 2001).

With the decline of the gold price, and the onset of economic recession in the 1980s, conglomerates found that geographical restrictions on their field of accumulation depressed their profits. Some of the conglomerates, such as Anglo-American, had been able partially to circumvent the spatial constraints of apartheid by illegal capital flight and by setting up offshore companies to undertake investment overseas (Summa, 1988; Fine and Rustomjee, 1996). However, given stark levels of income inequality in South Africa, these businesses had outgrown the domestic market. Whereas, by the 1990s, US corporations earned

30 percent of their profits overseas, the equivalent figure for South African companies was only 7 percent (Nitzan and Bichler, 2001). The biggest of these conglomerates, Anglo-American Corporation, is the world's largest natural resource company, with an annual turnover of over $20bn. In the mid-1990s, it had 100 subsidiaries in South Africa, and manufacturing accounts for about 30 percent of its revenues (*The Economist*, 1995b; *Wrights Investor Service*, 2001). Consequently, large-scale Anglophone and Afrikaner capital pressed for a negotiated settlement with the ANC, so that they could globalize their activities (O'Meara, 1996). The other way to alleviate the problem of overaccumulation would have been a development strategy that focused on widening and deepening domestic markets, but as this would have required substantial asset redistribution to be effective, the conglomerates preferred globalization, with little questioning of private property.

Some of the conglomerates, such as Anglo-American, with operations in all six continents, were already global companies. However, with the liberalization of the economy and the end of sanctions, these conglomerates lost little time in further globalizing their operations. At first this primarily took the form of regionalization.

From 1991 to 1995, South African firms increased their total investment in sub-Saharan Africa fivefold to account for 25 percent of the total (IMF, 1995 and Loxton, 1996, cited in Reno, 1998). From 1994 to 1998, Africa received 42 percent of the outward investments by South African companies, while the European Union received 18 percent (Hesse, 2000). Whereas many mines in South Africa are close to being worked out, this is not the case for new acquisitions in the rest of Africa. As one South African businessman explained in reference to Southern Africa: 'South African firms want to conquer it before anyone else does and before they themselves move into more competitive markets' (quoted in *The Economist*, 1995a, p. 17, cited in Reno, 1998, p. 56). Already by 1998 South African firms had overtaken British ones as the leading foreign business licensees in the Southern African region (Duke, 1997, cited in Hentz, 2005). Thus, South African companies used their locational advantages in Africa to achieve economies of scale, and boost profits: using the region as a springboard to globalize (Simon, 2001).

By some estimates South African exports to the rest of Africa rose from 1.7 percent of its total in 1991 to 12.8 percent by 2000 (Associated Bank of South Africa, 2001, making it the continent South Africa's fourth largest export market by 2001 (South African Department of Trade and Industry Statistics cited in Daniel *et al.*, 2004). Already by 1998 about 70 percent of intra-SADC trade took place at tariff levels below 10 percent

(Martin, 2002), and by 2001 the balance of trade with the rest of SADC was 9 to 1 in South Africa's favor (*Business Report*, 2002, cited in Daniel *et al.*, 2004). In recent years, SADC exports to South Africa have fallen (Gibb, 2004).

While SADC countries' share of South African investment in Africa was 63.9 percent in 1997, it had grown to 90.1 percent in 2001 (Palloti, 2004). However, while bringing benefits, South African investment to the rest of the region also has disadvantages in that it may displace local companies in markets and access to loans, profits are repatriated and it is not in sectors, for the most part, likely to result in many linkages and structural transformation. South African supermarkets in SADC import most of their products from South Africa, displacing local production (*South African Labour Bulletin*, 2003, cited in Palloti, 2004). Southern Africa is South Africa's most important market for manufactured goods and services (Department of Trade and Industry, 1998, cited in Hirsch, 2005).

Conglomerate regionalization strategies have also dovetailed with other aspects of globalization, particularly SAPs. Currency devaluations, as part of SAPs, serve to reduce labor costs for the conglomerates in Africa, and privatization opens up new investment opportunities. For example, as one of the conditions of its structural adjustment program, Zambia was to be forced to sell its state-owned copper mines to Anglo-American for only $90m, half the original negotiated price (*African Eye News Service*, 1999). Although Anglo subsequently pulled out though as even at this price it was felt not to be sufficiently profitable. The majority stake was subsequently bought by a London registered Indian company, which has since reaped the profits of the recent copper boom (UN-IRIN, 2003b). In Southern Africa, many such assets were previously owned by South African conglomerates before they were nationalized.[22] In this way former divisions of power, as described in the previous chapter in relation to Zimbabwe, are reinscribed. The South African government wanted the DRC included in SADC and was highly involved in the peace process there perhaps partly to open up mineral extraction for its companies there who were excluded during the war (Bond, 2005a). Peace plus neoliberalism facilitated this in the DRC.[23]

The globalization strategies of South African conglomerates have gone further than those of other multinationals worldwide. Despite an 'improvement of the business climate' in South Africa, with liberalization many of the main business groups, such as Anglo-American, Old Mutual, SA Breweries, Billiton, and Dimension Data, have shifted their primary stock market listings and headquarters to London in recent years. They did this to access cheaper capital and to facilitate their foreign expansion

(Van Rensburg, 1999). Off-shore listing was meant to improve their global competitiveness and facilitate increased investment in the South Africa economy. By 1998 the five largest conglomerates controlled 'only' 55 percent of the shares on the JSE (Hesse, 2000).

By moving their headquarters to London, and financially delinking from South Africa, these companies are able to unlock 'shareholder value' (*Mining Magazine*, 1998). While the stock market capitalization of many companies in advanced capitalist countries, such as the US, are above their net asset values, on the basis of projected future profits, Anglo's market capitalization was 22 percent below its net asset value in 1995 (*The Economist*, 1995b). By moving to London these company's assets became denominated in more secure hard currency, which increased asset values and consequently share prices. Additionally those conglomerates which became part of the Financial Times Stock Exchange (FTSE) 100 index, received an additional boost to their share prices as tracker funds, which mirror movements in such indices, are required to invest in such companies (*Mail and Guardian*, 1999). While Anglo's stock price has been erratic, based on price movements in commodity markets, by early 2001 the value of its shares were 37 percent above its asset value (*411 Stocks*, 2001). By mid-2005, with the high gold price, this had skyrocketed, so that its shares were worth 270 percent of its assets (*Stockselector.com*, 2005). According to the Chief Financial Officer of SABMiller (formerly South African Breweries), its big global acquisitions of recent years would not have been possible without the London listing (*The Economist*, 2006a).

There are also complementarities between different elements of conglomerate globalization. In addition to demutualizing and listing in London, an increasing proportion of Old Mutual's (one of the largest financial services companies) operations are now overseas, and consequently its share price has become at least partially delinked from the South African market (*Africa News Service*, 2001). The core element of Old Mutual's business is life assurance, and as the prevalence[24] of HIV/AIDS rises in South Africa, it is under pressure from international financial capital to diversify geographically, by buying banks in the US, for example.[25] The direct workforce costs associated with the HIV/AIDS pandemic also undoubtedly encourage corporate delinking.[26]

The political economy of conglomerate restructuring

GEAR assumed that FDI would act as a developmental *deus ex machina*, and register a ninefold increase to enable its employment targets were to be met (Harris and Michie, 1998). However, the median foreign company in South Africa is small, employing only 90 people, with a capital stock of US$1.94m (Gelb and Black, 2004). Furthermore South African companies invested $1.6bn more abroad than came into the country between 1994 and 1999 (*The Economist*, 2001b), thereby deepening dependence on portfolio capital. Thus the policy was self-defeating. However, the strategy of conglomerate globalization also serves political purposes. It was facilitated by élite pacting, with Anglo-American taking prominent opponents of apartheid, such as Mamphela Ramphele and Cyril Ramaphosa on to its board. Also after coming to power, in order to redress the legacy of racial exclusion, and to consolidate its own power base, the ANC sought the development of a new indigenous entrepreneurial class through 'black economic empowerment.' In order to achieve this quickly, there was a redistribution of assets from white to emergent black capital through 'unbundling' – that is white dominated conglomerates selling off 'noncore' areas of their business to black economic empowerment companies, and also to foreign multinationals. They were keen to unbundled because of falling rates of profit and the desire to pre-empt domestic competition action (Nitzan and Bichlet, 2001); gaining political capital in the process. From 1995 to 1998, the proportion of shares on the JSE owned by black economic empowerment companies rose, by some estimates, from 0.5 percent to almost 20 percent (*Sunday Times Business Times*, 1998, cited in Lodge, 1999). Conglomerates were allowed to use the proceeds from 'unbundling' to invest overseas.

There is a political imperative for the ANC to build an indigenous business class, both as a source of support for the party, and in order to legitimate ANC rule by showing the deracialization of the economy. The strength of this imperative is evidenced by the fact that in the 2003 budget 10bn rand was budgeted for black economic empowerment, versus only a fifth of that for HIV/AIDS (McKinley, 2004). In part this is justified on the basis that political order is at stake; that there is a need to avoid another Zimbabwe (C. Ramaphosa, quoted in Business.iafrica, 2001, cited in Southhall, 2004).

At one level, there are similarities between this process of indigenous business class formation and the creation of a large-scale Afrikaner business class which took place after the Nationalist government came to power in the 1940s (see Magubane, 1979). However, the direct beneficiaries of unbundling were very few, numbering roughly 200 (Lodge, 1999). In 1999, a single company, Johnnic accounted for 78 percent of market capitalization of black-controlled companies on the JSE (Southhall, 2004), although there are also substantial holdings from union pension funds. Also in a globalizing political economy, one of the effects of unbundling was to transfer some of the risks associated with South Africa's semi-peripheral location (as expressed through its currency)[27] from white conglomerate to emergent black capital, and to labor.

In its first year as a London listed company (1999–2000) Anglo-American posted a 24 percent increase in its profits (*Times of Zambia*, 2000). This was largely as a result of the appreciation of the dollar, the currency in which commodities are traded, versus the rand, the currency in which the bulk of its operating costs are paid. On the other hand, 'black economic empowerment' companies had had to borrow heavily to pay for their unbundled assets (Kunnie, 2000), making them 'capitalists without capital' (Andreasson, 2006). In the wake of the East Asian crisis, and given that the economy had already been substantially liberalized to attract international investment, the Reserve Bank pushed interest rates to 25 percent to try to keep portfolio capital in the country. This effectively transferred income from productive capital, consumers and government to financial investors. Given that 'black chip' companies were so highly leveraged, most of them experienced severe financial difficulty. Meanwhile, many of the conglomerates had substantial cash reserves, and had transferred the proceeds from unbundling overseas. In some cases they bought back assets which they had previously sold, at heavily discounted prices. Anglo-American had sold Johannesburg Consolidated Investments (JCI) at R54 per share, but after the dramatic fall in the gold price, Anglo bought back JCI's 'best assets': two gold mines. Consequently the 'only smile belong(ed) to Anglo, which . . . made a handsome profit on a sale it had originally declared would be a magnanimous gesture towards wealth sharing' (*The Economist*, 1998). By early 1998 JCI shares were trading at R21 each.[28] Conglomerate profit outflows were later implicated in further currency instability in 2000–2001 when the rand fell from 6 to 14 to the dollar, leading to a tightening of currency exchange regulations (Bond, 2002a).

Afrikaner businessmen with pre-existing capital were less exposed to interest rates. Consequently their ownership share of the JSE rose from 24 to 36 percent from 1996 to 1999, as large-scale Anglophone capital divested (Swarns, 2000). Thus, paradoxically, one of the objectives of apartheid – raising Afrikaners to a position of economic parity with English-speaking whites – is being furthered by its demise.[29] Although some statistics now suggest that there are more people of color who are multimillionaires in South Africa than 'whites' (*Sake Rapport*, 2005, cited in Hirsch, 2005).

Changes in share ownership coincide with other forms of socio-spatial restructuring. Nicky Oppenheimer (cited in Johnson, 1998) argued that with it its move to London, Anglo-American has now taken its 'rightful place' among the world's top corporations. On the other hand, others see it as a form of recolonization as London is re-established as the dominant command and control center for the South African economy (Johnson, 1998). Thus aspects of both South Africa's colonial and apartheid history are being reinscribed or reinforced by current restructuring (Lester *et al.*, 2000). Indeed Nelson Mandela (quoted in Bond, 2004b) has argued that 'Cecil John Rhodes would have given his approval to this effort to make the South African economy of the early 21st century appropriate and fit for its time.'

While South African companies pressed to be able to globalize their activities, they are now also being shaped by globalization, through direct competition with other MNCs, and through competition for financial capital. In 1995, the chairman of Anglo-American (quoted in *The Economist*, 1995b, p. 67) argued that a core operation was one that 'earns a better rate of return than something else you could do.' However, by 1998 the group stated that its core strategy would be 'to develop as a global operating mining and natural resource company, with related industrial activities' (*Mining Magazine*, 1998). This change in orientation is because international financial capital wants the conglomerates to become more tightly focused 'investment vehicles' – to focus on their core operations, diversify geographically, and to abolish the pyramid structure of cross-holdings between companies. In Anglo-American's case this attempt 'to create a structure that meets the needs and wishes of today's investors,' led to the conglomerate being split up into separate business units with different managements (S. Thompson, quoted in *Weekly Mail and Guardian*, 1997). The new chairman of Anglo-American promised to dispose of roughly $4bn of industrial and financial assets over the course of a year, and pulled the company out of sugar production in Zimbabwe, for example (*The Economist*, 2000, *PanAfrican News Agency*, 2000). There have also been dramatic reductions in crossholdings, between De Beers and Anglo-American, for example, with De Beers becoming a private company in 2001 (Cowell and Swarns, 2001).

In addition to unbundling there has also been a process of what has been called 'rebundling' as conglomerates merge and acquire new assets in core sectors to try to meet global competition, with Billiton merging with the Australian mining house BHP, for example (Field, 1998; *The Economist*, 2001e). In 2004 Anglo-Gold merged with Ashanti Goldfields of Ghana, Africa's only substantial multinational corporation, outside of South Africa (Goodman Nikoi, 2004). 'South African' conglomerates are also further inter-twining with international capital to overcome their relative technological backwardness. Sanlam has outsourced all of its information technology infrastructure to Daimler–Chrysler, for example (*Sanlam*, 2001) and Old Mutual, in partnership with Nokia, IBM and Dimension Data, became the first unit trust company in the world to offer online trading via cell phone in 2000 (*ITWeb*, 2001). Thus as globalization from the 'outside in' and 'inside out' intertwine with one another, South African conglomerates and state élites are being absorbed into a broader transnational capitalist class project where global financial capital, given its greater fungibility and mobility, and hence structural power, sets the agenda (Glassman, 1999; Sklair, 2001).

Globalization and economic restructuring in South Africa: boom or bust?

Fine and Rustomjee (1996) have argued that South Africa's political economy has been dominated by a 'minerals-energy complex' (MEC) which has blocked the diversification of the economy beyond a focus on mining, mineral processing and the production of energy. For example, heavy investment in energy self-sufficiency by the apartheid regime in South Africa has given that country very low energy costs; and corporations in South Africa have been able to access electricity at a quarter the price paid by low-income rural households, for example (Bond, 2002b). Consequently some international conglomerates remain willing to invest in 'mega-projects' such as aluminum processing, which require a lot of energy.

Others have disputed the centrality of the MEC, arguing that economic diversification progressed substantially beyond that (Bell and Farrell, 1997). Irrespective of which of these positions was correct, some clear trends on the nature of restructuring have emerged now that policy increasingly responds to global capital,[30] rather than a domestically embedded MEC or manufacturing.

While the government's emphasis on FDI can be read as a desire to recreate aspects of the 'economic boom' years of apartheid, it misreads the current conjuncture. In the 1960s, multi-national corporations (MNCs) engaged in 'tariff jumping' investment in South Africa to service the market provided by affluent 'whites.' High rates of profit could be achieved based on the low wages of 'black' workers (Seidman and Seidman, 1977). However, with trade liberalization, underdevelopment of skills in the workforce, higher wage costs than in most of Asia and

Latin America and the relative insignificance of the South African market, there is relatively little incentive to locate new investments there, as it can be served from other, more cost effective locations (Mbekeani, 1997; Bond, 2000). Foreign investment has also been discouraged in the past by the domestic ownership structure, as conglomerates have monopolized markets.

There have been some successes in attracting FDI in export-oriented industries – as some previous 'tariff jumping' investment has also been transformed into export platform investment. In the late 1990s, the value of car exports rose almost 30 percent a year (Seidman Makgetla, 2004), and all 3 series BMWs and C class Mercedes are now assembled in South Africa (*The Economist*, 2001b). Rather than write off their sunk costs both companies have invested heavily in upgrading and expanding their facilities there. Also trade liberalization has reduced the cost of importing components and currency depreciation has reduced wage costs. The South Africa–European Union free trade agreement also serves to 'lock-in' access to that market. Also, the fact that components are purchased on international markets in hard currency, and that the most of the output is likewise sold in international markets means these companies are not adversely affected by the depreciation of the rand, even if this serves to immiserize growth more generally (Kaplinsky *et al.*, 2001).

While there have been some growth areas, such as call centers which now employ 80,000 people (Brenner, 2006),[31] most FDI has also taken the form of acquisitions which do not create substantial numbers of new jobs (Fine, 1997).[32] Furthermore, despite attempts to attract FDI through infrastructural investment in SDIs (see Gelb and Manning, 1998), inflows started to fall in 1998 as many state enterprises such as the fixed line telecommunications monopoly, Telkom, were already partially privatized (ILO, 1999). Inward FDI fell by almost half from 1996 to 1998, putting South Africa behind Nigeria, Egypt, Tunisia, Algeria, Zimbabwe and Angola as a recipient of FDI (*Business Day*, 1999, cited in Marais, 2003). However, private acquisitions have become more important in recent years. FDI rose by 807 percent in 2005 on the previous year as a result of the acquisition of the Associated Bank of South Africa by Barclays for US $5bn (see *The Economist*, 2005b). This meant South Africa attracted more FDI than India in that year.

There have also been other costs to the attraction of FDI. In the car industry, a study by Nicolau (1998) found that vehicle assembly has benefited from trade liberalization, whereas domestic component manufacturers have been subject to competitive displacement. Final assembly for export gained from lower tariffs on inputs and the depreciation of the rand which have made exports cheaper (Coetzee *et al.*, 1997). However, Nicolau (1998, p. 52) argues that 'this is a dangerous predicament to be in and will eventually lead to the total eradication of the [domestic] South African motor vehicle industry.' In other cases, previous 'tariff jumping' investments, such as a Philips television manufacturing plant, have closed as a result of trade liberalization. Production of televisions fell 19 percent from 1995 to 1998.[33] Local firms also found it difficult to meet competition from foreign investors with tax holidays. For example, in Natal a new Chinese investment in fridge manufacturing had a tax holiday, whereas the local company, Defy, did not and was consequently downsizing in 1999 (Interview with National Union of Metalworkers of South Africa negotiator, Johannesburg, 20 June, 1999). This policy of preferential treatment for foreign investors was abolished in 1998 for new investors (Boyd *et al.*, 2001).

South Africa spends roughly 1 percent of its GDP on research and development (R and D), a higher proportion than many developed countries, and there is evidence of innovation among South African firms (Foundation for Research and Development, 1996 and 1997). Surveys have found some South African companies to be operating at the frontiers of 'international best practice' (Schoenberger, 1996), and the country has some strengths in noncommodity-based manufactured exports. For example, in the 'aluminum cluster,' alloy wheels, catalytic converters and tanktainers are growing strongly.[34] Interestingly though President Mbeki (quoted in McKinley, 2005) has argued that the owners of the new catalytic converter plant in Port Elizabeth, the multinational Corning, would not be able to maintain R and D facilities to keep up with global technological developments, making this a role for publicly funded South African technikons, universities and 'specialized public sector bodies.' South Africa is also the world's largest exporter of leather car seats, related to BMW's investment. However, several studies have shown the deindustrializing impacts of globalization on different sub-sectors of industry (Kaplinsky and Barnes, 2000; Kaplinsky and Morris, 1999; Kaplan and Kaplinsky, 1999). It is not competitive in labor-intensive exportable goods industries such as textiles, clothing, footwear and electronic assembly (Gibbon, 2001a). Consequently, it is not capturing substantial foreign investment in these areas and as its own industries have been exposed to trade liberalization it is experiencing increasing marginalization in these subsectors. Some industries, such as bicycle and ship production, have been completely eliminated by foreign competition (Interview with Industrial Development Corporation manager,

Sandton, 15 July, 1999; IDC and DTI, 1998). Import competition from China has been particularly important in recent years.

Africa has recently been hit with a Chinese 'Textile tsunami.' Out of every 100 t-shirts exported to South Africa, 80 are from China (Lyman, 2005).[35] South Africa's clothing exports to the US fell from $26m in the first quarter of 2004 to $12m for the first quarter of 2005, with 30,000 people losing their jobs as Chinese companies reacted to the phasing out of the Multi-Fiber Arrangement by no longer sourcing in Africa (*Asia News*, 2005).[36] This was reflective of a broader problem in manufacturing which, based on estimates, was 'still not competitive in most sectors [sic] in the late 1990s' (Edwards and Golub, 2004, p. 1333).

The Chinese have noted that 'the fundamental reason for the increase in Chinese textile and clothing imports [into Africa] is the high demand for Chinese goods' (Guixan, 2006). Some argue though that this represents a fresh neocolonialism, disguised as South–South co-operation. According to Moletsi Mbeki (quoted in Mooney, 2005, cited in Servant, 2005), 'we sell them raw materials and they sell us manufactured goods with a predictable result – an unfavorable trade balance against South Africa.'

South Africa accounts for more than 20 percent of total Chinese trade with Africa, more than doubling over a six-year period (*Xinhua*, 2004b). China and South Africa are negotiating a free trade deal and the Chinese have expressed support for NEPAD and regional integration (*Xinhua*, 2004a). This may seem paradoxical, as does the fact that China sends election observers to Africa (*Financial Times*, 2006), but the fact is that both the Chinese and South Africans privilege regional economic integration over the governance procedures of NEPAD as evidenced by their mutually reinforcing approach to Zimbabwe, where both have been supportive of President Mugabe (Taylor, 2005b; see also Alden, 2002).

The solution put forward to the Chinese competitive threat by Trevor Manuel, Minister for Finance in South Africa, is for South African industry to identify new niche markets and improve its competitiveness to gain access to the Chinese market (Guixan, 2006). However, in 2005 the Chinese, ostensibly in order to ease the pressure on African countries, introduced export tariffs on 148 lines of textile and clothing exports and also prohibited additional investment in 28 categories of textile investment (Guixan, 2006). In part this may have been in response to the threat of 'safeguard measures' in Africa, and to prevent over-heating of the domestic economy. They also lowered the import tariffs on textiles entering China to 11.4 percent on the basis of WTO commitments, and abolished tariffs on 190 goods imported from 25 African countries (Bartholomew, 2005). This is part of an effort to expand and balance bilateral trade, while 'optimizing' [a neocolonial] trade structure (Chinese Ministry of Foreign Affairs, 2006). However, China also warned the South Africans that 'unfair and discriminative restrictions will never be accepted by China' (China's Economic and Commercial Counselor in South Africa quoted in Lyman, 2005). 'There's no question that for upper classes it's a boon . . . the problem is any lower-class South African's would rather have a job' (N. Seidman Makgetla, quoted in *Washington Post Foreign Service*, 2006). Thus while Thabo Mbeki argues that on the basis of economic growth of over 5 percent, Africa has 'irreversibly turned the corner' (*African Business*, 2006a), the growth of China may further exacerbate unemployment and income inequality in South Africa, reinforcing the previous growth path.

Some areas of manufacturing in South Africa, particularly mineral processing, continue to attract substantial conglomerate investment (Thompson, 2000). For example, conglomerates, catalyzed by state capital in the form of the Industrial Development Corporation are willing to invest in new 'mega-projects,' such as steel and aluminum processing (Fine and Rustomjee, 1996; Fitschen, 1998; IDC, 1998). Consequently, the South African case is not one of straight deindustrialization, as in much of the rest of Africa, as industrial output continues to expand slowly in most years (Stein, 1992)[37]. However, 'reintegration into the world market is . . . reinforc(ing) dependence on resource intensive industries' (Nordas, 1996, p. 715), with negative implications for sustainability.

The capital goods and engineering industry, which has historically been critically important in the structural diversification of industrializing economies, has been very hard hit by trade liberalization. In the metal and engineering industry employment declined by 9.2 percent from 1994 to 1999 (National Union of Metalworkers of South Africa, 1999). Thus rather than the touted labor-absorptive growth pattern emerging, there is evidence of increased capital-intensity in investment, although this represents a deepening of a pre-existing trend (National Productivity Institute, 1998; Kaplinsky, 1995). Indeed there is a path dependency in this as the Industrial Development Corporation which was set up in 1939 sought to deepen industrialization, without creating additional demand for skilled black labor (Hentz, 2005).

Under GEAR, manufactured export volumes were erratic, rising and falling depending on the value of the currency and global economic conditions (SARB, 1998, cited in Habib and Padayachee, 2000; SARB, 2001), but 'most of the sub-sectors in which net exports have been improving have experienced decreasing production' (Roberts, 1998, p. 46). On the back of a depreciating currency, manufactured exports grew by an astounding 18.2 percent a year in real terms from 1996 to 2000, but extroverted development resulted in rising unemployment (Terreblanche, 2002). The dramatic rise of the gold price and the rand after September 11, 2001 meant South Africa recorded a massive trade deficit of over US $9bn in 2004 (WTO, 2005), storing up a future debt problem and also making import competition in manufacturing in particular more intense (Hirsch, 2005). The overall impact of the strong rand has been 'employment stunting' (Nevin, 2006b).

A recent IMF study found substantial increases in total factor productivity as the capital intensity of investment has increased, and employment has contracted (Jonsson and Subramanian, 2000, cited in Subramanian *et al.*, 2000). Thus, although the relationship is denied by the IMF, the current pattern of growth could be described as 'job destroying.' Given the orthodoxy of macroeconomic management, a World Bank funded report attributes massive job losses in South Africa to 'the hassle factor' associated with 'excessive' labor market regulation and crime, rather than the impacts of globalization and conglomerate restructuring (Greater Johannesburg Metropolitan Council and World Bank Partnership, 2000). The substitution of capital for labor is also undoubtedly related to the impacts of HIV/AIDS (Simon, Rosen *et al.*, 2001).

In contrast to the 1980s, South Africa continues to achieve positive economic growth, averaging 1.5 percent p.a. from 1996 to 2000 and 3.5 percent from 2001 to 2005.[38] This enabled government to reduce corporate tax rates from 48 percent to 30 percent from 1994 to 1999 (Bond, 2002b), while maintaining its tax revenue from them, with Exchequer receipts rising from R146bn in 1996/7 to R160bn in 2000–2001 in real terms.[39] However, GEAR was implicated in a substantial slowing of growth from the immediate postapartheid period and massive job losses, as very tight monetary and fiscal policies, combined with trade liberalization have been deflationary (Weeks, 1999). One of the architects of GEAR, Stephen Gelb (1999, p. 155) wrote that 'it has manifestly failed to provide a credible framework for productive investors.' Indeed he has written of the economy's 'slow rotting' (Gelb, 2003, cited in Bond, 2004b), although economic growth has been over 5 percent for the last few years largely on the basis of Chinese demand for minerals. High real interest rates, now being somewhat reduced, and job losses increase government expenditure and decrease the tax take from workers, making the state more responsive to capital.

The South African government has identified high technology as a strategic sector of the economy as it attempts to move toward an 'information society' (Van der Walt and Blankley, 1999; van Audenhove, 1999). South Africa has an advanced telecommunication infrastructure, and there have been examples of successful 'high-tech' start-up companies, such as Dimension Data and Thawte, which was sold in 1999 for $575m (Wangwe and Musonda, 1998; *The Economist*, 2001d).[40] A major new private sector company also emerged in the form of Telkom, the former state-owned monopoly which has been partly sold to US and Malaysian investors (*Telkom*, n.d.).[41] In its policy programs and focus on high technology, the South African state may be trying to emulate the success of high-tech export platforms, such as the Republic of Ireland (Ó'Riain, 2000).[42] However, this would appear to be dependent on the attraction of massive foreign investment, which has not materialized, and is unlikely to materialize.

Mirroring trends in the rest of Africa, the financial sector of the economy has grown disproportionately under economic liberalization, as new investment opportunities are opened up, in currency speculation for example, to the detriment of production (Mamdani, 1991; Carmody, 2001) (Figure 7.1). While employment in financial services grew by 300 percent in the 1990s (SARB, 2005, cited in Hirsch, 2005), there are few examples of new hard industries which would create substantial numbers of jobs, and rebalance the income distribution structure (Fingleton, 1999). The (post)apartheid economy is experiencing deepening sectoral disarticulation, or structural dualism, as the conglomerates continue to invest in some major mineral processing projects, but divest from other subsectors, and the information economy is confined to the élite.

There are two sets of institutional types which can foster endogenous capitalist industrialization: diversified business groups, which have synergies across divisions, and regional industrial complexes based on high levels of trust and cooperation between small firms (Amsden, 1989). To date, South African industrialization has been dominated by large business groups, but these are now specializing and delinking. This in turn has knock-on effects. Given the importance of big business to the South African economy, since 1994 'a substantial number of SMMEs (small, micro and medium enterprises) have not been able to grow' and 'the growth that does take place in the SMMEs is, to a large extent, jobless' (A. Kesper quoted in Barrell, 2000).

Within government, some recognize that the results of the supply-side industrial strategy have 'not been that good unless you do something fundamentally different' (Interview with DTI official, Pretoria, 30 June,

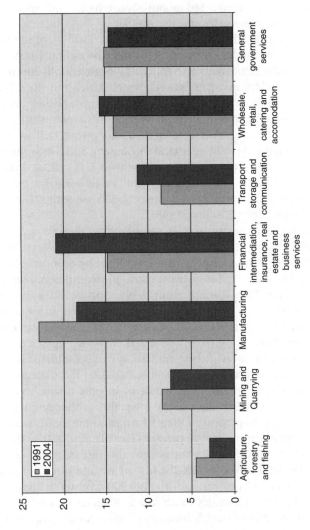

Figure 7.1   Percentage contribution to South African GDP by sector.

1999).[43] This concern is shared by the private sector and trade unions (Interview with Steel and Engineering Industrial Federation Association economist, Johannesburg, 9 July 1999; Joint Employer/Trade Union Initiative, 1999). In the wake of the East Asian crisis, even the major conglomerates were concerned about over-reliance on speculative short-term capital inflows (Thompson, 2000).

Globalization in South Africa has resulted in a rescaling of the forces driving uneven (economic) development from the national state/market complex to the global market. Neoliberal globalization is continuing to widen the development gap between South Africa and the OECD – globalizing economic apartheid – and resulting in repeated currency crises. It is also creating new patterns of uneven development within South Africa as globalization results in a 'hollowing out' of South Africa's traditional industrial heartland in Gauteng and a movement of manufacturing toward the coast (Interview with DTI official, Pretoria, 30 June, 1999), with ISCOR closing its Pretoria steelworks, for example, and investing in a new one at Sultana Bay (Interview with DTI official, Pretoria, 30 June, 1999; Fitschen, 1998).

In terms of the social impacts of restructuring, despite progressive government initiatives such as participatory budgeting with a gender focus, women tend to be disproportionately hurt by economic liberalization as the costs of adjustment are passed 'down the line' (Budlender, 2000; Thomas-Emeagwali, 1995; Shiva, 1989). In South African manufacturing, women's employment is more heavily concentrated in intensive–intensive sector, such as clothing, which have been most adversely affected by trade liberalization. Those segments of the MEC that have experienced growth are heavily male dominated in terms of employment (Valodia, 2000). Also, although inter-racial inequality is falling, South Africa has the highest rate of income inequality in the world, and this is rising.[44] The scale of inequality is shocking with the incomes of the top 20 percent of ['black'] African households is around 40 times as high as the poorest 40 percent (Terreblanche, 2002). The proportion of 'black' Africans under the poverty line rose from 50 to 62 percent from 1993 to 2001 (Bond, 2002b). Indeed average 'black' household income declined by 19 percent from 1995 to 2000, versus an increase for 'whites' of 15 percent (Statistics South Africa, 2002, cited in Andreasson, 2006). The deepening of (raced) inequality[45] gives rise to other patterns of uneven development as neoapartheid 'gated communities' proliferate. While there are other reasons for the extent of crime in South Africa (see Ellis, 1999), increased inequality undoubtedly contributes. Thus conglomerate (selective) delinking becomes a self-fulfilling prophecy as it contributes to increased inequality, crime and the narrowing of markets, which further increase incentives to disinvest. The inequality embedded in the neoliberal model, and the 'Anglo-Americanization' of South Africa is particularly inappropriate given the pre-existing extent of inequality (Terreblanche, 2002).

While the legitimation element of South Africa's organic crisis has been temporarily solved, the accumulation crisis has not, and the social crisis has worsened (Terreblanche, 2002). The fact that GEAR was not brought before the National Economic Development and Labor Advisory Committee (NEDLAC) for consideration effectively killed that institution, undermining prospects for a neocorporatist labor accord (Interview with Stephen Gelb in Andreasson, 2003).[46] Ultimately economic liberalization may undo South Africa's consociational compact, and in the longer term forebode further social instability, associated economic costs and a shift toward more authoritarian modes of governance (Mengisteab, 1999; Habib and Padayachee, 2000). Given skyrocketing crime rates there are calls among business for 'a *return* to law and order' (my emphasis) (Campbell, 1998, p. 2). The informalization of the economy (Rogerson, 2000) means that in the medium-term tax revenues may be undercut and the South African state weakened.

Alan Hirsch, the South African president's chief economic advisor argues that South Africa has now entered onto a new growth path based on a Keynesian virtuous circle between increased social expenditure, infrastructure provision, small business development and black economic empowerment. There have been notable achievements, with social grants, focused on children in particular, almost quadrupling from 1994 to 2003 and the percentage of people with access to clean water and electricity rising from 60 to 85 percent and 32 to 70 percent, respectively from 1996 to 2001 (Policy Co-ordination and Advisory Services, The Presidency, 2003, cited in Hirsch, 2005). A major new infrastructural investment program has also recently been announced by the government: the Accelerated and Shared Growth Initiative.[47] Hirsch notes that while unemployment has continued to rise as a result of an increased economically active population as African women define themselves as being in the labor force, formal sector nonagricultural employment increased by 17 percent from 2000 to 2003. However, whether such improvements are structural or conjunctural based on a temporarily improved global economy is open to question. Historically low interest rates of 7 percent have fed a consumption and property boom and a rising rand has increased real incomes, although as *Africa Confidential* notes only half of

South Africans have 'real' incomes (*Africa Confidential*, 2005a).[48] Indeed South Africa had the world's highest percentage increase in property prices in the early 2000s (Bond, 2006). If Chinese demand for minerals falters, or there is 'correction' in the US market,[49] the picture for South Africa could look very different.

NEPAD and the political economy of a new South Africa

South Africa's experience has important implications for globalization theory, which can inform praxis. In the literature, there has been a debate about whether globalization is weak or strong. Held *et al.* have transcended this debate by showing that there are different types of globalization which vary across space in terms of their extensity, intensity, velocity and impact (Held *et al.*, 1999). However, globalization is not just a horizontal-relational phenomenon. It originates within particular places, materializes in national institutions and reshapes hierarchies between places (Sassen, 1999; Held *et al.*, 1999; Held and McGrew, 2000). As South Africa's experience shows, globalization may originate from either the 'outside in' or the 'inside out.' It is generally strongest in its impacts where it is largely driven from outside, and economies are extraverted as in Singapore, Ireland or much of sub-Saharan Africa. It tends to be the weakest in quantitative terms where capital is the most developed and trade to GDP ratios are low, as in the major industrial countries.

South Africa is unusual in that globalization was initially largely 'from the inside out,' but its impacts have been strong in terms of job loss and economic diversification. Typically where globalization originates from within, those places are in dominant positions within subsequent networks. However, the shift of major conglomerate headquarters to London has negated this in the South African case. Thus as the nature of globalization is restructured, South Africa increasingly experiences it from the 'outside in' (dependence). Also South African investment in the rest of the continent, while bringing some benefits, will not lay the basis for economic renewal as it increases dependence on South Africa and displaces local enterprises (Bullen, 1999, cited in Ryklief, 2002). It is thus necessary to tame globalization.

SDIs could be seen as an element of a 'new regionalism' in Southern Africa. The 'new regionalism' is created not only by the actions of states, but by private sectors and civil societies. Carol Thompson (2000) argues that the SADC is a 'regional challenge to globalization.' She notes the importance of inter-state cooperation in issues like military and regional environmental security, such as access to water. Thus she sees political action as co-equal with economic exchange. However, an exclusive focus on the region neglects the importance of wider global processes.

Bertil Odén (1999) argues that for the 'new regionalism' to be effective in Southern Africa, South Africa must play the role of benevolent regional hegemon. However, the South African state has made it clear that it places its own national interests above those of the region. It is pursuing global integration more vigorously through the WTO and a free trade deal with the European Union more than regional integration. The free trade agreement will cost the other members of the Southern African Customs Union substantial tariff revenues. This is consistent with South Africa's approach more generally, which saw its government bring pressure to bear to get car assembly plants closed in Botswana, so that it would remain the regional hub for such investment (Good and Hughes, 2002).

While James Hentz argues that South Africa has combined a variety of different approaches to regional integration, based on a domestic class compromise (Hentz, 2005), the 'South African economy first' strategy can be justified on pragmatic electoral grounds and also on the basis of regional 'trickle out' economic strategy.

Within South Africa, there has been a continuing debate around what constitutes an appropriate economic development strategy. In 1997, Stephen Gelb argued that South Africa's development strategy must embody a compromised between capital and labor, given the power of both parties to disrupt a settlement not in their interest through strikes or a refusal to undertake new investment. Webster and Adler (1999) argue for a deepening of South Africa's corporatist institutions to facilitate 'bargained liberalization' where efficiency on the shop-floor is matched by redistributive mechanisms at the national level to offset the effects of any economic adjustments. However, they acknowledge that this would require the reintroduction of Keynesian solutions at national and international levels, making it difficult to achieve. More recently the government has shown a renewed interest in Keynesian strategies through the Accelerated and Shared Growth Initiative, (Government of South Africa, 2006) which will invest $66bn, largely in infrastructure (Nevin, 2006a). This shift in economic orientation is partly based on a recognition from the President's office that if the 'dynamic of economic inclusion and exclusion' were to continue in the same direction 'we could soon reach a point where the negatives [of the postapartheid period] start to overwhelm the positives' (Government of South Africa, 2003, cited in Bond, 2005a, p. 288).

Nicoli Nattrass (1996) has argued that neither Keynesian nor neoliberal strategies are likely to achieve their goals, but that the neoliberal ones are more realistic and less damaging. She argues persuasively that a Keynesian-inspired public investment program would likely result in unsustainably increased public debt and that an investor response would not necessarily be forthcoming. However, her limited endorsement of GEAR is difficult to sustain given the impacts of current neoliberal restructuring.

While replicating the Asian experience of industrialization is not possible, the potential for effective state intervention in the economy remains (Pempel, 1999; Streak, 1997; Kaplinsky and Mhlongo, 1997; Chang, 1998; Edwards, 1998; Mkandawire and Soludo, 1999). In the wake of the East Asian crisis, even the IMF acknowledged that (short term) capital controls can be beneficial (see Michie and Grieve Smith, 1999). Particularly given that the HIV/AIDS pandemic will discourage foreign investment, the state must reassert control over conglomerate and financial capital if currently deepening inequality in, and marginalization of, South Africa are to be reversed. Achieving greater autonomy from global financial capital will require the mobilization of domestic resources through enforced saving, such as that pursued by Chile (Green, 1995a).[50]

While James Mittelman (2000) argues that new technologies have enabled capital to transcend national regulation, Saskia Sassen (1998) has noted that the high level of territorialization of financial trading, combined with its computerization, have created possibilities for reregulation. Reasserting control over the conglomerates remains possible given the extent of their sunk costs in fixed investments, with Anglo-American retaining two thirds of its assets in South Africa (Arnold, 2000).

The South African state is trying to resolve some of the problems created by apartheid by upscaling economic development processes to the level of the global market. However, it has ended up reinforcing many of them. Given changed global conditions, particularly the constraints imposed by the WTO on export-oriented industrialization, as liberalization is required for market access, some downscaling may be a more appropriate response.[51] South Africa's financial institutions were perhaps too sophisticated and able to integrate globally, for its level of development (Terreblanche, 2002).

Some political economists such as Gibbon (2001b, p. 348) also argue for a strategy of upgrading to penetrate export markets. However, this logic is subject to a fallacy of composition, given that export markets are limited. According to Sampie Terreblanche (2002, p. 464), 'in building a truly developmental state to address the dismal legacy of colonialism and apartheid, the government will have no choice but to assume control over a far larger part of the South African economy.' However, 46 percent of South Africa's capital stock was in public hands in 2001, down from 51 percent in 1994 (Gelb and Black, 2004). While conglomerates may still play a useful role, alternative economic institutions to conglomerate capital, such as community-based corporations, co-ops and small businesses must be constructed (Shuman, 1998). This will require the nature of the South African settlement to be revisited. If alternative economic institutions are to be constructed across locales this will require the development of synergy between the state and civil society, between different levels of government, and the strengthening of state institutions.[52]

It is ironic that the 'political capital' built up by the ANC during the liberation struggle is now being spent to enforce neoliberal structural reforms. While organizing to embed the state and market in society, and to transform them, may be more difficult than organizing against apartheid, it is imperative (Adler and Steinberg, 2000). So far, however, counter-hegemonic civil society in South Africa has been focused on single-issue campaigns, such as the HIV by the Treatment Action Campaign (Habib, 2005). The impetus for embedding the market in society must come from globalization's and (post)apartheid's counter-movements in South Africa. However, in order to be successful the national and international contexts must become more conducive.

Patrick Bond (2004a) has noted the attempt by the South African government to elide its responsibility for often disimproving socio-economic conditions in South Africa by appealing for 'global reforms,' which are frustrated. With the failure of GEAR and SDIs, NEPAD is now presented as the solution to (South) Africa's problems (Terreblanche, 2002). Indeed we can see a neoliberal progression from national (GEAR) and regional (SDIs) to continental/global (NEPAD) in the South African state's policies, over which it has increasingly less control. However, this is equally unlikely to be effective, as the effects of neoliberalism in South Africa have shown. South Africa, while combining neoliberal economic principles with 'good governance' has failed to redress its jobs crisis or rising inequality, despite its regionally dominant position.

NEPAD has missing dimensions, particularly HIV/AIDS and gender (Taylor, 2005b). One of the impacts of HIV will be that savings rates will likely plummet, making NEPAD's goals unattainable (de Waal, 2006), and perhaps explaining President Mbeki's denialism in relation to the pandemic. Successful global reforms must ultimately transcend neoliberalism. It is to a viable strategy of 'scaling up' and particularly the changed geopolitical context in which global reform might take place that we now turn.

8
Governing Globalization for Human Security Post-9–11

> If the US wants to make the world a safer place, it will eventually have to offer, or force other governments to provide, the population of the entire world with the means to participate in global society. This will involve real constraints on the operation of the market, particularly finance capital. *Tuesday, 11 September 2001 may prove to be the date at which Neoliberalism and globalization parted company* (emphasis added).
>
> (Bull, 2001, cited in Moore, 2003a)

Globalization is the extension of social relations across the world. It is a dialectical process leading to the complex de- and reterritorialization of power along different dimensions. For some, what is new about globalization is the degree of the penetration of global phenomenon into national economic policies (Mittleman, 1995). However, since September 11, 2001 another dimension of globalization has been strengthened: the degree of penetration of global phenomenon into security policies.

Africa has traditionally been regarded as a 'backwater' in US diplomatic circles (Adebayo, 2003a), but since 9/11 the United States has taken a greater interest in African affairs for two reasons: oil and the potential terrorist threat. (Stevenson, 2003).[1] According to a Pentagon official (cited in Malan, 2002) 40 out of 48 countries in sub-Saharan Africa are not in control of their borders and could harbor terrorists. Consequently the former US Assistant Secretary of State for African Affairs considers that 'Africa is the soft underbelly for global terrorism' (S. Rice quoted in EIU, 2002b). Is there now a new international security regime[2] in construction, or are US relations with Africa taking a realist turn to contain 'anarchy?'

September 11 and its impact on Africa

Economically, politically and militarily, the attacks of September 11 had direct and indirect impacts on Africa. Some of these impacts are ephemeral; others will prove more long lasting. According to the World Bank, an additional 20,000–40,000 children under aged five, mostly in Africa, would die because of the more severe global economic downturn caused by the attacks, and an additional 10m people would fall below the poverty line of US $1 a day (*Africa Recovery*, 2001, cited in Ssemakula, 2002; Pogge, 2002). While most sub-Saharan African countries benefited from recent low real international interest rates on their foreign debts, economic growth for the sub-continent fell from 3.3 to 2.4 percent from 2002 to 2003, largely as a result of depressed international economic conditions (World Bank, 2004a). However, the economic effects on Africa were geographically and sectorally variegated. For example, tourism to North Africa fell by 4 percent from 2001 to 2002, while it rose in sub-Saharan Africa by 8.5 percent, as this was perceived to be a 'safe' destination (African Development Bank, 2003). The South African tourist market, in particular, boomed after September 11, as Europeans forewent travel to the US (*Moneyweb*, 2003). Tourist arrivals continued to increase in 2003 in some countries, although at a slower rate,[3] and Kenya and Tanzania, the sites of the US embassy bombings in 1998 were affected by terror alerts.

Capital moved out of North American stock markets into South Africa, particularly into gold stocks: a traditional investment haven in times of uncertainty. Gold stocks rose between 100 to 300 percent in the wake of September 11 and this, combined with increases in the price of gold, temporarily boosted South African and other African gold producers' economic growth (*Business Center*, 2002). Combined with China's rapid industrialization and consequent demand for minerals, this has resulted in a rapid appreciation of 'commodity currencies,' such as the South African rand (Morrison, 2004). More recently, oil-importing countries have also been adversely affected by higher oil prices.

There has been a marked increase in US private and state sector interest in oil production, particularly in West Africa. In 2002 the US Assistant Secretary of State with responsibility for Africa noted that

> oil and gas is [sic] one natural resource that Africa does have. And what we would like to see is Africa use those resources, and we are very interested in helping African governments use those resources and prioritize how they might build on a successful national resource economy.
> (Katzensteiner, 2002)

Indeed the Bush administration has declared that African oil is 'of national strategic interest' to the US, given that the United States is likely to import two out of every three barrels of its oil by 2020 (Servant, 2003).

It takes about six weeks for oil from the Persian Gulf to reach the US, but only two weeks from West Africa (Ruppert, 2005).[5] Political instability in the Middle East and potential supply disruption through the Suez Canal and Sumed pipeline are additional considerations (USEIA, n.d.).[6] West African oil is 'light and sweet,' with a low sulfur content, particularly suitable for burning in cars. Seventeen percent of US oil imports currently originate in West and Central Africa; and major new investments are being undertaken in Nigeria, Angola, Sao Tomé and Equatorial Guinea. Nigeria is currently the fifth largest crude oil exporter to the US; Angola is ninth and there are now direct weekly flights from Texas to Equatorial Guinea, which in 2003 had the world's fastest growing economy (*Sixty Minutes*, 2003).[7] It has a population of half a million people, but US oil firms have invested $5bn there. According to Human Rights Watch, continued human rights abuses have not deterred US investment and it is geo-strategically attractive to the US because it is a non-Muslim, non-OPEC (Organization for Petroleum Exporting Countries). The size of oil revenues is a state secret, but in the first year of its contract with ExxonMobil, Equatorial Guinea got to keep only 12 percent of its oil revenues (Klein, 2005).[8]

The US has also dropped, or is in the process of dropping, sanctions against some African oil producers and after the September 11 attacks Colonel Gadaffi asking Libyans to 'bleed for the US' (Sapa-AP, 2004). After Libya abandoned its nuclear weapons program, the UN lifted its sanctions and diplomatic relations between Libya and the US resumed (Fidler *et al.*, 2004). Fearing American coercive power, Sudan cooperated with the US by providing intelligence in the 'war-on-terror,' and both the US and UN lifted sanctions against Sudan (de Waal and Abdel Salam, 2004). The US executive branch may have been eager, in competition with China, to gain access to Sudan's oil supply, which was set to double from 2002 to 2005, but the US Congressional politics prevented it from doing so (Volman, 2003b).[9] The UN recently imposed an arms embargo and targeted sanctions on human-rights violators in Darfur, at the US instigation, although close cooperation between Khartoum and Western intelligence agencies may be blocking war crimes prosecutions there (*Planetguru.com*, 2005; *Africa Confidential*, 2006).

The US suspended military assistance to Nigeria after President Obasanjo published a letter critical of the any US action in Iraq. Before that Nigeria had been the main recipient of US military aid in sub-Saharan Africa. The aim of increased military assistance to sub-Saharan Africa is now to 'bolster the capacity of African military forces to protect oil production and transportation facilities' (Volman, 2003b, p. 579). The Central Intelligence Agency (CIA) estimates that by 2015 West Africa alone will supply 25 percent of America's imported oil (CIA and National Security Council, 2000, cited in Volman, 2003b).[10]

Overall net FDI inflows to Africa fell from 2001 to 2002 – from US $172bn to $151bn – partly because of the slowing pace of privatizations (African Development Bank, 2003, p. 11). Thus the intensity of some global private-sector flows decreased, while others increased. The US state has sought to leverage these flows by selectively encouraging, de- and re-regulating private financial flows to Africa in recent years. On the one hand, the Bush Administration contracted with Fitch, a principal global credit rating agencies, to fix sovereign-debt credit ratings for 15 African countries so that they can more easily access global financial capital (Katzensteiner, 2002);[11] on the other hand, the US government has eliminated some financial flows, through, for example, the closure of al-Bearcat, the Somali bank and money-transfer service in the US, as it was said to be a source of revenue for al-Qaeda. Estimates of the size of this financial flow varied from $200 to $500m per year, versus $60m in humanitarian assistance per annum to Somalia (UN-IRIN, 2001). Up to 80 percent of the Somali population relied on these funds for basic survival (De Sio, 2001, cited in Mercer *et al.*, 2003), and Somalia's biggest orphanage was forced to close (*The Economist*, 2004a).[12]

The American response to September 11 led to the establishment of a direct military presence, with a new US military base set up in Djibouti, and also to bolstering the military capabilities of proxy state and nonstate actors. According to Baregu, under the previous security regime prior to 9/11, lead nations were appointed by the US to engage in regional military interventions in Africa, with Nigeria being the lead nation in West Africa and South Africa in Southern Africa (Baregu, 2003). This was, in part, a response to the failure of the US mission in Somalia in the early 1990s, which also contributed to the US setting up the African Crisis Response Initiative to train an African Rapid Reaction Force (US Department of State, 2000). However, the US is now taking up a more aggressive forward posture in Africa. In part, this has been justified by casting doubt on South African military capabilities because of the impacts of AIDS.

Strategically situated, the military base in Djibouti houses a rapid reaction force capable of conducting operations in Kenya, Somalia, Tanzania or Yemen. Djibouti hosts a Voice of America transmitter (used recently to threaten bombing of 'terrorist camps' in the Sahel), and in return will receive $30m a year in US aid (Bollee, 2003). The US possibly plans to build a naval base on Sao Tomé, which may have oil reserves of 4bn barrels (Johnson, 2004). An offshore base would provide logistical support for U.S. Special Forces to operate on mainland West Africa (Ellis, 2004). The US sent a small intervention force to Liberia in 2003, as it was thought to be the center of al-Qaeda's operations in West Africa (Lyman and Morrison, 2004).

In the spring of 2002, the Bush Administration developed a new military assistance programme: African Contingency Operations Training Assistance (ACOTA), which differs from its predecessor by providing training for offensive military operations and offensive weaponry, such as machine guns and mortars (Volman, 2003c). In 2004 Angola and Nigeria, the two largest African oil exporters to the US became eligible to receive free weapons under the Pentagon's Excess Defense Articles Program (Klare and Volman, 2006). This increased military assistance, and the decreased emphasis on human rights, has led Harvey Glickman (2003) to argue that the response of the United States to September 11 is remarkably similar to the early days of the Cold War.[13]

There has also been the development of the Pan-Sahel Initiative (later renamed the Trans-Sahara Counter Terrorism Initiative) to train the militaries of Chad, Niger, Mauritania and Mali in counter terrorism to prevent the Sahara becoming a haven for global terrorists. The initiative, through training and basing rights, secures an American military presence between oil-rich North and West Africa and the 'encirclement of Islamic Africa' (Kennan, 2004; Martin, 2004).[14] One thousand American special-forces troops have been sent to the Sahel, and attacks on suspected Islamic militants have taken place by African armies, but under US command (Ellis, 2004).

In tandem with formal initiatives, the US stepped up assistance to some military nonstate actors. In Somalia, it funds General Aidid's son, because he claims he can lead them to Al-Qaeda terrorists (Pilger, 2002). Peter Little notes that the power of warlords in Somalia has been greatly strengthened since September 11 (Little, 2003). He is reported to have been paid $500,000 by the United States for 41 Strela missiles to ensure that they do not fall into al-Qaeda's hands (*The Economist*, 2004a). Thus the US is funding warlord politics, as long as they are 'our warlords.' The power of warlords in Somalia has greatly strengthened since late 2001 (Little, 2003).

The US state has developed a campaign to 'win hearts and minds in Africa.' In January 2003, President Bush announced a $15bn contribution to the global battle against AIDS and substantial increases in aid (Adebayo, 2003b). The President's Emergency Plan for AIDS Relief (PEPFAR) bypasses the United Nations, and will purchase only those drugs that are in conformity with US patent law. PEPFAR was budgeted to spend US$2.4bn in 2004, mostly in Africa (US Department of State, 2004). In June 2003, President Bush announced a $100m counter-terrorism package for the Horn of Africa: it would support a coastal and border security program, a Kenyan antiterror police unit, and Muslim education, but Muslim leaders rejected the money for education (Lyman and Morrison, 2004).

The potential impacts of increased aid are being undercut by the lack of 'joined-up thinking,' however, with short-term US domestic politics continuing to take priority (Hope, 2002; Nye, 2004). The main indirect impact on Africa from September 11 was the protectionist response to the economic downturn in the US; particularly the $190bn farm subsidy bill, which affects some African produced products, such as cotton (Robinson, 2004). After this, US cotton farmers received three times more in subsidies than total US aid for sub-Saharan Africa and this contributed to further immiseration (Oxfam International, 2002). US cotton subsidies were more than the GDP of Burkina Faso, where 3m people are dependent on cotton for their livelihoods.

Some observers, such as the former President of the World Bank Jim Wolfensohn (n.d.), see a link between poverty and terrorism, but others argue that the links are very tenuous, as most of the September 11 perpetrators came from a wealthy state, Saudi Arabia (Clapham, 2003). This calculus may be feeding into the dominant US security response to September 11 of policing global exclusion, while making side payments to select developing country governments, rather than promoting inclusion. Simultaneously positing poverty as causal of terrorism allows political rationales for terrorism to be downplayed (Howell, 2006). Neoconservatives and others have written openly of the 'new imperialism.' This open embracing of imperialism has been skillfully exploited by the demagogues, such as Robert Mugabe (Phimister and Raftopolous, 2004). Indeed Mugabe's rhetoric draws from the same register as NEPAD – ridding the continent of neo-colonial interests (Moseley and Ikubolajeh Logan, 2004, cited in Moseley and Ikubolajeh Logan, 2006).

From hegemony to hegemony?

With the collapse of the Soviet bloc, African elites were encouraged to 'own' downsizing neoliberal economic reforms. However, 'when governments no longer provide public goods and services, [state] failure looms' (Rotberg, 2002, p. 131). Thus, neoliberalism proved unable to secure African state hegemony, with the result that 'underdevelopment turned dangerous.'

One of Tony Blair's key advisors, Robert Cooper, who was subsequently 'promoted' to advise the EU foreign policy representative, divides the world into three zones 'pre-modern,' 'modern' and 'post-modern' (Cooper, 2003). He argues that the 'alien' must be contained and that 'victory in the pre-modern world would mean empire' (Cooper, 2003, p. 74): among 'ourselves, we keep the law but when we are operating in the jungle, we must also use the law of the jungle' (Cooper, 2002). Cooper's threefold division neglects the interacting nature of regions and their mutual co-constitution, but his theory has had concrete application with recent Western military interventions: by Britain in Sierra Leone, by the United States in Liberia, and by France in Côte D'Ivoire.

This is a form of what Mark Duffield (2001) has called 'network war' where terrorist networks and now networks of states confront each other. According to Richard Falk (2003, p. 6) 'al-Qaeda exemplifie(s) the organizational form of the current era of globalization: a network that c(an) operate anywhere and everywhere, and yet (i)s definitely situated nowhere.'

States for the most part have lined up behind the US, including China, taking September 11 as an attack on the entire state system (Falk, 2003). Thus there is inter-network competition for control or influence over regions, and a globalization of 'new' postmodern war; which has already been a feature of some African countries over the past decades. However, the ability of the network of 'coalition' states to win in this new variable geometry of power is open to question (Cox, 2004). As Fareed Zakaria (2000) notes the United States may be the Goliath in the world, but David won in that story.

According to John MacKinlay (2001, p. 145) 'the currently assembling coalition of likeminded states to "wage war on terrorism" is an old fashioned emergency structure that would address a Clausewitzian threat to security, but not the virus of its own condition.'

The over-generalized US response to a very specific kind of extremist trans-national violence has had the unfortunate effect of sending a green light to governments around the world to intensify their own violence against opposition and resistance activity branded as terrorism, and even to wage war against neighboring states that allegedly support anti-state forces.

(Falk, 2003, p. xix)

In Africa, it has served to exempt state terrorism from scrutiny.[15] Under US pressure, but confronting popular resistance, Kenya, South Africa and other African states have passed antiterror laws (Kraxberger, 2005). Draconian antiterrorist laws have been passed in Morocco for example; and Eritrea and Ethiopia have both accused dissident groups of being linked to al-Qaeda (Adebayo, 2003b). The US is working closely with the Ethiopian secret service in Somali (*The Economist*, 2005f). Foreign terrorist suspects are now extradited from the United States, or kidnapped in third countries, through the procedure of 'extraordinary rendition,' and sent to countries such as Egypt, known for using torture in interrogation (Tretter, 2005). However, the more the new coalition aligns itself with autocratic regimes, the more it risks creating long-term instability. US Vice-President Dick Cheney (quoted in Ruppert, 2005) has spoken about the war on terror as a 'war which will not end in our lifetimes.'

The 'new imperialism' also invokes pre-emptive military activity. However, both support for repressive governments and direct and indirect military action, in dialectical fashion, are likely to prove unstable as they generate 'blowback' (Falk, 2003),[16] unintended negative consequences for the instigators of policies, itself a form of globalization. The activity of the US military in West Africa may result in the extroversion of Muslim–Christian conflict in Nigeria, which to date has centered on local disputes (Ellis, 2004). The radicalization of Islam and blowback against the region's governments are already in evidence in the Sahel, partly as a result of the destruction of the region's main industry, tourism, because of the terror-zone label associated with the Pan-Sahel Initiative (Kennan, 2004). 'Islamic social movements are both a moment of, and a reaction to, neoliberal globalization' (Kamal Pasha, 2001, p. 242). Blowback is perhaps most in evidence in Somalia where US funding of warlords helped the Islamic Courts Union come to power there in 2006, sparking an Ethiopian invasion which may portend renewed civil war, while also serving to distract from domestic tensions in Ethiopia (*The Economist*, 2006b).

Stephen Gill (2003, p. 141) has identified under globalization 'a growing contradiction between the tendency towards the universality of capital in the neoliberal form and the particularity of the legitimation and enforcement of its key exploitative relations by the state.' This was displaced in the initial era of neoliberalism as the US was able to engage in 'meta-steering' or regime creation which had global effects (Jessop, 2002). It can no longer do this because of a more assertive neoliberal multilateralism by Southern countries, demanding better market access in the WTO, in evidence in Seattle and Cancun, and because the previous regimes did not contain transnational terrorism. September 11 demonstrated the fragility of this fix as the global contradiction between the state and the market is expressed in elements of civil society-transnational terrorists-and is not amenable displacement. This is particularly so because the institutions of global legitimation, the United Nations in particular, are weak when compared to those of global accumulation (the World Bank, IMF and WTO) (Mittleman, 1988; see also Peet *et al.*, 2003).

Stephen Gill claims that panopticism, where the United States can 'look into' terrorist networks using satellites and 'forensic accounting,' as a strategy is a means of coercively containing 'the contradictions between capital accumulation and social reproduction' (Gill, 2003, p. 196).[17] However in Somalia in the early 1990s, clansmen used digital phones that the US was unable to tap (Kaldor, 1999). In this way the technology of corporate globalization is being used against it, with the power of surveillance and violence into society at large (Castells, 1997).[18] This diffusion, which reached the United States on September 11, 2001, combined with the fact that the globalized economy is tied to territorially fixed resource extraction, oil in particular (Zalik, 2004), has given rise to the imperative of a more-aggressive military forward posture by the United States in Africa. Thus, the previous strategy, of coercion (structural-adjustment conditionality) informed by consent (funding to NGOs) (Farah, 2005), is now losing ground to US hegemony in the realist sense, or 'dominance,' which relies more on force (Sparke, 2004). However, new contradictions are generated as the neoconservative synthesis involves both constitutionalizing (neoliberal economic) and deconstitutionalizing (neorealist) tendencies. The emphasis on democratization among bilateral and multilateral donors may now also be reduced in favor of effective territorial control as an objective.[19]

Unilateralism is in evidence in US policy toward Africa as the United States deploys its 'hard' power to selectively regulate, promote, eliminate and deregulate global flows, contributing to both globalization and deglobalization; while seeking to extend US state power. The US state is trying to reinforce security boundaries within Africa and certain flows (foreign investment, aid and trade) to Africa. However, flows in this context are contradictory, as they work within and against the geopolitical codes of spatial sovereignty (Luke, 1993, cited in Agnew and Corbridge, 1995, p. 215).

Remilitarization and stateness in Africa

Stateness 'refers to the functional ability of institutions to organize constraints and effect compliance to orient human action toward certain expectations and rules of procedure' (Khadiagala, 1995, p. 35). As recent work has shown there is a range of state types in Africa from the failed (Somalia) to the developmental (Botswana) (Samatar and Samatar, 2002a). There are three different strategies of state rule: hegemony, repression and clientelism. Neoliberal global forces sought to build a new hegemony based in rural areas in Africa and to reduce direct repression and clientelism. The failure of this hegemonic project, because of the shallow nature of the transnational historic bloc with which it is associated, accounts in part for political instability in Africa. In parts of Africa security had previously been at least partially privatized through the development of private military companies, and states struggled to maintain their monopoly on violence. According to Christopher Clapham (2001) in parts of Africa 'military power has shifted very significantly away from formally constituted armies, under the control of state governments in the capital cities, towards rural-based groups that exercise direct control over local economic resources.' He also argues that 'it would be wise to recognize that the brief period in which states covered the whole of the inhabited world has now passed, and that a reversion to patterns of international activity characteristic of previous eras is now called for' (Clapham, 2000). Others do not go this far but argue that there has been a general erosion of stateness in Africa and that the era of the 'postcolonial state' is over (Young, 2004). According to Mark Duffield (2001, p. 164) 'especially in Africa, the strategic complexes of liberal governance have occupied the space previously controlled by national economic and welfare actors.'

Private military and security companies have also filled part of the void filled by state security retraction. The role of South African private military companies in the civil war in Sierra Leone has been well explored, for example (see Reno, 1998). With the end of the civil war, after British military intervention, the security regime there has been reconfigured, with both a private security company and armed police guarding the important Koidu diamond mine (Abrahamsen and Williams, 2005b).

Growing inequality has also prompted the growth of private security companies. As a percentage of its GDP, South Africa has the largest security market in the world (Abrahamsen and Williams, 2005a), with the turnover for the industry being roughly the same as the national police budget (Kruger, 2004). However, September 11 may result globally in the renationalization of security policy regimes (Mann, 1999).

The increased emphasis on 'hard' or military security may result in further 'arms pollution' in Africa, although remilitarization was already in evidence in parts of the continent. As Agnew and Corrbridge (1995, p. 24) note, 'the other side to the economic "globalization" of the "core" industrial states has been the militarization of many regions in the "periphery."' There was a sharp growth in military expenditure in Africa in the late 1990s (Omitoogun, 2000), and the UK has quadrupled its arms sales to Africa since 1999 (Talbot, 2002, cited in Mercer *et al.*, 2003). Rwanda had 1298 percent more people in the armed forces in 2001 than in 1985; whereas the figures for Djibouti and Cameroon are 328 percent and 316 percent, respectively (UNDP, 2003b, p. 306–7). Previous US training of the Rwandan armed forces, after the 1994 genocide, facilitated their later involvement in the war in the Democratic Republic of the Congo, which has claimed the lives of several million people, directly and indirectly (Hartung and Berrigan, 2005).

Peter Little (2003, p. 2) notes, 'international bodies, such as the UN and World Bank, need governments to operate, accept their loans and aid and impose their policies in the same way that colonialism often required 'traditional' authorities and bounded polities to operate.' It could now be added that the US now requires states in Africa to maintain security. Thus there is likely to be less tolerance by the US state for the deliberate instrumentalizing of disorder (Chabal and Daloz, 1999). The global security regime changed after the end of the Cold War in important ways, and it has been further revised since 9/11.

Former US President Bill Clinton says that the failure to intervene in Rwanda during the 1994 genocide is the greatest regret of his time in office (Clinton, 2005a).[20] His administration forbade officials from referring to the events which unfolded there during 1994 as "genocide" lest it inflame American public opinion and provoke demands for intervention. The administration blocked the sending of 5,500 troops requested by the UN Secretary General (Schraeder, 2000). However, since the genocide there the American government has been a strong support of Paul Kagame's regime, which has sometimes acted as a proxy for the

Americans in their competition with the French for resources and influence in Central Africa.

The failure of the international community to prevent genocide in Rwanda led to greater prominence for the doctrine of humanitarian intervention – the 'right to interfere' – to prevent massive abuses of human rights at the United Nations. The right to interfere has now been written into 150 resolutions of the UN, sometimes retroactively as in the case of France's recent military intervention in Côte d'Ivoire. (B. Kouchner, cited in Allen and Styan, 2000). This 'right' has proven to be very contentious, however, as developing countries often see this as a cover for Western neoimperialism. Moreover, if not explicitly authorized by the UN Security Council this 'right,' or in a stronger forumulation, 'duty' has been sometimes been used as a cover to breach the UN Charter.[21]

More recently, the UN (2005) has recast the 'right to interfere' as 'the responsibility to protect' (R2P) people who are experiencing acute breaches of their human rights. In the first instance, it is meant to be national states which have the responsibility to protect their populations. However if the state is judged to be ineffective, or complicit in human rights abuses, the responsibility extends to the other countries acting through the United Nations.

The extent to which this new responsibility is acted on depends on geopolitics. For example, despite claiming that the current conflict in Darfur, Sudan is 'genocide,' the American Administration argues that UN troops should 'not fight their way in' (Frazer, 2006). While Africa has become an increasingly important source of oil supplies for the US, it still pales compared to the Gulf (Klare, 2005). Thus the US prefers to act through proxy states in Africa, rather than taking direct military action, and has stepped up military assistance to them since 9/11.

Increased military assistance by the US may dialectically promote disorder as military strengthening of African states may lead to further societal disengagement, thereby further weakening the state in the long-term (Rothchild and Lawson, 1994). 'Of the twenty four countries that experienced at least one armed conflict in 1997 . . . the United States sold weapons and/or provided military training to twenty one of them at some point during the 1990s' (Tabb, 2001, p. 98). September 11 may also consolidate the emergence of illiberal democracies, where regular, competitive multiparty elections are held but the daily business of the state is marked by abuses (Zakaria, 2000).[22]

Investment in oil production can fuel conflict, as there is political competition to control access to oil rents and governments can afford to buy new arms. In Chad, despite agreements with the World Bank to invest in the social sector, the government used $4m out of the first payment of $25m of oil revenue to buy arms (Volman, 2003a). It subsequently has completely abrogated the agreement.

The end of the North–South Sudanese civil war in 2003 was based on a power and oil revenue sharing agreement between the Northern, and new Southern government, to exclusion of the West and East of the country. The exclusion of Darfur in the West from the benefits of oil revenues was one of the factors which prompted rebels to attack the government troops there in 2003 (El-Tom, 2005).

Often only negligible proportions of oil revenue are reinvested in source areas, which have to bear the negative environmental consequences of oil flaring and spills. For example, despite producing massive oil wealth, Ogoniland, in Nigeria, has no water or electricity infrastructure (Harrison, 2002). These conditions may generate local resistance movements MOSOP. The suppression of MOSOP and the execution of its leaders in the early 1990s led to the development of violent movements, such as the Niger Delta People's Volunteer Force, which have recently succeeded in reducing Nigeria's oil output by half, pushing global oil prices higher (Seager and Macalister, 2004; Watts, 2004). Unless it is well managed, oil investment may thus lead to further conflict between state and society and a crisis of national development (see Auty [2001] on managing resource booms), and in turn discourage other forms of FDI.

September 11 and development strategy

According to Kidane Mengisteab (2002, p. 189):

> African countries are caught in a seemingly impossible vicious circle. State building in this era requires democratization and internal economic integration. Democratization and internal economic integration, in turn, depend on state building. The task of breaking this vicious circle is indeed daunting.

This suggests that responses to Africa's problems must be multiscalar; internal and external. President Bush has expressed the opinion that free trade fights terrorism as it promotes widespread prosperity (Sandbrook, 2003) and that its promotion is a 'moral imperative.' Nonetheless he has pressed forward with a neoliberal agenda internationally, but a protectionist one domestically. Unlike the International Financing Facility, proposed by Britain's Chancellor of the Exchequer, Gordon Brown, the US Millennium Challenge Account (MCA) is a unilateral aid initiative, with its own management structure, independent of USAID (Owusu, 2004). Drawing on World Bank theory which suggests aid should be concentrated on those countries which are already 'well governed' and will use it efficiently the MCA represents a shift to 'pre-emptive development' (Soederberg, 2004).

The MCA has been well received among NGDOs in the US with the former President and CEO of InterAction, the alliance of US international development and humanitarian organizations, noting that it 'targets a limited number of high performing countries . . . [and that this was] free of political and security imperatives' (McClymont, 2005). She also argued that the fact that there were four seats on the board of the Millennium Challenge Fund, which administers the MCA, for NGOs was 'good news for us.'

The challenge is arguably for developing countries to gain access to the account, given the strict conditions attached to it, despite it being touted by President Bush as 'a new global compact' for global development (Carbone, 2004). Madagascar became the first country to receive a disbursement from it, in April 2005 (*The Economist*, 2005d). Several other compacts were subsequently concluded (Mawdsley, 2005). However, in each of the bilateral compacts so far approved export agribusiness receives heavy emphasis, and no welfare/poverty-reduction mechanisms are included.

Nonetheless, through political conditionality, Washington may be seeking an expanded 'democratic peace' on the basis that democracies, by allowing for dissent, do not foster terrorism. The bilateralism and high level of surveillance of the MCA, and its break with the emergent global aid regime of 'common pooling' and donor coordination, could be seen as an attempt by Washington to rebuild its network of patron–client ties, which had been allowed to ossify with the end of the Cold War. It is now left to the World Bank to reengage with 'fragile' (failing) states through the Low Income Country under Stress Program, designed in 2002 (World Bank, 2005b).[23]

It remains to be seen how securitization will affect development strategies more generally in Africa and in particular the new metathemes of 'participation' and partnership.[24] The appointment of Paul Wolfowitz, formerly US Deputy Secretary of Defense, as President of the World Bank, in line with other rounds of securitization of development policy after the Second World War and during the Cold War, is bound to bring US security concerns to the fore in that institution (Mallaby, 2005). It may reinforce the emerging trend in development research and policy toward greater emphasis on the state.

Bread (or at least health and education) for the (pre)quiescent masses is the flip-side of force for the resistant. The formula of poor relief and riot control is being reworked to fit new circumstances. Development for Africa humanizes the 'war-on-terror,' which home delivers democracy with daisy cutters (Sparke, 2004). It was in October 2001 that Tony Blair spoke of Africa as 'a scar on the conscience of the world' (quoted in Monbiot, 2003). However, competing budgetary demands, such as the wars in Afghanistan and Iraq resulted in the recent closure of several British diplomatic missions in Africa (Vines and Cargill, 2006).

The necessity of, yet greater, trade liberalization is also justified in reference to Africa's needs, although even of World Bank figures Africa suffered huge losses through the abolition of preferences under the Lome Convention and the adoption of the Cotonou Agreement which is WTO conforming. To some extent this has been compensated for by the EU's 'Everything But Arms' Initiative and the US African Growth and Opportunity Act.

There has been a marked shift on the part of some donors, particularly the United Kingdom and the World Bank, toward direct budgetary support of African governments, with roughly a third of Bank support now taking this form (Interview with development-assistance official, Addis Ababa, September 11, 2004; Murphy, 2005). By strengthening the state, this aid modality may dovetail with the new security agenda. USAID is investigating the potential of budget support (USAID, 2004), although its impact on poverty may be limited (Unwin, 2004). USAID found that 70 percent of aid to Mozambique went to the Maputo region, the richest in the country. Thus direct budget support, may, somewhat ironically revive 'urban bias.'

The state retraction phase of neoliberalism has now passed its high watermark. According to Chang (2003), extensive state intervention to correct for pervasive market failures and externalities is permissible within the neoclassical framework (but not in the Austrian-Libertarian tradition).[25] As Ben Fine (2001) notes, the PWC seeks an alternative in where state intervention is deeper and wider. This opens up space for somewhat more interventionist domestic economic policy regimes.[26]

Africa and America: accelerating, reversing or transforming globalization?

The responses to the attacks of September 11 are altering globalization. States are imbricated in many networks, other than those associated with security, with African leaders now regularly appearing at

G8 summits, for example. A strong statist shift has occurred in American policy (Gallagher, 2003) and reinforced the development of the transnational state, with a greater hard security focus world-wide. William Robinson (2002, p. 215) defines the transnational state as 'an emerging network that comprises transformed and externally integrated national states, together with the supranational economic and political forums and that has not yet acquired any centralized institutional form.' Thus empire has assumed a new network form involving states, transnational corporations and NGOs (Hardt and Negri, 2000).[27] Arguably the contradictions in the new structure of empire have given rise the imperative of direct, unilateral military power projection by the United States. As Bob Jessop (2002) notes, other priorities can override the imperative of capital accumulation, such as national security. The limits of this transnational state in effectively addressing security in African-American relations are important issues, as America's commercial and security interests can prosper only in a context in which global poverty is effectively addressed (Malloch-Brown, 2001).

Megaterrorism, or terrorism of such a scale that it is difficult to dis-tinguish from war (Falk, 2003), poses a structural challenge, which can be met effectively only by dealing with the sources of conflict, includ-ing poverty. Excessive military expenditure will reduce US economic competitiveness. From record surpluses, the US budget deficit from 2005 to 2014 is now projected to be $1,900bn (Congressional Budget Office cited in Swann, 2004). While the proportion of US GDP spent on the military is still less than during the Cold War, in the medium-term Paul Kennedy's (1988) thesis about the decline of great powers may yet be proven right for the US as it engages in military overstretch.[28] In 2002, US defense spending was raised by $300bn, almost the size of the economy of the Russian Federation (Chossudovsky, 2002). The US econ-omy has grown on the basis of openness, but it is also slipping in global competitiveness ratings due to increased visa restrictions on students and high-tech workers.[29]

According to Christopher Clapham (2003, p. 6), while conditions conducive to the growth of terrorism are increasing in sub-Saharan Africa, Africa remains unlikely to foster anti-Western terrorism because of the absence of an 'alternative indigenous vision of the future, of the kind that is provided by radical Islam in parts of the Arab world.'[30] Nonetheless the US state, partly because of its reliance on African oil, should be concerned about conditions – Islamic fundamentalism in Africa,[31] 'failed states' and lack of effective territorial control – that can provide high quality operating conditions for transnational terrorists. From a position of 'enlightened self-interest,' what is the appropriate response to this?

In the aftermath of September 11, Stephen Morrison (2001) argued that existing initiatives by the US should be 'brought to scale':

> That will mean overt, strong U.S. diplomatic leadership to support the New Africa Initiative [NAI]. It will also mean deepening and broadening the trade and investment opportunities of the Africa Growth and Opportunity Act (AGOA); increasing debt relief and facilities through the IMF and World Bank; steadily enlarging U.S. commitments to battle HIV/AIDS, so that they surpass $1 billion within a year, and otherwise doubling bilateral assistance in support of economic growth, conflict reconciliation and rule of law. It means elaborating a serious energy strategy for Africa that focuses upon building management capacity, transparency and accountability, power generation and regional integration of energy grids. It is less important, post-September 11, that the United States embarks on wholly new initiatives than that it protect and bring to scale existing policy priorities that require substantially higher commitments to be effective, and to earn credibility and leverage in Africa.

It is interesting that the NAI got its new, less autocentric, name, NEPAD a month after 9/11 in October 2001 at the meeting of the implementation committee in Abuja (African Development Bank, 2003). However, because of the severity and depth of the problems, bringing existing initiatives to scale is unlikely to accomplish its goal of achieving hard security for the US, through better human security in Africa.[32] The unilateralism, nature and small-scale, relative to need, of the new MCA and PEPFAR will not address these problems.

Glickman (2003) argues that African states need to adopt a 'maximalist-realist' position in relation to the United States where they extract concessions on aid and trade in return for oil, strategic location and information. In particular, he argues that the Economic Support Funds (a type of budget support that accompanies military aid) should be directed in good part to trade skills and technical training. He also argues for foregrounding human rights by the US compensating the victims of al-Qaeda attacks in Africa with seized funds. In contrast, Peter Uvin (1998) argues that development aid is symbiotic with exclusion and structural violence, and therefore debt relief may be preferable to aid (Bond, 2001b). However, there is a need to go further than debt relief, because some of its benefits may be appropriated by corrupt political elites, inappropriate conditions have been attached to it (Storey, 2005), and debt is programmed into the structure of most African economies by virtue of their specialization in exporting low-value-added agricultural products (Lewis, 1985).

African state leaders should be pragmatic in their dealings with the US (Owusu, 2003) and take advantage of any new space for more nationally oriented accumulation strategies (Chang and Grabel, 2004). Political stability is in part dependent on the *effective* implementation of heterodox alternatives and dealing with the HIV/AIDS crisis, which has increased the numbers of people living in poverty in some African countries by up to 5 percent (Sandbrook and Romano, 2004; Amoako, 2004). However, the ending of global network war will require the actualization of new conceptions of security, and deepening US engagement with Africa and other parts of the developing world.

States in general serve three functions: to promote accumulation, to establish security and ensure legitimation. The US state has promoted global accumulation, and its multinationals have moved back up the rankings of the largest companies in the world (*Financial Times*, 1999, cited in Petras and Veltmeyer, 2001).[33] Before September 11, 2001, given dramatic reductions in aid, the necessity of greater economic engagement with Africa was recognized by the OECD through AGOA and the EU 'Everything But Arms' Initiative (both of which are market driven, in contrast to the Lome Conventions, as they must be WTO compatible). However, there is a danger inherent in the free trade agenda as noted in the Focke Report on the Lome Conventions in 1980 as 'the rule of free trade is meaningless for countries which at the present stage of their production structures, have practically nothing to export to the Community' (Focke Report, 1980, p. 14, cited in Holland, 2002, p. 39).

The US is becoming more economically linked with Africa through AGOA. AGOA has also changed production structures in parts of Africa, to some degree, by attracting some new FDI from Asia (Gibbon, 2003).[34] For example, exports of textiles from Madagascar more than doubled from the first six months of 2000 to the same period in 2001.[35] Some estimates suggest that 200,000 new jobs were created in Africa between 2000 and 2002 because of AGOA (Versi, 2003, cited in Adebayo, 2003b).[36] However, the act has not been that favorable for Africa. In 2001, the first full year of AGOA, exports from sub-Saharan Africa to the US actually declined, and 83 percent of eligible exports are in the energy sector, largely accounted for by Nigerian oil (African Development Bank, 2003, p. 197). However, exports from the US to Africa increased, partly as a result of US textile content requirements for clothing, for some more developed African countries (Tabb, 2001).

From 2002 to 2004, exports to the United States from Africa under AGOA almost doubled, partly because Angola, and its oil, became AGOA-eligible (Trade Law Center for Southern Africa, 2005). However, the previous benefits for African textile and clothing industries are likely to be short-lived as a result of the phasing out of the Multi-Fiber Arrangement, which permitted importers to impose quotas, in 2005 (Thompson, 2004). In January 2005, Chinese textile exports to the United States were 75 percent higher than they had been in the previous month (*Newsweek*, 2005). While restrictions on the 'import surge' from China have been negotiated with the EU and the US, these will expire in the next few years. Nonetheless, the US now trades more with Africa than with the former Soviet Union and Eastern Europe combined (African Development Bank, 2003).

The internationalization of the US state has also proceeded apace along the security dimension, with invasions of Afghanistan and Iraq, and new military cooperation agreements signed with many countries around the world. However, the fact that the US is concerned with its own, rather than African, security is evidenced by the fact that it deployed only 200 troops to Liberia (for two months) in 2003, in contrast to its operations in Iraq, where there are 140,000 troops (Adebayo, 2003b).[37] With the US military stretched in Afghanistan and Iraq, the implicit division of labor is that the Europeans and the United Nations will handle peacekeeping and humanitarian assistance elsewhere (de Waal and Abdel Salam, 2004). However, some branches of the US government, particularly the CIA, understand that security is multidimensional and interlinked (Sachs, 2002). The United States should step-up active support for conflict resolution, and particularly prevention in Africa. One estimate suggests that it would have cost US $1.5bn to prevent the outbreak of conflict in Somalia versus the US $7.3bn it cost to respond to it (Commission for Africa, 2005). This does not include the costs in lives and money to the people of Somalia themselves. American and European governments should not remain inactive, as they did during the Rwandan genocide (Power, 2003).[38]

Conflict resolution is a prerequisite for socioeconomic development in countries affected by conflict (Stewart, 2000). Co-regulationist agreements such as the Kimberly Process Certification Scheme, which brought together NGOs, business, governments and international organizations, may also have an important role to play in conflict reduction (Böge *et al.*, 2006). Gavin Kitching (2001) also suggests that peace keeping should not be left to the vagaries of US presidential politics but that there should be a permanent standing strong global peace keeping force, with a transnational basis of funding.[39] Some argue that another genocide is under way in Darfur, Sudan, although there has been success in ending wars in the Congo, Burundi, Sierra Leone, Liberia, among others (Frazer, 2006).

It is at the level of legitimation that the internationalization of the US state is at its weakest. Humanity faces multiple interlinked threats. These take the forms of hunger, disease, terrorism and war. All of these result from power asymmetries and contestation over these (Sen, 1999).[40] 'The key world order problem for the future might be said to involve the creation of a peaceful and tolerant co-existence between differentiated forms of civilization, in ways that provide material and political conditions of high quality' (Gill, 2003, p. 142). This solution can be achieved through the 'operationalization' of human security, which the United Nations Development Program defines as referring 'to two mutually reinforcing concepts: (i) safety from such chronic threats as hunger, disease and repression, and (ii) protection from sudden and hurtful disruptions in the patterns of daily life' (Mohamed Salih, 2001, p. 68).[41] There is thus a need for a new holistic international-security regime to rebalance the different 'legs' of globalization.

At the moment the global system is in a condition of dynamic disequilibrium as there is a globalization of both direct and structural forms of violence (Chossudovsky, 1997; Gautney, 2003, Mann, 1999). There is thus a need to transcend fundamentalisms of all types, including market fundamentalism and its societal disembedding effect. In the US, a bipartisan panel report issued in 2003 noted that in the Muslim world 'hostility towards America has reached shocking levels. What is required is not merely tactical adaptation, but strategic and radical transformation' (cited in Nye, 2004, p. 43). Olukoshi (2003) argues that the resolution of the crisis of governance in Africa will depend on the articulation and implementation of a new social compact that is sensitive to the welfare aspirations of the populace. The transformations needed in US relations with Africa depend on a reconceptualization of power to achieve human security, which 'becomes possible if its four pillars—order, justice, peace and economics—coexist in a condition of dynamic equilibrium' (Zacarias, 2003, p. 43). Thus the solution is power sharing and substantial resource redistribution. This may be achieved, in part, through the deployment of the 'gentle art of persuasion' (Cheru, 2002). Giovanni Arrighi has noted a distinction between

> 'distributive' and 'collective' power. The former has the character of a zero-sum game in which competition can improve the position of the hegemon by taking power away from others. . . . But to be truly hegemonic in a global sense entails the use of leadership to create a non-zero-sum game in which all parties benefit, either out of mutual gains from their own interactions (such as trade) or through their enhanced collective power vis-à-vis nature.
>
> (Harvey, 2003, p. 37)

The US state is confronted by three different types of 'globalization from below' (Falk, 2000): by transnational terrorist groups; by a coalition of developing countries seeking better market access in the WTO,[42] with South Africa playing a leading, and sometimes contradictory, role; and by the global social justice movement. In order to be sustainable, globalization, as it is being currently constituted, needs to be reconfigured. 'In the search for a new spatial-institutional fix, neoliberals risk depriving themselves of an Archimedean point from which to coordinate the different scales of economic, social and political actions and to develop compensatory and flanking measures on other scales in response to changes pursued on other levels' (Jessop, 2002, p. 171).

There should be a synthesis of corporate 'globalization from above' with the latter two 'globalizations from below': with developing countries being given better market access for their products,[43] and that the social dimension of globalization should be strengthened if the project is to succeed in being legitimated.[44] This has important implications for US foreign policy.

While the urge to help among international leaders is undoubtedly genuine (see for example Brown, 2004), it also serves a variety of instrumental functions. The proposed IFF represents an attempt to indirectly renovate the productive base of African economies through investment in health and education. This combined with debt relief is meant to establish a new 'virtuous circle' of development in Africa and reduce 'negative externalities' for the international system, such as terrorism. However, debt is a feature of the global political economy because of both the programming of unequal trade, and consequently debt, into Africa's political economy as a result of colonialism, and because of the tendency of the global market system to produce excess capital which must then be on-lent, thereby providing a 'temporal fix' for the global economic system.[45] The IFF is based on debt, although this time to be taken out by developed country governments and secured against future aid budgets. But it represents a gamble that the rates of return on its initial investments will outstrip interest payments in the future. However, there is some cause for skepticism of future 'indebted development' models, given previous experience.[46]

Christopher Chase Dunn (1998) has argued for a global state to undertake global legitimation, whereas Deacon *et al.* (1997) argue for a more limited 'international welfare state.' Others have argued for the globalization of social democracy and the development of a cosmopolitan social identity to facilitate this global transformation. (Mittelman, 2000; Held and McGrew, 2002). The United Nations is the obvious vehicle from which to launch the extension of global legitimation. It could be strengthened through the development of a Human Security Council (Held and McGrew, 2002), and better funding and more enforcement power for elements of the UN system such as UNCTAD and the International Labor Organization (Bello, 2002).

The UN MDGs, which are a mild form of a new rights-based constitutionalism, aim to reduce the number of people living in extreme poverty by half by 2015. In Africa, on current trends, the number of people living in absolute poverty (less than US $1 a day) is projected to increase by 30 percent by 2015 (African Development Bank, 2003, p. 34).[47] Even if it were fully funded, the Millennium Development project's approach reflects a somewhat static view of poverty, which does not adequately address the structural nature of poverty (see Sachs and McArthur, 2005). Peter Uvin (1998) argues that development aid is symbiotic with exclusion and structural violence, thus debt relief may be preferable to aid (Bond, 2001b). However, there is a need to go further than debt relief to utilize new socioeconomic policy innovations.

In sub-Saharan Africa and South Asia, social security personal coverage is estimated at only 5 to 10 percent of the working population (ILO, 2001). Recent World Bank studies have underscored the importance of social security in poverty reduction strategies (Christiaensen *et al.*, 2002). Development is about resource creation and redistribution, not just voice and 'participation,' although these are also important. There is a need to create 'win–win' games. The reconstruction of collective power will require a speeding up of debt relief and the introduction of new social policy innovations.[48] Better human security would reduce the necessity of US military expenditure and free up resources from the military in African countries for the social sector.[49]

On current trends, 23 African countries will not meet any of the eight MDGs by 2015 (Commission for Africa, 2004). One way to ensure the delivery of the MDGs in Africa would be through the development of basic incomes or minimum income guarantees.[50] One way to achieve this would be through employment guarantee schemes, like that in Maharashtra in India, combined with targeted welfare payments for those not able to participate in the labor-force (Joshi and Moore, 2001). Public works programs could include road construction using labor-intensive methods, such as in the Kenya Rural Access Roads Programme (James, 2002). Ethiopia has recently introduced a program like this, with the support of donors (UN-IRIN, 2005a). Although the disadvantage of a public works program relative to a basic income grant is that typically 40–50 percent of resources are absorbed by administration (Nattrass, 2004).

Improved infrastructure would also facilitate tourism and foreign investment and the development of indigenous wage-goods industries, and attract back Africa's masses of 'flight capital,' estimated to be up to 40 percent of the continent's wealth.[51] The most recent *World Development Report* (World Bank, 2004b) found that institutional factors and infrastructure are more important than the economic policy regime in determining economic performance.

It has been estimated that in Southern Africa, 33 foreign tourists create one job opportunity directly and two indirectly (Tourism South Africa, 1999, cited in Jordan, 2001). However tourism does not exist in isolation. Political and social stability are important in creating an environment in which tourist arrivals and stays can increase. This suggests the importance of paying attention to the productive sectors of the economy.

While foreign direct investment to Africa is minimal, it has very high profit rates of up to 25 percent (Keet, 1998, cited in Thompson, 2000). Higher profit rates are required by investors to offset the risks associated with political and economic instability on the continent. Investment is also crucially needed in the manufacturing sector. Such a program would also accord with the IMF's 'social liberal' approach. Substantial inflows of money for social expenditure, might of course appreciate the real exchange rate, discouraging private sector exports. This suggests the necessity of a non-market determined exchange rate regime.

The economic policy regime in African countries must be informed by justice. George de Martino (2000, p. 144) defines an economic policy regime as just 'if and to the degree that it promotes harmonization of capabilities to achieve functionings at a level that is sufficient, universally attainable and sustainable.' Nederveen Pieterse (2001, p. 57) claims that: 'at present levels of technology, industrialization without foreign investment has become unrealistic: the cost and quality differential between domestic and end products has become too great.' However, foreign investment need not be unconditional. This will require that multilateral economic organizations, such as the WTO expand, rather than contract, 'special and differential treatment' for developing countries (Wade, 2004). It is possible for African governments working collectively to influence trade agreements, for example. The shift toward outcome-based conditionality on the part of the UK offers potential as the UK government 'will not make our aid conditional on specific policy decisions by partner governments, or attempt to impose policy choices on them (including in sensitive economic areas such as privatization or trade liberalization)' (Department for International Development and Her Majesty's Treasury, 2005, cited in Wood, 2005, p. 5). As the Commission for Africa (2005) rightly notes, if African governments are to be accountable to their people they must have control over economic policy.

Previous aid approaches have undermined efficiency and democracy by emphasizing external accountability (Leonard and Strauss, 2003). However, a reprioritization of aid toward social protection, combined with opportunities for recipient publics to influence aid allocations and monitor outcomes substantively would strengthen democracy (de Waal, 2004). Better human security would help relegitimate African states, and free up resources from the military for the social sector. In Angola in the early 1990s, for example, the military consumed 20 percent of GDP (Willett, 1998). With societal cooperation, African states could thereby attend to their 'hard' (police and military) security functions and rebuild their capacity, which is essential for sustained development (Leftwich, 2000).

This might be also quite cost-effective for the US and the EU as it was estimated that even prior to September 11 it would only take 12 percent of global military spending to eliminate severe malnutrition, reduce moderate malnutrition by half, and provide safe drinking water and primary health care for all (UNDP, 1994, cited in Pick, 1999).[52] The US now spends $450bn a year on the military, or 43 percent of global military expenditure, but only $15bn on development assistance (Sachs, 2004; SIPRI, 2005).[53] During the Cold War the US Defense Department became the world's single largest organization (Chafe and Sitkoff, 1999, cited in Hanahoe, 2003). However, the United States is unlikely to cut its military budget back in the short term, given the current priority attached to its 'hard' security needs. Thus other funding modalities, based on the actualization of human rights, are required.

The head of the IMF's Department of Fiscal Affairs has called for a world taxing authority (Tanzi, 1999). The most politically feasible way of raising substantial revenue for global development—the so-called 'Landau proposals,' recently mooted by the French government—would be a value-added tax on the 3bn airplane tickets sold yearly, or on airplane fuel (Deacon *et al.*, 1997). The French government has recently introduced this 'solidarity tax' on airplane tickets to raise money for international development. If it were to become generalized, it would raise substantial funds, thereby linking immanent with imminent development. It would mean that the technology of corporate globalization was being used to enhance, rather than undermine equity, thereby contributing to security.

The introduction of a basic or minimum income guarantee by the developed countries would thus be funded in a way which would impose minimal costs on the global economy, be distributively just by taxing upper income groups, have environmental benefits and be cost effective. The synthesis of globalization from above and below would result in a global system of flexible labor markets and social security systems ('flexicurity') (Kongshøj Madsen, n.d). Such a programme would also accord well with Islamic social values (Kamal Pasha and Samatar, 1998). However, the US should take the lead in having the EU and Japan 'burden share' the costs of a reformed NEPAD, as it will have the most to gain from it. NEPAD, in turn, should incorporate minimum income guarantees. The danger in all of this is that revenues raised globally would be diverted into pervasive neopatrimonial networks in Africa (Taylor, 2005b). Some accountability mechanisms are already in place, but this is where (civil) society can indeed play a critical monitoring role and decision-making role, through participatory budgeting mechanisms pioneered in Porto Alegre, Brazil, although this is not a panacea as it has failed in other Brazilian cities (Center for the Future State, 2005). Another innovation that might be replicated is the Law of Popular Participation in Bolivia through which fiscal responsibility and resources were devolved to municipal level. Oversight of this was given to local communities, with NGOs providing training in techniques such as participatory needs assessment (Narayan, 2002).

This program would create a win–win game, whereby the hard security of the United States is achieved through better human security in Africa.

The danger is that a hard security response to September 11 brings short-term returns more in line with the American electoral cycle (a political military cycle), whereas social investment only brings security benefits in the longer-term. Short-term military gains, however, as this paper has demonstrated, may be at the expense of longer-term security.

Conclusion

The African Union notes that security is interdependent and multidimensional (Kwasi Tieku, 2004). There is increasing recognition of this internationally (Stedman, 2004), and the empirical linking of different aspects of security is a logical outcome of increased interdependence, or globalization.

The United States now faces unprecedented threats to its national security in the form of megaterrorism. The proliferation of weapons of mass destruction, from box cutters and planes, to nuclear 'dirty bombs,' rightly cause its policymakers concern. The question is how to respond most effectively to these challenges. The 'silent violence' of malnutrition and preventable diseases are massive failures of entitlements and human rights (Watts, 1983), which compromise African state effectiveness, and ultimately US economic and military security. As this book has argued, it is in the medium- and long-term interest of the United States to reverse this situation.

As the Second World War drew to a close, the vision of the US and British delegations at the Bretton Woods Conference enabled a progressive global economic-policy regime to be put in place, a regime that facilitated unprecedented, and globally shared, economic growth (Panić, 1995). When President Nixon broke the dollar's link to gold in 1971 he said there 'was a need for fair competition in the world and the fact that we need to compete' (R. Nixon quoted in *Orebody*, 1971, p. 7). As it was put at the time, the US had shared its prosperity with the world; it would now share its problems. The problem was that many African economies were not at the starting blocks to compete fairly and that they were hampered from doing so by domestic protectionism in the US and other developed country markets. This pattern of protectionism at home and free trade abroad has been reinforced since September 11. However, there is a need for wider global prosperity, as the formula developed under President Clinton in the US of 'humanitarianism abroad, prosperity at home' is no longer tenable (Clinton, 2005b).

Objective economic conditions have changed since the time of the Bretton Woods agreement, and the economically unipolar world of the postwar era has been replaced by economic multipolarity. Consequently, the United States can no longer, by itself, underwrite a new global socioeconomic compact. Nonetheless, more than 30 years after the breakdown of the Bretton Woods system, a new grand vision, beyond neoliberalism and war, is called for. The United States is having cosmopolitanism forced upon it. Patriotism, in part reawakened by the attack of September 11, 2001, will require long-term global social investments and greater freedom for developing countries in their economic policies.[54] As the late George F. Kennan (1947, p. 582) put it after the Second World War, American security depends on the American people's 'pulling themselves together and accepting the responsibility of . . . political leadership.'

Notes

Introduction

1. Although the extent of marginalization should not be over-stated. See Shaw (2000) and Grant (2002).
2. Context is again important here. Where state cut-backs undermined patronage networks this fed conflict (See Reno, 1998). On the other hand where state collapse preceded national neoliberalism and the 'trough factor,' where it was difficult for things to get worse, came into play, as in Ghana or Uganda in the 1980s, or Mozambique in the 1990s this has not been the case. In these cases, when combined with substantial aid, neoliberalism has been coincident with state reconstruction and strengthening (Callaghy, 1990).
3. Defined as 'the rapid reinstatement of state power and sovereign control in the face of a traumatic challenge to the state's monopolization' of violence (Edkins, 2002, p. 243).
4. Again as noted earlier context is important here. In postconflict societies coming off a desperately low base, with substantial aid, neoliberal economic reform may have resulted in economic stabilization. Its impacts in more developed countries in Africa, as will be discussed later, has often been deindustrializing and destabilizing.
5. The best and most thorough account is Taylor (2005b).

1 The Rise of Non-Governmental Organizations and the Civilization of Neoliberalism?

1. This term has different definitions. For Ha-Joon Chang (2003) it is a marriage of convenience between neoclassical economics and the Austrian Libertarian tradition. Others have noted, however, that neoliberal economics is distinct from neoclassical economics because of the revival of the 19th-century bankers' emphasis on 'sound money' in the former (Nederveen Pieterse, 2001). For Björn Beckman (1993) what is 'neo' is the emphasis on state retraction, which distinguishes it from other liberal development strategies such as those inspired by modernization theory. Neoliberalism represents '(a) good householding (don't spend more than you earn), (b) technical expertise, (c) a theoretical legacy, (d) an ideological mindset and (e) an interest coalition' (Nederveen Pieterse, 2001, p. 165).
2. Harriss (2002, p. 17) notes a problem with methodological individualism, which is that its frame of reference is tautological: 'interests are what people appear to be trying to maximise.'
3. On the landless movement see Kingsnorth (2003).
4. He sees two main global social movements: those for and against social protection.
5. For an excellent review of this see Hanahoe (2003).

6. This proposition of course depends on one's definition of civil society.
7. NGOs are not associational and as such could be excluded from definitions of civil society. Some, often called 'gap-fillers,' might better be conceived as 'not-for-profit businesses/charities.' Some refer to this as the 'third sector.'
8. However, NGDOs have also developed monitoring and evaluation techniques from which the public sector can learn (Fowler, 2002).
9. There are different definitions of what constitutes a discourse. For some it is a linked set of language and actions. For others they are inter-linked sets of ideas with an internal coherence. For Hilhorst (2003, p. 11), 'discourses are both the medium and outcome of the practices they organize.'
10. Hidden transcripts are 'speeches, gestures, and practices of sub-ordinate people that confirm, contradict, or inflect what appears in open interactions between subordinates and superiors' (Scott, 1990, p. 4).

2. Civil Society, Governance and Transformation

1. For a discussion of the World Bank's and others changing political analysis see Leftwich (2005).
2. The individual integrity of board members in Cameroon is not in question with some NGO members saying they will resign if there is any impropriety with funds (*National Geographic*, 2005). *National Geographic* notes that the members of the *Collège du Contrôlle* in Chad are some of the most powerful people in the country. However, they are unelected.
3. The AIDS crisis has recently undermined Botswana's achievements, although a comprehensive anti-retroviral treatment program has recently been rolled out with the support of the Global Alliance for Vaccines and Immunizations.
4. The World Development reports do not officially represent corporate World Bank positions, but in practice guide it.
5. The traditional definition of this is dominance; whereas Gramsci saw it as coercion informed by consent (Marais, 1998).
6. For an excellent discussion on the need for NGOs to improve their economic and political analysis see Lockwood (2005).
7. The US also funds government economic research through the Support for Economic Growth Analysis (SEGA) administered by Nathan Associates, in which the current author participated. The research analysis to be undertaken is decided by the South African ministries in this however.
8. On Botswana see Iliffe (1983) and Samatar (1999).
9. A fuller list of major investment projects in Mozambique is available at www.dfat.gov.au/geo/mozambique. Accessed 12 July 2004.
10. In Mozambique, the International Monetary Fund (IMF) blocked rebuilding of schools and hospitals as this would create 'excessive demand' in the economy. It has recently blocked hiring of HIV/AIDS workers for the same reason.
11. For more detail see Chaplin and Mathews (2005). The compensation being offered is minimal, compared to the losses that will be incurred.
12. Such as World Bank (2002a) *Ethiopia: The Woreda Studies* which was in part funded by Action Aid.

3 The Theory of Civil Society in Poverty Reduction or the Social Capitalization of Neoliberalism

1. Default rates for these are between 0.1 percent and 2.5 percent in Tanzania, versus 80 percent for commercial banks (Aryeetey *et al.*, 1997, cited in Mari Tripp, 2003).
2. Kanbur (2005) identifies SEWA as pragmatic and postideological, with one of their best known pamphlets entitled 'Liberalizing for the Poor' ('Economic Policy').
3. The previous political economy of reform had suggested that these constituencies (trade unions, protected businesses) could be bought off through side-payments in the forms of social funds for retrenched workers, for example. However, it is now thought that more extensive social engineering is needed to 'lock in' and deepen reform.
4. This is based on a study of 30 African countries by Ndikumana and Boyce (2002, cited in Taylor, 2005a). Some estimates put the figure much higher at $700–800bn, with possibly $300bn of this coming from Nigerian oil revenue alone (Mistry, 2005).
5. 'Communitarians . . . believe in private ownership but nevertheless stress the need for cooperation among neighbors and a greater degree of caring and sharing among community members' (Midgley, 1998, p. 91). Its most well-known current proponent is Amitai Etzioni.
6. The Johns Hopkins Center for the Study of Civil Society has been at the forefront of 'third sector' research (Howell and Pearce, 2001). An alternative perspective, that nonetheless presents itself as postideological is that put forward by Schumann (1998).
7. However, social cohesion is enforced not only by trust and reciprocity, but also force.
8. Government expenditure in the OECD rose from under 30 percent of GDP in 1960 to nearly 50 percent in 1995 (OECD 1998, cited in Deacon, 2000, p. viii).
9. See de Soto (1989 and 2001) on how the poor may be integrated into the market through their own production. In the context of saturated global markets there is now interest among TNCs on how to sell to the 'bottom of the pyramid' through selling individualized products, rather than packets, for example. This may reduce the scope of the informal economy.
10. They also distinguish a type of binding social capital as between ethnic groups in Tanzania, which is nonetheless not civic.
11. Others translate it as those who attack together. Robert Putnam (1994) recognizes this problem when there is bonding but not bridging social capital.
12. Vertical corruption is aid, bribes, tax and natural resource revenues going to elites, whereas horizontal corruption refers to day-to-day corruption among police, civil servants, etc. (de Sardan, 1999).
13. Karl Polanyi (1957) might refer to trust as a fictitious commodity as it cannot be produced solely by market mechanisms.
14. See G. Parayil (1996) for a balanced assessment.
15. Conceived in the narrow sense of parties, government and state, rather than as including civil society.

16. Peter Evans (1996b, p. 1122) argues that synergy is where 'active government and mobilized communities can enhance each others' development efforts.' Sometimes this is called 'interactive policy-making.'
17. Some World Bank staff are favorable toward co-production, however (see Narayan, 2002).
18. The experience of water privatization in Tanzania has also been disastrous and has had to be recently reversed. Water privatization has been associated with outbreaks of cholera in South Africa.
19. For more detail see Globalization Challenge Initiative (2002).

4   Participatory Poverty: Poverty Re(pro)duction Strategy Papers

1. This phrase is from George Stephanopoulis, President Clinton's former advisor, on American television at the time.
2. Some World Bank economists have launched a vigorous defense of the primary importance of economic growth, however, claiming that the poor benefit equally from economic growth (See Dollar and Kraay, 2005). However, this is dependent on the structure of the economy. The Statistics office of Zimbabwe found that the poverty elasticity for that country in the first half of the 1990s was –0.477; meaning that poverty only reduced by this percentage for every 1 percent of economic growth (cited in World Bank, 2004c). Dollar and Kraay (2005) also found that democratic institutions or public expenditure on health and education do not have systematic effects on the incomes of the poor.
3. This is not without contradictions, however. Despite talking of 'cores' and 'peripheries,' exploitation of the third world and acknowledging that neo-classical trade models are wrong, unmediated integration into the global market is still presented as the best policy option (Sachs, 2003, 2005).
4. Ironically, given its poverty, Madagascar plays an important role in the curative cancer treatment as Eli Lilly has developed an anticancer drug from the rosy periwinkle found in its tropical rainforests. Madagascar has 'not received "as much as a penny of compensation for the expropriation of one of its natural resources."' (Rifkin, 1999, cited in Campbell, 2003, p. 150).
5. In West Bengal the ruling Communist party has banned strikes to attract investment, drawing inspiration from China's model where trade unions are banned (*The Economist*, 2004e). Whether such strategies represent an accommodation to capitalism or a transition to capitalism is open to debate (see Schweickart, 1999).
6. Under HIPC, debt reduction can be up to 80 percent in present value terms (Obadan, 2004). African external debt as a percentage of exports will have fallen from roughly 240 percent in 1998 to 110 percent by 2005 and the debt service ratio from roughly 23 percent to 10 percent (IMF, cited in *The Economist*, 2004c). Although some claim that the initiative will only write off $19bn of the $230bn owed by Africa (Anon., 2004a). More recently 100 percent debt relief was announced for 18 low-income countries, mostly in Africa. However, many conditions attach to this.
7. CIVICUS and USAID have both developed indices to measure the 'health of civil society' (Howell and Pearce, 2001).

8. The proportion of people in Uganda living below the poverty line fell from 56 to 35 percent from 1992 to 2000 (Craig and Porter, 2002). This may be due to the nature of economic policies, the massive extent of external funding and an economic 'trough factor,' facilitating a rebound (on the political trough factor see T. Callaghy, 1990). The poverty rate may also not reflect the availability of public services.

9. Defined as 'those instances in which "interventions or events throw up new opportunities, reconfiguring relationships between actors within these spaces, or bringing in new actors, and opening the possibility of a shift in direction"' (Grindle and Thomas, 1991, cited in Brock *et al.*, 2001, cited in McGee, 2002a, pp. 190–191).

10. 'Populist ideology claims that the best society is one in which an ambiguously defined entity, the people, is accorded primary importance' (Midgley, 1998, p. 90).

11. To undertake unpopular neoliberal economic management 'efficiently.'

12. For the most comprehensive statement of this position see N. van de Walle (2001).

13. Defined as liberalism modified in the interests of domestic stability (Ruggie, 1983).

14. This is an adaptation of the idea of a 'lump of labor fallacy' which posits that there is a set amount of work to be done in a society. Likewise there is not a given amount of poverty to be created or distributed.

15. I am grateful to Diana Mitlin for this point.

16. Camdessus is now head of the private sector civil society group promoting water privatization, the World Water Council (*Africa Confidential*, 2005b).

17. Privatization conditions are often attached to World Bank Poverty Reduction Support Credits, despite the Bank's recognition these are often in direct conflict with public opinion and parliamentary motions (Wood, 2005).

18. A. Fowler (1993, cited in Hulme and Edwards, 1997a, p. 366) defines this as the 'organic link between the state and citizens,' which he sees as missing in much of sub-Saharan Africa.

19. This group includes 'many economic analysts, economic policy managers and operational managers in the IFIs and the Regional Multilateral Banks' and the financial press. In civil society he includes those working in NGOs, some of the UN specialized agencies, aid ministries in the North and social sector ministries in the South and academic noneconomists (Kanbur, 2005). A better description of the first category might be global financial capital.

20. The Berg Report makes such an argument (World Bank, 1981).

21. A recent assessment concludes: 'government interpretations of participation are typically confined to information-gathering or consultation, with little or no recognition of the right to participate in dialogue on policy decisions affecting the lives of the poor, including macro-economic policies. The latter is an arena from which civil society is almost uniformly excluded' (International Cooperation for Development and Solidarity and Caritas International, 2003, p. 32).

22. While Japan has favored the development of strategic industrial policies these are not included in the new consensus (see B. Fine, 1999). The World Bank does countenance functional industrial policies, for skills and infrastructure

upgrading without 'picking winners' (for a discussion of this see P. Carmody, 2001).

23. It is sometimes forgotten that industrial policy is an important element of social democracy, such as the Rehn–Meidner policy in Sweden, which tied wages in domestic economic sectors to those in the export sector to encourage productivity increases (Weiss, 1998). Arguably in some developing countries, which perform well on social indicators, the productive sector has been taxed without raising productivity, as in the plantation sector in Sri Lanka, thereby undermining the economic base.

24. This echoes earlier critics of structural adjustment (see for example, Mengisteab, 1995).

25. The former administrator of the UNDP, Mark Malloch Brown, characterized the link between the PRSPs and MDGs as a 'big bargain' between developed and developing countries (UNDP, 2003a). The choice of Chile and Mexico as the sites of the new consensus is perhaps not accidental. Both are considered to be success stories of globalization, with Mexico receiving massive US investment, and Chile receiving massive Japanese investment. For a problematization of this 'success' see J. Glassman and P. Carmody (2001).

26. In this sense PRSPs may be net destructive of social capital.

27. For a discussion on the constraints to microenterprise development in Africa see Alila and Pedersen (2001).

28. Oxfam helped the World Bank resecure funding from the US Congress, for example. This argument is in contrast to Stephen Gill's view (2003) that the emergent transnational historic bloc is shallow. While this was true initially, it is now striking deeper roots into society to stabilize itself.

29. Initially this was an Irish charity, but is now 'Concern Worldwide.'

30. Paul Ladd (2003) notes that some PRSPs do deviate from Washington Consensus trade prescriptions, such as Ethiopia's Agricultural Development Led (ADLI) program, which advocates the use of industrial protection with offsetting measures for exporters.

31. The IMF now posts the consultations on these on its website: a form of 'virtual participation?'

32. These have been renamed Poverty Reduction Support Credits but allow extra conditionality to PRSPs through the Letter of Development Policy which accompany them (Stewart and Wang, 2003).

33. Abrahamson (2002, cited in Mercer, 2003) suggests that the same ability to 'rule at a distance' is achieved through 'partnership' in relation to African states.

34. This is the view of the Tanzanian Coalition for Debt and Development and the Feminist Action Coalition in relation to civil society participation in the Tanzanian PRSP (Mercer, 2003).

35. The Utstein group is a group of donors who have agreed to co-ordinate their policies (UK, Holland, Norway, Germany, Sweden and Canada).

5 Remaking African Civil Societies and PRSP in Action: Ethiopia

1. More accurately Euro-American. It is interesting that de Tocqueville was a Frenchman analyzing America, whereas in its more recent incarnation Robert Putnam (an American) examines Italy. As a normative, ideal civil society may

be more visible in foreign contexts. De Tocqueville's study was aimed at Europe, and particularly France (Renshaw, 1998). This feature of civil society may explain Putnam's dehistoricized account (See Harriss, 2002).

2. Between Cadbury and cocoa farmers in the Gold Coast (Ghana), for example (Beckman, 1993).

3. This qualification is necessary to avoid the 'territorial trap' through which social phenomena are viewed through a national lens, in a period of intense globalization (see Corbridge and Agnew, 1995).

4. In Uganda force is often used to extract 'graduated personal taxes' on all adult males and salaried females. There are similarities with colonial hut taxes here. Increased central revenues flows have reduced incentives to collect local taxes, arguably also reducing local officials accountability, and creating 'mini rentier states' (Craig and Porter, 2002).

5. This is something which also applies to contexts outside of Africa. For example, McGee describes how a truant teacher in India was protected by a district-level official. For her, this encapsulated 'the gap between macro-level strategies and ground-level realities in the poverty reduction discourse.' (McGee, 2002b, p. 28).

6. The elections were held off a single party list.

7. Adverse selection arises in a context of information failure. For example, the people most eager to sell their second-hand cars may want to do so because the cars are 'lemons.'

8. In people's minds the two may often be coterminous.

9. A measure of income inequality, where if there is perfectly equal distribution among the population it would be 0 and if all income accrues to one person it would be 1.

10. State capacity is weak however, with only 17 percent of civil servants having a college diploma and above (Gabriel, 2002).

11. The Oromo Liberation Front was initially part of the Transitional Government of Ethiopia, along with the EPRDF and other groups, but left in 1992 (F. Joireman, 1997, cited in Doyle, 2004).

12. Many of the regions do not contain absolute ethnic majorities. The most anomalous example of this is the Harari region whose population is 52 percent Oromo, 33 percent Amhara but only 7 percent Harari (Central Statistics Agency, 1995, cited in Zewdu, 2005). The main political office holders in the region are Harari, however. The 'Southern Nations, Nationalities and Peoples' region has 45 nationalities.

13. Although Abdi Samatar (2005) notes that the establishment of ethnic regions also helped establish a degree of legitimacy for the TPLF, with the regional primary schools able to use their own languages for the first time, for example.

14. He campaigned for EPRDF in the 2005 election and appears to have joint business interests with the American oil company Unocal (Chossudovsky, 2002). According to *Forbes Magazine* (2006) his net worth is $1.5bn. Of that, according to *The Reporter* (*Ethiosports*, n.d.), $1bn is invested in Ethiopia. Much of this derives from his ownership of the 'finest hotel in Africa,' the Addis Ababa Sheraton, which by some estimates cost $400m to build.

15. This was confirmed to me in conversations in Ethiopia.

16. Ethiopia compares well with other low-income countries in sub-Saharan Africa on 'control of corruption' and 'rule of law' in the World Bank's governance indicators (World Bank, 2002b, cited in DCI, 2004).

17. In relation to the application of tariffs, for example (Geda, 2004).

18. In Tanzania one donor drew a distinction between the 'shop-window' talk of good governance and PRSPs, and the 'smoke-filled rooms' where meetings of the ruling party really decided on priorities (Kelsall, 2004, cited in Lockwood, 2005).

19. As predicted the suppression of dissent may be feeding regional instability (BBC News, 2005a).

20. R. Joseph (1999b, p. 63) defines this as a state that allows 'some space for independent civic and political action, while guaranteeing order and protecting the sway of economically dominant groups.' Thus he argues 'good governance' has been diluted to 'acceptable governance.'

21. A study by the German aid agency GTZ in 2002 suggested that *iddrs* have around 39 million members, *equbs* 21 million and 9 million in other self-help groups (Ministry of Capacity Building, 2004).

22. Calculated based on exchange rate in CIA (2002).

23. While Ethiopia is expected to more than meet the MDG for primary education, concerns have been expressed about quality and Abegaz notes a 'secular deterioration' in peasant living standards ('Ethiopia'). This conclusion is supported by other studies (e.g. E. Mebrahtu, 2004).

24. For a fuller discussion see P. Gibbon *et al.* (1993).

25. These include the Poverty Action Network, Civil Society Against Famine in Ethiopia, Consortium of Reproductive Health Association, Initiative Africa, Pastoralists Forum and Sustainable Land Use Forum.

26. I was told one story by a development assistance official about how they had asked the CRDA for comments on a report. The CRDA wanted to hire a consultant to do the commentary, but wanted the donor to pay for it. Eventually the CRDA paid for the consultant, but submitted the comments four months too late, so that they could not be incorporated into the review of programs. Some argue that NGOs need 'to move beyond advocacy to policy analysis' (Interview with United Nations official, Addis Ababa, September 15, 2004).

27. Different organizations have different emphases. The International Monetary Fund (IMF) and International Development Association (IDA) argue that while 'there was a wide-ranging set of consultations in drafting the original PRSP, the participatory process has been slower to take root during implementation, due in part to capacity constraints in both the government and' NGOs (IMF and IDA, 2004, p. 2).

6   The Making of a Zimbabwean Rogue (State): Robert Mugabe, Neoliberalism, Civil Society and NEPAD

1. This included kidnapping and beating opposition members of Parliament and the charging of the opposition presidential candidate Morgan Tsvingarai with treason (*Irish Times*, February 8, 2002).

2. Authoritarian tendencies were in evidence earlier in the suppression of dissent in Matabeleland from 1982 to 1985, and the attempt to move to a one-party state in the late 1980s.

3. Mugabe has announced that he will retire. He may, of course, prove to be 'indispensable' and have to stay on for 'the sake of the country'.

4. Museveni conducted a state visit to Zimbabwe in 2004 to make up with Mugabe over the 'little misunderstanding' over the war in the Democratic Republic of the Congo, which cost the lives of five million people (*News24*, 2004).

5. For the most detailed analysis of this see Potts (2006).

6. The most important study of this is Herbst (1990). As a simple illustration, Clark Gibson (1999, p. 78) found that 'Not confronting severe economic contraction, and not possessing the type of patronage politics found in well-entrenched one-party systems, Zimbabwe did not endure poaching to the same extent' as Kenya and Zambia.

7. Translated as the clearing out of chaff in Shona. This entailed the massacre of tens of thousands of people in Matableland.

8. This was only successful arguably because of local conditions. See Larsen (2002).

9. Elsewhere in this report it is noted that 'the government was strongly independent, wanting to reform at its own pace' (p. 27). Thus ownership takes on an interesting connotation roughly corresponding to being able to divine what the World Bank wants you to do and doing it when it wants you to, without being told to. The ministers in question may have believed in the markets ability to redistribute wealth – upwards.

10. This terminology is taken from Reno (2000).

11. Although there was 'outright conflict' in the East of the country before that in 1993 (Nest *et al.*, 2006).

12. The dominant role of Zimbabwe in the security organ of SADC may be partly responsible for South Africa, Mozambique and Botswana's push to have SADC restructured to conform to NEPAD and AU priorities (Landsberg, 2003).

13. Western mining corporations, such as American Mineral Fields, had rushed in to the Congo after the fall of Mobutu but were subsequently left 'licking their wounds,' as Kabila would not enforce their property rights (*African Business*, 1998; Lokongo, 2005).

14. For a good discussion of this, see Helen Suzman Foundation (n.d.).

15. Although privatization in the energy sector failed (see Mangwengwende, 2002).

16. This is the home region of Solomon Mujuru, former army commander and MP and husband of recently promoted Vice-President, Comrade 'Spill Blood,' Joyce Mujuru (Gandu, 2005).

17. This *nomme de guerre* is from her shooting down a Rhodesian army helicopter during the liberation war.

18. On this see Taylor (1999).

19. For his analysis see Gwisai, (2002).

20. Unfortunately the US does have the capability to alter weather patterns (See *craigslist.org*, 2005).

21. The prospect was advanced in Economist Intelligence Unit (2005a).
22. Mugabe was also made an honorary professor of the Chinese Foreign Affairs College on this trip.
23. Mahathir sent a $40,000 shipment of rare Malaysian timber, at taxpayers expense to Mugabe for his new mansion (Baker, 2004).
24. Welshman Ncube of the MDC says that they have not asked the South African government to do this as it would 'not be the right approach.' They have, however, asked South African's 'not to dissuade other countries' from getting involved, thereby placing its hopes it would seem in the US and the UK (Ncube, 2003). This would seem a forlorn hope given that US President Bush appointed South African President Mbeki 'point man' on Zimbabwe when he visited in 2003 (*SouthAfrica.info*, 2003). Some have speculated this was because Jendayi Frazer of the US National Security Council was friendly with Jonathon Moyo, Mugabe's minister of Information at the time, having been students together in the US (David Moore, in conversation, Dublin, October 2004). Moyo subsequently fell out with Mugabe, and Frazer was appointed US ambassador to South Africa where she said that South African and US interests in Africa 'coincide almost entirely – Zimbabwe being one exception insofar as we have the same interest but different strategy and tactics for pursuing that interest' (quoted in P. Bond, 2005b). Nonetheless, to further its overall interests, the US may be willing to let South Africa make the running on Zimbabwe. Now Secretary of State Rice has declared Zimbabwe an 'out-post of tyranny.' Frazer has become Assistant Secretary of State for Africa.
25. A search of the NEPAD website reveals zero 'hits' for Zimbabwe. Available at http://www.nepad.org. Accessed 26 July, 2005.
26. Some donors provide emergency aid, such as that provided by UNDP and USAID to keep Harare's water purification system working (*afrolNews*, 2005a).
27. The Ethiopian government has also engaged in recent, controversial and unpopular slum clearance programs in Ethiopia (Adow, 2005).
28. The Irish company African Mining is also continuing to invest in Zimbabwe (personal communication from chairman, March 2004), despite numerous invasions of its mine (*BBC News*, 2002). Investors may be put off by statements by Mugabe about mining companies having to give 49 per cent of their investments to black empowerment groups (cited in *Zimbabwe Standard*, 19 September, 2004, cited in Dansereau, 2005).

7   Regionalizing Neoliberalism: The New Partnership for African Development and the Political Economy of Restructuring in South Africa

1. It also talks about Africa's archaeology, and its rainforests as a global 'lung.'
2. For example, Macroeconomic Research Group (1993); N. Nattrass (1994); R. Kaplinsky (1994); J. Sender (1994); X. Carim (1995).
3. The South African economy is 17 times the next largest in the region: Zimbabwe (World Bank, 2000b). In 1981 Anglo-American Corporation

controlled assets bigger than the economies of the nine countries closest to South Africa (Murray, 1987).

4. Comment attributed to the South African Minister of Industry Alec Irwin by a South African consultant (in conversation, Pretoria, July, 1999). Gauteng, a tiny province accounts for 34 percent of South Africa's GDP.

5. In agriculture part of the reason for job losses relates to the government's redirection of subsidies away from heavily subsidized commercial farming to social expenditures (Lodge, 1999). Recent high commodity prices have resulted in higher rates of economic growth and some limited employment growth (Statistics South Africa, 2006a).

6. The JSE is the 10th largest stock exchange in the world – bigger than China, Brazil's or Hong Kong's (*The Economist*, 2006a). Fine and Rustomjee (1996) argue that the economy has been dominated by six conglomerates or 'axes of capital': SA Mutual, Sanlam, Anglo-American Corporation, Liberty/Standard, Rembrandt/Volkskas and Anglovaal.

7. Harris and Michie (1998) argue that the fall of the rand in 1996 was largely the result of sales by domestic finance houses – another example of globalization from within.

8. An official of the Ministry of Finance (in conversation, 14 July, 1999, Midrand) noted that reduction of the budget deficit was facilitated by higher than expected growth in incomes, and hence tax returns, among upper-income groups.

9. The one area where the South African state has most explicitly challenged globalization is in relation to AIDS drugs patents (see Bond, 1999) and perhaps also through the nationalization of mineral deposits in 2002 (Bond, 2002b).

10. South Africa was part of the coalition of developing countries which derailed the Millennium Round of the WTO.

11. The government's position has changed somewhat since the collapse of the Millennium Round of the WTO and the reinvigoration of the G77, as it now seeks to diversify its trade, particularly to Latin America (Cauvin, 2000).

12. African National Congress, South African Communist Party and Congress of South African Trade Unions.

13. The government achieved deficit reduction, while still increasing the rate of public investment by retargeting expenditure away from commercial farming (Harris and Michie, 1998; Lodge, 1999). However, the government is also investing heavily in upgrading military hardware, by buying $6bn in weaponry, such as new submarines for example, which cannot be used in regional peace-keeping operations (Bond, 2004d). This seemingly illogical expenditure may reflect ideas within the international community of states about what major and middle powers 'should do' (Wendt, 1999).

14. These aim to improve competitiveness through training and other interventions along the production chain (See Joffe *et al.*, 1995) and have been financially supported by the World Bank (1997b).

15. Wage increase were offset by the depreciation of the rand which 'immiserized growth' (Kaplinsky and Morris, 1999).

16. Manufacturing wages have risen 65 percent since 1995 (SARB, n.d.).

17. This terminology draws from Evans's (1995) idea of 'embedded autonomy.'

18. This council does not include any South African members, and relations with Anglo-American remain somewhat terse as a recent spat over the fact that its chairman declared there was still 'a political risk' in South Africa demonstrated (See Mbeki, 2005). Tony Trahar may have been trying to displace the blame for low investment from corporations to the government (Mohamed Salih, 2004).

19. Peter Evans (1995) has argued that developmental states are characterized by 'embedded autonomy,' where there are dense networks of interaction between the state and domestic industrial capital, with the state in dominant position.

20. The state also tries to encourage social development and offset the impacts of the global market by other elements of its policy regime, such as increased social service provision (see Bond and Khosa, [1999] for an assessment of how well RDP targets were met).

21. Although the role of embedded institutions is also critically important (see Amin and Thrift, 1994; Rogers Hollingsworth and Boyer, 1997; Storper, 1997).

22. I am grateful to David Simon for this point.

23. The DRC already had an Interim PRSP in March 2002 (DRC, 2002) a full year before the final peace deal was signed in South Africa in April 2003. Previously the South African government had given a loan to the Congo to pay off IMF arrears. Within a year and a half Pretoria had secured a US $10bn trade and investment deal, and US $4bn worth of World Bank tenders for its companies in the Congo (Bond, 2006).

24. Prevalence refers to the proportion of the population infected. Incidence is the new infection rate in a given year.

25. In HSBC Bank's analysis, sterling investors should apply a 20 percent risk premium to Old Mutual shares in part because of 'an increased exposure to the Aids risk as sales of protection products increases' (quoted in *Zimbabwe Standard*, 1999).

26. Whereas the migratory labor system served the needs of mining capital in the past, it has now facilitated the spread of HIV (Webb, 1998).

27. Ultimately a currency is a claim on production of goods and services produced within a national territory, and exchange rates reflect that over the long-term.

28. The share of the JSE owned by black economic empowerment companies fell, by some estimates, from 6 percent in 1998 to 1.5 percent in 2000 (*The Economist*, 2001a). Politically, Anglo could not let JCI fail, and so arranged a share swap with Lonrho shares to keep it afloat (*Weekly Mail and Guardian*, 1997).

29. Fine and Davis (1990) cautioned 15 years ago against such an outcome.

30. This does not imply that this capital is everywhere, but that its field of action is global (Jessop, 2000).

31. The bookseller Amazon has recently set up a call center in South Africa, for example (*The Economist*, 2005c).

32. For example, Ford buying Samcor back from Anglo-American (*Business Day*, 2000).

33. Calculated from Statistics South Africa (1997, 1999).

34. Tank-tainers are aluminum road tankers with a 'return load capability (i.e., fuel out and general freight in)' (Moore, 1999, p. 33; Interview with DTI official,

Pretoria, 30 June 1999; and DTI official in conversation, Midrand, 15 July, 1999). One of the legacies of the apartheid era was heavy investment in military and 'strategic' industries. See IDC and DTI (1998) for an assessment of different industries.

35. South Africa has the largest Chinese population in Africa at 160,000 (*The Guardian*, 2006).

36. This displacement was the result of the 'failure to create sustainable comparative or competitive advantages,' despite preferences (Curran, 2006).

37. Manufacturing output declined in 1999, however (Statistics South Africa, 2001b).

38. Calculated from SARB (various) and Statistics South Africa (2006b).

39. Calculated in constant 1997 Rand from SARB (1997, 2001) and Statistics South Africa (2001a).

40. The attempt to create an information society included reducing tariffs on telecommunication equipment (a key hard industry) to zero, far below the 20 percent required by the WTO (Marais, 1998), perhaps because of US technology executives who advise Mbeki (Mervin Gumede, 2002). However, as the US experience has shown, the internet economy largely represented a displacement of over-accumulation into the sphere of circulation and was not a sustainable basis for economic development. A DTI official argued that Nokia, the Finnish telecommunication giant may have been able to develop because it had a 'technology road-map' (in conversation, Midrand, 15 July, 1999).

41. Thirty percent of the shares were sold to black South Africans (*The Economist*, 2001a).

42. President Mbeki has written of the Republic of Ireland's 'outstanding economic success,' but South Africa's location under globalization is very different (Mbeki, 2001).

43. Bell (1995) had predicted this.

44. Brazil's may be higher (Statistics South Africa, 2000).

45. Although inter-racial inequality is falling, this reflects the creation of a new indigenous entrepreneurial and managerial class and the absorption of indigenous people into paid employment by the state. See Nattrass and Seekings (2001). Inequality remains profoundly gendered and raced in the sense that poverty remains heavily concentrated among rural black women and that it is predominantly the black working class that has had to bear the burden of retrenchments, while white conglomerate capital has benefited from globalization. See May *et al.* (2000).

46. Harcourt and Wood (2003) nonetheless feel this route to be a promising one.

47. Available at http://www.info.gov.za/asgisa/asgisa.pdf. Accessed July 24, 2006.

48. By 'real' here Africa Confidential mean are involved in the formal sector.

49. The US budget deficit is currently running at $2.8bn dollars a day, or about $1m dollars a minute, drawing in about 80 percent of world savings. The extent of this debt raises questions about its sustainability, particularly in a context in which the US 'big three' auto-makers' stock has been downgraded to 'junk' status (Nederveen Pieterse, 2005). More recently the budget deficit has fallen.

50. Whereas Malaysia responded to the global economic crisis of 1997–99 by imposing capital controls, Chile liberalized its controls to try to attract more

investment. This implies transcending dependence on foreign portfolio investment (Bond, 2001a).

51. Prescription is always fraught with danger, but alternatives are possible at different scales. Gillian Hart (2002, p. 12) reminds us that 'local political dynamics assume sharply divergent forms, even in places that are structurally very similar.'

52. On synergy see Evans (1996a, b) and Tendler (1997). However, Tendler neglects the importance of synergy between scales: particularly national macroeconomic strategy in the sustainability of local/regional projects. See also Samatar (1999).

8   Governing Globalization for Human Security Post-9–11

1. According to a US Air Force General the terrorist threat in Africa is growing (*Etaiwannews.com*, 2005).

2. Volger (1995, cited in Johnston *et al.*, 2002, p. 681) defines a regime as 'an institution, or more precisely, a set of norms, principles, rules and decision making procedures that govern a particular issue area.'

3. Holiday arrivals in South Africa rose from 507,033 in 2002 to 513,523 to 2003 (Statistics South Africa, 2003).

4. On the dangers and difficulties of a natural resource-based economy, such as 'Dutch disease' and potential for increased corruption, see Auty (2001). The Economist Intelligence Unit (2002a, p. 2) notes that because sub-Saharan 'resource-based industries are growing faster than the rest of manufacturing industry, the region has downgraded technologically.'

5. West African oil is also 'light and sweet,' with a low sulfur content particularly suitable for burning in cars.

6. The canal recently had a temporary closure for two weeks (Scott-Joynt, 2004).

7. In 2002, its economy grew an astonishing 24 percent (UNECA, 2003). Despite having the 13th highest GDP per capita in the world (over US $30,000 at purchasing power parity), it ranks 121st on the UNDP Human Development Index, suggesting an unequal distribution of income (Available at http://hdr.undp.org/statistics/data/cty/cty_f_GNQ.html. Accessed 4 April 2007).

   A U.S. Senate investigation found that President Obiang and his family held between $400 and $700m in US bank accounts. South African companies, particularly from the Western Cape, are hoping to cash in as service providers in the West African oil boom (*Xinhua*, 2004b).

8. In Angola six former or current ministers are estimated to be worth over $100m each because of oil revenues, and the President would rank as one of the top 10 richest people in Brazil (*The Economist*, 2004d). Meanwhile one in four children die before their fifth birthday (UNICEF cited in UN-IRIN, 2003a). On the consequences of oil revenues for Nigeria see Watts (1994).

9. An oil refinery in Sudan has been built with Chinese loans and Sudan is now China's fourth largest supplier of oil (A. Osman El-Tom, in conversation, Dublin, March 2005).

10. The other area in which the US has shown substantial interest is the Caspian Basin, with an estimated 6 percent of world oil reserves (Johnson, 2004). Thus Africa is not unique as there is a broader 'politics of Pipelinestan' at

play (I am grateful to Diane Rocheleau for this point). As a result of scarcity, some estimates suggest global oil production is set to decline from 2008 onward (Douthwaite, 2004b).

11. The United Nations has a similar program.

12. This article quotes a Somali militiaman as saying that because of resulting hardships 'we must become terrorists.'

13. An essential difference though is that during the Cold War the US was willing to tolerate illiberal economic policies among its client states. This is no longer the case (see Bello *et al.*, 1994).

14. There are also other initiatives (see Abrahamsen, 2004a; Abromovici, 2004; Hartung and Berrigan, 2005).

15. Unless the government involved is Islamic, as in Sudan, where the US government has rightly declared the atrocities in Darfur to be 'genocide' (see Steidle, 2005).

16. Blowback is unintended negative consequences for the instigators of policies. For a discussion of the nature of blowback (see Johnson, 2000).

17. Panopticism involves using surveillance technology such as satellites to 'see' down into terrorist networks, or 'forensic accounting,' for example.

18. Al-quada ('The Base') has a double meaning of the volunteers who will engage in war and the computer database which holds their names (Gregory, 2004).

19. On the difficulties of this, see Herbst (2000).

20. For excellent discussion of the reasons behind the genocide, see Longman (1999).

21. For a discussion of the grave consequences of the breach of the UN Charter, see Mandel, (2004).

22. A. Adebayo (2003b) notes that many of the 'new leaders' celebrated by President Clinton were autocrats.

23. In relation to Zimbabwe, World Bank management noted that prior to LICUS there were 'no markers for what to do in a country in rapid decline and political turmoil' (World Bank, 2004b, p. 61). Before structural adjustment Zimbabwe was a middle-income country.

24. Mark Duffield has written of the merging of development and security and this trend looks set to increase post-9/11.

25. According to John Sender (2002) the 'Post-Washington Consensus' fits comfortably within the framework of neoclassical economics.

26. For the possibilities of greater state intervention in a market framework in Africa see Cheru, (2002). As Dani Rodrik (1999, cited in White and Killick, 2001, p. 41) notes, 'countries that have done well . . . are those that have been able to formulate a domestic investment strategy to kick-start growth and those that have had appropriate institutions to handle adverse external shocks, not those that have relied on reduced barriers to trade and capital flow.' Thus, the quality of intervention is of paramount importance. Better interventions will require the relegitimation and capacitation of African states.

27. For a discussion of whether Hardt and Negri's theory applies to Africa see Kevin Dunn (2003).

28. The Bush Administration's resistance to UN involvement in Iraq is estimated to have cost the US $100bn or roughly $1,000 per American household (Nye, 2004).

29. The Pentagon also now wants compulsory notification of all foreign takeovers in the US worth more than $100m (Johnson, 2004, p. 122).

30. However, Clapham notes that conditions conducive to terrorism are increasing in sub-Saharan Africa. Most Muslims in sub-Saharan Africa, however, belong to the Sufi sect, which is not associated with Islamic radicalism (Durac, 2004).

31. However, Samir Amin (1990, p. 109, cited in Nederveen Pieterse, 2001, p. 55) has noted that 'there is an element of hypocrisy on the part of the West in lamenting current Islamic fundamentalism when it has fought in every way possible against the progressive alternative.'

32. Using the UNDP definition, 'human security refers to two mutually reinforcing concepts: (i) safety from such chronic threats as hunger, disease and repression, and (ii) protection from sudden and hurtful disruptions in the patterns of daily life' (Mohamed Salih, 2001, p. 68). 'Human security' as a concept may also be used, however, to legitimize external intervention (Duffield, 2005a).

33. Nearly half of the top 500 companies in the world are American (Coggan, n.d., cited in Nye, 2004).

34. This is an example of a 'globalization chain' where politics, trade and investment are linked. This investment may also have further developmental effects (see Bräutigam, 2003).

35. To reach a total of US$178m in 2001. However, they were halved against a background of civil conflict in 2002 (Gibbon, 2003).

36. Former US President Clinton feels AGOA to be 'the best thing' he ever did for Africa (William Jefferson Clinton, in conversation, Dublin, July 2003).

37. However, some elements of the US state apparatus, particularly the Central Intelligence Agency, understand the interlinked nature of security and the fact that AIDS in Africa, for example, poses a national security threat to the US (Sachs, 2002).

38. Of course, the French government was deeply implicated in the genocide to begin with by training and arming the Interahamwe militias. President Clinton apologized for this inaction in 1998 when he visited Kigali for three and a half hours, and presented a plaque to the Rwandan President honoring the victims. During his visit the engines of Air Force One were never shut down (*PBS*, 1999).

39. The UN peacekeeping budget fell from $3,346m in 1995 to $900m in 1999 (McDermott, 2001, cited in Pugh, 2002).

40. On AIDS and power see (Campbell, 2003).

41. Mark Duffield (2005b) is less sanguine about the concept arguing that it allows for continuing imperialism by drawing a distinction between effective states, which provide human security and ineffective states, which do not. Human security then provides the rationale for intervention by the former in the latter.

42. This might be better described as 'globalization from the middle,' as it is conducted by elites, but from less powerful countries.

43. This might include the reintroduction of commodity agreements to stabilize prices. Currently the only one which functions is in natural rubber. Kitching (2001, p. 267) argues that in 'the short- to medium-term

beneficiaries of the genuine globalization of capitalist economic relations [through totally free trade and capital mobility] commencing now would be the presently poor and poorer workers of the world.' However, the danger in such a scenario is that more advanced developing countries, or efficient agricultural producers such as Australia and New Zealand, capture market share at the expense of low income ones, as has already happened under globalization (Kennedy, 1993). This recently led a group of the 49 least developed countries to ask the EU to consider returning to fixed quotas for their exports to the EU (Denny and Moore, 2004). Kitching falls into the neoclassical economic trap of neglecting the importance of non-price factors such as technology and skills (See Lall and Pietrobelli, 2003). The World Bank is progressive on the question of market access, arguing that African 'exporters should be granted full, tariff-free access to OECD markets, with exemptions from antidumping measures, countervailing duties, and other safeguards that create uncertainties about market access' (World Bank, 2000a, p. 257). Phytosanitary measures are particularly important nontariff barriers to African agricultural exports (Gibbon, 2002).

44. The origins of the Global Social Justice movement can be traced to the Zapatista organized 'Intergalactic Encounters for Humanity and Against Neoliberalism.' While elements of the resistance movement may not want to synthesize, even Zapatistas drink Coke (Kingsworth, 2003).

45. Unequal trade is where the prices of a country's exports tend to go down, while import prices go up. (Lewis, 1985).

46. It is interesting that if adopted this would strengthen the role and profitability of global financial capital. At least 20 percent of employment in New York and London is in financial services, with 443,000 and 617,000 workers, respectively (Fine, 2004).

47. There are also substantial 'poverty gaps.' In Uganda, the average person living on less than a dollar a day earned less than 60 cents a day from 1990–2001 (UNDP, 2003b).

48. David Moore (2004) argues that a welfarist approach by itself will be insufficient and that full employment is a global public good. This will require 'sophisticated industrial strategies.'

49. In 1993, military spending in Angola took up 20 percent of GDP (Willett, 1998, cited in Power, 2004).

50. A basic income is given to all members of society, whereas a minimum income guarantees a floor (Standing, 2002). Standing (1999) also outlines plans to achieve greater economic democracy. On the difficulties of achieving a redistributive politics in the US, given the strength of the Lockian political tradition there, see Hutton (2002).

51. This is in stark contrast to East Asia where only 4 percent of private sector savings are held overseas (Commission for Africa, 2005).

52. In addition to 'resource switching' away from the military, new funds for social spending could be provided by a Tobin tax or 'global resource dividend' (see Pogge, 2002). Another alternative, particularly given the extent of the global climate crisis, would be to establish a 'global carbon fund' (see White, 2003). Probably the most politically feasible would be a value added

tax on airplane travel (Deacon *et al.*, 1997). In this way immanent and imminent development can be linked.

53. This is equivalent to the military budgets of the next 27 highest spenders
and by one estimate is 16 times more than the US spends trying to prevent
war (Johnson, 2004, p. 63, p. 307). The Pentagon's Space Command recent
policy statement notes that the globalization of the world economy will
continue, with a growing gulf between the 'haves and have nots' and that
its mission is to dominate space to 'protect US interests and investments'
(Johnson, 2004, p. 81).

54. US leaders will have to become 'cosmopolitan patriots' and promote this
among the American Public (Anthony Appiah, 1999).

Bibliography

411 Stocks (n.d.) Available at 411stocks.stockselector.com. Accessed 18 June 2001.

Aalen, L. (2002) *Ethnic Federalism in a Dominant Party State: The Ethiopian Experience 1991–2000*, Bergen: Chr. Michelsen Institute.

Abbay, A. (2004) 'Diversity and State-Building in Ethiopia,' *African Affairs* 103 (413), 593–694.

Abbink, J. (2006) 'Discomfiture of Democracy? The 2005 Election Crisis in Ethiopia and its Aftermath,' *African Affairs* 105 (419), 173–199.

Abegaz, B. (2001) 'Ethiopia,' in S. Devarajan, D. Dollar and T. Holmgren. (eds) *Aid and Reform in Africa*, Washington, D.C.: World Bank.

Abraham, K. (2001) *Ethiopia: The Dynamics of Economic Reforms: Economic Liberalization and Political Transformation*, Addis Ababa: Ethiopian International Institute for Peace and Development.

—— (2002) *Ethiopia: From Empire to Federation*, Addis Ababa: Ethiopian International Institute for Peace and Development.

Abrahamsen, R. (2000) *Disciplining Democracy: Development Discourse and Good Governance in Africa*, London: Zed Books.

—— (2002) 'Who Governs? Sovereignty, Governmentality and Development in Sub-Saharan Africa,' Paper Presented at the African Studies Association, Washington, D.C., 5–8 December.

—— (2004a) 'A Breeding Ground for Terrorists? Africa and Britain's "War on Terrorism,"' *Review of African Political Economy* 102, 677–684.

—— (2004b) 'The Power of Partnerships in Global Governance,' *Third World Quarterly* 25 (8), 1453–1467.

—— and M. Williams (2005a) 'The Globalization of Private Security,' in *Chatham House and Economic and Social Research Council ISP/NSC Briefing Paper* 05/02, October.

—— (2005b) *The Globalization of Private Security: Country Report: Sierra Leone.* Available at http://users.aber.ac.uk/rbh/privatesecurity/country%20report-sierra%20leone.pdf. Accessed 26 October 2006.

Abromovici, P. (2004) 'Briefing: United States: The New Scramble for Africa,' *Review of African Political Economy* 102, 685–691.

Abugre, C. (2000) 'Still Sapping the Poor: A Critique of IMF Poverty Reduction Strategies.' Available at http://www.wdm.org.uk/campaigns/cambriefs/debt/PRSPcrit.htm. Accessed 31 July 2005.

Ackerman, J. (2004) 'Co-Governance for Accountability: Beyond "Exit" and "Voice,"' *World Development* 32 (3), 447–463.

Adam, C. S. and J. W. Gunning (2002) 'Redesigning the Aid Contract: Donor's Use of Performance Indicators in Uganda,' *World Development* 30 (12), 2045–2056.

Adan, A., K. Brock, P. Kabakcheiva, A. Kidanu, M. Melo, C. Turk and H. Yusuf (2002) 'Who is Listening? The Impact of Participatory Poverty Research on Policy,' in K. Brock and R. McGee (eds) *Knowing Poverty: Critical Reflections on Participatory Research and Poverty*, London: Earthscan.

267

Addison, T. and L. Laakso (2003) 'The Political Economy of Zimbabwe's Descent into Conflict,' *Journal of International Development* 15, 457–470.

Adebayo, A. (2003a) 'Africa, African Americans and the Avuncular Sam,' *Africa Today* 50 (3), 93–110.

—— (2003b) 'Africa and America in the Age of Terror,' *Journal of Asian and African Studies* 38 (2–3), 175–191.

—— (2003c) 'A Western Wolf in African Sheepskin,' *Mail and Guardian*, 14 November 2003, p. 15.

Adedeji, A., O. Otite, K. Amuwo, S. Egwu, I. Eteng, S. Kawonise, N. Ofundu, A. Okorie and N. Yaqub (1997) *Nigeria: Renewal from the Roots? The Struggle for Democratic Development*, London and Ijebu Ode: Zed Books and ACDESS.

Adelzadeh, A. (1996) *From the RDP to GEAR: The Gradual Embracing of Neo-Liberalism in South Africa*, National Institute for Economic Policy Occasional Paper Series, No. 3 August.

Adler, G. and J. Steinberg (eds) (2000) *From Comrades to Citizens: The South African Civics Movement and the Transition to Democracy*, New York: St. Martin's Press.

—— and E. Webster (2000) 'Introduction: Consolidating Democracy in a Liberalizing World – Trade Unions and Democratization in South Africa,' in G. Adler and E. Webster (eds), *Trade Unions and Democratization in South Africa, 1985–1997* (New York: St. Martin's Press).

Adow, M., 'Ethiopia Poll Reveals Rural–Urban Divide.' BBC News, Addis Ababa. Available at http://news.bbc.co.uk/2/hi/africa/4576325.stm. Accessed 26 September 2005.

Africa Confidential (2005a) 'South Africa: A Good Week for Mbeki,' December, 46 (7), 3–4.

—— (2005b) 'Water: Privatization Flood,' December, 46 (7), 6–7.

—— (2005c) 'What Is the MDC for?' May, 46 (10), 3.

—— (2005d) 'Zimbabwe: The Dam Bursts,' May, 46 (10), 2–3.

—— (2006) 'Sudan: Oddest Bedfellows,' 47 (9), 8.

Africa News Service (2001) 'Old Mutual Loses Made in South Africa Tag,' 31 January. Available at web7.infotrac.galegroup.com. Accessed 21 June 2001.

African Business (1998) 'Carving up the Congo,' October 1998. Available at http://www.africaasia.co.uk. Accessed 28 June 2006.

—— (2004) 'African Super-Rich on the Rise,' August/September (301), p. 8.

—— (2006a) 'Africa Has Irreversibly Turned the Corner,' July 2006. Available at http://www.africasia.co.uk/africanbusiness/ab.php?ID=963. Accessed 12 July 2006.

—— (2006b) 'Zimbabwe: Inflation Heading for Orbit,' March 2006, No. 318, p. 47.

African Development (1971) 'Trade Account Is Always in Deficit,' *African Development*, November, London: African Buyer and Trader Limited, p. E. 9.

African Development Bank (2000) *Cooperation with Civil Society Organizations: Policy and Guidelines* Abidjan: ADB.

—— (2003) *African Development Report 2003*, Oxford: Oxford University Press.

Africa News Archives (2005) 'Dr Kenneth Kaunda: Blair is More of a Devil than Mugabe,' 26 April, Lusaka: *The Post*. Available at http://afgen.com/zimbabwe_land3. html. Accessed 26 July 2005.

African Eye News Service (1999) 'Zambia and the IMF will Discuss New Economic Strategy,' 23 September. Available at web7.infotrac.galegroup.com. Accessed 23 June 2000.

Africa Recovery (2001) 'Africans Anxious over Terrorism War,' October, 15 (3), 3, United Nations.

Africa Today (2004) 'Under a Spell.' Available at http://www.africatody.com/feb04/feb04underaspell.htm. Accessed 28 September 2004.

afrolNews (2005a) 'Harare Water Quality Rescued by Foreign Aid,' 15 January 2005. Available at http://www.afrol.com/articles/10785. Accessed 27 July 2005.

—— (2005b) 'IMF Gives Zimbabwe Last Chance,' 17 November 2005. Available at http;//www.afrol.com/articles/14826. Accessed 27 July 2006.

—— (2005c) 'Mugabe Leaves Libya Empty Handed,' 1 July 2005. Available at http://www.afrol.com/articles/10444. Accessed 27 July 2006.

Agamben, G. (1998) *Homo Sacer: Sovereign Power and Bare Life*, Stanford: Stanford University Press.

Agénor, P-R. (2005) 'The Macroeconomics of Poverty Reduction,' *The Manchester School* 73 (4), 369–434.

Agnew, J. and S. Corbridge (1995) *Mastering Space: Hegemony, Territory and International Political Economy*, London: Routledge.

AGOA (African Growth and Opportunity Act) (2003) 'Second US-SSA AGOA Forum.' Available at http://www.agoa.mu/ethiopia.htm. Accessed 31 July 2005.

Ake, C. (1996) *Democracy and Development in Africa*, Washington, D.C.: Brookings Institution.

Akeroyd, A. V. (2004) 'Coercion, Constraint, and "Cultural Entrapments": A Further Look at the Gendered and Occupational Factors Pertinent to the Transmission of HIV in Africa,' in E. Kalipeni, S. Craddock, J. R. Oppong and J. Ghosh (eds) *HIV and AIDS in Africa: Beyond Epidemiology*, Oxford, Malden and Victoria: Blackwell.

Akkerman, T., M. Hajer and J. Grin (2004) 'The Interactive State: Democratization from Above?' *Political Studies* 52, 82–95.

Alagiah, G. (2005) 'Dreaming of a New Dawn,' *The Observer*, 3 July, p. 22.

Alavi, H. (1972) 'The State in Post-Colonial Societies: Pakistan and Bangladesh,' *New Left Review* I (74), 59–81.

Alden, C. (2002) 'South Africa's "Quiet Diplomacy" and the Crisis in Zimbabwe,' *Cadernos de Estudos Africanos* 2, 189–211.

Alexander, J. C. (1998) 'Introduction: Civil Society I, II, III: Constructing an Empirical Concept from Normative Controversies and Historical Transformations,' in J. C. Alexander (ed.) *Real Civil Societies: Dilemmas of Institutionalization*, SAGE Studies in International Sociology, London: Thousand Oaks and New Dehli: SAGE.

Alila, P. O. and P. O. Pedersen (eds) (2001) *Negotiating Social Space: East African Micro Enterprises*, Trenton, NJ: Africa World Press.

Allen, C. (1995) 'Understanding Africa Politics,' *Review of Africa Political Economy* 65, 301–320.

—— (2004) 'Who Needs Civil Society' in G. Mohan and T. Zack-Williams (eds) *The Politics of Transition in Africa*, ROAPE African Readers, Oxford and Trenton: James Currey and Africa World Press.

Allen, T. and D. Styan (2000) 'A Right to Intervene? – Bernard Kouchner and the "New Humanitarianism,"' *Journal of International Development* 12, 825–842.

Altangerel, T. and S. Bae (2004) *Results of the Survey on World Bank – Civil Society Engagement*, Report Prepared for CIVICUS – The World Alliance for Civil Participation. Available at http://www.civicus.org/new/media/ResultsJFCSurvey.doc. Accessed 13 September 2005.

Alwang, J., B. F. Mills and N. Taruvinga (2002) *Why Has Poverty Increased in Zimbabwe?* Washington, D.C.: World Bank.

Amaïzo, Y. E. (2004) 'Poverty and HIV/AIDS: Instruments for Regulating African Insecurity?' in B. Onimode (ed.) *African Development and Governance Strategies in the 21st Century: Looking Back to Move Forward, Essays in Honor of Adebayo Adedeji at Seventy*, London and New York: Zed Books.

Amin, A. (2004) 'Regulating Economic Globalization,' in *Transactions of the Institute of British Geographers* New Series, 29 (2), 217–233.

—— and N. Thrift (eds) (1994) *Regional Development in Western Europe*, Oxford and New York: Oxford University Press.

Amin, S. (1990) *Maldevelopment: Anatomy of a Global Failure*, London: Zed Books.

Amnesty International, (2002) *Making a Killing: The Diamond Trade in Government-Controlled DRC*. Available at http://web.amnesty.org/library/index/engafr620172002.

Amoako, K. (2004) 'The Capable State: A Pillar of Development in Africa,' *New Economy* 13 (3), 132(137.

Amsden, A. (1989) *Asia's Next Giant: South Korea and Late Industrialization*, New York: Oxford University Press.

anclist (1999) Press statement issued by anclist@lists.sn.apc.org, 13 December.

Andersson, J. (2001) 'Reinterpreting the Rural–Urban Connection: Migration Practices and Socio-Cultural Dispositions of Buhera Workers in Harare,' *Africa* 71 (1), 82–112.

Andreassen, B. A., W. Maina and M. Ngunyi (1996) *Supporting Human Rights in Times of Democratic Transitions: External Aid to the DG Sector in Kenya*, Oslo: The Norwegian Institute of Human Rights.

Andreasson, S. (2003) 'Economic Reforms and "Virtual Democracy" in South Africa and Zimbabwe: The Incompatibility of Liberalization, Inclusion and Development,' *Journal of Contemporary African Studies*, 21 (3), 383–486.

—— (2006) 'The African National Congress and its Critics: "Predatory Liberalism," Black Empowerment and Intra-Alliance Tensions in Post-Apartheid South Africa,' *Democratization* 13 (2), 302–322.

Anheier, H. K. (2000) 'Managing Non-Profit Organizations: Towards a New Approach,' *Civil Society Working Papers*, Center for Civil Society, No. 1, London: LSE.

Anon. (2004a) 'NEPAD,' in B. Onimode *et al.*, *African Development and Governance Strategies in the 21st Century: Looking Back to Move Forward, Essays in Honor of Adebayo Adedeji at Seventy*, London and New York: Zed Books.

Anon. (2004b) 'NEPAD: Yet Another Plan, Another Initiative and New Partnership,' in B. Onimode (ed.) *African Development and Governance Strategies in the 21st Century: Looking Back to Move Forward, Essays in Honor of Adebayo Adedeji at Seventy*, London and New York: Zed Books.

—— (2004c) 'Professor Adebayo Adedeji, CFR: A Profile,' in B. Onimode *et al.*, *African Development and Governance Strategies in the 21st Century: Looking Back to Move Forward, Essays in Honor of Adebayo Adedeji at Seventy*, London and New York: Zed Books.

Anthony Appiah, K. (1999) 'Cosmopolitan Patriots,' in L. Wohlgemuth, S. Gibson, S. Klasen and E. Rothchild (eds) *Common Security and Civil Society in Africa*, Uppsala: Nordiska Afrikainstitutet.

Arnold, G. (2000) *New South Africa*, Basingstoke and New York: Palgrave Macmillan.

Arrighi, G. (2004) 'Globalization and Uneven Development,' Paper Presented at the Overcoming Underdevelopment in South Africa's Second Economy, Development Bank of Southern Africa, Midrand, 28–29 October. Available at www.dbsa.org/document/powercomagenda/popgovannarrighthi.rtf. Accessed 12 September 2005.

Arruda, M. (1996) 'Globalization and Civil Society: Rethinking Cooperativism in the Context of Active Citizenship,' Rio de Janerior: PACS.

Asea, P. (2003) 'Uganda: A Tale of Two Economies,' in Economic Commission for Africa and Economic Policy Research Center, *Key Components of Pro-Poor Growth Strategies*, Proceedings of Expert Group Meeting, Munyonyo Speke Resort, Kampala, Uganda, 23–24 June.

Asia News (2005) 'Chinese Textile "Tsunami" Hits Africa and Asia,' 26 April. Available at http://www.asianews.it. Accessed 18 September 2006.

Aspen, H. (2002) 'Models of Democracy – Perceptions of Power: Government and Peasantry in Ethiopia,' in B. Zewde and S. Pausewang (eds) *Ethiopia: The Challenge of Democracy from Below*, Stockholm: Nordiska Afrikaininstitutet and Forum for Social Studies.

Associated Bank of South Africa (2001) *South Africa's Foreign Trade*, 2001 edn, SA Financial Sector Forum: Rivonia.

Auty, R. M. (ed.) (2001) *Resource Abundance and Economic Development*, Oxford and New York: Oxford University Press.

Azarya, V. (1994) 'Civil Society and Disengagement in Africa,' in J. Harbeson, D. Rothchild and N. Chazan (eds) *Civil Society and the State in Africa*, Boulder, CO: Lynne Rienner.

Bach, D. C. (2003) 'New Regionalism as an Alias: Regionalization Through Trans-State Networks,' in J. A. Grant and F. Söderbaum (eds) *The New Regionalism in Africa*, London: Ashgate.

Baker, M. (2004) 'Mahathir Defends Gift to Mugabe,' *Sidney Morning Herald*. Available at http://www.smh.com.au. Accessed 26 July 2005.

Bangura, Y. and B. Beckman (1993) 'African Workers and Structural Adjustment: A Nigerian Case-Study,' in A. O. Olokoshi (ed.) *The Politics of Structural Adjustment in Nigeria*, London, Ibadan and Portsmouth: James Currey, Heinemann Educational Books Nigeria Plc and Heinemann.

Bank/NetherlandsWater Partnership Program (n.d.) *Water Rights Concept Note*. Available at: http://www.worldbank.org/water.

Baregu, M. (2003) 'Economic and Military Security,' in M. Baregu and C. Landsberg (eds) *From Cape to Congo: Southern Africa's Evolving Security Challenges*, Boulder and London: Lynne Rienner.

Barkan, J. D. (1994) 'Resurrecting Modernization Theory,' in D. E. Apter and C. G. Rosberg (eds) *Political Development and the New Realism in Sub-Saharan Africa*, Charlottesville and London: University of Virginia Press.

Barkawi, T. (2006) *Globalization and War*, Lanham, Maryland: Rowman and Littlefield.

Barnett, M. and R. Duvall (2004) 'Power in Global Governance,' in M. Barnett and R. Duvall (eds) *Power in Global Governance*, Cambridge and New York: Cambridge University Press.

Barr, A. and J. Toye (2000) 'It's not What You Know – It's Who You Know! Economic Analysis of Social Capital,' Insights Issue No.34, September. Available at http://www.id21.org/insights/insights34/insights-iss34-art01.html. Accessed 24 June 2004.

Barrell, H. (2000a) 'Mbeki: Talking Left and Doing Right,' *Mail and Guardian*, 21 January.

—— (2000b) 'SA's Economy Geared for Growth,' *Daily Mail and Guardian*, 23 October.

Bartholomew, C. (2005) 'U.S. China Economic and Security Review Commission Hearings on China's Influence in Africa,' Testimony to the US House of Representatives Committee on International Relations, Subcommittee on Africa, Global Human Rights and International Operations, 28 July 2005. Available at www.uscc.gov. Accessed 18 September 2006.

Bates, R. (1984) *Markets and States in Tropical Africa: The Political Basis of Agricultural Policies*, Berkeley: University of California Press.

—— (1987) *Essays on the Political Economy of Rural Africa*, Berkeley: University of California Press.

Bauer, G. and S. Taylor (2005) *Politics in Southern Africa: State and Society in Transition*, Boulder and London: Lynne Rienner.

Bayart, J-F. (1986) 'Civil Society in Africa,' in P. Chabal (ed.) *Political Domination in Africa: Reflections on the Limits of Power*, Cambridge: Cambridge University Press.

—— (1993) *The State in Africa: The Politics of the Belly*, London: Longman.

—— (2000) 'Africa in the World: A History of Extraversion,' *African Affairs* 395 (99), 217–267.

——, B. Hibou and S. Ellis (1999) *The Criminalization of the State in Africa*, Bloomington and Indianapolis: International African Institute, James Currey and Indiana University Press.

BBC News (2000) 25 July edition.

—— (2002) 'Miner Bemoans Zimbabwe's Decline,' 20 September. Available at http://news.bbc.co.uk/2/hi/business/2271187.stm. Accessed 12 March 2004.

—— (2004) 'Zimbabwe Reveals China Arms Deal,' 14 June. Available at http://news.bbc.co.uk/1/hi/world/africa/3804629.stm. Accessed 3 April 2007.

—— (2005a) 'Blasts Kill Five in East Ethiopia.' 25 July. Available at http://news.bbc.co.uk/2/hi/africa/4714155.stm. Accessed 26 July 2005.

—— (2005b) 'Britain Wastes Aid Money to Malawi – Report,' 28 August. Available at http://news.bbc.co.uk/1/hi/uk_politics/4191950.stm. Accessed 14 September 2005.

—— (2005c) 'Callous Raids Anger Mugabe Ally,' 5 July. Available at http://news.bbc.co.uk/2/hi/africa/4651603.stm. Accessed 24 July 2005.

—— (2005d) 'Ethiopia "Frees Poll Protestors,"' 24 June. Available at http://news.bbc.co.uk/2/hi/africa/4620239.stm. Accessed 26 July 2005.

—— (2005e) 'Q and A: Zimbabwe Election,' 29 March. Available at http://news.bbc.co.uk/1/hi/world/africa/4372311.stm. Accessed 26 July 2005.

—— (2005f) 'S Africa "Not Zimbabwean Broker,"' 20 April. Available at http://news.bbc.co.uk/1/hi/world/africa/4465767.stm. Accessed 26 July 2005.

—— (2005g) 'UK, US "Caused Zimbabwe Drought,"' 28 June. Available at http://news.bbc.co.uk/2/hi/africa/4630443.stm. Accessed 29 June 2005.

Bebbington, A. and R. Riddell (1997) 'Heavy Hands, Hidden Hands, Holding Hands? Donors, Intermediary NGOs and Civil Society Organizations,' in D. Hulme and M. Edwards (eds) *NGOs, States and Donors: Too Close for Comfort?*, New York: St. Martin's Press.

Beck, U. (1992) *The Risk Society: Towards a New Modernity*, London, Thousand Oaks and New Dehli: SAGE.

Beckman, B. (1993) 'The Liberation of Civil Society: Neo-liberal Ideology and Political Theory in an African Context,' in M. Mohanty and P. Nath Mukherji with O. Törnquist (eds) *People's Rights: Social Movements and the State in the Third World*, New Dehli, Thousand Oaks, London: SAGE.

Bell, T. (1995) 'Improving Manufacturing Performance in South Africa: A Contrary View,' *Transformation: Critical Perspectives on Southern Africa* 28, 1–34.

—— (1997) 'Trade Policy,' in J. Michie and V. Padayachee (eds) *The Political Economy of South Africa's Transition*, London: Dryden Press.

—— and G. Farrell (1997) 'The Minerals-Energy Complex and South African Industrialization,' *Development Southern Africa* 14 (4), 591–613.

Belli, P., M. Finger and A. Ballivan (1993) *South Africa: A Review of Trade Policies*, Informal Discussion Papers on Aspect of the Economy of South Africa, Discussion Paper No. 4, Washington, D.C.: World Bank.

Bello, W. (2002) *Deglobalization: Ideas for a New World Economy*, London: Zed Books.

—— with S. Cunningham and B. Rau (1994) *Dark Victory: The United States, Structural Adjustment and Global Poverty*, Pluto: London.

Bergeron, S. (2003) 'Challenging the World Bank's Narrative of Inclusion,' in A. Kumar (ed.), *World Bank Literature*, Minneapolis: University of Minnesota Press.

Berhanu, K. (2002) 'The Role of NGOs in Promoting Democratic Values: The Ethiopian Experience,' in B. Zewde and S. Pausewang (eds) *Ethiopia: The Challenge of Democracy from Below*, Stockholm: Nordiska Afrikaininstitutet and Forum for Social Studies.

Bernal, M. (1987) *Black Athena: Afroasiatic Roots of Classical Civilization: The Fabrication of Ancient Greece 1785–1985*, London: Free Press Association.

Bevan, P. (2000) *Poverty in Ethiopia*, Discussion Paper Prepared for the Dept. for International Development, University of Bath.

Bierschenk, T., J. P. Chauveau and J. P. Olivier de Sardan (2000) *Coutiers en développement: les villages africains en quête de projets*, Paris: Karthala.

Bigsten, A., B. Kebebe and A. Shimeles (2003) 'Growth and Poverty Reduction in Ethiopia: Evidence from the Household Panel Surveys,' *World Development*, 31 (1), 87–106.

—— (2005a) 'Introduction,' in A. Bigsten, A. Shimeles and B. Kebebe (eds) *Poverty, Income Distribution and Labor Markets in Ethiopia*, Uppsala: Nordiska Afrikainstitutet.

—— (2005b) 'Overview of the Economy,' in A. Bigsten, A. Shimeles and B. Kebebe (eds) *Poverty, Income Distribution and Labor Markets in Ethiopia*, Uppsala: Nordiska Afrikainstitutet.

——, K. Kronlid and N. Makonnen (2005) 'Dynamics of Income Distribution in Urban Ethiopia 1994–1997,' in A. Bigsten, A. Shimeles and B. Kebebe (eds), *Poverty, Income Distribution and Labor Markets in Ethiopia*, Uppsala: Nordiska Afrikainstitutet.

——, A. Shimeles and B. Kebebe (2005) 'Conclusions and Policy Implications,' in A. Bigsten, A. Shimeles and B. Kebebe (eds) *Poverty, Income Distribution and Labor Markets in Ethiopia*, Uppsala: Nordiska Afrikainstitutet.

Bird, G. (2004) 'Growth, Poverty and the IMF,' *Journal of International Development* 16, 621–636.

Birdsall, N. (1993) *Social Development in Economic Development*, Washington, D.C.: World Bank.

Blair, D. (2002) *Degrees in Violence: Robert Mugabe and the Struggle for Power in Zimbabwe*, London: Continuum.

Blanq, B. (1994) 'Congo: Corruption et Résistance au Changement,' in D. Darbon and P. Ouartin (eds) *L'Afrique Politique: Vue sure la Démocratisation a marée Basse*, Paris: Karthala.

Boagang, H. (1997) *The Democratic Implications of Civil Society in China*, Basingstoke: Macmillan.

Böge, V., C. Fitzpatrick, W. Jaspers and W-C Paes (2006) *Who's Minding the Store? The Business of Private, Public and Civil Actors in Zones of Conflict*, Fatal Transactions Brief No. 32, Bonn: Bonn International Center for Conversion.

Bolderson, C. (2005) 'Ethiopia "Right" to Stop Protests,' *BBC News*, Addis Ababa, 6 July. Available at http://news.bbc.co.uk/2/hi/africa/4655243.stm. Accessed 26 July 2005.

Bollee, A. (2003) 'Djibouti: From French Outpost to US Base,' *Review of African Political Economy* 97, 481–484.

Bond, P. (1998) *Uneven Zimbabwe*, Trenton and Asmara: Africa World Press.

—— (1999) 'Globalization, Pharmaceutical Pricing and South African Health Policy: Managing Confrontation with US Firms and Politicians,' *International Journal of Health Services* 29 (3), 765–792.

—— (2000) *Elite Transition: From Apartheid to Neoliberalism in South Africa*, London and Pietermaritzburg: Pluto Press and University of Natal Press.

—— (2001a) 'A Case for Capital Controls,' in *Against Global Apartheid: South Africa Confronts the World Bank, IMF and International Finance*, London and Cape Town: Pluto and UCT Press.

—— (2001b) *Against Global Apartheid: South Africa meets the World Bank, IMF and International Finance*, Cape Town: University of Cape Town Press.

—— (2002a) 'Thabo Mbeki and NEPAD: Breaking or Shining the Chains of Global Apartheid,' in S. Jacobs and R. Calland (eds) *Thabo Mbeki's World: The Politics and Ideology of the South African President*, London and Pietermaritzberg: Zed Books and University of Natal Press.

—— (2002b) *Unsustainable South Africa: Environment, Development and Social Protest*, Scottsville and London: University of Natal Press and Merlin.

—— (2002c) 'Zimbabwe: On the Brink of Change, or of a Coup?' Available at http://www.zmag.org/Sustainers/content/2002–01/30bond.cfm. Accessed 4 April 2007.

—— (2003) 'Africa in Evian: If the G8 is Meeting, It Must be Time to "Dignify" NEPAD (again).' Available at http://www.focusweb.org/popups/articleswindow. php?id=324. Accessed 14 September 2005.

—— (2004a) *Talk Left, Walk Right: South Africa's Frustrated Global Reforms*, Durban: University of Kwa-Zulu Natal Press.

—— (2004b) 'The ANC's "Left Turn" and South African Sub-Imperialism,' *Review of African Political Economy*, 102, 599–616.

—— (2004c) 'The ANC's "Left Turn" and South African Sub-Imperialism,' *Review of African Political Economy* 102, 599–616.

—— (2004d) '"The George Bush of Africa': Pretoria Chooses Subimperialism,' *Foreign Policy in Focus* 13 July, 1–8.

—— (2005a) 'Afterword,' in P. Bond (ed.) *Fanon's Warning: A Civil Society Reader on the New Partnership for Africa's Development*, 2nd edn, Trenton and Asmara: Africa World Press.

—— (2005b) 'Imperialism's African Helpers,' *Socialist Review*, June 2005. Available at http//:www.socialistreview.org/article.php?articlenumber=9431. Accessed 18 September 2006.

—— (2005c) 'Zimbabwe: Loan Request Gives SA Leverage to Press for Change.' Available at http://www/irinnews.org. Accessed 28 July 2005.

—— (2006) *Looting Africa: The Economics of Exploitation* (London: Zed Books).

—— and M. Manyanya (2002) *Zimbabwe's Plunge: Exhausted Nationalism, Neoliberalism and the Search for Social Justice*, Scottsville and London: University of Natal Press and Merlin Press.

—— and R. Saunders (2005) 'Labor, the State and the Struggle for a Democratic Zimbabwe,' *Monthly Review*, December 2005. Available at http://www.monthlyreview.org. Accessed 20 June 2006.

—— and M. Khosa (eds) (1999) *An RDP Policy Audit*, Pretoria: HSRC.

Boone, C. (1994) 'States and Ruling Classes in Post-Colonial Africa,' in J. Migdal (ed.) *State Power and Social Forces: Domination and Transformation in the Third World*, New York: Cambridge University Press.

Booth, D. (2003a) *Fighting Poverty in Africa: Are PRSPs Making a Difference?* London: Overseas Development Institute.

—— (2003b) 'Patterns of Difference and Practical Theory: Researching The New Poverty Strategy Process in Africa,' *Journal of International Development* 15, 863–877.

Boschma, R. A. and J. G. Lambooy (1999) 'Evolutionary Economics and Economic Geography,' *Journal of Evolutionary Economics* 9, 411–429.

Boyd, L., M. Spicer and G. Keeton (2001) 'Economic Scenarios for South Africa: A Business Perspective,' *Daedalus*, Winter, 71–89.

Boyer, R. and J. Hollingsworth (eds) (1997) *Contemporary Capitalism: The Embeddedness of Institutions*, Cambridge: Cambridge University Press.

Braathen, E. (2000) 'New Social Corporatism – A Discursive-Comparative Perspective on the World Development Report 2000/2001 "Attacking Poverty."' Available at http://www.crop.org/publications/files/report/Comments_to_WDR 2001_2002_ny.pdf. Accessed 12 September 2005.

BRAC (Bangladesh Rural Advancement Committee) (1999) *Annual Report 1999*, BRAC, Dhaka.

Bracking, S. (2005) 'Development Denied: Autocratic Militarism in Post-Election Zimbabwe,' *Review of African Political Economy* 32 (104/5), 341–357.

—— and L. Sachikonye (2006) 'Remittances, Poverty Reduction and the Informalization of Household Well-Being in Zimbabwe,' GPRG-WPS-045. Available at http://www.gprg.org/pubs/workingpapers/pdfs/gprg-wps-045.pdf. Accessed 27 July 2006.

Bratton, M. (1989a) 'Beyond the State: Civil Society and Associational Life in Africa,' *World Politics* 41 (3), 407–430.

—— (1989b) 'The Politics of Government – NGO Relations in Africa,' *World Development* 17 (4), 569–587.

—— and N. van de Walle (1997) *Democratic Experiments in Africa: Regime Transitions in Comparative Perspective*, Cambridge and New York: Cambridge University Press.

Bräutigam, D. (2003) 'Close Encounters: Chinese Business Networks as Industrial Catalysts in Sub-Saharan Africa,' *African Affairs* 102, 447–467.

Brecher, J., T. Costello and B. Smith (2000) *Globalization from Below: The Power of Solidarity*, Boston: Beacon Books.

Brenner, C. (2006) '"South Africa On-Call": Information Technology and Labor Restructuring in South African Call Centers,' *Regional Studies*, 40 (9), 1025–1040.

Brenner, R. (1998) 'The Economics of Global Turbulence: A Special Report on the World Economy, 1950–98,' Special Issue of *New Left Review*, 229.

Breslin, S. (2000) 'Decentralization, Globalization and China's Partial Re-Engagement with the Global Economy,' *New Political Economy* 5 (2), 205–226.

Brett, E. A. (2005) 'From Corporatism to Liberalization in Zimbabwe: Economic Policy Regimes and Political Crisis (1980–1997),' Crisis States Programme, London School of Economics, Working Paper No. 58. Available at http://www.crisisstates.com/Research/projects/africa04.htm. Accessed 22 September 2006.

Bretton Woods Project (2001) 'PRSPs are Just PR says Civil Society Groups.' Available at http://www.BrettonWoodsproject.org/topic/adjustment/a23rspsstats.html.

—— (2004) 'Bank Review: "One-Size Fits All" Solutions Persist,' 26 July. Available at http://www.globalpolicy.org/socecon/bwi-wto/wbank/2004/0823worldbank.htm. Accessed 30 August 2004.

Brinkerhoff, D. W. and A. Goldsmith (2003) 'How Citizens Participate in Macroeconomic Policy: International Experience and Implications for Poverty Reduction,' *World Development* 31 (4), 685–701.

—— with assistance from N. P. Kulibaba (1996) 'Perspectives on Participation in Economic Policy Reform in Africa,' *Studies in Comparative International Development* 31 (3), 123–151.

British Council (2004) *Mapping NSAs* (Non-State Actors) *in Ethiopia*, Executive Summary.

Brock, K. (2002) 'Introduction,' in K. Brock and R. McGee (eds) *Knowing Poverty: Critical Reflections on Participatory Research and Poverty*, London: Earthscan.

——, A. Cornwall and J. Gaventa (2001) *Power, Knowledge and Political Spaces in the Framing of Poverty Policy*, Working Paper 143, Brighton: Institute of Development Studies.

Brown, D. (2004) 'Participation in Poverty Reduction Strategies: Democracy Strengthened or Democracy Undermined?' in S. Hickey and G. Mohan (eds) *Participation: From Tyranny to Transformation*, London: Zed Books.

Brown, G. (1999) 'Rediscovering Public Purpose in the Global Economy,' *Social Development Review* 3 (1) March, 3–7. Available at http:///www.icsw.org/publications/sdr1999_march/rules_game.htm. Accessed 25 August 2005.

—— (2004) 'The Challenges of 2005: Forging a New Compact for Africa,' *New Economy* 13 (3), 127–131.

Budlender, D. (2000) 'The Political Economy of Women's Budgets in the South,' *World Development* 28 (7), 1365–1378.

Bull, M. (2001) 'You Can't Build a New Society with a Stanley Knife,' *London Review of Books*, 4 October.

Bullen, A. (1999) *The African Renaissance: An Assessment of the African Renaissance Discourse as a Unique Strategy for Development in Africa*. Honours dissertation, School of African Studies, University of Cape Town.

Burt, R. S. (2000) 'The Network Structure of Social Capital,' in R. I. Sutton and B. M. Straw (eds) *Organizational Behavior*, Greenwich, CT: JAI Press.

Business Africa, Issue of 1–15 September 2002, 2.

Business Center (2002) CNBC, 29 May 2002. Available at web.lexis-nexis.com. Accessed 19 June 2005.

Business Day (1999) Issue of 28 September.

—— (2000) 'Ford Doubles Its Stake,' 26 January. Available at web7.infotrac. galegroup.com. Accessed 21 July 2001.

—— (2004) Issue of 26 March, 599–616.

Business.iafrica (2001) Edition of 8 August.

Business Report (2002) Edition of 19 June.

Bustelo, E. S. (2001) 'Expansion of Citizenship and Democratic Construction,' in W. van Genugten and C. Perez-Bustillo (eds) *The Poverty of Rights: Human Rights and the Eradication of Poverty*, Comparative Research Programme on Poverty, London and New York: Zed Books.

Callaghy, T. (1990) 'Lost Between the State and the Market: The Politics of Economic Adjustment in Ghana, Zambia and Nigeria,' in J. Nelson (ed.) *Economic Crisis and Policy Choice: The Politics of Adjustment in the Third World*, Princeton, NJ: Princeton University Press.

—— (1994) 'A Dissenting Opinion About Resurgent Societies,' in J. W. Harbeson, D. Rothchild and N. Chazan (eds) *Civil Society and the State in Africa*, Boulder, CO: Lynne Rienner.

—— (2001) 'Networks and Governance in Africa: Innovation in the Debt Regime,' in T. M. Callaghy, R. Kassimir and R. Latham (eds) *Intervention and Transnationalism in Africa: Global-Local Networks of Power*, Cambridge: Cambridge University Press.

Callinicos, A. (2000) *Against the Third Way*, Cambridge: Polity.

Cammack, P. (2004) 'What the World Bank Means by Poverty Reduction, and Why It Matters,' *New Political Economy* 9 (2), 189–211.

Campbell, C. (1998) 'Presidential Address,' Steel and Engineering Industry Federation of South Africa, 12 October 1998, Johannesburg, *SEIFSA Annual Report*, p. 2.

—— (2003) *Letting Them Die: Why HIV/AIDS Prevention Programmers Fail*, London: James Currey.

Campbell, H. (2003) *Reclaiming Zimbabwe: The Exhaustion of the Patriarchal Model of Liberation*, Cape Town: David Phillip.

Campbell, J. (2001) 'Autonomy and Governance in Ethiopia: The State, Civil Society and NGOs,' in O. Barrow and M. Jennings (eds) *The Charitable Impulse: NGOs and Development in East and Northeastern Africa*, London: James Currey.

Carbone, M. (2004) 'Briefing: The Millennium Challenge Account,' *Review of African Political Economy* 101, 536–542.

Cardoso, F. H. (1993) 'North-South Relations in the Present Context: A New Dependency?' in M. Carnoy, M. Castells, S. S. Cohen and F. H. Cardoso (eds) *The New Global Economy in the Information Age*, University Park: Pennsylvania Press.

Carim, X. (1995) 'Engaging the Bretton Woods Institutions: Policy Implications for South Africa,' *Development Southern Africa* 12 (3), 333–346.

Carley, M. and I. Christie (2000) *Managing Sustainable Development*, 2nd edn, London: Earthscan.

Carmody, P. (2001) *Tearing the Social Fabric: Neoliberalism, Deindustrialization and the Crisis of Governance in Zimbabwe*, Portsmouth, NH: Heinemann.

—— (2002) 'The Liberalization of Underdevelopment or the Criminalization of the State? Contrasting Explanations of Africa's Politico-Economic Crisis under Globalization,' in B. Ikubolajeh Logan (ed.) *Globalization, the Third World State and Poverty Alleviation in the Twenty-First Century*, London: Ashgate.

—— and S. Taylor (2003) 'Industry and the Urban Sector in Zimbabwe's Political Economy,' *African Studies Quarterly* 7 (2 and 3), 1–28. Available at http://web.africa.ufl.edu/asq/v7/v7i2a3.htm. Accessed 15 July 2004.

Carnoy, M. (1984) *The State and Political Theory* (Princeton: Princeton University Press.

Carrier, J. G. and D. Miller (eds) (1998) *Virtualism: A New Political Economy*, Oxford: Berg.

Castells, M. (1983) *The City and the Grassroots: A Cross-Cultural Theory of Urban Social Movements*, Berkeley: University of California Press.

—— (1996) *The End of Millennium*, London: Blackwell.

—— (1997) *The Power of Identity*, Oxford: Blackwell.

Castro-Leal, F., J. Dayton, L. Demery and K. Mehra (2000) 'Public Spending on Health Care in Africa: Do the Poor Benefit?' *Bulletin of the World Health Organization* 78 (1), 66–74.

Cattell, V. and M. Evans (1999) *Neighborhood Images in East London: Social Capital and Social Networks on Two East London Estates*, York: York Publishing Services for the Joseph Rowntree Foundation.

Cauvin, H. (2000) 'South Africa Looks West for Some Economic Muscle,' *New York Times*, 31 December, p. 12.

Center for the Future State (2005) *Signposts to More Effective States: Responding to Governance Challenges in Developing Countries*, Sussex: Institute of Development Studies.

Central Statistics Agency (1995) Ethiopian Population and Housing Census, Addis Ababa: Central Statistics Agency.

Chabal, P. and J.-P. Daloz (1999) *Africa Works: Disorder as Political Instrument*, Oxford, Bloomington and Indianapolis: International African Institute, James Currey and Indiana University Press.

Chafe, W. H. and H. Sitkoff (eds) (1999) *A History of Our Time: Readings on Postwar America*, New York: Oxford University Press.

Chambers, R. (2002) 'Power, Knowledge and Policy Influence: Reflections on an Experience,' in K. Brock and R. McGee (eds) *Knowing Poverty: Critical Reflections on Participatory Research and Poverty*, London: Earthscan.

—— (2006) *Ideas for Development*, London: Earthscan.

Chandhoke, N. (2001) 'The "Civil" and the "Political" in Civil Society,' *Democratization* 8 (2), 1–24.

Chang H.-J. (1998) 'Evaluating the Current Industrial Policy of South Africa,' *Transformation: Critical Perspectives on Southern Africa* 36, 51–72.

—— (2003) *Globalization, Institutions and Economic Development*, London: Zed Books.

—— and I. Grabel (2004) *Reclaiming Development: An Alternative Economic Policy Manual*, London: Zed Books.

Chaplin, H. and A. Mathews (2005) 'Coping with the Fallout for Preference-Receiving Countries from EU Sugar Reform,' Policy Coherence Working Paper No. 1, Dublin: Institute for International Integration Studies, Trinity College, Dublin.

Chase Dunn, C. (1998) *Global Formation: Structures of the World Economy*, London: Rowman and Littlefield.

Chazan, N. (1988) 'State and Society in Africa: Images and Challenges,' in D. Rothchild and N. Chazan (eds) *The Precarious Balance: State and Society in Africa*, Boulder, CO: Lynne Rienner.

—— (1992) 'Liberalization, Governance and Political Space in Ghana,' in G. Hyden and M. Bratton (eds) *Governance and Politics in Africa*, Boulder, CO: Lynne Rienner.

——, P. Lewis, R. A. Mortimer, D. Rothchild and S. J. Stedman (1999) *Politics and Society in Contemporary Africa*, 3rd edn, Boulder, CO: Lynne Rienner.

Cheru, F. (1989) *The Silent Revolution in Africa: Debt and Development*, London: Zed Books.

—— (2001) *Economic, Social and Cultural Rights – The Highly Indebted Poor Countries (HIPC) Initiative: A Human Rights Assessment of the Poverty Reduction Strategy Papers (PRSPs)*, Report submitted to the 57th session of the Economic and Social Council of the United Nations, Commission on Human Rights. Available at www.unhchr.ch/tbs/doc.nsf/0/d66450e1d7b27564c1256a45004ca1c6/$FILE/G0140960.pdf.

—— (2002) *African Renaissance: Roadmaps to the Challenge of Globalization*, Cape Town and London: David Phillip and Zed Books.

Chikwanha, A., T. Sithole and M. Bratton (2004) *The Power of Propaganda: Public Opinion in Zimbabwe, 2004*, AfroBarometer Working Paper No. 42. Cape Town, Legon-Accra and East Lansing: IDASA, CDD-Ghana and MSU.

Chimakikire, D. P. (2003) 'Foreign and Security Policy of Zimbabwe: From Independence to the DRC,' in S. Darnolf and L. Laakso (eds) *Twenty Years of Independence in Zimbabwe: From Liberation to Authoritarianism*, Basingstoke and New York: Palgrave Macmillan, International Political Economy Series, 2003.

Chinese Ministry of Foreign Affairs (2006) 'China's Africa Policy,' 12 January. Available at http://news.xinhuanet.com. Accessed 18 September 2006.

Chossudovsky, M. (1997) *The Globalization of Poverty*, London and New York: Zed Books.

—— (2002) *War and Globalization: The Truth Behind September 11th*, Canada: Global Outlook.

Christiaensen, L., L. Demery and S. Paternostro (2002) *Growth, Distribution and Poverty in Africa: Messages from the 1990s*, Poverty Dynamics in Africa Series, Washington, D.C.: World Bank.

Chua, A. (2004) *World On Fire: How Exporting Free Market Democracy Breeds Ethnic Hatred and Global Instability*, New York: Anchor Books.

CIA (Central Intelligence Agency of the United States) (2002) *World FactBook 2002*. Available at http://www.umsl.edu/services/govdocs/wofact2002/fields/2076.html. Accessed 24 May 2005.

—— and National Security Council (2000) 'Global Trends 2015,' (December). Available at http://www.eia.doe.gov.

Clapham, C. (2000) 'Failed States and Non-States in the Modern International Order.' Available at www.ippu.purdue.edu/failed_states/2000/papers/clapham.html. Accessed 18 April 2005.

—— (2001) 'Rethinking African States,' *African Security Review* 10 (3). Available at www.is.co.za. Accessed 18 April 2005.

—— (2003) 'Terrorism in Africa: Problems of Definition, History and Development.' Paper presented at 'Africa after 9/11: Strategies for Engagement and Co-operation,' Alakawayn University, Ifrane, Morocco, July.

—— (2004) 'Background to Civil Society in Ethiopia,' in European Commission, *Mapping Non-State Actors in Ethiopia*. Available at http://www.deleth.

cec.eu.int/en/sections/Political%20and%20Information/mapping_non_state_ actors.htm. Accessed 15 July 2005.

Cleaver, F. (2004) 'Paradoxes of Participation: Questioning Participatory Approaches to Development,' in M. Edwards and A. Fowler (eds) *The Earthscan Reader on NGO Management*, London: Earthscan.

Clinton, B. (2005a) Interview with Miriam O'Callaghan on *Prime Time*, RTE, Irish Television.

—— (2005b) *My Life*, London: Arrow Books.

CNN (Cable Network News) (2006) Interview with J. Frazer, Undersecretary of State for African Affairs, September.

Coetzee, Z. R., K. Gwaradam, W. Naudé and J. Swanepoel (1997) 'Currency Depreciation, Trade Liberalization and Economic Development,' *South African Journal of Economics* 65 (2), 165–191.

Cogburn, D. (1998) 'Globalization and State Autonomy in the Information Age: Telecommunication Restructuring in South Africa,' *Journal of International Affairs* 51 (2), 583–604.

Coggan, P. (n.d.) 'Uncle Sam Stands Above the Rest,' *Financial Times*, FT Report-FT 500, p. 3.

Colcough, C. and J. Manor (eds) (1991) *States or Markets: Neo-Liberalism and the Development Policy Debate*, Oxford: Clarendon Paperbacks.

Coleman, J. (1988) 'Social Capital and the Creation of Human Capital,' *American Journal of Sociology* 94, Supplement, S95–S120.

—— (1990) *Foundations of Social Theory*, Cambridge: Harvard University Press.

Coleman, M. (2002) 'Thinking about the World Bank's "Accordion" Geography of Financial Globalization,' *Political Geography* 21, 495–524.

Colletta, N. and M. Cullen (2002) 'Resilient Communities: Building Social Foundations of Human Security,' in J. Isham, T. Kelly and S. Ramaswamy (eds) *Social Capital and Economic Development: On Well Being in Developing Countries*, Northampton, MA: Edward Elgar.

Comhlámh (2005) *Europe's New Free Trade Areas with Developing Countries*, Comhlámh Briefing Paper, Dublin: Comhlámh.

Commission for Africa (2004) *An Overview of Evidence*, Secretariat paper presented for the first meeting of the Commission on 4 May, available at http://www. commissionforafrica.org/english/about/meetings/first/trends_and_evidence. pdf. Accessed 13 September 2005.

—— (2005) *Our Common Interest: An Argument*, London: Penguin Books.

Cooke, B. (2004) 'Rules of Thumb for Participatory Change,' in S. Hickey and G. Mohan (eds) *Participation: From Tyranny to Transformation*, London: Zed Books.

Cooper, R. (2002) 'The New Liberal Imperialism,' *Observer World View Extra*, 7 April. Available at http://www.observer.co.uk. Accessed 3 February 2004.

—— (2003) *The Breaking of Nations: Order and Chaos in the Twenty-First Century*, Atlantic Books: London.

Corbridge, S. and J. Agnew (1995) *Mastering Space: Hegemony, Territory and International Political Economy*, London: Routledge.

Corcoran, B. (2005a) 'Mbeki Admits Failure of Zimbabwe Strategy,' *Irish Times*, 20 August, p. 9.

—— (2005b) 'Police Raze Homes, Mass Arrests in Harare,' *Irish Times*, 27 May, p. 13.

Cornwall, A. (2000) 'Beneficiary, Consumer, Citizen: Perspectives on Participation in Poverty Reduction,' *Sida Studies* 2, Stockholm: Sida.

—— (2003) 'Whose Voices? Whose Choices? Reflections on Gender and Participatory Development,' *World Development* 31 (8), 1325–1342.

—— (2004a) 'Spaces for Transformation? Reflections on Issues of Power and Difference in Participation in Development,' in S. Hickey and G. Mohan (eds) *Participation: From Tyranny to Transformation*, London: Zed Books.

—— (2004b) 'Introduction: New Democratic Spaces? The Politics and Dynamics of Institutionalized Participation,' IDS Bulletin 35 (2), 1–9.

—— and C. Nyamu-Musembi (2004) 'Putting the "Rights-Based Approach" to Development into Perspective,' *Third World Quarterly* 25 (8), 1415–1437.

—— and K. Brock (2005) *Beyond Buzzwords: 'Poverty Reduction,' 'Participation' and 'Empowerment' in Development Policy*. Overarching Concerns Programme Paper Number 10, Geneva: UNRISD.

Corporate Watch (2003) 'Farms, Fascism and Famine: Land Reform and the Politics of Disintegration in Zimbabwe,' Corporate Watch Newsletter, Issue 14, July–August. Available at http://archive.corporatewatch.org. Accessed 10 August 2006.

Cowell, A. and R. Swarns (2001) '\$17.6 Billion Deal to Make De Beers Private Company,' *New York Times*, 16 February, p. W1.

Cowen, M. and R. Shenton (1996) *Doctrines of Development*, London: Routledge.

Cox, R. (1987) *Production, Power and World Order: Social Forces in the Making of History*, New York: Columbia University Press.

—— (2004) 'Beyond Empire and Terror: Critical Reflections on the Political Economy of World Order,' *New Political Economy* 9 (3), 307–323.

Coyle, E., Z. Curran and A. Evans (2003) *PRSP synthesis note 7*, Monitoring and Synthesis Project, June, London.

Craig, D. and D. Porter (2002) 'Poverty Reduction Strategy Papers: A New Convergence,' in *World Development* 30 (12), 53–69.

—— (2006) *Development Beyond Neoliberalism: Governance, Poverty Reduction and Political Economy*, London: Routledge.

Craigslist.org (2005) 'High-Frequency Active Aural Research Program.' Available at http://seattle.craigslist.org/pol/97813474.html. Accessed 26 September 2005.

Cramer, C. (1999) 'Can Africa Industrialize by Processing Primary Commodities? The Case of Mozambican Cashew Nuts,' *World Development* 27 (7), 1247–1266.

—— (2006) *Civil War is Not a Stupid Thing*, London: Hurst.

Crawford, G. (1996) *Promoting Democracy, Human Rights and Good Governance Through Development Aid: A Comparative Study of the Policies of Four Northern Donors*, Working Paper on Democratization, Leeds: Centre for Democratization Studies.

CRDA (Christian Relief and Development Association) (1998) *25 Years of Service to the People of Ethiopia, Silver Jubilee Anniversary Issue*, Addis Ababa: CRDA.

—— (2002) *CRDA News*, 18 (9).

Cross, E. (n.d.) 'The Truth About Zimbabwe's Theft of Private Assets and NEPAD.' Available at http://africantears.netfirms.com/eddiecross.htm Accessed 27 June 2005.

Cunill, N. (n.d.) 'Responsabilización por el control social,' United Nations Online Network in Public Administration and Finance (UNPAN). Available at http://unpan1.un.org/intradoc/groups/public/documents/clad/unpan000183.pdf.

Curran, L. (2006) 'The Impact of Liberalisation of the EU Textiles and Clothing Trade on Key Developing Country Suppliers,' Paper Presented at 'Linking the

Local and the Global: Education for Development in a Globalizing World,' March 23–24, Dublin City University.

DAG (Development Assistance Group) (2002) *Key Elements of a Strategic Framework for DAG Support to Civil Society Engagement in the SDPRP*, UNDP.

Dailami, M. and M. Walton (1989) *Private Investment, Government Policy and Foreign Capital in Zimbabwe*, World Bank Policy, Planning and Research Working Paper 248, Washington, D.C.: World Bank.

Daily Graphic (2005) 'Ideals of NEPAD to be Taught as SSS (senior secondary school) Level.' Available at: http://www.kumasimetro.org/kmanews/cn_kma_more.cfm?tblNewsID=773&tblNewsCatID=62. Accessed 28 July 2005.

Daniel, J., J. Lutchman and S. Naidu (2004) 'Post-Apartheid South Africa's Corporate Expansion into Africa,' *Review of African Political Economy* 100, 343–378.

Dansereau, S. (2005) 'Between a Rock and a Hard Place: Zimbabwe's Development Impasse,' in H. Melber (ed.) *Zimbabwe – The Political Economy of Decline*, Uppsala: Nordiska Afrikainstitutet.

Dashwood, H. (1996) 'The Relevance of Class to the Evolution of Zimbabwe's Development Strategy 1980–1991,' *Journal of Southern African Studies* 22 (1), 27–48.

—— (2000) *Zimbabwe: The Political Economy of Transformation*, Toronto: University of Toronto Press.

Davidson, B. (1993) *The Black Man's Burden: Africa and the Curse of the Nation State*, Three Rivers Press.

Davies, R. (1996) 'New Sources for Growth and Hope: Prospects for Southern Africa,' *Development* 2, 24–28.

—— (2004) 'Memories of Underdevelopment: A Personal Interpretation of Zimbabwe's Economic Decline,' in B. Raftopolous and T. Savage (eds) *Zimbabwe: Injustice and Political Reconciliation*, Ann Arbor: Michigan State University Press.

DCI (Development Co-operation Ireland) (2004) *Bridging the Gap between People and Power in Ethiopia*, Participatory Development and Governance Programme Strategy Paper., Addis Ababa: DCI.

Deacon, B. (2000) *Globalization and Social Policy: The Threat to Equitable Welfare*, United Nations Research Institute for Social Development Occasional Paper No. 5, Geneva: UNSRID. Available at http://www.unrisd.org/unrisd/website/document.nsf/0/815BC5D09E74323A80256B67005B740A?OpenDocument. Accessed 13 September 2005.

—— with M. Hulse and P. Stubbs (1997) *Global Social Policy: International Organisations and the Future of Welfare*, London: SAGE.

Debt and Development Coalition Ireland (2004) *How Does the European Commission Engage with Poverty Reduction Process*, Dublin: Debt and Development Coalition.

Degefe, B. and B. Nega (eds) (2000) *Annual Report on the Ethiopian Economy 1999/2000*, vol. 1, Addis Abba: Ethiopian Economic Association.

de Herdt, T. and J. Dastiaensen (2004) 'Aid as an Encounter at the Interface: The Complexity of the Global Fight against Poverty,' *Third World Quarterly* 25 (5), 871–885.

de Martino, G. (2000) *Global Economy, Global Justice Theoretical Objections and Policy Alternatives to Neoliberalism*, London: Routledge.

Denny, C. (2002) 'Nestle Claims £3.7m from Famine Hit Ethiopia,' *The Guardian*, 19 December. Available at http://www.guardian.co.uk/famine/story/0,12128, 862655,00.html. Accessed 1 August 2005.

—— and C. Moore (2004) 'Family's £25m Sugar Bonanza: Westons Profit from Rigged Market, Says Oxfam Report,' *The Guardian*, 14 April, p. 16.

Department for International Development and Her Majesty's Treasury (2005) 'Partnerships for Poverty Reduction: Rethinking Conditionality,' London: Department for International Development.

Department of Finance (1996) *Growth, Employment and Redistribution: A Macroeconomic Strategy*, Pretoria: Government Printers. Available at http://www.treasury.gov.za/documents/gear/all.pdf. Accessed 3 April 2007.

Department of Trade and Industry (1998) South African Foreign Trade: Selected Statistics, July 1998 (unpublished).

—— (1999) 'Preparing for WTO Multilateral Trade Negotiations in 2000: Towards a South African Framework' (photocopy).

Dercon, S., T. Gebre Selassie and P. Krishnan (2005) 'The Urban Labor Market during Structural Adjustment in Ethiopia 1990–1997,' in A. Bigsten, A. Shimeles and B. Kebebe (eds), *Poverty, Income Distribution and Labor Markets in Ethiopia*, Uppsala: Nordiska Afrikainstitutet.

de Sardan, O. (1999) 'A Moral Economy of Corruption in Africa?' *Journal of Modern African Studies* 37 (1), 25–52.

De Sio (2001) 'Somalia's Internet is Casualty of War on Terrorism,' *Digital Freedom Network*, 29 November. Available at www.dfn.org/news/somalia/internet-casualty.htm.

de Soto, H. (1989) *The Other Path: The Invisible Revolution in the Third World*, London: Tauris.

—— (2001) *The Mystery of Capital: Why Capitalism Triumphs in the West and Fails Everywhere Else*, London: Black Swan.

de Waal, A. (2002) 'What's New in the "New Partnership for Africa's Development?"' *International Affairs* 101 (404), 463–474.

—— (2004) 'Rethinking Aid: Developing a Human Security Package for Africa,' *New Economy* 13 (2), 158–163.

—— (2006) 'The Challenge of HIV/AIDS,' in C. Toulmin, B. Wisner and R. Chitiga (eds) *Towards a New Map of Africa*, London: Earthscan and IIED.

—— and A. H. Abdel Salam (2004) 'Africa, Islamism and America's "War on Terror" after September 11,' in A. de Waal (ed.), *Islamism and Its Enemies in the Horn of Africa*, London: Hurst and Company.

Dia, M. (1996) *Africa's Management in the 1990s and Beyond: Reconciling Indigenous and Transplanted Institutions*, Directions in Development Series, Washington, D.C.: World Bank.

Diamond, L. (1988) 'Introduction: Roots of Failure, Seeds of Hope,' in L. Diamond, J. J. Linz and M. Lipset (eds) *Democracy in Developing Countries: Africa*, vol. II, Boulder, CO: Lynne Rienner.

—— (1994) 'Rethinking Civil Society: Toward Democratic Consolidation,' *Journal of Democracy* 5, 4–17.

—— (1997) *Prospects for Democratic Development in Africa*, Stanford, CA: Hoover Institution.

Dicklitch, S. (1998) *The Elusive Promise of NGOs in Africa: Lessons from Uganda*, International Political Economy Series, Basingstoke: Macmillan.

Dollar, D. and A. Kraay (2005) 'Growth is Good for the Poor.' Available at http://www.worldbank.org/research/growth/pdfiles/growthgoodforpoor.pdf. Accessed 12 September 2005.

Dorman, S. R. (n.d.) 'NGOs and State in Zimbabwe: Implications for Civil-Society Theory,' in B. Beckman, A. Sjogren and E. Hannsen (eds), (forthcoming) *Civil Society, Authoritarianism and Globalization.*

—— (2001) *Inclusion and Exclusion: NGOs and Politics in Zimbabwe*, D.Phil thesis, Oxford University.

—— (2002) 'Rocking the Boat?: Church NGOs and Democratization in Zimbabwe,' *African Affairs* 101, 75–92.

Douthwaite, R. (2004a) 'Kerala.' Available at http://www.greenbooks.co.uk/ Douthwaite/kerala.htm. Accessed 8 January 2004.

—— (2004b) Lecture, St. Patrick's College, Dublin City University, 29 April.

Doyle, D. (2004) 'Ethiopia Briefing Paper,' for 'Civil Society Engagement for Poverty Reduction' Project, Center for International Studies, Dublin City University.

DRC (Democratic Republic of the Congo) (2002) *Interim Poverty Reduction Strategy Paper.* Available at http://www.imf.org/external/np/prsp/2002/cod/01/index. htm. Accessed 24 July 2006.

Drinkwater, M. (1991) *The State and Agrarian Change in Zimbabwe's Communal Areas*, London: Palgrave Macmillan.

Duffield, M. (1993) 'NGOs, Disaster Relief and Asset Transfer in the Horn: Political Survival in a Permanent Emergency,' *Development and Change* 24, 131–151.

—— (2001) *Global Governance and the New Wars*, London: Zed Books.

—— (2005a) 'Human Security: Linking Development and Security in an Age of Terror,' Paper for the 11th General Conference of the EADI, Bonn 21–24 September.

—— (2005b) 'Native Administration Past and Present,' Paper presented to the Royal Geographical Society/Institute of British Geographers Conference, 31 August–2 September, London.

—— and J. Prendergaast (1994) *Without Troops and Tanks: Humanitarian Intervention in Eritrea and Ethiopia*, Asmara: Red Sea Press.

Duke, L. (1997) 'South Africans Look North, Invests in Neighbors,' Washington Post, 6 November, p. A30.

Dunn, K. (2003) 'Africa's Ambiguous Relation to Empire,' in P. Passavant and J. Dean (eds) *Empire's New Clothes: Reading Hardt and Negri*, London: Routledge.

Durac, V. (2004) Lecture, St. Patrick's College, Dublin City University, 20th April.

Economic Commission for Africa and Economic Policy Research Center (2003) *Key Components of Pro-Poor Growth Strategies*, Proceedings of Expert Group Meeting, Munyonyo Speke Resort, Kampala, Uganda, 23–24 June.

Economic Focus: Bulletin of the Ethiopian Economics Association (2002) Issue 5 (2), July–August.

Economist, The (1995a) 'Investing in Africa: A New Scramble,' 12 August, 17.

—— (1995b) 'Not a Golden Titan, More a Pig in Poke,' 7 October, 67–68.

—— (1996) 'Latin America's Backlash,' 30 November.

—— (1998) 'Cautionary Tale of Black Business: South Africa,' 10 January, 38.

—— (2000) 'The Inside Outsider,' 22 July, 65.

—— (2001a) 'Inequality Changes Colour,' A Survey of South Africa, 24 February, 10.

—— (2001b) 'Jobless and Joyless,' A Survey of South Africa, 24 February, 11.

—— (2001c) 'Minefield,' 17 March, 61–62.

—— (2001d) 'Over the Rainbow,' A Survey of South Africa, 24 February, 14–15.

—— (2001e) Issue of 24 March.

—— (2004a) 'Coke and al-Qaeda,' 3 April, 44.

—— (2004b) 'Counting the Cost: The Price of Zimbabwe's Collapse for the Rest of Africa,' 19 July 2004. Available at http://www.economist.com/displaystory.cfm?story_id= 2194218. Accessed 19 July 2004.

—— (2004c) Issue of 6 November, 106.

—— (2004d) 'The Shameless Rich and Voiceless Poor: Stomach Churning Allegations about Angola's Rulers,' 22 January, 42–43.

—— (2004e) 'The Thin Red Line: A Bastion of Indian Communism Rebrands Itself,' 6 May. Available at http://www.economist.com.

—— (2004f) 'Zimbabwe: Where Have All the People Gone,' 27 November, 42.

—— (2005a) 'A Taste for Democracy,' 21 May, 43–45.

—— (2005b) 'Banking in South Africa: Absa's Allure,' 28 April. Available at www.economist.com. Accessed 24 July 2006.

—— (2005c) 'Into Africa,' 27 August, 5.

—— (2005d) 'Is America's Millennium Challenge Account Too Challenging for Its Own Good?' 21 April. Available from http://www.economist.com/displaystory.cfm?story_id=3887385. Accessed 19 May 2005.

—— (2005e) *Old-Age Income Support in the 21st Century*, quoted in 'Second Thoughts on the Third Age,' 19 February, 63.

—— (2005f) 'Somaliland: Trying to Behave Like a Proper State,' 1–7 October, 41.

—— (2005g) 'The $25 Billion Dollar Question,' 2–8 July, 25–27.

—— (2006a) 'South African Business: Going Global,' 15 July, 55–56.

—— (2006b) 'The Rising Fear of a War of Proxies,' 15 July, 39–40.

—— (2006c) 15 July, 86.

Economist Intelligence Unit (1997) *Business Africa*, London: EIU.

—— (2000) *Country Report: South Africa*, 1st quarter 2000, London: EIU.

—— (2002a) *Business Africa*, 1–15 September, 2.

—— (2002b) 'September 11th, One Year on: How US-African Relations Have Changed,' *Business Africa*, 1, 15 September, 1.

—— (2003) *Zimbabwe: Country Report*, December 2003, draft, London: EIU.

—— (2005a) *Country Report June 2005: Zimbabwe*, London: EIU.

—— (2005b) *Country Report March 2005: Zimbabwe*, London: EIU.

Edge, W. and M. Kekorwe (eds) (1998) *Botswana: Politics and Society*, Pretoria: J. L. van Schaik Publishers.

Edkins, J. (2002) 'Forget Trauma? Responses to September 11,' *International Relations* 16 (2), 243–256.

Edwards, C. (1998) 'Financing Faster Growth in South Africa: The Case for Reforming the Financial Sector,' *Transformation: Critical Perspectives on Southern Africa* 35, 49–76.

Edwards, M. (2000) *NGO Rights and Responsibilities: A New Deal for Global Governance*, London: Foreign Policy Center, 2000.

—— (2004a) 'Beyond Partnership: Getting Real about NGO Relationships in the Aid System,' in M. Edwards and A. Fowler (eds) *The Earthscan Reader on NGO Management*, London: Earthscan.

—— (2004b) 'International Development NGOs: Agents of Foreign Aid or Vehicles for International Cooperation?' in M. Edwards and A. Fowler (eds) *The Earthscan Reader on NGO Management*, London: Earthscan.

—— (2004c) 'NGO Performance: What Breeds Success? New Evidence from South Asia,' in M. Edwards and A. Fowler (eds) *The Earthscan Reader on NGO Management*, London: Earthscan.

—— (2004d) 'Organizational Learning in Non-Governmental Organizations: What Have We Learned?' in M. Edwards and A. Fowler (eds) *The Earthscan Reader on NGO Management*, London: Earthscan.

—— and A. Fowler (2004) 'Introduction: Changing Challenges for NGDO Management,' in M. Edwards and A. Fowler (eds) *The Earthscan Reader on NGO Management*, London: Earthscan.

—— and D. Hulme (2000) 'Too Close for Comfort? The Impact of Official Aid on Nongovernmental Organizations,' *World Development* 24 (6), 961–973, reprinted in S. Corrbridge (ed.) *Development: Critical Concepts in the Social Sciences*, vol. IV, *States Politics and Civil Society*, London: Routledge.

—— (2004) 'Making a Difference: Scaling-up the Developmental Impact of NGOs – Concepts and Experiences,' in M. Edwards and A. Fowler (eds) *The Earthscan Reader on NGO Management*, London: Earthscan.

—— and D. Hulme (eds) (1992) *Making a Difference: NGOs and Development in a Changing World*, London: Earthscan.

—— and S. Golub (2004) 'South Africa's International Cost Competitiveness and Exports in Manufacturing,' *World Development* 32 (8), 1323–1339.

EEA (Ethiopian Economics Association) (2004) *Report on the Ethiopian Economy, Volume III 2003/2004: Industrialization and Industrial Policy in Ethiopia*, Addis Ababa: Ethiopian Economics Association.

Ege, S. (2002) 'Peasant Participation in Land Reform: The Amhara Land Redistribution of 1997,' in B. Zewde and S. Pausewang (eds) *Ethiopia: The Challenge of Democracy from Below*, Nordiska Afrikainstitutet and Forum for Social Studies: Stockholm.

Ehrenber, J. (1999) *Civil Society: The Critical History of an Idea*, New York: New York University Press.

Elbadawi, I. and A. Gelb (2003) 'Financing Africa's Development: Toward a Business Plan?' in N. van de Walle, N. Ball and V. Ramachandran (eds) *Beyond Structural Adjustment: The Institutional Context of Development*, New York: Palgrave Macmillan.

Electionworld (2005) Elections database. Available at http://www.electionworld. org/ethiopia.htm. Accessed 1 August 2005.

Elliot, E. and D. Kiel (1997) 'Nonlinear Dynamics, Complexity and Public Policy,' in R. A. Eve, S. Horsfall and M. E. Lee (eds) *Chaos, Complexity and Sociology*, London: SAGE.

Ellis, F. and G. Bahigwa (2003) 'Livelihoods and Rural Poverty Reduction in Uganda,' *World Development* 31 (6), 997–1013.

Ellis, S. (1999) 'The New Frontiers of Crime in South Africa,' in J.-F. Bayart, S. Ellis and B. Hibou (eds) *The Criminalization of the State in Africa*, Oxford, Bloomington and Indianapolis: James Currey and Indiana University Press.

—— (2004) 'Briefing: The Pan-Sahel Initiative,' *African Affairs* 103 (12), 459–466.

El-Tom, A. (2005) 'Darfur, Race and the Arab-Islamic Project,' African Studies Association of Ireland Seminar, Dublin, 18 April.

Encarnación, O. (2000) 'Tocqueville's Missionaries: Civil Society and the Promotion of Democracy,' *World Policy Journal* XVII (1), 9–18.

Engberg-Pedersen, L. (2002) 'The Limitations of Political Space in Burkina Faso: Local Organizations, Decentralization and Poverty Reduction,' in N. Webster and L. Engberg-Pedersen (eds) *In the Name of the Poor: Contesting Political Space for Poverty Reduction*, London: Zed Books.

—— and N. Webster (2002) 'Introduction to Political Space,' in N. Webster and L. Engberg-Pedersen (eds) *In the Name of the Poor: Contesting Political Space for Poverty Reduction*, London: Zed Books.

Escobar, A. (1995) *Encountering Development: The Making and Unmaking of the Third World*, Princeton, NJ: Princeton University Press.

Esping-Andersson, G. (1999) *The Social Foundations of Post-Industrial Economies*, Oxford and New York: Oxford University Press.

Esteva, G. and M. Suri Prakesh (1998) *Grassroots Post-Modernism: Remaking the Soil of Cultures*, London: Zed Books.

Etaiwannews.com (2005) 'United States Increases Its Military Clout across Africa.' Available at http://www.etaiwannews.com/World/2004/02/29/1078026919. htm. Accessed 19 June 2005.

Ethiopian Civil Society Organizations (n.d.) 'Recommendations to the Second Annual Progress Report (APR) (2003/2004) of the Sustainable Development and Poverty Reduction Program (SDPRP).' Available at http://www.crda. ethiopia.org. Accessed 31 July 2005.

Ethiopian News and Views (2005) 'The Hijacked Election,' 16 July. Available at http://www.geocities.com/~dagmawi/Zebenya/05/Hijacked_Kercha.html. Accessed 31 July 2005.

Ethiosports (n.d.) 'Profile of Sheikh Mohammed Hussein Al-Amoudi.' Available at http://www.ethiosports.com/Sheikh_Mohammed_Hussein_Al_Amoudi.html. Accessed 24 June 2005.

Eurodad (European Network on Debt and Development) (2004) 'Eurodad Analysis of the 2004 World Bank and IMF PRSP Evaluations from a Donor Perspective.' Available at http://www.eurodad.org/articles/default.aspx?id=557. Accessed 19 October 2004.

European Commission (2000) 'The Lisbon Agenda.' The Lisbon European Council – An Agenda of Economic and Social Renewal for Europe. Contribution of the European Commission to the Special European Council in Lisbon, 23–24 March 2000. Available at http://ec.europa.eu/growthandjobs/ pdf/lisbon_en.pdf. Accessed 28 July 2005.

—— (2001) *Ethiopia – European Community: Country Strategy Paper and Indicative Programme for the Period 2002–2007*. Available at http://www.euforic.org/ by_place/et.htm. Accessed 13 September 2005.

Evans, P. (1995) *Embedded Autonomy: States and Industrial Transformation*, Princeton, NJ: Princeton University Press.

—— (1996a) 'Development Strategies Across the Public–Private Divide,' *World Development* 24 (6), 1033–1037.

—— (1996b) 'Government Action, Social Capital and Development: Reviewing the Evidence on Synergy,' *World Development* 24 (6), 1119–1132.

—— (2004) 'Development as Institutional Change: The Pitfalls of Monocropping and the Potentials of Deliberation,' *Studies in Comparative International Development* 38 (4), 30–52.

—— (2005) 'Global Social Movements: Capability Politics in an Era of Bit Driven Growth,' Sociology Seminar, National University of Ireland, Maynooth, 25 April.

Express, The (2001) 'NGO Congestion Creates Chaos,' 26 July–1 August, Dar es Salaam.

Fairtrade (2002) 'Coffee Prices and Famine in Ethiopia.' Available at http://www.fairtrade.org.uk/pr191102.htm.

Fajertag, G. and P. Pochet (eds) (1997) *Social Pacts in Europe: New Dynamics*, Brussels: OSE.

Falk, R. (2000) 'Humane Governance for the World: Reviving the Quest,' in J. Nederveen Pieterse (ed.) *Global Futures: Shaping Globalization*, London: Zed Books.

—— (2003) *The Great Terror War*, Gloucestershire: Arris Books.

Fallon, P. and R. Lucas (1998) *South Africa: Labor Markets, Adjustment and Inequality*, Discussion Paper No. 12, Informal Discussion Papers on Aspects of the Economy of South Africa, World Bank Southern Africa Department, Washington, D.C.: World Bank.

Farah, M. (2005) 'The Impacts of Foreign Aid on Mozambique. Unpublished Essay for Africa Module on Masters of Arts in Globalisation,' Dublin City University.

Farrington, J. and A. Bebbington with K. Wills and D. Lewis (1993) *Reluctant Partners? NGOs, the State and Sustainable Agricultural Development*, London: Routledge.

—— and D. Lewis (eds) with S. Satish and A. Miclat-Teves (1993) *NGOs and the State in Asia: Rethinking Roles in Sustainable Agricultural Development*, London: Routledge.

Fatton, R. (1995) 'Africa in the Age of Democratization: The Civic Limitations of Civil Society,' *African Studies Review* 38 (2), 67–99.

Ferguson, J. (1994) *The Anti-Politics Machine: 'Development', Depoliticization and Bureaucratic Power in Lesotho*, Minneapolis and London: University of Minnesota Press.

—— (2006) *Global Shadows: Africa in the Neoliberal World Order*, Durham, NC: Duke University Press.

—— (n.d.) 'Transnational Topographies of Power: Beyond "the State" and "Civil Society" in the Study of African Politics,' draft mimeo, Department of Anthropology, University of California, Irvine.

Fidler, S., R. Khalaf and M. Huband (2004) 'Return to the Fold: How Gadaffi Was Persuaded to Give up His Nuclear Goals,' *Financial Times*, 27 January, p. 17.

Field, G. (1998) 'South Africa's Next Revolution,' *Worldlink* January/February. Available at http://backissues.worldlink.co.uk.

Financial Gazette (2003), Harare.

Financial Times, The (1999) 'Global 500,' 28 January.

—— (2004) '"Curse of Oil" Puts African States in Sticky Situation,' 24 March, p. 16.

—— (2006) 'Friend or Forager? How China Is Winning Resources and the Loyalties of Africa,' 23 February, p. 15.

Fine, B. (1997) *Industrial Policy and South Africa: A Strategic View*, National Institute for Economic Policy Occasional Paper Series, No. 5, April 1997.

—— (1999) 'The Developmental State Is Dead – Long Live Social Capital?' *Development and Change* 3, 1–19.

—— (2001) *Social Capital Versus Social Theory: Political Economy and Social Science at the Turn of the Millennium*, London: Routledge.

—— (2003) 'The Social Capital of the World Bank,' in B. Fine, C. Lapavitsas and J. Pincus (eds) *Development Policy in the Twenty-First Century: Beyond the Post-Washington Consensus*, London: Routledge.

—— (2004) 'Examining the Ideas of Globalization and Development Critically: What Role for Political Economy?' *New Political Economy* 9 (2), 213–231.

—— with D. Davis (1990) *Beyond Apartheid: Labor and Liberation in South Africa*, London: Pluto Press.

—— and Z. Rustomjee (1996) *The Political Economy of South Africa: From Minerals-Energy Complex to Industrialization*, London: Hurst and Company.

Fingleton, E. (1999) *In Praise of Hard Industries: Why Manufacturing not the New Economy Is the Key to Future Prosperity*, London: Orion Business Books.

Fitschen, A. (1998) 'The Impact of the Saldanha Steel Project on the West Coast Economy,' in 'Spatial Development Initiatives: Unlocking Economic Potential,' Special Issue of *Development Southern Africa* 15 (5), 771–786.

Focke Report, The (1980) *From Lome I to Lome II; Texts of the Report of the Resolution Adopted on 26 September 1980 by the ACP-EEC Consultative Assembly*, Luxembourg: European Parliament.

Focus on Trade (2000) Issue No. 51, June.

Forbes Magazine (2006) March issue.

Ford, N. (2005) 'Crucial Trade Issues Ignored by G8,' *African Business*, August/September, 312, 18–20.

Forrest, J. (1998) 'State Inversion and Nonstate Politics,' in L. Villalón and P. Huxtable (eds) *The African State at a Critical Juncture* Boulder, CO: Lynne Rienner.

Foundation for Research and Development (1996) *SA Science and Technology Indicators*, FRD, Pretoria.

—— and Industrial Strategy Project (1997) *Innovation Patterns in South African Manufacturing Firms – Report on the Survey of Innovative Activity in South African Manufacturing Firms*, FRD and ISP: Pretoria and Cape Town.

Fowler, A. (1993) 'NGOs as Agents of Democratization: An African Perspective,' *Journal of International Development* 5 (3).

—— (1997) *Striking a Balance: A Guide to Enhancing the Effectiveness of Non-Governmental Organisations in International Development*, London: Earthscan.

—— (1998) 'Authentic NGDO Partnerships in the New Policy Agency for International Aid: Dead End or Light Ahead?' *Development and Change* 29 (1), 137–159.

—— (2000) *NGOs, Civil Society and Development: Changing the Rules of the Game*, Geneva: United Nations Research Institute for Social Development.

—— (2002) 'Performance Measurement for Development Interventions: NGDO Experience,' in K. van der Molen, A. van Rooyen and B. van Wyk (eds) *Outcomes-Based Governance: Assessing the Results*, Sandown: Heinemann.

—— (2004a) 'An NGDO Strategy: Learning for Leverage,' in M. Edwards and A. Fowler (eds) *The Earthscan Reader on NGO Management*, London: Earthscan.

—— (2004b) 'Assessing NGO Performance: Difficulties, Dilemmas and a Way Ahead,' in M. Edwards and A. Fowler (eds) *The Earthscan Reader on NGO Management*, London: Earthscan.

—— (2004c) 'Beyond Partnership: Getting Real about NGO Relationships in the Aid System,' in M. Edwards and A. Fowler (eds) *The Earthscan Reader on NGO Management*, London: Earthscan.

—— (2004d) 'NGO Futures – Beyond Aid: NGDO Values and the Fourth Position,' in M. Edwards and A. Fowler (eds) *The Earthscan Reader on NGO Management*, London: Earthscan.

Francis, P. and R. James (2003) 'Balancing Rural Poverty Reduction and Citizen Participation: The Contradictions of Uganda's Decentralization Program,' *World Development* 31 (2), 325–337.

Frazer, J. (2006) 'Current Themes in U.S.–Africa Policy,' Address given at Chatham House, London, 16 May 2006. Available at www.state.gov. Accessed 29 August 2006.

Freeman, L. (2005a) 'Contradictory Constructions of the Crisis in Zimbabwe,' *Historia* 2, 287–310.

—— (2005b) 'Unraveling the Contradictions – South Africa's Zimbabwe Policy,' *Journal of Contemporary African Studies* 23 (2), 147–172.

Friedmann, J. (1992) *Empowerment: The Politics of Alternative Development*, Oxford: Basil Blackwell.

Fuller, D. and A. E. G. Jonas (2003) 'Alternative Financial Spaces,' in A. Leyshon, R. Lee and C. C. Williams (eds) *Alternative Economic Spaces*, London, Thousand Oaks and New Delhi: SAGE.

Gabriel, A. H. (2002) *The PRSP Process in Ethiopia: Second Meeting of the African Learning Group on the Poverty Reduction Strategy Papers*, 18–21 November, Brussels, Addis Ababa: UNECA.

Gabriel, N. (n.d.) 'Monterrey: Spinning the Washington Consensus All the Way to Johannesburg.' Available at: http://www.holycrossjustice.org/monterrey.htm. Accessed 28 July 2005.

Gallagher, K. (ed.) (2005) *Putting Development First: The Importance of Policy Space*, London: Zed Books.

Gallagher, T. (2003) 'Is Big Government Back? The Political Economy of Activist Government Policy,' *Business Economics*, July, pp. 25–37.

Gallin, D. (2000) *Trade Unions and NGOs: A Necessary Partnership for Social Development*, Civil Society and Social Movements Programme Paper Number 1, Geneva: UNRISD.

Gandu, G. (2005) '"Vendetta" Points to Zanu-PF Split,' *Mail and Guardian*, 22 July. Available at http://www.mg.co.za. Accessed 24 June 2005.

Garbutt, A. and B. Pratt (2003) 'Official Agency Interaction with Civil Society,' A Report of the Two Day Official AgencyWorkshop/Forum for the Dutch Foreign Ministry, 4–5 December, Oxford: INTRAC.

Garrison, J. (2000) *From Confrontation to Collaboration: Civil Society–Government–World Bank Relations in Brazil*, Washington, D.C.: World Bank.

GATT (General Agreement on Tariffs and Trade) (1993) *Trade Policy Review: The Republic of South Africa*, vol. 1, Geneva: GATT.

Gautney, H. (2003) 'The Globalization of Violence in the 21st Century: Israel, Palestine and the War on Terror,' in S. Aronowitz and H. Gautney (eds) *Implicating Empire: Globalization and Resistance in the 21st Century*, New York, Basic Books.

Gaventa, J. (2004) 'Towards Participatory Governance: Assessing the Transformative Possibilities,' in S. Hickey and G. Mohan (eds) *Participation: From Tyranny to Transformation*, London: Zed Books.

Geda, A. and J. Weeks (2002) *Evaluation of UNDP's Role in the PRSP Process: Ethiopia*, Addis Ababa: UNDP.

Geda, T. (2004) 'Businesses Unhappy with Customs' Performance,' *Capital: The Paper that Promotes Free Enterprise* 6 (301), 12–18 September, p. 1.

Gelb, S. (ed) (1991) *South Africa's Economic Crisis*, Cape Town, London and New Jersey: David Philip and Zed Books.

—— (1997) 'South Africa's Post-Apartheid Political Economy,' in L. Swatuk and D. Black (eds) *Bridging the Rift: The New South Africa in Africa*, Boulder, CO: Westview Press.

—— (1999) 'Economic Growth, People and the Environment,' in G. Maharaj (ed.) *Between Unity and Diversity: Essays on Nation-Building in Post-Apartheid South Africa*, Cape Town: Idasa and David Philip.

—— (2003) 'Inequality in South Africa: Nature, Causes and Responses,' DFID Policy Initiative on Addressing Inequality in Middle-Income Countries, Johannesburg: The Edge Institute.

—— and C. Manning (eds) (1998) 'Spatial Development Initiatives: Unlocking Economic Potential,' Special Issue of *Development Southern Africa* 15 (5), 717–942.

—— and A. Black (2004) 'Foreign Direct Investment in South Africa,' in S. Entrin and K. Meyer (eds) (2004) *Investment Strategies in Emerging Markets*, Cheltenham: Edgar Elgar.

Gibb, R. (2004) 'International and Regional Trade in Eastern and Southern Africa,' in D. Potts and T. Boyer-Bower (eds) *Eastern and Southern African: Development Challenges in a Volatile Region*, New York: Prentice Hall.

Gibbon, P. (1992) 'The World Bank and African Poverty,' *The Journal of Modern African Studies* 30 (2), 193–220.

—— (1996) 'Structural Adjustment and Structural Change in Sub-Saharan Africa: Some Provisional Conclusions,' *Development and Change* 27, 751–784.

—— (2001a) *At the Cutting Edge: UK Clothing Retailers and Global Sourcing*, Centre for Development Research Working Paper, 01.4, Copenhagen.

—— (2001b) 'Upgrading Primary Production: A Global Commodity Chain Approach,' *World Development* 29 (2), 345–363.

—— (2002) 'Present-Day Capitalism, the New International Trade Regime and Africa,' *Review of African Political Economy* 91, 95–112.

—— (2003) 'The African Growth and Opportunity Act and the Global Commodity Chain for Clothing,' *World Development* 31 (11), 1809–1827.

—— and S. Ponte (2005) *Trading Down: Africa, Value Chains and the Global Economy*, Philadelphia: Temple University Press.

—— K. J. Havenevik and K. Hermele (1993) *A Blighted Harvest: The World Bank and African Agriculture in the 1980s*, Trenton, NJ: Africa World Press.

Gibbs, C. (1999) *Politicians and Poachers: The Political Economy of Wildlife Policy in Africa*, Cambridge and New York: Cambridge University Press.

——, C. Fumo and T. Kuby (1999) *Non-Governmental Organizations in World Bank-Supported Projects: A Review*, Washington, D.C.: World Bank Operations Evaluation Department.

Gibson, S. (1999) 'Aid and Politics in Malawi and Kenya: Political Conditionality and Donor Support to the "Human Rights, Democracy and Governance" Sector,' in L. Wohlgemuth, S. Gibson, S. Klasen and E. Rothchild (eds) *Common Security and Civil Society in Africa*, Uppsala: Nordiska Afrikainstitutet.

Gill, S. (2003) *Power and Resistance in the New World Order*, Basingstoke and New York: Palgrave Macmillan.

Glassman, J. (1999) 'State Power Beyond the "Territorial Trap": The Internationalization of the State,' *Political Geography* 18, 669–696.

—— and P. Carmody (2001) 'Structural Adjustment in East and South-East Asia: Lessons from Latin America,' *Geoforum* 32 (1), 77–90.

Glickman, H. (2003) 'Africa in the War on Terrorism,' *Journal of Asian and African Studies* 38 (2–3), 162–174.

Globalization Challenge Initiative (2002) 'Growing Dangers of Service Apartheid: How the World Bank Group's Private Sector (PSD) Strategy Threatens Infrastructure and Basic Service Provision,' *News and Notices for IMF and World Bank Watchers* 2 (5), Winter, entire issue.

Good, K. and S. Hughes (2002) 'Globalization and Diversification: Two Cases in Southern Africa,' *African Affairs* 101 (402), 39–59.

Goodman Nikoi, E. (2004) 'Globalization from the "Inside Out": The Case of Ashanti Goldfields Company of Ghana,' MA, University of Vermont.

Götz, G. (2000) 'Shoot Anything That Flies, Claim Anything That Falls: Labor and the Changing Definition of the Reconstruction and Development Programme,' in G. Adler and E. Webster (eds). *Trade Unions and Democratization in South Africa, 1985–1997*, New York: St. Martin's Press.

Gould, J. (2005a) 'Conclusion: The Politics of Consultation,' in J. Gould (ed.) *The New Conditionality: The Politics of Poverty Reduction Strategy Papers*, London: Zed Books.

—— (2005b) 'Poverty, Politics and States of Partnership,' in J. Gould (ed.) *The New Conditionality: The Politics of Poverty Reduction Strategy Papers*, London: Zed Books.

—— and J. Ojanen (2003) *'Merging the Circle': The Politics of Tanzania's Poverty Reduction Strategy, Policy Papers 2/2003*, University of Helsinki: Institute of Development Studies. Available at http://www.valt.helsinki.fi/kmi/policy/merging.pdf. Accessed 13 September 2005.

—— (2005) 'Tanzania: Merging in the Circle,' in J. Gould (ed.) *The New Conditionality: The Politics of Poverty Reduction Strategy Papers*, London: Zed Books.

Government of South Africa (1996) *Growth, Employment and Redistribution*. Available at http://www.southafrica.net/economy/finance/macro1.html. Accessed 30 June 2002.

—— (2000) Notes on the First Meeting of the International Investment Council, 24–25 June. Office of the President, Republic of South Africa, Available at http://www.info.gove.za/speeches/2000/000627110p1010.htm. Accessed 24 June 2005.

—— (2001) 'New Partnership for African Development.' Available at www.un.org/esa/africa/NEPADenglish.pdf. Accessed 10 June 2002.

—— (2003) *Towards a Ten Year Review*, The Presidency, South Africa.

—— (2006) Background Document: A Catalyst for Accelerated and Shared Growth-South Africa. Available at http://www.pmg.org.za. Accessed 5 July 2006.

Government of Zimbabwe (1990) *Budget Statement*, Harare: Government Printers

—— (1991) *Zimbabwe: A Framework for Economic Reform (1991–95)*, Harare: Government Printers.

—— (2003) 'Report of the Presidential Land Review Committee on the Implementation of the Fast Track Land Reform Programme, 2000–2002,' Zimbabwe, August.

Granoveter, M. (1973) 'The Strength of Weak Ties,' *American Journal of Sociology* 78 (6), 1360–1380.

Grant, R. (2002) 'Foreign Companies and Glocalizations: Evidence from Accra, Ghana,' in R. Grant and J. R. Short (eds) *Globalization and the Margins*, New York: Palgrave Macmillan.

Grant, J. A. and F. Söderbaum (2003) 'Introduction: The New Regionalism in Africa,' in J. A. Grant and F. Söderbaum (eds) *The New Regionalism in Africa*, Aldershot and Burlington: Ashgate.

Greater Johannesburg Metropolitan Council and World Bank Partnership (2000) *Constraints to Growth and Employment in South Africa*. Available at www.tips.org.za/lfs9. Accessed 10 July 2005.

Green, D. (1995a) 'Flexibility and Repression: The Chilean Model,' in F. Rosen and D. McFadyen (eds) *Free Trade and Economic Restructuring in Latin America*, Washington, D.C.: NACLA Report on the Americas.
—— (1995b) *Silent Revolution: The Rise of Market Economics in Latin America*, London: Continuum International Publishers.
Gregory, D. (2004) *The Colonial Present: Afghanistan, Palestine, Iraq*, Oxford: Blackwell.
Grillo, R. D. and R. L. Stirrat (eds) (1997) *Discourses of Development*, Oxford: Berg.
Grindle, M. and J. Thomas (1991) *Public Choices and Policy Change*, Baltimore: Johns Hopkins University Press.
Grootaert, C. (1997) 'Social Capital: The Missing Link?' in World Bank *Expanding the Measure of Wealth – Indicators of Environmentally Sustainable Development*, Washington, D.C.: World Bank.
—— with G. Oh and A. Swamy (2002) 'Social Capital, Education and Credit Markets: Empirical Evidence from Burkina Faso,' in J. Isham, T. Kelly and S. Ramaswamy (eds) *Social Capital and Economic Development: On Well Being in Developing Countries*, Northampton, MA: Edward Elgar.
Guardian, The (2006) 'China's Goldmine,' March 28. Available at http://www.guardian.co.uk. Accessed 18 September 2006.
Guixan, L. (2006) 'Perspectives on China–Africa Trade and Economic Cooperation – Presentation by Minister Counsellor Liang Guixan at the 4th Tswalu Dialogue.' Available at www.chinese-embassy.org.za/eng/znjl/tl94633.htm. Accessed 18 September 2006.
Gwisai, M. (2002) *Revolutionaries, Resistance and Crisis in Zimbabwe: Anti-Neoliberal Struggles in Periphery Capitalism*, Harare: International Socialist Organization.
Habermas, J. (1990) *Moral Consciousness and Communicative Action*, Cambridge: Polity Press.
Habib, A. (2005) 'State-Civil Society Relations in Post-Apartheid South Africa,' *Social research*, 72 (3), 671–692.
—— and V. Padayachee (2000) 'Economic Policy and Power Relations in South Africa's Transition to Democracy,' *World Development*, 28 (2), 245–263.
Hadenius, A. and F. Uggla (1996) 'Making Civil Society Work, Promoting Democratic Development: What Can States and Donors Do?' *World Development* 24 (10), 1621–1639.
Hakkarainen, O., H. Katsui, C. B. Kessey, T. Kontinen, T. Kyllonen, S. Rovaniemi and R. Wamia (2002) *Voices from Southern Civil Societies: Interplay of National and Global Contexts in the Performance of Civil Society Organisations in the South*, A Report Prepared for the Department for International Development Co-operation, the Ministry for Foreign Affairs of Finland, Helsinki: Institute for Development Studies.
Hall, J. A. (1995) 'In Search of Civil Society,' in J. A. Hall (ed.) *Civil Society: Theory, History, Comparison*, Cambridge: Polity.
Hanahoe, T. (2003) *America Rules: US Foreign Policy, Globalization and Corporate USA*, Dingle, Kerry: Brandon.
Hanlon, J. (1996) *Peace Without Profit: How the IMF Blocks Rebuilding in Mozambique*, Portsmouth, NH: Heinemann.
—— (2000) 'An "Ambitious and Extensive Political Agenda": The Role of NGOs in the AID Industry,' in K. Stiles (ed.) *Global Institutions and Local Empowerment: Competing Theoretical Perspectives*, International Political Economy Series, Basingstoke: Macmillan.

—— (2001) 'Mozambique Wins Long Battle over Cashew Nuts and Sugar,' *Review of African Political Economy* 87, 111–112.

—— (2004) 'Do Donors Promote Corruption: The Case of Mozambique,' *Third World Quarterly* 25 (4), 747–763.

Hanson, M. and J. Hentz (1999) 'Neocolonialism and Neoliberalism in South Africa and Zambia,' *Political Science Quarterly* 114 (3), 479–502.

Harbeson, J. (1988) *The Ethiopian Transformation: The Quest for the Post-Imperial State*, Boulder, CO: Westview.

Harcourt, M. and G. Wood (2003) 'Is There a Future for a Labour Accord in South Africa?' *Capital and Class* 79, 81–106.

Hardt, M. and A. Negri (2000) *Empire*, Cambridge: Harvard University Press.

Hard Talk (2006) Interview with J. Moyo, BBC World, 21 September 2006.

Harris, L. and J. Michie (1998) 'The Effects of Globalization on Policy Formation in South Africa,' in D. Baker, G. Epstein and R. Pollin (eds) *Globalization and Progressive Economic Policy*, Cambridge and New York: Cambridge University Press.

Harris, N. (2003) *The Return of Cosmopolitan Capital: Globalization, the State and War*, London: IB Taurus.

Harrison, G. (1999) 'Mozambique Between Two Elections: A Political Economy of Transition,' *Democratization* 6 (4), 166–180.

—— (2002) *Issues in the Contemporary Politics of Sub-Saharan Africa*, Basingstoke: Palgrave Macmillan.

—— (2004a) 'Introduction: Globalization, Governance and Development,' *New Political Economy* 9 (2), 155–162.

—— (2004b) *The World Bank and Africa: The Construction of Governance States*, London: Routledge.

—— (2005) 'Neoliberalism and the Persistence of Clientelism in Africa,' in R. Robinson (ed.) *The Neoliberal Revolution*, International Political Economy Series, Basingstoke and New York: Palgrave Macmillan.

Harriss, J. (2002) *Depoliticizing Development: The World Bank and Social Capital*, London: Anthem Press.

Hart, G. (n.d.) 'Reworking Apartheid Legacies: Global Competition, Gender and Social Wages in South Africa, 1980–2000,' Draft Paper for United Nations Research Institute for Social Development.

—— (2002) *Disabling Globalization: Places of Power in Post-Apartheid South Africa*, Berkeley: University of California Press.

—— and A. Todes (1997) 'Industrial Decentralization Revisited,' *Transformation: Critical Perspectives on Southern Africa* 32, 31–53.

Hartung, W. D. and F. Berrigan (2005) 'Militarization of US Africa Policy 2000 to 2005.' Available at http://www.worldpolicy.org/projects/arms/reports/Africa_Fact_Sheet_EAD_March_2005.pdf. Accessed 23 March 2005.

Harvey, D. (2003) *The New Imperialism*, Oxford and New York: Oxford University Press.

—— (2005) *A Brief History of Neoliberalism*, Oxford: Oxford University Press.

Hass P. M. (1992) 'Introduction: Epistemic Communities and International Policy Co-Ordination,' *International Organization* 46 (1), 1–36.

Hearn, J. (1999) 'Foreign Aid, Democratization and Civil Society in Africa: A Study of South Africa, Ghana and Uganda,' Institute of Development Studies, Discussion Paper 368, Brighton: IDS.

—— (2000) 'Aiding Democracy? Donors and Civil Society in South Africa,' *Third World Quarterly* 21 (5), 815–830.

Held, D. and A. McGrew (2000) 'The Great Globalisation Debate: An Introduction,' in D. Held and A. McGrew (eds) *The Global Transformations Reader: An Introduction to the Globalisation Debate*, Cambridge: Polity Press.

—— (2002) *Globalization/Anti-Globalization*, Oxford: Polity Press.

—— A. McGrew, D. Goldblatt and J. Perraton (1999) *Global Transformations: Politics, Economics and Culture*, Stanford: Stanford University Press.

Helen Suzman Foundation (n.d.) 'Inside Zimbabwe Inc.' Available at http://www.zimbabwesituation.com. Accessed 22 June 2006.

Hentz, J. J. (2000) 'The Two Faces of Privatization: Political and Economic Logics in Transitional South Africa,' *The Journal of Modern African Studies* 38 (2), 203–223.

—— (2005) *South Africa and the Logic of Regional Cooperation*, Bloomington and Indianapolis: Indiana University Press.

Herald, The (2006) 'Zimbabwe: Zimplats Nets Operating Profit of US $25.4 Million,' 2 August 2006. Available at http://allafrica.com/stories/200608020249. html. Accessed 9 August 2006.

Herbst, J. (1990) *State Politics in Zimbabwe*, Berkeley, Los Angeles and Oxford: University of California Press.

—— (2000) *States and Power in Africa: Comparative Lessons in Authority and Control*, Princeton: Princeton University Press.

Hertz, N. (2004) *I.O.U.: The Debt Threat and Why We Must Defuse it*, London and New York: Fourth Estate.

Hesse, K. (2000) 'Foreign Direct Investment in South Africa (1994–1999) – Confronting Globalization,' *Development Southern Africa* 17 (3), 389–400.

Hickey, S. and G. Mohan (2004a) 'Relocating Participation within a Radical Politics of Development: Insights from Political Action and Practice,' in S. Hickey and G. Mohan (eds) *Participation: From Tyranny to Transformation*, London: Zed Books.

—— (2004b) 'Towards Participation as Transformation: Critical Themes and Challenges,' in S. Hickey and G. Mohan (eds) *Participation: From Tyranny to Transformation*, London: Zed Books.

Hilhorst, D. (2003) *The Real World of NGOs: Discourses, Diversity and Development*, London: Zed Books.

Hill, G. (2005) *What Happens After Mugabe: Can Zimbabwe Rise From the Ashes?* Cape Town: Zebra Books.

Hirsch, A. (2005) *Season of Hope: Economic Reform under Mandela and Mbeki*, Durban: IDRC and University of Kwa-Zulu Natal Press.

—— and S. Hanival (1998) 'Industrial Restructuring in South Africa: The Perspective From Government,' Paper Presented at the TIPS 1998 Annual Forum, 20–22 September at Muldersrift.

Holland, M. (2002) *The European Union and the Third World*, London: Palgrave Macmillan.

Holm, J. D. and P. Molutsi (1992) 'State-Society Relations in Botswana: Beginning Liberalization,' in G. Hyden and M. Bratton (eds) *Governance and Politics in Africa*, Boulder, CO: Lynne Rienner.

Hope, K. R. Sr. (1997) *African Political Economy: Contemporary Issues in Development*, Armonk, NY: M.E. Sharpe.

—— (2001) 'From Crisis to Renewal: Towards a Successful Implementation of the New Partnership for Africa's Development,' *African Affairs* 101 (404), 387–402.

—— (2002) *From Crisis to Renewal: Development Policy and Management in Africa*, Leiden: Brill.

Howell, J. (2000) 'Making Civil Society from the Outside – Challenges for Donors,' *The European Journal of Development Research* 12 (1), 3–22.

—— (2006) 'The Global War on Terror, Development and Civil Society,' *Journal of International Development* 18, 121–135.

—— and J. Pearce (2001) *Civil Society and Development: A Critical Exploration*, Boulder, CO: Lynne Rienner.

Hulme, D. and M. Edwards (1997a) 'NGOs, States and Donors: An Overview,' in D. Hulme and M. Edwards (eds) *NGOs, States and Donors: Too Close for Comfort?* Basingstoke: Macmillan.

—— (1997b) 'Conclusion: Too Close to the Powerful, Too Far from the Powerless?' in D. Hulme and M. Edwards (eds) *NGOs, States and Donors: Too Close for Comfort?* Basingstoke: Macmillan.

Hume, C. R. (2004) 'A Message from Ambassador Hume,' *Safundi: The Journal of South African and American Comparative Studies*, Special Issue on Ten Years of the New South Africa, 13/14, 3. Available at http://www.safundi.com. Accessed 24 September 2004.

Hunter Wade (2004a) 'Is Globalization Reducing Poverty and Inequality?' *World Development* 32 (4), 567–589.

Hutchful, E. (2002) *Ghana's Adjustment Experience: The Paradox of Reform*, Oxford, Portsmouth, NH and Accra: UNRISD in association with James Currey, Heinemann and Woeli Publishing Services.

Hutchinson Country Facts (n.d.) 'Ethiopia.' Available at http://www.tiscali.co.uk/reference/encyclopaedia/countryfacts/ethiopia.html. Accessed 31 July 2005.

Hutton, W. (2002) *The World We're In*, London: Little Brown.

Hyden, G. and M. Hailemariam (2002) 'Voluntarism and Civil Society: Ethiopia in Comparative Perspective,' *Afrika Spectrum* 38 (2), 215–234.

——, J. Court and K. Mease (2003) 'Civil Society and Governance in 16 Developing Countries,' World Governance Survey Discussion Paper 4, July. Available at http://www.odi.org.uk/wga_governance/Findings.html. Accessed 12 September 2005.

ICG (International Crisis Group) (2000) *Scramble for Congo: Anatomy of an Ugly War*, ICG Africa Report No. 26, Brussels: ICG.

IDC (Industrial Development Corporation) (1998) *The Richards Bay Spatial Development Initiative: Industrial Appraisal*, Sandton: IDC.

—— and DTI (Department of Trade and Industry) (1998) *Sectoral Prospects: Growth Guidelines for South Africa's 80 Industries – 1997–2001*, IDC: Sandton.

Illich, I. (1969) 'Outwitting the "Developed" Countries,' *New York Review of Books*, 6 November, 20–24, reprinted in H. Bernstein (ed.) (1978) *Underdevelopment and Development: The Third World Today*, London: Penguin Books.

Iliffe, J. (1983) *The Emergence of African Capitalism*, Minneapolis: University of Minnesota Press.

—— (1999) 'The South African Economy, 1652–1997,' *Economic History Review* LII (1), 87–103.

ILO (International Labor Office) (1999) *South Africa, Studies on the Social Dimensions of Globalization*, Geneva: ILO.

—— (2001) *Social Security: A New Consensus*, Geneva, ILO.

IMF (International Monetary Fund) (1995) *International Financial Statistics*, Washington, D.C.: IMF.

—— (1996) *South Africa – Selected Economic Issues*, IMF Staff Country Report No. 96/94, Washington, D.C.: IMF.

—— (2002) Staff Review of PRGF, 5 July 2002. Washington, D.C.: IMF.

—— (2004) *IMF Statement on the Conclusion of 2004 Article IV Consultation Discussions with Zimbabwe*, 31 March. Available at http://imf.org/external/np/sec/pr/2004/pr0467.htm.

—— and IDA (International Development Association) (2004) *Poverty Reduction Strategy Paper Annual Progress Report Joint Staff Assessment*, Washington, D.C.: IMF and World Bank.

—— and World Bank (2002) *Review of the Poverty Reduction Strategy Paper Approach: Early Experiences with Interim and Full PRSPs*, 26 March, Washington, D.C.: IMF and World Bank.

Inter-Africa Group (2001) *Civic Engagement in the PRSP*, Addis Ababa: IAG.

—— (2002) 'Civic Engagement in Key Policy Processes: UNDP and the PRSP: An Examination of Seven Countries in Central and Eastern Africa,' May, IAG: Addis Ababa.

Interaction (American Council for Voluntary International Action) (2003) *Synopses of Forum 2003 Panels, Overview of Forum 2003 – The Challenge of Global Commitments: Advancing Relief and Development Goals through Advocacy and Action.* Available at http://www.interaction.org/forum2003/panels.html#Natsios.

International Cooperation for Development and Solidarity and Caritas International (2003) 'Input to the International Monetary Fund Independent Evaluation Office and the World Bank's Operations Evaluation Department Evaluation of Poverty Reduction Strategy Papers,' mimeo, August.

International Development Association and IMF (2002) 'Review of the Poverty Reduction Strategy Paper (PRSP) Approach: Main Findings,' 15 March. Available at www.worldbank.org/prsp/PRSP_Policy_Papers/prsp_policy-papers.html.

International Forum on Globalization (2002) *Alternatives to Economic Globalization: A Better World is Possible*, San Francisco: Berrett-Koehler.

INTRAC (International Non-Governmental Training and Research Center) (2004) 'Case Studies of Effective Empowerment in Ethiopia,' commissioned by the World Bank, Draft 1, 03/06/04.

ITWeb (2001) 'Old Mutual Unit Trusts Go Wireless in World First.' Available at web7.infotrac.galegroup.com. Accessed 16 July 2001.

Irish Times, The (2002) 'Claims of Political Violence in Zimbabwe,' 8 February, p. 10.

—— (2005a) 'Norway Cuts Aid to Uganda by $4m,' 20 July, p. 11.

—— (2005b) 'S. Africa Considers Aid to Zimbabwe,' 25 July, p. 9.

—— (2005c) 27 July.

—— (2006) 'Zimbabwe Revalues to Dampen Inflation,' 17 August, p. 11.

Isham, J., T. Kelly and S. Ramaswamy (eds) (2002) *Social Capital and Economic Development: On Well Being in Developing Countries*, Northampton, MA: Edward Elgar.

IWPR (Institute for War and Peace Reporting) (2005) On-line Image of Miss Tourism World Competition, Zimbabwe. Available at http://www.iwpr.net/africa_zimba_photos.html. Accessed 27 July 2006.

Jackson, R. H. and C. G. Rosberg (1982) *Personal Rule in Black Africa*, Berkeley and London: University of California Press.

Jamal, V. and J. Weeks (1993) *Africa Misunderstood or Whatever Happened to the Rural–Urban Gap?* London: Macmillan.

James, J. (2002) *Globalization, Technology and Poverty*, Cheltenham: Edward Elgar.

Jega, A. (1993) 'Professional Associations and Structural Adjustment,' in A. O. Olokoshi (ed.) *The Politics of Structural Adjustment in Nigeria*, London, Ibadan and Portsmouth: James Currey, Heinemann Educational Books Nigeria Plc and Heinemann.

Jenkins, C. and N. Siwisa (1997) 'Overview of Trade Policy in South Africa,' Paper Prepared for the TIPS 1997 Annual Forum, Muldersrift.

Jenkins, R. (2001) 'Mistaking "Governance" for Politics: Foreign Aid, Democracy and the Construction of Civil Society,' in S. Kaviraj and S. Khilnani (eds) *Civil Society: History and Possibilities*, Cambridge: Cambridge University Press.

Jessop, B. (2000) 'The Crisis of the National Spatio-Temporal Fix and the Tendential Ecological Dominance of Globalizing Capital,' *International Journal of Urban and Regional Research* 24 (2), 223–260.

—— (2002) *The Future of the Capitalist State*, Oxford: Polity.

Jochnick, C. (2001) 'The Human Rights Challenge to Global Poverty,' in W. van Genugten and C. Perez-Bustillo (eds) *The Poverty of Rights: Human Rights and the Eradication of Poverty*, Comparative Research Programme on Poverty, London and New York: Zed Books.

Joffe, A., D. Kaplan, R. Kaplinsky and D. Lewis (1995) *Improving Manufacturing Performance in South Africa: Report of the Industrial Strategy Project*, Cape Town and Ottawa: University of Cape Town Press and International Development Research Center.

Johnson, C. (2000) *Blowback: The Costs and Consequences of American Empire*, New York: Owl Books.

—— (2004) *The Sorrows of Empire: Militarism, Secrecy and the End of the Republic*, New York: Metropolitan Books, Henry Holt and Company.

Johnson, K. (2002) 'State and Civil Society in contemporary South Africa: Redefining the Rules of the Game,' in S. Jacobs and R. Calland (eds) *Thabo Mbeki's World: The Politics and Ideology of the South African President*, Pietermaritzberg: University of Natal Press.

Johnson, R. W. (1998) 'Colonialism Returns to South Africa.' *New Statesman*, 13 November, 21.

Johnston, R. J., D. Gregory, G. Pratt and M. Watts (2002) *The Dictionary of Human Geography*, 4th edn, Oxford: Blackwell.

Johwa, W. (n.d.) 'Zimbabwe's Secret War in the DRC,' *Mail and Guardian online*. Available at http://www.mg.co.za. Accessed 27 July 2006.

Joint Employer/Trade Union Initiative (1999) 'Draft Letter for Consideration to Minister of Trade and Industry,' 12 October (photocopied).

Joireman, F. ((1997) 'Opposition Politics and Ethnicity in Ethiopia: We Will All Go down Together,' *Journal of Modern African Studies* 35 (2), 387–407.

Jones, S. (ed.) (1992) *Financial Enterprise in South Africa since 1950*, Basingstoke: Macmillan.

Jonsson, G. and A. Subramanian (2000) *Dynamic Gains from Trade: Evidence from South Africa*, IMF Working Paper, Washington, D.C.: IMF.

Jordan, A. (2001) 'The Challenges of Globalization for Development in Southern Africa,' *Development Southern Africa* 18 (1), 79–92.

Jordan, L. and P. van Tujil (2000) 'Political Responsibility in Transnational NGO Advocacy,' *World Development* 28 (12), 2051–2065.

Joseph, R. (1999a) 'State, Conflict and Democracy in Africa,' in R. Joseph (ed.) *State, Conflict and Democracy in Africa*, Boulder, CO: Lynne Rienner.

—— (1999b) 'The Reconfiguration of Power in Late Twentieth Century Africa,' in R. Joseph (ed.) *State, Conflict and Democracy in Africa*, Boulder, CO: Lynne Rienner.

Joshi, A. and M. Moore (2001) 'Enabling Environments and Effective Anti-Poverty Programmes,' in E. Øyen *et al.* (eds) *Best Practices in Poverty Reduction: An Analytical Framework*, London: Zed Books.

Kaldor, M. (1999) 'The Structure of Conflict,' in L. Wohlgemuth, S. Gibson, S. Klasen and E. Rothschild (eds) *Common Security and Civil Society in Africa*, Uppsala: Nordiska Afrikiainstitutet.

—— (2003) 'Civil Society and Accountability,' *Journal of Human Development* 4 (1), 5–27.

Kamal Pasha, M. (2001) 'Globalisation, Islam and Resistance,' in B. Gills (ed.) *Globalisation and the Politics of Resistance*, Basingstoke and New York: Palgrave Macmillan.

—— and A. Samatar (1998) 'The Resurgence of Islam,' in J. Mittelman (ed.), *Globalization: Critical Reflections*, Boulder, CO: Lynne Rienner.

Kamete, A. (2005) 'Zimbabwe,' in A. Mehler, H. Melber and K. Van Walraven (eds) *Africa Yearbook 2004*, Leiden: Brill.

Kanbur, R. (2005) 'Economic Policy, Distribution and Poverty: The Nature of the Disagreements.' Available at http://www.ifad.org/poverty/lecture.pdf. Accessed 12 September 2005.

Kankwenda, M. (2004) 'Forty Years of Development Illusions: Revisiting Development Policies and Practices in Africa,' in B. Onimode (ed.) *African Development and Governance Strategies in the 21st Century: Looking Back to Move Forward, Essays in Honor of Adebayo Adedeji at Seventy*, London and New York: Zed Books.

Kanyenze, G. (2003) 'The Performance of the Zimbabwean Economy, 1980–2000,' in S. Darnolf and L. Laakso (eds) *Twenty Years of Independence in Zimbabwe: From Liberation to Authoritarianism*, Basingstoke and New York: Palgrave Macmillan.

Kaplan, D. and R. Kaplinsky (1999) 'Trade and Industrial Policy on an Uneven Playing Field: The Case of the Deciduous Fruit Canning Industry in South Africa,' *World Development* 27 (10), 1781–1801.

Kaplinsky, R. (1994) '"Economic Restructuring in South Africa: The Debate Continues": A Response,' *Journal of Southern African Studies* 20 (4), 533–537.

—— (1995) 'Capital Intensity in South African Manufacturing and Unemployment, 1972–90,' *World Development* 23 (2), 179–192.

—— and J. Barnes (2000) 'Globalisation and the Death of the Local Firm? The Automobile Components Sector in South Africa,' *Regional Studies* 34 (9), 797–812.

—— and C. Manning (1998) 'Concentration, Competition Policy and the Role of Small and Medium Sized Enterprises in South Africa's Industrial Development,' *Journal of Development Studies* 35 (1), 139–161.

—— and E. Mhlongo (1997) 'Infant Industries and Industrial Policy: A Lesson From South Africa,' *Transformation: Critical Perspectives on Southern Africa* 34, 57–85.

—— and M. Morris (1999) 'Trade Policy Reform and the Competitive Response in Kwazulu Natal Province, South Africa,' *World Development* 27 (4), 777–837.

——, M. Morris and J. Readman (2001) 'The Globalization of Product Markets and Immiserizing Growth: Lessons from South Africa's Furniture Industry,' mimeograph.

Karlstrom, M. (1999) 'Civil Society and Its Presuppositions: Lessons from Uganda,' in J. L. Comaroff and J. Comaroff (eds) *Civil Society and the Critical Imagination in Africa: Critical Perspectives*, Chicago: University of Chicago Press.

Kasfir, N. (1983) 'Designs and Dilemmas: An Overview,' in P. Mahwood (ed.) *Local Government in the Third World: The Experience of Tropical Africa*, New York: John Wiley.

Katzensteiner, W. (2002) State Department Briefing, 18 November. Available at web.lexis-nexis.com. Accessed 19 June 2005.

Kaufmann, D., A. Kraay and M. Mastruzzi (2003) *Governance Matters III: Governance Indicators for 1996–2002*, World Bank Policy Research Working Paper 3106. Available at http://web.worldbank.org/WBSITE/EXTERNAL/WBI/EXTWBIGOVANTCOR/0,contentMDK:20773686~menuPK:1976990~pagePK:64168445~piPK:64168309~theSitePK:1740530,00.html.

Kebebe, B., A. Shimeles and M. Taddesse (2005) 'Rural and Urban Poverty Profiles,' in A. Bigsten, A. Shimeles and B. Kebebe (eds) *Poverty, Income Distribution and Labor Markets in Ethiopia*, Uppsala: Nordiska Afrikainstitutet.

Keen, D. (2000) 'Incentives and Disincentives for Violence,' in M. Berdal and D. M. Malone (eds) *Greed and Grievance: Economic Agendas in Civil Wars*, Boulder, CO: Lynne Rienner for the International Development Research Center.

Keet, D. (1998) 'Integrating the World Community: Political Challenges and Opportunities for Developing Countries,' *Southern African Perspectives* 70, 28–29.

Kelly, M. V. (1993) *Financial Institutions in South Africa*, Johannesburg: Juta Press.

Kennan, G. F. (1947) 'The Sources of Soviet Conduct,' *Foreign Affairs* 25 (July), 566–582.

Kennan, J. (2004) 'Terror in the Sahara: The Implications of US Imperialism for North and West Africa,' *Review of African Political Economy* 101, 475–496.

Kelsall, T. (2002) 'Shop Windows and Smoke-Filled Rooms: Governance and the Re-Politicization of Tanzania,' *Journal of Modern African Studies* 40 (4), 597–619.

Kennedy, P. (1988) *The Rise and Fall of the Great Powers: Economic Change and Military Conflict from 1500 to 2000*, London: Fontana Press.

—— (1993) *Preparing for the Twenty-First Century*, London: Harper Collins.

Khadiagala, G. M. (1995) 'State Collapse and Reconstruction in Uganda,' in I. William Zartman (ed.) *Collapsed States: The Disintegration and Restoration of Legitimate Authority*, Boulder, CO.: Lynne Rienner.

Kiely, R. (2005) *Empire in the Age of Globalization: US Hegemony and Neoliberal Disorder*, London: Pluto.

Killick, T. (1998) *Aid and the Political Economy of Reform*, London: ODI.

—— with R. Gunatilaka and A. Marr (1998) *Aid and the Political Economy of Policy Change*, London: Routledge for the Overseas Development Institute.

Kingsworth, P. (2003) *One No, Many Yeses: A Journey to the Heart of the Global Resistance Movement*, New York: Free Press.

Kirby, P. (2002) *The Celtic Tiger in Distress*, International Political Economy Series, London: Palgrave Macmillan.

—— (2006) *Vulnerability and Violence: The Impact of Globalization*, London: Pluto.

Kitching, G. (2001) *Seeking Social Justice through Globalization: Escaping a Nationalist Perspective*, Pennsylvania Park, PA: Penn State University Press.

Klare, M. T. (2001) *Resource Wars: The New Landscape of Global Conflict*, Owl Books: New York.

—— (2005) *Blood and Oil: How America's Thirst for Petrol is Killing Us*, London: Penguin.

—— and D. Volman (2006) 'The African "Oil Rush" and US National Security,' *Third World Quarterly* 27 (4), 609–628.

Klein, N. (2005) 'A Noose, not a Bracelet,' *The Guardian*, 10 June. Available at http://www.guardian.co.uk/print/0,3858,5212562–103390,00.html. Accessed 20 June 2005.

KMP (Kilusan Magbubukid ng Pilipinas) (1994) 'Development Divergence: Reform in the Philippine NGO Community,' Quezon City: Peasant Update Philippines.

Koeble, T. (1998) *The Global Economy and Democracy in South Africa*, New Jersey: Rutgers University Press.

Kohn, M. (2002) 'Panacea or Privilege? New Approaches to Democracy and Association,' *Political Theory* 30 (2), 289–298.

Kolodziej, E. A. (2005) *Security and International Relations*, Cambridge and New York: Cambridge University Press.

Kongshøj Madsen, P. (n.d.) 'Security and Flexibility: Friends or Foes?: Some Observations from the Case of Denmark.' Available at http://www-ilo-mirror.cornell.edu/public/english/bureau/inst/download/madsen.pdf. Accessed 13 June 2005.

Korten, D. C. (1990) *Getting to the 21st Century: Voluntary Action and the Global Agenda*, West Hartford: Kumarian Press.

—— (1995) *When Corporations Rule the World*, New York: Kumarian Press.

Krasner, S. D. (1985) *Structural Conflict: The Third World Against Global Liberalism*, Berkeley: University of California Press.

Kraxberger, B. (2005) 'The United States and Africa: Shifting Geopolitics in an "Age of Terror,"' *Africa Today* 52 (1), 47–70.

Kriger, N. (2001) 'Les vétérans et la parti au pouvour: une coopération conflictuelle dans la longue durée,' *Politique Africaine* 81, 80–100.

—— (2003a) 'War Veterans: Continuities Between Past and Present,' *African Studies Quarterly* 7 (2). Available at http://www.africa.ufl.edu/asq/v7/v7i2a7.htm. Accessed 18 September 2006.

—— (2003b) 'Zimbabwe's War Veterans and the Ruling Party: Continuities in Political Dynamics,' in S. Darnolf and L. Laakso (eds) *Twenty Years of Independence in Zimbabwe: From Liberation to Authoritarianism*, International Political Economy Series, Basingstoke and New York: Palgrave Macmillan.

Kruger, F. (2004) 'South Africa's Growing Private Army,' *BBC News*, Johannesburg. Available at http://news.bbc.co.uk/1/hi/world/africa/3519352.stm. Accessed 27 October 2006.

Krugmann, H. (1995) 'Overcoming Africa's Crisis: Adjusting Structural Adjustment towards Sustainable Development in Africa,' in K. Mengisteab and B. Ikubolajeh Logan (eds) *Beyond Economic Liberalization in Africa: Structural Adjustment and the Alternatives*, London: Zed Books.

Kumar, R. (2002) 'Indian Union Leaders Open the Door for Tough Austerity Measures in Kerala.' Available at http://www.wsws.org/articles/2002apr2002/indi-a02_prm.shtml. Accessed 1 August 2005.

Kunnie, J. (2000) *Is Apartheid Really Dead? Pan-Africanist Working Class Cultural Critical Perspectives*, Boulder: Westview.

Kwasi Tieku, T. (2004) 'Explaining the Clash and Accommodation of Interests of Major Actors in the Creation of the African Union,' *African Affairs* 103 (411), 249–267.

Laakso, L. (2003) 'Regional Voting and Cabinet Formation,' in S. Darnolf and L. Laakso (eds) *Twenty Years of Independence in Zimbabwe: From Liberation to Authoritarianism*, Basingstoke and New York: Palgrave Macmillan.

Ladd, P. (2003) 'Too Hot to Handle? The Absence of Trade Policy from PRSPs.' Available at http://www.christianaid.org.uk/indepth/0304toohot/intro.htm. Accessed 13 September 2005.

Lall, S. and C. Pietrobelli (2003) *Failing to Compete: Technology Development and Technology Systems in Africa*, Cheltenham: Edward Elgar.

Landsberg, D. C. (2003) 'In Search of a Sub-Regional Political and Security Community: The Institutional and Governance Dimensions of SADC,' in D. Olowu and R. Mukwena (eds) *Governance in Southern Africa and Beyond: Experiences of Institutional and Public Policy Reform in Developing Countries*, Windhoek: Gamsberg Macmillan.

Larsen, M. (2002) 'Is Oligopoly a Condition of Successful Privatization? – The Case of Cotton in Zimbabwe,' *Journal of Agrarian Change* 2 (2), 185–205.

Lee, R. (2003) 'The Marginalization of Everywhere?' in J. Peck and H. Wai-chung Yeung (eds) *Remaking the Global Economy: Economic-Geographical Perspectives*, London, Thousand Oaks, Dehli: SAGE.

Leftwich, A. (2000) *States of Development: On the Primacy of Politics in Development*, Oxford: Polity Press.

—— (2005) 'Politics in Command: Development Studies and the Rediscovery of Social Science,' *New Political Economy* 10 (4), 573 –607.

Leithead, A. (2005) 'Zimbabwe's Muted Opposition,' *BBC News*, 3 April 2005. Available at http://news.bbc.co.uk/1/hi/world/africa/4407331.stm. Accessed 26 July 2005.

Lemarchand, R. (1972) 'Political Cientelism and Ethnicity in Tropical Africa: Competing Solidarities in Nation-Building,' *American Political Science Review* 64 (1), 68–90.

—— (1991) 'The Political Economy of Informal Economies,' *Africa Insight* 21 (4), 214–222.

Lemke, T. (2001) 'The Birth of Bio-Politics: Michel Foucault's Lecture at the Collège de France on Neoliberal Governmentality,' *Economy and Society* 30 (2), 190–207.

Lensink, R. (1996), *Structural Adjustment in Africa*, London and New York: Longman.

Leonard, D. K. and S. Strauss (2003) *Africa's Stalled Development: International Causes and Cures*, Boulder, CO: Lynne Rienner.

Lester, A., E. Nel and T. Binns (2000) 'South Africa's Current Transition in Temporal and Spatial Context,' *Antipode*, 32 (2), 135–151.

Lesufi, I. (2005) 'Six Years of Neoliberal Socioeconomic Policies in South Africa,' in A. Zegeye, R. Harris and P. Lauderdale (eds) *Globalization and Post-Apartheid South Africa*, Whitby, Ontario: de Sitter.

Levy, B. (1996) *South Africa: The Business Environment for Industrial and Small and Medium Enterprises*, Informal Discussion Papers on Aspects of the Economy of South Africa, Washington, D.C.: World Bank.

Lewis, D. (2002) 'Civil Society in African Contexts: Reflections on the Usefulness of a Concept,' *Development and Change* 34 (3), 569–586.

Lewis, W. A. (1985) *Racial Conflict and Economic Development*, Cambridge: Harvard University Press.

Leyshon, A. and R. Lee (2003) 'Introduction: Alternative Economic Geographies,' in A. Leyshon, R. Lee and C. C. Williams (eds) *Alternative Economic Spaces*, London, Thousand Oaks and New Delhi: SAGE.

Lieven, A. (2004) *America Right or Wrong: An anatomy of American Nationalism*, New York: Harper Collins.

Little, P. D. (2003) *Somalia: Economy without State*, Bloomington, IN: Indiana University Press.

Lloyd Roberts, S. (2005) 'Zimbabwe Army "Moves onto the Land,"' *BBC News*, 16 December. Available at http://news.bbc.co.uk/1/hi/world/africa/4534716.stm. Accessed 22 June 2006.

Lockwood, M. (2005) *The State They're In: An Agenda for International Action on Poverty in Africa*, Wiltshire: ITDG Publishing.

Lodge, G. and C. Wilson (2006) *A Corporate Solution to Global Poverty: How Multinationals Can Help the Poor and Invigorate Their Own Legitimacy*, Princeton: Princeton University Press.

Lodge, T. (1999) *South African Politics Since 1994*, Cape Town and Johannesburg: David Philip.

Logan, B. and D. Tevera (2001) 'Neoliberalism, Regime Survival, and the Environment: Economic Reform and Agricultural Transformation in Zimbabwe in the 1990s,' *Canadian Journal of African Studies* 35 (1), 99–138.

Lokongo, A. R. (2005) 'Why President Mugabe got involved in Congo and How It Was Portrayed by the Western media,' Paper Presented at the Reporting Zimbabwe: Before and After Conference, February 25th, University of Westminster. Available at http://www.wmin.ac.um. Accessed 28 June 2006.

Longman, T. (1998) 'Rwanda: Chaos from Above,' in L. Villalon and P. Huxtable (eds) *The African State at a Critical Juncture: Between Disintegration and Reconfiguration*, Boulder, CO: Lynne Rienner.

—— (1999) 'State, Civil Society and Genocide in Rwanda,' in R. Joseph (ed.) *State, Conflict and Democracy in Africa*, Boulder, CO: Lynne Rienner.

Lonsdale, J. (1981) 'State and Social Processes in Africa: A Historical Survey,' *African Studies Review* XXIV (2/3), 139–226.

Loxton, L. (1996) 'Africa Takes Its Place on the Mining Map,' *Mail and Guardian*, 9 February.

Lugard, F. (1922) *The Dual Mandate in British Tropical Africa*, Edinburgh: Frank Cass.

Luke, T. W. (1993) 'Discourses of Disintegration, Texts of Transformation: Re-Reading Realism in the New World Order,' *Alternatives* 18, 229–258.

Luiz, J. (2006) 'The New Partnership for African Development: Questions Regarding Africa's Response to Its Underdevelopment,' *Journal of International Development* 18, 223–236.

Lyman, P. (2005) 'China's Rising Role in Africa.' Presentation to the US-China Commission, 21 July. Available at http://www.cfr.org/publication/8436/. Accessed 18 September 2006.

—— and J. Stephen Morrison (2004) 'The Terrorist Threat in Africa,' *Foreign Affairs* 83 (1), 75–86.

MacGaffey, J. (1991) 'Historical, Cultural and Structural Dimensions of Zaire's Unrecorded Trade,' in J. MacGaffey, with V. Mukohya, R. wa Nkera, M. ma Mavambuye Beda, B. Gundfest Schoepf and W. Engundu. *The Real Economy of Zaire: The Contribution of Smuggling and Other Unofficial Activities to National Wealth*, London: James Currey.

MacKinlay, J. (2001) 'Osama bin Laden: Global Insurgent,' *African Security Review* 10 (4). Available at http://www.iss.co.za/Pubs/ASR/10No4/Mackinlay.html. Accessed 21 June 2005.

MacLean, S. J. (2002) 'Mugabe at War: The Political Economy of Conflict in Zimbabwe,' *Third World Quarterly* 23 (3), 513–538.

——, F. Quadir and T. Shaw (1997) 'Structural Adjustment and the Response of Civil Society in Bangladesh and Zimbabwe: A Comparative Analysis,' *New Political Economy* 2 (1), 149–164.

Macroeconomic Research Group (1993) *Making Democracy Work: A Framework for Macroeconomic Policy in South Africa*, Belville: Center for Development Studies.

Madziwa, M. (2006) 'Dignity. Period!' *Mail and Guardian online*, 12 July. Available at www.mg.co.za. Accessed 12 July 2006.

Magubane, B. (1979) *The Political Economy of Race and Class in South Africa*, New York: Monthly Review.

Mail and Guardian (1999) 'Old Mutual Hopes to Shine on the World Stage,' 29 January. Available at web7.infotrac.galegroup.com. Accessed 18 June 2001.

Maina Peter, C. (n.d.) *The State and Independent Civil Organizations: The Case of Tanzania Women's Council (BAWATA). A Case Study Prepared for the Civil Society and Governance in East Asia Project*, unpublished.

Makumbe, J. Mw. (1998) 'Is There a Civil Society in Africa?' *Journal of International Affairs* 74 (2), 305–317.

Malan, M. (2002) 'The Post 9/11 Security Agenda and Peacekeeping in Africa,' *African Security Review* 11 (3). Available at www.iss.co.za. Accessed 19 June 2005.

Malawi Economic Justice Network (2001) 'The Status of Civil Society in the Malawi PRSP,' *World Bank Watch* 3. Available at www.aidc.org.za.

Mallaby, S. (2005) 'The World's Banker: A Story of Failed States, Financial Crises, and the Wealth and Poverty of Nations.' Edited Transcript of Remarks, 27 January, Carnegie Council Books for Breakfast. Available at http://www.cceia.org. Accessed 16 April 2005.

Malloch-Brown, M. (2001) 'In the Wake of September 11th: Human Security and Human Development in the 21st Century,' Paper Presented to the Carnegie Council, Washington, D.C., 19 November. Available at http://www.cceia.org. Accessed 28 January 2004.

Mamdani, M. (1991) 'Uganda: Contradictions in the IMF Programme and Perspective,' in D. Ghai (ed.) *The IMF and the South: The Social Impact of Crisis and Adjustment*, London: Zed Books.

—— (1996) *Citizen and Subject: Contemporary Africa and the Legacy of Late Colonialism*, New Haven: Princeton University Press.

—— (2006) 'Identity and National Governance,' in C. Toulmin, B. Wisner and R. Chitiga (eds) *Towards a New Map of Africa*, London: Earthscan and IIED.

Mandel, M. (2004) *How American Gets Away With Murder: Illegal Wars, Collateral Damage and Crimes Against Humanity*, London: Pluto.

Mangwengwende, S. E. (2002) 'Tariffs and Subsidies in Zimbabwe's Reforming Electricity Industry: Steering a Utility through Turbulent Times,' *Energy Policy*, 30 (11–12), 947–948. Available at http://www.afrepren.org/SI/pdfs/spmm.pdf. Accessed 30 August 2004.

Mann, M. (1986) *The Sources of Social Power*, vol. II, Cambridge and New York: Cambridge University Press.

—— (1999) 'Globalisation as Violence.' Available at http://www.sscnet.ucla.edu/soc/faculty/mann/globasviol%5B1%5D.pdf. Accessed 17 March 2004.

Manor, J. (1999) 'The Political Economy of Democratic Decentralization,' Washington, D.C.: World Bank.

Manuel, T. (2003) 'Africa and the Washington Consensus,' *Finance and Development: A Quarterly Magazine of the IMF* 10 (3), 18–20.

Marais, H. (1998) *South Africa: Limits to Change: The Political Economy of Transition*, Cape Town: University of Cape Town Press.

—— (2003) 'The Logic of Expediency: Post-Apartheid Shifts in Macro-Economic Policy,' in S. Jacobs and R. Calland (eds) *Thabo Mbeki's World: The Politics and Ideology of the South African President*, London and Pietermaritzburg: Zed Books and University of Natal Press.

Mari Tripp, A. (2003) 'Forging Developmental Synergies Between States and Associations,' in N. van de Walle, N. Ball and V. Ramachandran (eds) *Beyond Structural Adjustment: The Institutional Context of Development*, New York: Palgrave Macmillan.

Mark, S. (2006) 'China in Africa – The New Imperialism,' *Pambuzuka News 244*. Available at http://www.pambazuka.org/eng/category/features/32432. Accessed 18 September 2006.

Martin, G. (2002) *Africa in World Politics: A Pan-African Perspective*. Trenton, NJ: Africa World Press.

Martin, W. G. (2004) 'Beyond Bush: The Future of Popular Movements and US Africa Policy,' *Review of African Political Economy* 102, 585–597.

Marx, A. (1992) *Lessons of Struggle: South African Internal Opposition, 1960–1990*, New York and Oxford: Oxford University Press.

Masland, T. (2005) 'A Despot Clings to Power,' *Newsweek*, 28 March, 20–24.

Masunda, D. (2001) 'ZANU-PF, Kabila in Secret US $300m deal,' *Financial Gazette*, 30 August.

Mathews, S. (2004) 'Investigating NEPAD's Development Assumptions,' *Review of African Political Economy* 101, 497–511.

Maundeni, Z. (2004) 'Why the African Renaissance Is Likely to Fail: The Case of Zimbabwe,' *Journal of Contemporary African Studies* 22 (2), 189–212.

Mawdsley, E. (2005) 'The Millennium Challenge Account: Neo-Liberalism, Poverty and Security,' Paper Presented at the Royal Geographical Society/Institute of British Geographers Conference, London, 31 August to 2 September.

—— and J. Rigg (2003) 'The World Development Report Series II: Continuity and Change in Development Orthodoxies,' *Progress in Development Studies* 3 (4), 271–286.

——, J. Townsend, G. Porter and P. Oakley (2001) *Knowledge, Power and Development Agendas: NGOs North and South*, Oxford: INTRAC.

Maxwell, D. (1998) '"Delivered from the Spirit of Poverty?" Pentecostalism, Prosperity and Modernity in Zimbabwe,' *Journal of Religion in Africa* XXVIII (3), 350–373.

Maxwell, S. (2003) 'Heaven or Hubris: Reflections on the New "New Poverty Agenda,"' *Development Policy Review* 21 (1), 5–25.

—— and R. Riddell (2002) 'Conditionality or Contract: Perspectives on Partnership for Development,' *Journal of International Development* 10, 257–268.

May, J., I. Woolard and S. Klasen (2000) 'The Nature and Measurement of Poverty and Inequality,' in J. May (ed.), *Poverty and Inequality in South Africa: Meeting the Challenge*, Claremont and New York: David Philip and Zed Books.

Mayer, P. (2000) '"An Italy of Asiatic Dimensions": What 19th Century Italy Can Tell Us about India in the 21st Century,' Seminar Paper, Department of Politics, University of Adelaide, Australia.

Mbekeani, K. (1997) *Foreign Direct Investment and Economic Growth*, National Institute for Economic Policy Occasional Paper Series no. 11, Johannesburg: NIEP.

Mbeki, M. (2005) *Perpetuating Poverty in Sub-Saharan Africa: How African Political Elites Undermine Entrepreneurship and Economic Development*, London: International Policy Press.

Mbeki, T. (1998) Statement at the African Renaissance Conference, Johannesburg, September 28th 1998. Available at http://www.anc.org.za/ancdocs/history/mbeki/1998/tm0928.html.

—— (1999) Statement at the 35th Ordinary Session of the OAU Assembly of Heads of State and Governments, 12–14 July, Algiers.

—— (2001) 'Clamour over Zimbabwe Reveals Continuing Racial Prejudice in SA,' *ANC Today*, 23–29 March. Available at www.anc.org.az/ancdocs/anctoday. Accessed 21 July 2001.

—— (2005) Thabo Mbeki, 'Letter of the President.' Available at http://www.saembassy.org/Letter%20of%20Question%20that%20demand%20answer.htm. Accessed 28 July 2005.

Mbendi Information Services (n.d.) 'South Africa-Mining: Chromite Mining.' Available at http://www.mbendi.co.za/indy/ming/chrm/af/sa/p0005.htm. Accessed 28 July 2005.

Mberi, R. (2005) 'Murewa Has His Job Cut out for Him,' *Financial Gazette*, 14 July. Available at http://www.fingaz.co.zw/fingaz/2005/July/July14/8943.shtml. Accessed 31 August.

Mbiba, B. (2006) 'Untold Stories: The Commission for Africa and Zimbabwe,' *The Round Table: The Commonwealth Journal of International Affairs* 95 (384), 201–218.

McCann, J. (2002) 'Prospects for Democracy, Agro-Ecology and Civil Society: The Elections in Amhara Region, Ethiopia's Rural/Urban Hinterland,' in S. Pausewang, K. Tronvall and L. Aalen (eds) *Ethiopia Since the Derg: A Decade of Democratic Pretension and Performance*, London: Zed Books.

McClymont, M. E. (2005) Presentation to the Conference on 'Meeting Global Development Challenges,' 15 June, Trinity College, Dublin.

McDermott, A. (2001) 'UN Finances: What Are the Costs and Who Pays the Bills?' in E. Newman and P. P. Richmond (eds) *The United Nations and Human Security*, Basingstoke: Palgrave Macmillan.

McGee, R. (2002a) 'Conclusion: Participatory Poverty Research: Opening Spaces for Change,' in K. Brock and R. McGee (eds) *Knowing Poverty: Critical Reflections on Participatory Research and Poverty*, London: Earthscan.

—— (2002b) 'The Self in Participatory Poverty Research,' in K. Brock and R. McGee (eds) *Knowing Poverty: Critical Reflections on Participatory Research and Poverty*, London: Earthscan.

—— and A. Norton (1999) *Participation in Poverty Reduction Strategies: A Synthesis of Experience with Participatory Approaches to Policy Design, Implementation and Monitoring*, Working Paper 109, Brighton: Institute of Development Studies.

McGregor, J. (2002) 'The Politics of Disruption: War Veterans and the Local State in Zimbabwe,' *African Affairs* 101, 9–37.

McGuirk, P. (2005) Panel presentation on 'International Perspectives on Globalization,' Royal Geographical Society/Institute of British Geographers Conference, 31 August–2 September, London.

McIlwaine, C. (1998a) 'Civil Society and Development Geography,' *Progress in Human Geography* 22 (3), 415–424.

—— (1998b) 'Contesting Civil Society: Reflections from El Salvador,' *Third World Quarterly* 19 (4), 651–672.

MacKinlay, J. (2001) 'Osama bin Laden: Global Insurgent,' *African Security Review* 10 (4). Available at http://www.iss.co.za/Pubs/ASR/10No4/Mackinlay.html. Accessed 21 June 2005.

McKinley, D. (1997) *The ANC and the Liberation Struggle: A Critical Political Biography*, London and Chicago: Pluto Press.

—— (2003) 'Commodifying Oppression: South African Foreign Policy towards Zimbabwe under Mbeki.' Available at http://spip.red.m2014.net/article.phs3?id_article=60. Accessed 28 July 2005.

—— (2004) 'South African Foreign Policy towards Zimbabwe under Mbeki,' *Review of African Political Economy* 100, 357–364.

—— (2005) 'Mbeki Leapfrogs into Economic Cul-de-Sac.' Available at http://spip.red.m2014.net/article.phs3?id_article=1–6. Accessed 28 July 2005.

McKinley, T. (2003) Response to A. Gueye and A. Gauci, 'Pro-Poor Educational Policies and the Demand for Labor,' in Economic Commission for Africa and Economic Policy Research Center, *Key Components of Pro-Poor Growth Strategies*, Proceedings of Expert Group Meeting Munyonyo Speke Resort, Kampala, Uganda, 23–24 June 2003.

McLaughlin, L. (2004) 'Feminism and the Political Economy of Transnational Public Space,' *Sociological Review* 52, Supplement 1, 156–175.

McMichael, P. (2000) 'Sleepless since Seattle: What is the WTO About?' *Review of International Political Economy* 7 (3), 466–474.

McNeill, D. (2000) 'Does Social Capital help the World Bank in Understanding and Alleviating Poverty?' Available at http://www.crop.org/publications/files/report/Comments_to_WDR2001_2002_ny.pdf. Accessed 12 September 2005.

Mebrahtu, E. (2004) *Making the Connection Between Power and Poverty: Ethiopia Case Study*, Oxford: INTRAC, 2004.

Mehrotra, S. (2001) 'Some Methodological Issues in Determining Good Practices in Social Policy: The Case of High-Achieving Countries,' in E. Øyen and A. D. Cimadore (eds) *Best Practices in Poverty Reduction: An Analytical Framework*, CROP International Studies in Poverty Research, London and New York: Zed Books.

Mekay, E. (2004) 'Fewer Conditions, World Bank Promises' August 24th. Available at http://www.global policy.org. Accessed 20 September 2004.

Meldrum, A. and J. Watts (2006) 'China Gives Zimbabwe Economic Lifeline,' *The Guardian*, 16 June, p. 19.

Mengisteab, K. (1995) 'A Partnership of the State and Market in African Development: What Is an Appropriate Strategy Mix?' in K. Mensisteab and B. I. Logan (eds) *Beyond Economic Liberalization in Africa: Structural Adjustment and the* Alternatives, London and Cape Town: Zed Books and SAPES.

—— (1999) 'Globalization and South Africa's Transition through Consociational Arrangement,' in F. Adams, S. Dev Gupta and K. Mengisteab (eds) *Globalization and the Dilemmas of the State in the South*, New York: St. Martin's Press.

—— (2002) 'Ethiopia: State Building or Imperial Revival?' in A. I. Samatar and A. Samatar (eds) *The African State: Reconsiderations*, Portsmouth, NH: Heinemann.

Mercer, C. (2002) 'NGOs, Civil Society and Democratization: A Critical Review of the Literature,' *Progress in Development Studies* 2 (1), 5–22.

—— (2003) 'Performing Partnership: Civil Society and the Illusions of Good Governance in Tanzania,' *Political Geography* 22, 741–763.

——, G. Mohan and M. Power (2003) 'Towards A Critical Political Geography of African Development,' *Geoforum* 34, 419–436.

Meredith, M. (2002) *Our Votes, Our Guns: Robert Mugabe and the Tragedy of Zimbabwe*, New York: Public Affairs.

—— (2005) *The State of Africa*, New York: Free Press.

Mervin Gumede, W. (2002) 'Down to Business, but Nothing to Show,' in S. Jacobs and R. Calland (eds) *Thabo Mbeki's World: The Politics and Ideology of the South African President*, London and Pietermaritzberg: Zed Books and University of Natal Press.

Michael, S. (2004) *Undermining Development: The Absence of Power Among Local NGOs in Africa*, Oxford, Bloomington and Indianapolis: James Currey and Indiana University Press.

Michie, J. and J. Grieve Smith (eds) (1999) *Global Instability: The Political Economy of World Economic Governance*, London and New York: Routledge.

Midgley, J. (1998) *Social Development: The Developmental Perspective in Social Welfare*, London, Thousand Oaks, New Delhi: SAGE.

Mining Magazine (1998) 'London – Home of the Giants,' November, 1998. Available at web7.infotrac.galegroup.com. Accessed 10 January 2001.

Ministry of Capacity Building, (2004) *Civil Society Organization's Capacity Building Programme*, Federal Democratic Republic of Ethiopia, Addis Ababa, Draft.

Ministry of Finance & Economic Development of the Federal Democratic Republic of Ethiopia (2004) *Civil Society Organization's Capacity Building Programme*, Addis Ababa, Draft.

—— and United Nations Country Team (2004) *Millennium Development Goals Report: Challenges and Prospects for Ethiopia*, Addis Ababa: MOFED.

Mistry, P. (2005) Letter to *The Economist*, 16–22 July, p. 18.

Mitchell, J. (1998) 'The Maputo Development Corridor: A Case Study of the SDI Process in Mpumalanga,' *Development Southern Africa* 15 (5), 757–769.

Mitter, S. (1994) 'On Organizing Women in Casualized Work: A Global Overview,' in S. Rowbotham and S. Mitter (ed.) *Dignity and Daily Bread: New Forms of Economic Organizing the Third World and the First*, London: Routledge.

Mittelman, J. (1988) *Out from Underdevelopment: Prospects for the Third World*, New York: St. Martin's Press.

—— (1995) 'Rethinking the International Divisions of Labour in the Context of Globalisation,' *Third World Quarterly* 16 (2), 273–295.

—— (2000) *The Globalization Syndrome: Transformation and Resistance*, New Haven, NJ: Princeton University Press.

Mkandawire, T. (1999) 'Crisis Management and the Making of "Choiceless Democracies,"' in R. Joseph (ed.) *State, Conflict and Democracy in Africa*, Boulder, CO: Lynne Rienner.

—— (2004) 'Social Policy in a Development Context: Introduction,' in T. Mkandawire (ed.) *Social Policy in a Development Context*, Basingstoke and New York: Palgrave Macmillan.

—— (2006) 'The Global Economic Context,' in C. Toulmin, B. Wisner and R. Chitiga (eds) *Towards a New Map of Africa*, London: Earthscan and IIED.

—— and C. Soludo (1999) *Our Continent, Our Future: African Voices on Structural Adjustment*, Trenton, NJ and Ottawa: Africa World Press and IDRC.

Mnyanda, L. (1999) 'Spiraling Job Crisis Besets Economy,' *Pretoria News Business Report*, 12 July, p. 11.

Mohamed Salih, M. A. (2001) 'Globalization and Human Insecurity in Africa,' in T. Assefa, S. Rugumamu and A. Ahmed (eds) *Globalization, Democracy and Development in Africa: Challenges and Prospects*, Addis Ababa: OSSREA.

Mohamed, S. (2004) 'Global Integration, not Political Risk Explains Low Investment,' *Policy and Law Online News*, 1 October. Available at http://www.polity.org.za/pol/ opinion/seeraj/?show=57189. Accessed 28 July 2005.

Mohan, G. (2002) 'The Disappointments of Civil Society: The Politics of NGO Intervention in Northern Ghana,' *Political Geography* 21, 125–154.

—— and K. Stokke (2000) 'Participatory Development and Empowerment: The Dangers of Localism,' *Third World Quarterly* 21 (2), 247–268.

Molutsi, P. (1999) 'The Interaction between State and Civil Society in Southern Africa: Prospects for Peace and Security,' in L. Wohlgemuth, S. Gibson, S. Klasen, E. Rothschild (eds) *Common Security and Civil Society in Africa*, Uppsala: Nordiska Afrikainstitutet.

—— and J. D. Holm (1990) 'Developing Democracy When Civil Society is Weak: The Case of Botswana,' *African Affairs* 89 (356), 323–340.

Monbiot, G. (2003) 'Africa's Scar Gets Angrier: At Evian the World's Rich Nations Missed a Golden Opportunity to Back Fair Trade,' *The Guardian*, 3 June. Available at http://www.guardian.co.uk/commentary/story/0,3604,969210,00. html. Accessed 25 August 2005.

Moneyweb (2003) *Africa News*, 3 January. Available at web.lexis-nexis.com. Accessed 19 June 2005.

Monga, C. (1995) 'Civil Society and Democratization in Francophone Africa,' *Journal of Modern African Studies* 33 (3), 359–379, reprinted in S. Corrbridge (ed.) (2000) *Development: Critical Concepts in the Social Sciences*, vol. IV, *States, Politics and Civil Society*, London: Routledge.

Mooney, P. (2005) 'China's African Safari,' *Yale Global*, New Haven, 3 January.

Moore, A. (1999) 'Aluminum Industry Comes of Age,' *South Africa: The Journal of Trade Industry and Investment*, 1st quarter, 33.

Moore, B. (1966) *The Social Origins of Dictatorship and Democracy*, Boston: Beacon Press.

Moore, D. (1999) 'Sail on, O Ship of State! Neoliberalism, Globalization and the Governance of Africa,' *Journal of Peasant Studies* 27 (1), 61–96.

—— (2001) 'Is Land the Economy and the Economy the Land? Primitive Accumulation in Zimbabwe,' *Journal of Contemporary African Studies* 19 (2), 253–266.

—— (2003a) 'Hardt and Negri's Empire and the Real Empire: The Terrors of 9–11 and After,' *ACME*, 2003. Available at www.acme-journal.org. Accessed 20 September 2006.

—— (2003b) 'Zimbabwe's Triple Crisis: Primitive Accumulation, Nation-State Formation and Democratization in the Age of Neoliberal Globalization,' *African Studies Quarterly* 7 (2 & 3). Available at http://web.africa.ufl.edu. Accessed 20 November 2004.

—— (2004) 'The Second Age of the Third World: From Primitive Accumulation to Global Public Goods?' *Third World Quarterly* 25 (1), 87–109.

Morgan, K. and C. Nauwelaers (eds) (1999) *Regional Innovation Strategies: The Challenge for Less-Favored Regions*, London and New York: Routledge.

Morrison, K. (2004) 'Output on Hold as "Commodity Currencies" Rise,' *Financial Times*, January 31/February 1, M20.

Morrison, S. J. (2001) 'Africa and the War on Global Terrorism,' Congressional Testimony, November 15th. Available at http://www.csis.org/hill/ts011115 morrison. htm. Accessed 21 July 2004.

Mosley, P., J. Harrigan and J. Toye (1991) *Aid and Power*, London: Routledge.

Moseley, W. and B. Ikubolajeh Logan (2004) *African Environment and Development*, Aldershot: Ashgate.

—— (2006) 'Food Security,' in C. Toulmin, B. Wisner and R. Chitiga (eds) *Towards a New Map of Africa*, London: Earthscan and IIED.

Moyo, S. (2000) *Land Reform under Structural Adjustment in Zimbabwe: Land Use Change in the Mashonaland Provinces*, Uppsala: Nordiska Afrikainstitutet.

—— (unpublished) 'Land and the Agrarian Question in Africa: The Case of Zimbabwe,' draft paper.

Muchie, M. (2003) 'Partnership or Self-Reliance: Does NEPAD Provide the Strategy for African Development?' CCS: 1–20. Available at http://www/nu/ac.za/ccs/default.asp?5,50,10,771. Accessed 19 September 2006.

Muir, A. (2004) 'Building Capacity in Ethiopia to Strengthen the Participation of Citizens' Associations in Development: A Study of the Organizational Associations of Citizens,' Draft report, INTRAC for the World Bank.

Munck, R. (2005) 'Neoliberalism and Politics,' in A. Saad-Filho and D. Johnston (eds) *Neoliberalism: A Critical Reader*, London: Pluto.

Murphy, P. (2005) 'Recent Trends in Development Cooperation, and on the Contribution of Higher Education Institutions and Suggestions for a Role for Universities Ireland in Africa.' Mimeograph.

Murray, M. (1987) *South Africa: Time of Agony, Time of Destiny*, London: Verso.

Mutume, G. (2003) 'A New Anti-Poverty Remedy for Africa? Adjustment Policies Weaken PRSP Goals, Critics Charge,' *Africa Recovery* 16 (4), 12–20. Available at http://www.un.org/ecosocdev/geninfo/afrec. Accessed 15 June 2005.

Muwonge, J., B. Geleta and S. Heliso (2002) 'Working Towards an Ethiopian PRSP,' in A. Whaites (ed.) *Masters of their Own Development? PRSPs and the Prospects for the Poor*, Monrovia, California: World Vision.

Narayan, D. (2002) 'Bonds and Bridges: Social Capital and Poverty,' in J. Isham, T. Kelly and S. Ramaswamy (eds) *Social Capital and Economic Development: On Well Being in Developing Countries*, Northampton, MA: Edward Elgar.

—— and K. Ebbe (1997) 'Design of Social Funds: Participation, Demand Orientation, and Local Operational Capacity,' Discussion Paper no. 375, Washington, D.C.: World Bank.

——, R. Patel, K. Schafft, A. Rademacher and S. Koch-Schulte (2000) *Voices of the Poor: Can Anyone Hear Us?*, Washington, D.C.: World Bank.

—— and L. Pritchett (1999) 'Cents and Sociability: Household Income and Social Capital in Rural Tanzania,' Economic Development and Cultural Change 47 (4), 871–878.

Narman, A. (2003) 'Education in Zimbabwe: A Matter of Success?' in S. Darnolf and L. Laakso (eds) *Twenty Years of Independence in Zimbabwe: From Liberation to Authoritarianism*, Basingstoke and New York: Palgrave Macmillan.

National Geographic (2005) 'African Oil: Whose Bonanza,' Special Issue on Africa, September, 50–65.

National Productivity Institute (1998) *Productivity Statistics*, Pretoria: NPI.

National Union of Metalworkers of South Africa (1999) Unpublished data.

Nattrass, N. (1994) 'Economic Restructuring in South Africa: The Debate Continues,' *Journal of Southern African Studies* 20 (4), 517–543.

—— (1996) 'Gambling on Investment: Competing Economic Strategies in South Africa,' *Transformation: Critical Perspectives on Southern Africa* 31, 25–42.

—— (2001) 'High Productivity Now: A Critical Review of South Africa's Growth Strategy,' *Transformation: Critical Perspectives on Southern Africa* 45, 1–24.

—— (2004) 'Unemployment and AIDs: The Social-Democratic Challenge for South Africa,' in G. Standing (ed.) *Confronting Economic Insecurity in Africa*, Geneva: ILO.

—— and J. Seekings (2001) '"Two Nations"? Race and Economic Inequality in South Africa Today,' *Daedalus*, Winter, 45–70.

Ncube, W. (2003) 'Zimbabwe: The Crisis and Beyond,' Royal African Society Lecture, 17 November, University of London.

Ndegwa, S. (1996) *The Two Faces of Civil Society: NGOs and Politics in Africa*, West Hartford, Connecticutt: Kumarian Press.

Ndikumana, L. and J. Boyce (2002) *Public Debts and Private Assets: Explaining Capital Flight from Sub-Saharan African Countries*, Working Paper no. 32, Amherst: Political Economy Research Institute, University of Massachusetts.

Nederveen Pieterse, J. (2001) *Development Theory: Deconstructions/Reconstructions*, London, Thousand Oaks and New Delhi: SAGE.

—— (2005) 'The Politics of Globalization Revisited: Flows, Scales and States,' Presentation to Plenary Session of The Royal Geographical Society/Institute of British Geographers, 31 August–2 September, London.

NEPAD Secretariat (2005) 'Africa's First NEPAD e-school Is Launched in Uganda,' *NEPAD Dialogue – Focus on Afric*a, Issue 101, 28 July. Available from http://www.nepad.org/2005/files/newsletterdisplay.php?ax=display&id=75.

Nest, M. (2001) 'Ambitions, Profits and Loss: Zimbabwean Economic Involvement in the Democratic Republic of Congo,' *African Affairs* 100, 469–490.

—— with F. Grignon and E. F. Kisangani (2006) *The Democratic Republic of Congo: Economic Dimensions of War and Peace*, Boulder, CO: Lynne Rienner and International Peace Academy.

Network Wizards (n.d.) Internet Survey. Available at http://www.nw.com.

Nevin, T. (2006a) 'Golden Boom only Benefits 20 percent,' *Africa Business*, 317 February, 44–45.

—— (2006b) 'Perils and Exhilaration of a Strong Rand,' *African Business* 318, March, 46–47.

News24 (2004) 'Uganda, Zim Make Up over DRC,' South Africa, 5 October. Available at http:www.news24.com/News24/Africa/News/0,2–11-1447_1599912,00.html. Accessed 22 June 2006.

Newsweek (2005) 'China's Not-So-Big Bang,' 28 March, p. 4.

NewZimbabwe.com (2005) 'Mugabe's Spies Implicated in Nkomo's Death.' Available at http://www.newzimbabwe.com/pages/mafuyana3.11921.html. Accessed 26 July 2005.

—— (2006) 'Mugabe's 1,400 per cent Pay Hike for Militia,' 11 March. Available at http://www.newzimbabwe.com/pages/army3.12232.html. Accessed 27 June 2006.

Nicolau, K. (1998) *An Evaluation of the MIDP (Motor Industry Development Program) Report No. 3625*, Johannesburg: NIEP.

Nitzan, J. and S. Bichler (2001) 'Going Global: Differential Accumulation and the Great U-turn in South Africa and Israel,' *Review of Radical Political Economics* 33, 21–55.

Nordas, H. (1996) 'South African Manufacturing Industries – Catching Up or Falling Behind?' *Journal of Development Studies* 32 (5), 715–731.

Nustad, K. G. (2000) 'On the theoretical framework of the World Development Report,' *A Critical Review of the World Bank Report: World Development Report 2000/2001: Attacking Poverty*, Comparative Research Programme on Poverty (CROP). Available at http://www.crop.org/publications/files/report/ Comments_ to_WDR2001_2002_ny.pdf. Accessed 12 September 2005.

Nyang'oro, J. E. (1993) 'Development, Democracy and NGOs in Africa,' *Scandinavian Journal of Development Alternatives* XII (2&3), 277–291.

Nye, J. (2004) *Soft Power: The Means to Success in World Politics*, New York: Public Affairs.

Obadan, M. I. (2004) 'The External Debt Crisis: Strategies and Policies,' in B. Onimode *et al. African Development and Governance Strategies in the 21st Century: Looking Back to Move Forward, Essays in Honor of Adebayo Adedeji at Seventy*, London and New York: Zed Books.

O'Brien, R., A. M. Goetz, J. A. Scholte and M. Williams (2000) *Contesting Global Governance: Multilateral Economic Institutions and Global Social Movements*, Cambridge and New York: Cambridge University Press.

Observer, The (1996) 'US Paid Burundi Coup Leader,' London, 28 July, p. 20.

Odén, B. (1999) 'New Regionalism in Southern Africa: Part of or Alternative to the Globalization of the World Ecnomomy,' in B. Hettne, Andras Inotai and Osvaldo Sunkel (eds) *Globalism and the New Regionalism*, St. Martin's Press: New York.

OECD (n.d.) Creditor Reporter System. Available at http://www.oecd.org/ dataoecd/50/15/5037782.htm.

—— (1998) *Background Document: The Caring World*, DEELSA/ELSA/MIN [98]3 prepared for a meeting of the Employment, Labor and Social Affairs Committee, 23–24 June.

Olukoshi, A. O. (ed.) (1998) *The Politics of Opposition in Contemporary Africa*, Nordiska Afrikaininstitute: Uppsala.

—— (2003) 'The Elusive Prince of Denmark: Structural Adjustment and the Crisis of Governance in Africa,' in T. Mkandawire and C. Soludo (eds) *African Voices on Structural Adjustment A Companion to Our Continent, Our Future*, Dakar, Ottowa, Trenton: CODESRIA, IDRC and Africa World Press.

Onimode, B. (2004) 'Mobilization for the Implementation of Alternative Development Paradigms in 21st Century Africa,' in B. Onimode *et al. African Development and Governance Strategies in the 21st Century: Looking Back to Move Forward, Essays in Honor of Adebayo Adedeji at Seventy*, London and New York: Zed Books.

O'Meara, D. (1996) *Forty Lost Years: The Apartheid State and the Politics of the National Party, 1948–1994*, Randburg, South Africa and Athens, OH: Ravan and Ohio University Press.

Omitoogun, W. (2000) 'Military Expenditure in Africa,' *SIPRI Yearbook 2000*. Available at http://projects.sipri.org/milex/mex_trends.html. Accessed 17 March 2004.

Onimode, B. (2004) 'Mobilization for the Implementation of Alternative Development Paradigms in 21st Century Africa,' in B. Onimode (ed.) *African Development and Governance Strategies in the 21st Century: Looking Back to Move Forward, Essays in Honor of Adebayo Adedeji at Seventy*, London and New York: Zed Books.

Orebody (1971) 'Now is the time for a new Bretton Woods,' *African Development* November, 7.

Ó'Riain, S. (2000) 'The Flexible Developmental State: Globalization, Information Technology and the "Celtic Tiger,"' *Politics and Society* 28 (2), 157–193.

OSG (Oromo Support Group) (1996) Press Release No. 10, February. Available at http://www.oromo.org/osg/pr100296.htm. Accessed 31 July 2005.

Owusu, F. (2003) 'Pragmatism and the Gradual Shift from Dependency to Neoliberalism: The World Bank, African Leaders and Development Policy in Africa,' *World Development* 31 (10), 1655–1672.

—— (2004) 'Falling Through the Cracks? US War-on-Terrorism and Poverty Reduction in Africa,' Paper Presented at the 100th Anniversary Meetings of the Association of American Geographers, 15 March, Philadelphia.

—— (2005) 'Livelihood Strategies and Performance in Ghana's Health and Education Sectors: Exploring the Connections,' *Public Administration and Development* 25, 157–174.

Oxfam International (1998) *Debt Relief and Poverty Reduction: Strengthening the Linkage*, Oxfam International Briefing Paper.

—— (2002) 'Cultivating Poverty; The Impact of US Cotton Subsidies on Africa.' Available at www.globalpolicy.org/globaliz/econ/2002/0927cotton.htm. Accessed 21 June 2005.

—— (2005) *Paying the Price: Why Rich Countries Must Invest now in a War on Poverty*, Oxford: Oxfam International.

Øyen, E. (n.d.) 'Social Capital Formation as a Poverty Reduction Strategy.' Available at http://www.crop.org/publications/files/report/Comments_to_WDR2001_2002_ny.pdf. Accessed 12 September 2005.

—— (2000a) 'Poverty Production: A Different Approach to Poverty Understanding,' in *A Critical Review of the World Bank Report: World Development Report 2000/2001: Attacking Poverty*, Norway: Comparative Research Programme on Poverty (CROP). Available at http:// www.crop.org/publications/files/report/Poverty_production.pdf. Accessed 13 September 2005.

—— (2000b) 'Social Capital Formation in Poverty Reduction Strategy: Which Role for Civil Society Organizations and the State?' Paper Presented at the UNESCO/MOST and CROP/ISSC Symposium at the UN World Summit for Social Development +5, Geneva, June 2000. Available at http://www.unesco.org/most/cophag5.htm. Accessed 13 September 2005.

—— (2001) 'A Methodological Approach to "Best Practices,"' in E. Øyen and A. D. Cimadore (eds) *Best Practices in Poverty Reduction: An Analytical Framework*, CROP International Studies in Poverty Research, London and New York: Zed Books.

Padayachee, V. (2000) 'South Africa: New Directions in Economic Policy,' *Economic and Political Weekly*, 15 April, 1357–1361.

—— and J. Michie (1998) 'Three Years After Apartheid: Growth Employment and Redistribution?' *Cambridge Journal of Economics* 22, 623–635.

Paes, W.-C. (2003) 'Towards a Political Economy of Soldiers in Business,' in J. Hentz and M. Bøås (eds) *New and Critical Security and Regionalism: Beyond the Nation State*, Hampshire: Ashgate.

Palloti, A. (2004) 'SADC: A Development Community without a Development Policy?' *Review of African Political Economy* 101, 513–531.

PanAfrican News Agency (2000) 'Anglo American Corp Pulls Out of Sugar in Zimbabwe,' 14 July 2000.

Panić, M. (1995) 'The Bretton Woods System: Concept and Practice,' in J. Michie and J. Grieve Smith (eds) *Managing the Global Economy*, Oxford and New York: Oxford University Press.

Pantoja, E. (2000) 'Exploring the Concept of Social Capital and Its Relevance for Community-Based Development, The Case of Coalmining Areas in Orissa, India,' World Bank Social Capital Initiative, Working Paper no. 18. Available at: http:// worldbank.org/socialdevelopment.

Parayil, G. (1996) 'The "Kerala model" of Development: Development and Sustainability in the Third World,"' *Third World Quarterly* 17 (5), 941–957.

Parfitt, T. (2002) *The End of Development: Modernity, Post-Modernity and Development*, London and Sterling Virginia: Pluto.

—— (2004) 'The Ambiguity of Participation: A Qualified Defense of Participatory Development,' *Third World Quarterly* 25 (3), 537–556.

Pausewang, S., K. Tronvoll and L. Aalen (2002a) 'A Process of Democratization or Control? The Historical and Political Context,' in S. Pausewang, K. Tronvoll and L. Aalen (eds) *Ethiopia Since the Derg: A Decade of Democratic Pretension and Performance*, London: Zed Books.

—— (2002b) 'Conclusion: Democracy Unfulfilled?' in S. Pausewang, K. Tronvoll and L. Aalen (eds) *Ethiopia Since the Derg: A Decade of Democratic Pretension and Performance*, London: Zed Books.

PBS (1999) 'The Triumph of Evil,' PBS Documentary, Aired 26 January. Transcript available at http://www.pbs.org/wgbh/pages/frontline/shows/evil/etc/script.html. Accessed 4 August 2005.

Pearce, J. (1997a) 'Between Co-option and Irrelevance? Latin American NGOs in the 1990s,' in D. Hulme and M. Edwards (eds) *NGOs, States and Donors: Too Close for Comfort?*, Basingstoke: Macmillan.

—— (1997b) 'Civil Society, the Market and Democracy in Latin America,' *Democratization* 4, 65–76.

Pedersen, P. O. (1998) 'Trading Agents and other Producer Services in African Industrialization and Globalization,' CDR Working Paper 98.14, Copenhagen: Center for Development Research.

—— (2004) 'Zimbabwe's Changing Freight Transport and Logistical System: Structural Adjustment and Political Change,' *Journal of Southern African Studies* 30 (3), 577–602.

Peet, R. (2003) *Unholy Trinity: The IMF, World Bank and WTO*, London: Zed Books.

Pempel, T. J. (1999) 'The Developmental Regime in a Changing World,' in M. Woo-Cummings (ed.) *The Developmental State*, Ithaca: Cornell University Press.

Pepper, D. (2006) 'Zimbabwe's Army Takes Over Black Farms,' *The Christian Science Monitor*, 5 June. Available at www.csmonitor.com. Accessed 21 June 2006.

Petras, J. and H. Veltmeyer (2001) *Globalization Unmasked: Imperialism in the 21st Century*, London and New York: Zed Books.

Phimister, I. and B. Raftopolous, (2004) 'Mugabe, Mbeki and the Politics of Anti-Imperialism,' *Review of African Political Economy* 31 (101), 385–400.

Phiri, G. and L. Dube (2004) 'War Vets defy Mugabe,' *Zimbabwe Independent*. Available at http://www.zimbabwesituation.com/dec17b_2004.html. Accessed 29 July 2005.

Pick, W. (1999) 'Health and Security in Sub-Saharan Africa,' in L. Wohlgemuth, S. Gibson, S. Klasen and E. Rothchild (eds) *Common Security and Civil Society in Africa*, Uppsala: Nordiska Afrikainstitutet.

Pilger, J. (2002) *New Rulers of the World*, London: Verso.

Pillay, V. (1997) 'South Africa's Monetary and Foreign Exchange Rate Policy,' in J. Michie and V. Padayachee (eds) *The Political Economy of South Africa's Transition*, London: Dryden Press.

Piron, L.-H. with A. Evans (2004) *Politics and the PRSP: Synthesis Paper*, Working Paper 237, London: Overseas Development Institute.

—— and A. Norton (2004) *Politics and the PRSP Approach: Uganda Case Study*, Working Paper 240, London: Overseas Development Institute.

Planetguru.com (2005) 'UN Tightens Sanctions on Sudan.' Available at http://planetguru.com/Articles/ArticleDetail.aspx?ChannelId=Politics&Article Id=12422. Accessed 26 March 2005.

Plaut, M. (2005) 'High Stakes in Ethiopia Stand-Off,' *BBC News*, 23 June. Available at http://news.bbc.co.uk/2/hi/africa/4122350.stm. Accessed 26 July 2005.

Pocock, I. (2005) 'Sugar Rush,' *Irish Times*, Weekend Review, 18 June, p. 3.

Pogge, T. (2002) *World Poverty and Human Rights: Cosmopolitan Responsibilities and Reforms*, Oxford: Polity Press.

Poku, Nana (2001) *Regionalization and Security in Southern Africa*, New York: Palgrave Macmillan.

Polanyi, K. (1957) *The Great Transformation: The Political and Economic Origins of Our Times*, Boston: Beacon Books.

Policy Co-ordination and Advisory Services, The Presidency (2003) *Towards a Ten Year Review: Synthesis Report of the Implementation of Government Programmes*, Pretoria: The Presidency.

Porteous, T. (2005) 'British Government Policy in Sub-Saharan Africa under New Labor,' *International Affairs* 81 (2), 281–297.

Potts, D. (2006) '"Restoring Order"? Operation Murambatsvina and the Urban Crisis in Zimbabwe,' *Journal of Southern African Studies* 32 (2), 273–291.

Power, M. (2004) 'Geographies of Governance and Regional Politics,' in D. Potts and T. Bowyer-Bower (eds) *Eastern and Southern Africa: Development Challenges in a Volatile Region*, Harlow: Pearson.

Power, S. (2003) *'A Problem from Hell': America and the Age of Genocide*, London: Flamingo.

Prakesh, M. and G. Esteva (1998) *Grassroots Post-Modernism*, London: Zed Books.

Pretorious, L. and S. Patel (n.d.) 'Policy Review: The New Partnership for Africa's Development (NE-PAD): A Critical Review.' Available at http://www.aidc.org.za/web/nepad/Irs.html.

Przeworski, A. (1991) *Democracy and the Market: Political and Economic Reforms in Eastern Europe and Latin America*, Cambridge: Cambridge University Press.

Pugh, M. (2002) 'Maintaining Peace and Security,' in D. Held and A. McGrew, *Governing Globalization: Power and Authority*, Oxford: Polity.

Putnam, R. (1994) *Making Democracy Work: Civic Traditions in Northern Italy*, New Haven: Princeton University Press.

Rademacher, A. and R. Patel (2002) 'Retelling Worlds of Poverty: Reflections on Transforming Participatory Research for a Global Narrative,' in K. Brock and R. McGee (eds) *Knowing Poverty: Critical Reflections on Participatory Research and Poverty*, London: Earthscan.

Raftopolous, B. (2004) 'Unreconciled Differences: The Limits of Reconciliation Politics in Zimbabwe,' in B. Raftopolous and T. Savage (eds) *Zimbabwe: Injustice and Political Reconciliation*, Ann Arbor: Michigan State University Press.

—— and D. Compagnon (2003) 'Indigenization, the State Bourgeoisie and Neo Authoritarian Politics,' in S. Darnolf and L. Laakso (eds) *Twenty Years of Independence in Zimbabwe: From Liberation to Authoritarianism*, Basingstoke and New York: Palgrave Macmillan.

—— and I. Phimister (2004) 'Zimbabwe Now: The Political Economy of Crisis and Coercion,' *Historical Materialism* 12 (2), 355–382.

Rahmato, D. (2002) 'Civil Society Organizations in Ethiopia,' in B. Zewde and S. Pausewang (eds) *Ethiopia: The Challenge of Democracy from Below*, Stockholm: Nordiska Afrikaininstitutet and Forum for Social Studies.

—— and M. Ayenew (2004) *Democratic Assistance to Post-Conflict Ethiopia: Impact and Limitations, FSS Monograph Series 3*, Addis Ababa: Forum for Social Studies.

Rahnema, M. (1992) 'Participation,' in Wolfgang Sachs (ed.) *The Development Dictionary: A Guide to Knowledge as Power*, London: Zed Books.

Rajani, R. (2004) 'Civil Society in Africa,' Annual Sean Lester Memorial Lecture, Dublin City University, 29 November.

Ravenhill, J. (1987) 'The Elusiveness of Development,' in John Ravenhill (ed.) *Africa in Economic Crisis*, London: Macmillan.

Reilly, C. (1995) (ed.) *New Paths to Democratic Development in Latin America: The Rise of NGO-Municipal Collaboration*, Boulder, CO: Lynne Rienner.

Reno, W. (1998) *Warlord Politics and African States*, Boulder, CO: Lynne Rienner.

—— (2000) 'Shadow States and the Political Economy of Civil Wars,' in M. Berdal and D. Malone (eds) *Greed and Grievance: Economic Agendas in Civil Wars*, Boulder, CO: Lynne Rienner and IDRC.

—— (2002) 'Uganda's Politics of War and Debt Relief,' *Review of International Political Economy* 9 (3), 415–435.

Renshaw, P. (1998) 'Introduction,' to A. de Tocqueville, *Democracy in America*, Hertfordshire: Wordsworth Classics.

Ribot, J. C. and P. R. Oyono (2006) 'The Politics of Decentralization,' in C. Toulmin, B. Wisner and R. Chitiga (eds) *Towards a New Map of Africa*, London: Earthscan and IIED.

Riddell, R. C. and A. J. Bebbington (1995) *Developing Country NGOs and Donor Governments, Report to the Overseas Development Administration*, London: Overseas Development Institute.

—— and M. Robinson (1995) *Non-Governmental Organizations and Rural Poverty Alleviation*, Oxford: Clarendon Press.

Ritchey-Vance, M. (2004) 'Social Capital, Sustainability and Working Democracy: New Yardsticks for Grassroots Development,' in M. Edwards and A. Fowler (eds) *The Earthscan Reader on NGO Management*, London: Earthscan.

Robb, C. M. (2002) *Can the Poor Influence Policy? Participatory Poverty Assessments in the Developing World*, Washington, D.C.: World Bank and International Monetary Fund.

Roberts, S. (1997) 'Monetary Policy Within Macroeconomic Policy: An Appraisal in the Context of Reconstruction and Development,' *Transformation: Critical Perspectives on Southern Africa* 32, 54–78.

—— (1998) *A Preliminary Analysis of the Impact of Trade Liberalisation on Manufacturing or 'Will Trade Liberalization Generate Export-Led Growth in South Africa?'* Trade and Industrial Policy Secretariate Working Paper No. 8, Februrary, Johannesburg: TIPS.

Robinson, G. (2004) *Geographies of Agriculture: Globalisation, Restructuring and Sustainability*, Essex: Prentice Hall.

Robinson, M. (1996) *Strengthening Civil Society Through Foreign Political Aid, ESCOR Research Report R6234*, Sussex: Institute of Development Studies.

—— (1997) 'Privatizing the Voluntary Sector: NGOs as Public Service Contractors,' in D. Hulme and M. Edwards (eds) *NGOs, States and Donors: Too Close for Comfort?*, New York: St. Martin's Press.

—— and S. Friedman (2005) 'Civil Society, Democratization and Foreign Aid in Africa,' IDS Discussion Paper 383, Sussex, IDS.

Robinson, P. (1996) 'Democratization: Understanding the Relationship between Regime Change and the Culture of Politics,' *African Studies Review* 37 (1), 39–68.

—— (2001) 'Macroeconomic Performance under the Economic Structural Adjustment Program: An Essay on Iatrogenic Effects,' in C. Mumbengegwei (ed.) *Macroeconomic and Structural Adjustment Policies in Zimbabwe*, Basingstoke, Hampshire and New York: Palgrave Macmillan.

Robinson, W. (1996a) *Promoting Polyarchy*, Cambridge and New York: Cambridge University Press.

—— (1996b) 'The Role of Aid Donors in Strengthening Civil Society,' in A. Clayton (ed.) *NGOs, Civil Society and the State: Building Democracy in Transitional Societies*, Oxford: INTRAC.

—— (2002) 'Capitalist Globalization and the Transnationalization of the State,' in M. Rupert and H. Smith (eds) *Historical Materialism and Globalization*, London and New York: Routledge.

Rodrik, D. (1999) 'The New Global Economy and Developing Countries: Making Openness Work,' ODC Policy Essay 24, Washington, D.C.

—— (2000) *Can Integration into the World Economy Substitute for a Development Strategy?*, Cambridge, MA: Harvard.

Rogers, D. (2006) 'Where a Beer Costs $150,000,' *Los Angeles Times*, 9 July. Available at http://www.latimes.com. Accessed 12 July 2006.

Rogers Hollingsworth, J. and R. Boyer (eds) (1997) *Contemporary Capitalism: The Embeddedness of Institutions*, Cambridge and New York: Cambridge University Press.

Rogerson, C. M. (2000) 'Emerging from Apartheid's Shadow: South Africa's Informal Economy,' *Journal of International Affairs* 53 (2), 673–695.

Romer, P. (1986) 'Increasing Returns and Long-Run Growth,' *Journal of Political Economy* 94 (5), 1002–1037.

Roper-Renshaw, L. (1994) 'Strengthening Civil Society: The Role of NGOs,' *Development* 4, 46–49.

Rotberg, R. I. (2000) 'Africa's Mess, Mugabe's Mayhem,' *Foreign Affairs* 79 (5), 47–61, reprinted in W. Moseley (ed.), (2003) *Taking Sides: Clashing Views on Controversial African Issues*, Connecticut: McGraw Hill.

—— (2002) 'Failed States in a World of Terror,' *Foreign Affairs* 81 (4), 127–140.

—— (ed.) (2005) *Battling Terrorism in the Horn of Africa*, Brookings Institution: Baltimore.

Rothchild, D. (1994) 'Structuring State-Society Relations in Africa: Toward and Enabling Political Environment,' in J. A. Widner (ed.) *Economic Change and Political Liberalization in Sub-Saharan Africa*, Baltimore: Johns Hopkins University Press.

—— and L. Lawson (1994) 'The Interactions Between State and Civil Society in Africa: From Deadlock to New Routines,' in J. W. Harbeson, D. Rothchild and N. Chazan (eds) *Civil Society and the State in Africa* Boulder, CO: Lynne Rienner.

Roy, A. (2003) 'When the Saints Go Marching Out,' *Znet*, 2 September. Available at http://www.zmag.org.

Rueschemeyer, D., E. Huber Stephans and J. Stephens (1992) *Capitalist Development and Democracy*, Chicago: University of Chicago Press.

Ruggie, J. G. (1983) 'International Regimes, Transactions, and Change: Embedded Liberalism in the Postwar Economic Order,' in S. Krasner (ed.) *International Regimes*, Ithaca, NY: Cornell University Press.

Ruppert, M. (2000) *Ideologies of Globalization*, London: Routledge.

—— (2005) 'Saudi Arabia, West Africa – Next Stop on the Infinite War for Oil.' Available at www.fromthewilderness.com/free/ww3/051503_saudi_africa. html. Accessed 19 June 2005.

Ruzvidzo, V. and B. Benza (2005) 'Gono Adjusts Exchange Rate.' Available at http://allafrica.com/stories/200507220493.html. Accessed 24 June 2005.

Ryklief, S. (2002) 'Does the emperor really have no clothes?' in S. Jacobs and R. Calland (eds) *Thabo Mbeki's World: The Politics and Ideology of the South African President*, Pietermaritzberg: University of Natal Press.

Sachs, J. (2002) 'Global Poverty and US Foreign Policy,' Paper Presented to the Carnegie Council, 6 November. Available at www.cceia.org. Accessed 21 July 2005.

—— (2003) 'The Millennium Development Goals,' Paper Presented at The Global Development Challenge, Trinity College Dublin, 10 July.

—— (2004) 'Doing the Sums on Africa,' *The Economist*, 22 May, 21–23.

—— (2005) *The End of Poverty: How We Can Make it Happen in Our Lifetime*, London: Penguin.

—— and J. W. McArthur (2005) 'The Millennium Project: A Plan for Meeting the Millennium Development Goals,' *The Lancet* 365, 347–353.

Sake Rapport (2005) Edition of 30 January.

Salamon, L. M. (1994) 'The Rise of the Nonprofit Sector,' *Foreign Affairs* July/August, 109–122.

Samatar, A. I. (1999) *An African Miracle: State and Class Leadership and Colonial Legacy in Botswana Development*, Portsmouth: Heinemann.
—— (2005) 'Ethiopian Federalism: Autonomy versus Control in the Somali Region,' *Third World Quarterly* 35 (6), 1131–1154.
—— (2005) 'The Ethiopian Election of 2005: A Bombshell & Turning Point?' *Review of African Political Economy*, 32, 104/5, 466–473.
—— and A. Samatar (2002a) 'Introduction,' in A. I. Samatar and A. Samatar (eds) *The African State: Reconsiderations*, Portsmouth, NH: Heinemann.
—— and A. Samatar (2002b) (eds) *The African State: Reconsiderations*, Portsmouth, NH: Heinemann.
——, B. Wisner, R. Chitiga, T. Smucker, E. Wangui and C. Toulmin (2006) 'Agenda for Action,' in C. Toulmin, B. Wisner and R. Chitiga (eds) *Towards a New Map of Africa*, London: Earthscan and IIED.
Sanchez, D. and K. Cash (2003) *Reducing Poverty or Repeating Mistakes: A Civil Society Critique of Poverty Reduction Strategy Papers*, Church of Sweden Aid, Save the Children Sweden and the Swedish Jubilee Network. Available at http://www.globalpolicy.org/socecon/develop/2003/12prspmistakes.pdf. Accessed 13 September 2005.
Sandbrook, R. (1993) *The Politics of Africa's Economic Recovery*, Cambridge and New York: Cambridge University Press.
—— (2003) 'A New Urgency: Civilising Globalisation in an Era of Terrorism,' in Richard Sandbrook (ed.) *Civilising Globalisation: A Survival Guide*, Albany: SUNY Press.
—— and D. Romano (2004) 'Globalization, Extremism and Violence in Poor Countries,' *Third World Quarterly* 25 (6), 1007–1030.
Sanlam (2001) 'Sanlam Outsources IT infrastructure.' Available at www.sanlam. co.za. Accessed 16 July 2001.
Sapa-AP (2004) 'Gaddafi Urges Libyans to "Bleed" for US.' Available at http://www.iol.co.za. Accessed 20 June 2005.
SAPRIN (Structural Adjustment Participatory Review International Network) (2002) *The Policy Roots of Economic Crisis*, London: Zed Books.
SARB (South African Reserve Bank) (n.d.) *Economic and Financial Data*. Available at www.reservebank.co.za. Accessed 15 October 2001.
—— (1997) *Quarterly Bulletin*, Pretoria: SARB.
—— (1998) *Quarterly Bulletin*, Pretoria: SARB.
—— (1999) *Quarterly Bulletin*, June 1999. Available at www.resbank.co.za. Accessed 30 July 2002.
—— (2001) *Quarterly Bulletin*, March 2001. Available at www.resbank.co.za. Accessed 30 July 2002.
—— (2005) *Quarterly Bulletin March 2005*, Pretoria: SARB.
Sassen, S. (1998) *Globalization and Its Discontents: Essays on the Mobility of People and Money*, New York: Free Press.
—— (1999) 'Servicing the Global Economy: Reconfigured States and Private Agents,' in K. Olds, P. Dicken, P. Kelly, L. Kong and H. Yeung (eds) *Globalisation and the Asia-Pacific*, London and New York: Routledge.
Saul, J. S. (2002) 'Cry for the Beloved Country: The Post-Apartheid Denouement,' in S. Jacobs and R. Calland (eds) *Thabo Mbeki's World: The Politics and Ideology of the South African President*, London and Pietermaritzberg: Zed Books and University of Natal Press.

—— (2004) 'The Hares, the Hounds and the African National Congress: on Joining the Third World in Post-Apartheid South Africa,' *Third World Quarterly* 25 (1), 73–86.

Saurin, J. (1995) 'The End of International Relations? The State and International Theory in the Age of Globalization,' in J. Macmillan and A. Linklater (eds), *Boundaries in Question*, London: Pinter.

Scarnecchia, T. (2006) 'The "Fascist Cycle" in Zimbabwe, 2000–2005,' *Journal of Southern African Studies* 32 (2), 221–237.

Schoeman, N., J. Clausen, Z. Robinson and T. J. de Wet (2000) 'Foreign Direct Investment Flows and Fiscal Discipline in South Africa,' *South African Journal of Economic and Management Science* 3 (2), 235–244.

Schoenberger, R. (1996) *World Class Manufacturing: The Next Decade*, New York: Free Press.

Schraeder, P. J. (2000) *African Politics and Society: A Mosaic in Transformation*, Boston and New York: Bedford/St. Martin's.

Schumann, M. (1998) *Going Local: Creating Self-Reliant Communities in a Global Age*, New York: Free Press.

Schweickart, D. (1999) 'Market Socialism: A Defense,' in B. Ollman (ed.) *Market Socialism: The Debate Among Socialists*, London: Routledge.

Scott, J. C. (1990) *Domination and the Arts of Resistance: Hidden Transcripts*, New Haven and London: Yale University Press.

—— (1998) *Seeing Like a State: Why Certain Schemes to Improve the Human Condition Have Failed*, New Haven: Yale University Press.

Scott-Joynt, J. (2004) 'Retailers Cash in on Playstations,' *BBC News*, 6 December. Available at http://news.bbc.co.uk/1/hi/business/4070755.stm. Accessed 21 April 2005.

Seager, A. and T. Macalister (2004) 'Nigeria Warning Pushes Oil Past $50,' *The Guardian*, 29 September.

Sefera, M. (2003) 'Mixed Reaction to Mugabe's New AU Post,' *The Star*, 14 July 2003. Available at http://www.zimbabwesituation.com/jul14a_2003.html#link8. Accessed 27 June 2006.

Seidman, A. and N. Seidman (1977) *South Africa and U.S. Multinational Corporations*, Dar es Salaam: Tanzania Publishing House.

Seidman Makgetla, N. (2004) 'The Post-Apartheid Economy,' *Review of African Political Economy* 100, 263–281.

Sen, A. K. (1999) *Development as Freedom*, New York: Alfred A. Knopf.

Sender, J. (1994) 'Economic Restructuring in South Africa: Reactionary Rhetoric Prevails,' *Journal of Southern African Studies* 20 (4), 539–543.

—— (2002) 'Reassessing the Role of the World Bank in Sub-Saharan Africa,' in J. Pincus and J. Winters (eds) *Reinventing the World Bank*, Ithaca: Cornell University Press.

Servant, J.-C. (2003) 'The New Gulf Oil States,' *Le Monde Diplomatique*, 8 January. Available at http://www.globalpolicy.org/security/natres/oil/2003/0114angola.htm. Accessed 21 June 2005.

—— (2005) 'China's Trade Safari in Africa,' *Le Monde Diplomatique*, May. Available at http://mondediplio.com. Accessed 18 September 2006.

Shaffer, P. (2002) 'Participatory Analyses of Poverty Dynamics: Reflections from the Myanmar PPA,' in K. Brock and R. McGee (eds) *Knowing Poverty: Critical Reflections on Participatory Research and Poverty*, London: Earthscan.

Shaw, G. B. (1905) Preface to *Major Barbara*.

Shaw, M. (2003) 'The State of Globalization: Towards a Theory of State Transformation,' in N. Brenner, B. Jessop, M. Jones and G. Macleod (eds) *State/Space: A Reader*, Oxford and Malden, MA: Blackwell.

Shaw, T. (2000) 'New Regionalisms in Africa in the New Millennium: Comparative Perspectives on Renaissance, Realisms and/or Regressions,' *New Political Economy* 5 (3), 399–414.

—— (2003) 'Towards a Political Economy of Conflict and Cooperation in Middle Africa at the Start of the Twenty-First Century,' in J. J. Hentz and M. Bøas (eds) *New and Critical Security and Regionalism: Beyond the Nation State*, London: Ashgate.

——, F. Soderbaum, J. Nyangoro and J. A. Grant (2003) 'The Future of New Regionalism in Africa: Regional Governance, Human Security/Development and Beyond,' in J. A. Grant and F. Söderbaum (eds) *The New Regionalism in Africa*, Aldershot and Burlington: Ashgate.

Shiva, V. (1989) *Staying Alive: Women, Ecology and Development*, London: Zed Books.

Shivji, I. (n.d.) 'African Integration in and for Civil Society: Bulletin 6.' Available at http://www.nu.ac.za/ccs/default.asp? Accessed 12 September 2005.

Shuman, M. (1998) *Going Local: Creating Self-Reliant Communities in a Global Age*, New York: Free Press.

Simkins, C. (2004) 'Employment and Unemployment in South Africa,' *Journal of Contemporary African Studies* 22 (2), 253–278.

Simon, D. (2001) 'Trading Spaces: Imagining and Positioning the "New" South Africa within the Regional and Global Economy,' *International Affairs* 77 (3), 377–405.

—— (2003) 'Regional Development-Environment Discourses, Policies and Practices in Post-Apartheid Southern Africa,' in J. A. Grant and F. Söderbaum (eds) *The New Regionalism in Africa*, London: Ashgate.

Simon, J., S. Rosen, J. Vincent, W. Macleod, M. Fox and D. Thea (2001) 'Estimating the Impacts of AIDS on Businesses in South Africa,' Paper Presented to the Boston University African Studies Seminar, 10 April.

Sinha, S. (2005) 'Neoliberalism and Civil Society: Project and Possibilities,' in A. Saad-Filho and D. Johnston (eds) *Neoliberalism: A Critical Reader*, London: Pluto.

SIPRI (Stockholm International Peace Research Institute) (2005) 'Recent Trends in Military Expenditure.' Available at http://projects.sipri.org/milex/mex_trends. html. Accessed 21 September 2006.

Sisulu, L. (2005) Presentation by Minister of Housing, Republic of South Africa at 'Stakeholder Consultation on Ireland's First White Paper on Development Cooperation: Tackling World Poverty,' Dublin Castle, 11 October.

Sixty Minutes (2003) 'The Kuwait of Africa,' CBS, 16 November. Available at web.lexis-nexis.com. Accessed 21 April 2005.

Skålnes, T. (1995) *The Politics of Economic Reform in Zimbabwe: Continuity and Change in Development*, International Political Economy Series, Basingstoke and New York: Palgrave Macmillan.

Skirbekk, G. and A. St. Clair (2005) 'A Philosophical Analysis of the World Bank's Conception of Poverty.' Available at http://www.crop.org/publications/ files/report/Comments_to_WDR2001_2002_ny.pdf. Accessed 12 September 2005.

Sklair, L. (2001) *The Transnational Capitalist Class*, Oxford, Malden, MA: Blackwell.

Smalberger, W. (2003) 'Lessons Learnt by South Africa during the Negotiations,' in T. Bertelsmann-Scott, G. Mills and E. Sidiropoulos (eds) *The EU-SA Agreement*, Johannesburg: South Africa Institute of International Affairs.

Smillie, I. and J. Hailey (2001) *Managing for Change*, London, Earthscan.

and H. Helmich (1993) *Non-Governmental Organisations and Governments: Stakeholders for Development*, Paris: OECD.

Smith, R. (2000) 'Profile: War Veterans' leader "Hitler" Hunzvi,' *BBC News*, 20 April. Available at http://news.bbc.co.uk/1/hi/world/africa/699951.stm. Accessed 31 July 2006.

Smith, S. (2005) *Ending Global Poverty: A Guide to What Works*, Basingstoke and New York: Palgrave Macmillan.

Soederberg, S. (2004) 'American Empire and "Excluded State": The Millennium Challenge Account and the Shift to Pre-Emptive Development,' *Third World Quarterly* 25 (2), 279–302.

—— (2006) *Global Governance in Question: Empire, Class and the New Common Sense in Managing North-South Relations*, London: Pluto, 2006.

Sunmonu, H. A. (2004) 'Implementation of Africa's Development Paradigms,' in B. Onimode (ed.) *African Development and Governance Strategies in the 21st Century: Looking Back to Move Forward, Essays in Honor of Adebayo Adedeji at Seventy*, London and New York: Zed Books.

SouthAfrica.info (2003) 'Mbeki, Bush Cement Relations,' 10 July. Available at http://www.southafrica.info/doing_business/sa_trade/agreements/bushsavisit. htm. Accessed 24 June 2005.

—— (n.d.) 'South Africa: Economic Overview.' Available at http://www. southafrica.info/doing_business/economy/econoverview.htm. Accessed 29 July 2005.

South African Labour Bulletin (2003) Umanyano Publications, Johannesburg.

Southern African Development Co-operation Conference (1986) *Annual Report*.

Southhall, R. (2004) 'The ANC and Black Capitalism in South Africa,' *Review of African Political Economy* 100, 313–328.

Sparke, M. (2004) 'Political Geography: Political Geographies of Globalization (1) – Dominance,' *Progress in Human Geography* 28 (6), 777–794.

Ssemakula, J. (2002) 'The Impact of 9/11 on HIV/AIDS Care in Africa and the Global Fund to Fight AIDS, Tuberculosis, and Malaria,' *Journal of the Association of Nurses in AIDS Care*, 13 (5), 45–56.

Standing, G. (1999) *Global Labor Flexibility: Seeking Distributive Justice*, London: Palgrave Macmillan.

—— (2002) *Beyond the New Paternalism: Basic Security as Equality*, London and New York: Verso.

——, J. Sender and J. Weeks (1996) *Restructuring the Labor Market: The South African Challenge*, An ILO Country Review, Geneva: International Labor Office.

Statistics South Africa (1997) *Statistical Release P3051.4: Manufacturing Statistics*, April, SSA: Pretoria.

—— (1999) *Statistical Release P3051.4: Manufacturing Statistics*, March, SSA: Pretoria.

—— (2000) *Measuring Poverty in South Africa*. Available at www.statssa.gov.za. Accessed 21 July 2001.

—— (2001a) 'Consumer Price Index.' Available at http://www.statssa.gov.za. Accessed 20 June 2001.

—— (2001b) *Statistical Release P0441: Gross Domestic Product*, February. Available at www.statssa.gov.za. Accessed 2 February 2002.

—— (2002) *Earning and Spending in South Africa*, Pretoria: SSA.

—— (2003) *Statistical Release PO 351: Tourism and Migration*, October. Available at www.statssa.gov.za. Accessed 19 June 2005.

—— (2006a) *Statistical Release PO 277: Quarterly Employment Statistics*, March. Available at www.statssa.gov.za. Accessed 10 July 2006.

—— (2006b) *Statistical Release PO 441: Gross Domestic Product, First Quarter.* Available at www.statsssa.gov.za. Accessed 10 July 2005.

Stedman, S. J. (ed.) (2004) *A More Secure World: Our Shared Responsibility*, Report of the UN Secretary General's High Level Panel on Threats, Challenges and Change. Available at http://www.un-globalsecurity.org. Accessed 12 March 2005.

Steidle, B. (2005) 'I Walked through a Field Filled with Human Bones,' *The Independent*, 1 April, 30–31.

Stein, H. (1992) 'Deindustrialization, Adjustment, the World Bank and the IMF in Africa,' *World Development* 20 (1), 83–95.

—— (2005) 'The Millennium Development Goals,' Paper Presented at the Millennium Development Goals Lecture Series, Trinity College, Dublin, 3 March.

Stephan, A. (1988) *Rethinking Military Politics: Brazil and the Southern Cone*, Princeton: Princeton University Press.

Stevenson, J. (2003) 'Africa's Growing Strategic Resonance,' *Survival* 45, 153–172.

Stewart, F. (2000) 'Civil Wars in Sub-Saharan Africa: Counting the Economic and Social Cost,' in D. Ghai (ed.) *Renewing Social and Economic Progress in Africa: Essays in Memory of Philip Ndegwa*, London: Macmillan.

—— and M. Wang (2003) 'Do PRSPs Empower Poor Countries and Disempower the World Bank, Or is it the Other Way Round?' Queen Elizabeth House Working Paper Series No. 108. Available at http://www.eurodad.org/uploadstore/cms/docs/WBevalMay03.pdf, p. 2. Accessed 13 September 2005.

Stiglitz, J. E. (2002) *Globalization and Its Discontents*, London: Allen Lane.

Stiles, K. (2002) 'International Support for NGOs in Bangladesh: Some Unintended Consequences,' *World Development* 30 (5), 835–846.

Stockselector.com (2005) 'Anglo-American PLC.' Available at http://www.stockselector.com/profile.asp?symbol=AAUK. Accessed 1 August 2005.

Stoneman, C. and L. Cliffe (1989) *Zimbabwe: Politics, Economics and Society*, London and New York: Pinter.

Stoppard, A. (2002) 'Civil society gives cautious nod of approval to African Union.' Available at http://www.woza.co.za.

Storey, A. (2001) 'Structural Adjustment, State Power and Genocide: The World Bank and Rwanda,' *Review of African Political Economy* 27 (89), 365–386.

Storey, A. (2005) 'The Price of Debt Relief,' *Village: Ireland's Current Affairs Weekly*, Issue 38, 17–23 June, p. 34.

Storper, M. (1997) *The Regional World: Territorial Development in a Global Economy*, London and New York: Guildford.

Streeten, P. (2002) 'Reflections on Social and Anti-Social Capital,' in J. Isham, T. Kelly and S. Ramaswamy (eds) *Social Capital and Economic Development: On Well Being in Developing Countries*, Northampton, MA: Edward Elgar.

Streak, J. (1997) 'The Counter-Counterrevolution in Development Theory on the Role of the State in Development: Inferences for South Africa?' *Development Southern Africa* 14 (3), 307–325.

Subramanian, A. with Enrique Gelbard, R. Harmsen, K. Elborgh-Woytek and P. Nagy (2000) *Trade and Trade Policies in Eastern and Southern Africa*, IMF Occasional Paper 196, Washington, D.C.: IMF.

Summa, J. (1988) 'Anglo-American Corporation: A Pillar of Apartheid,' *Multinational Monitor* 9 (9). Available at http://www.essential.org/monitor/hyper/issues/1988/09/mm0988_08.html. Accessed 20 April 2001.

Sunday Times Business Times (1998) 'Empowerment Deal Slowdown,' 18 October.

Swann, C. (2004) 'Projected US Budget Deficit "$1,000bn out,"' *Financial Times*, 27 January, p. 6.

Swarns, R. (2000) 'For South African Whites, Money Has No Color,' *New York Times*, 20 April, p. A4.

Swatuk, L. (1999) 'Remaking the State: Assessing South Africa's Developmental Agenda,' in K. Mengisteab and C. Daddieh (eds) *State Building and Democratization in Africa*, Westport, CT and London: Praeger.

Sylvester, C. (2003) 'Vacillations Around Women: The Overlapping Meanings of "Women" in the Zimbabwean Context,' in S. Darnolf and L. Laakso (eds) *Twenty Years of Independence in Zimbabwe: From Liberation to Authoritarianism*, Basingstoke and New York: Palgrave Macmillan.

—— (2006) 'Bare Life as a Development/Postcolonial Problematic,' *The Geographical Journal* 172, 66–77.

Tabb, W. K. (2001) *The Amoral Elephant: Globalisation and the Struggle for Social Justice in the Twenty-First Century*, New York: Monthly Review Press.

Talbot, C. (2002) 'Blair's Neocolonialist Vision for Africa.' Available from http://www.wsws.org/articles/2002/feb2002/.

Tandon, Y. (1996) 'An African Perspective,' in D. Sogge (ed.) *Compassion and Calculation: The Business of Private Foreign Aid*, London and Chicago: Pluto Press and Transnational Institute.

Tanzi, V. (1999) 'Globalization and the Financing of Social Protection,' Paper Presented at Conference on Financing Social Protection in Europe, Helsinki, 22–23 November.

Tarrow, S. (1994) *Power in Movement. Social Movements, Collective Action and Politics*, Cambridge: Cambridge University Press.

Taylor, I. (2001) *Stuck in Middle GEAR: South Africa's Post-Apartheid Foreign Relations*. Westport, CT and London: Praeger.

—— (2002) 'The NEPAD, Zimbabwe and Elites as Obstacles to Change,' *Foreign Policy in Focus*, 22 April, 1–3.

—— (2004) 'The "All-Weather Friend"? Sino-African Interaction in the Twenty First Century,' in I. Taylor and P. Williams (eds) *Africa in International Politics: External Involvement on the Continent*, London: Routledge.

—— (2005a) 'Advice is Judged by Results, Not by Intentions: Why Gordon Brown is Wrong about Africa,' *International Affairs* 81 (2), 299–310.

—— (2005b) *NEPAD: Towards Africa's Development or Another False Start*, Boulder, CO: Lynne Rienner.

—— (2005c) 'Zimbabwe and the Death of NEPAD,' in P. Bond (ed.) *Fanon's Warning: A Civil Society Reader on the New Partnership for Africa's Development*, 2nd edn., Trenton and Asmara: Africa World Press.

—— and P. Nel (2002) '"New Africa," Globalisation and the Confines of Elite Reformism: "Getting the Rhetoric Right," Getting the Strategy Wrong,' *Third World Quarterly* 23 (1), 163–180.

Taylor, S. D. (1999) 'Race, Class and Neopatrimonialism in Zimbabwe,' in R. Joseph (ed.) *State Conflict and Democracy in Africa*, Boulder, CO: Lynne Rienner.

Teivainen, T. (2002) *Enter Economism, Exit Politics: Experts, Economic Policy and the Damage to Democracy*, London: Zed Books.

Telkom (n.d.) 'Company Background.' Available at www.telkom.co.za. Accessed 21 July 2001.

Teljeur, E. (1998) 'Free Trade: Does South Africa Gain?' *Trade and Industry Monitor* 6, 1–6.

Temple, J. and P. Johnson (n.d.) 'Social Capability and Economic Development,' Unpublished Paper.

Tendler, J. (1997) *Good Government in the Tropics*, Baltimore, Johns Hopkins University Press.

Terreblanche, S. (2002) *South Africa: A History of Inequality in South Africa 1652–2002*, Scottsville and Sandton: KMM and University of Natal Press.

Thirkell-White, B. (2004) 'The International Monetary Fund and Civil Society,' *New Political Economy* 9 (2), 251–270.

Thomas, A., D. Humphreys and S. Carr (2001) 'Influence Thrust Upon Them? NGOs Role in Public Action on the Environment in Africa,' in A. Thomas, S. Carr and D. Humphreys (eds) *Environmental Policies and NGO Influence: Land Degradation and Sustainable Resource Management in Sub-Saharan Africa*, London: Routledge.

Thomas, N. H. (2003) 'Land Reform in Zimbabwe,' *Third World Quarterly* 24 (4), 691–712.

Thomas-Emeagwali, G. (ed.) (1995) *Women Pay the Price: Structural Adjustment in Africa and the Caribbean*, Trenton, NJ: Africa World Press.

Thomas Isaac, T. M., R. W. Franke and P. Raghavan (1998) *Democracy at Work in an Indian Industrial Cooperative: The Story of Kerala Dinesh Beedi*, Ithaca and London: Cornell University Press.

Thompson, C. (2000) 'Regional Challenges to Globalisation: Perspectives from Southern Africa,' *New Political Economy* 5 (1), 41–57.

—— (2004) 'US Trade with Africa: African Growth and Opportunity?' *Review of African Political Economy* 101, 457–474.

Thompson, J. (2000) 'South Africa: A Reasoned Case for Optimism,' Speech by the Chairman of the Anglo-American Corporation to the Instituto de Empresa, Madrid, 16 November. Available at www.barney.co.za/news/nov00/optimism17.htm. Accessed 12 July 2006.

Tieku, T. K. (2004) 'Explaining the Clash and Accommodation of Interests of Major Actors in the Creation of the African Union,' *African Affairs* 103, 249–267.

Times of Zambia (2000) 'Diamond Sales Earns Anglo $1.55 Billion Profit,' 28 March. Available at web7.infotrac.galegroup.com. Accessed 21 June 2001.

Tomasevski, K. (1997) *Between Sanctions and Elections: Aid Donors and Their Human Rights Performance*, London: Pinter.

Tomori, S. O. and O. W. Tomori (2004) 'Revisiting the African Alternative Framework to Structural Adjustment Programmers for Socio-Economic Recovery and Transformation in Contemporary Niger,' in B. Onimode (ed.)

African Development and Governance Strategies in the 21st Century: Looking Back to Move Forward, Essays in Honor of Adebayo Adedeji at Seventy, London and New York: Zed Books.

Toulmin, C. and B. Wisner (2006) 'Introduction,' in C. Toulmin, B. Wisner and R. Chitiga (eds) *Towards a New Map of Africa*, London: Earthscan and IIED.

Tourism South Africa (1999) *Executive Summary*, Pretoria: Satour.

Toussaint, E. (n.d.) *Debt in Sub-Saharan Africa on the Eve of the Third Millennium*. Unpublished Paper. Brussels: Committee for the Abolition of Third World Debt.

Toye, J. (1987) *Dilemmas of Development Reflections on the Counterrevolution in Development Theory and Policy*, Oxford: Blackwell.

Trade Law Center for Southern Africa (2005) *Total Trade between AGOA Countries and the US*. Available at http://www.agoa.info/index.php?view=trade_stats&story=all_trade. Accessed 19 May 2005.

Treanor, P. (n.d.) 'Neoliberalism: Origins, Theory, Definition.' Available at http://web.internl.net/users/Paul.Treanor/neoliberalism.html.

Tretter, E. (2005) Mailing List, available from: leftgeog@lsv.uky.edu. Accessed 18 April 2005.

Tucker, V. (1997) 'From Biomedicine to Holistic Health: Towards a New Health Model,' in A. Cleary and M. P. Treacy (eds) *The Sociology of Health and Illness in Ireland*, Dublin: University College Dublin Press.

United Nations (2005) *In Larger Freedom: Towards Development, Security and Human Rights for All*, Report of the Secretary General. Available at www.un.org/largerfreedom/contents.htm. Accessed 23 October 2006.

United Nations Commission on Global Governance (1995) *Our Common Neighborhood: The Report of the Commission on Global Governance*, Oxford: Oxford University Press.

UNCTAD (United Nations Conference on Trade and Development) (1996) *World Investment Report 1996: Investment, Trade and International Policy Arrangements*, New York: United Nations.

—— (2002) *Poverty Reduction Strategies in Africa: What is New?* Geneva: UNCTAD.

UNDP (United Nations Development Program) (1993) *Human Development Report 1993*, Oxford: Oxford University Press.

—— (1994) *Human Development Report 1994*, Oxford and New York: Oxford University Press.

—— (1996) *Human Development Report 1996*, New York and Oxford: Oxford University Press.

—— (2003a) *Evaluation of UNDP's Role in the PRSP Process*, Main Report, Draft.

—— (2003b) *Human Development Report, 2003: Millennium Development Goals: A compact among nations to end human poverty*. Available at http://hdr.undp.org/reports/global/2003/. Accessed 21 July 2005.

—— (2005) *The Millennium Development Goals Report 2005*, UN: New York. Available at http://unstats.un.org/unsd/mi/pdf/MDG%20Book.pdf. Accessed 24 July 2006.

UNECA (United Nations Economic Commission for Africa) (2003) *Economic Report on Africa 2003: Accelerating the Pace of Development*, Addis Ababa: UNECA.

UNESCO (United Nations Educational and Scientific and Cultural Organization) (2003) 'UNESCO Sector for the Social and Human Sciences/CROP Consultation,' Bergen, Norway, 5–6 June 2003 on the draft document 'Abolishing Poverty

Through the International Human Rights Framework: Towards an Integrated Strategy for the Social and Human Sciences.' Available at http://www.crop.org/publications/reports.cfm. Accessed 13 September 2005.

UN-IRIN (United Nations-Integrated Regional Information Network) (2001) '"Disaster" Beckons as US Cuts Lifeline.' Available at http://www.africaaction.org/docs01/som0111.htm. Accessed 21 April 2006.

—— (2003a) 'Angola: Dos Santos at the Helm.' Available at http://www.irinnews.org/report.asp?ReportID=38470. Accessed 20 June 2005.

—— (2003b) 'ZAMBIA: Surprise Sale of State-Owned Copper Mine,' 16 May. Available at http://www.irinnews/org. Accessed 26 July 2005.

—— (2005a) 'Delays in Safety Nets Creating "Disaster" – Report,' 29 July 2005. Available from listserv IRIN@irinnews.org,.

—— (2005b) 'South Africa: Evictions Worsen Low-Cost Housing Crisis, NGOs.' UN-IRIN, 27 July 2005. Available from IRIN@irinnews.org.

—— (2005c) 'Zimbabwe: Crucial IMF Assessment Will Put Membership in the Balance,' 28 June. Available at http://www.irinnews.org. Accessed 28 June 2006.

—— (2005d) 'Zimbabwe: "Look East" Policy Staves Off Collapse with Grants and Deals,' 31 July. Available at http://www.irinnews.org/print.asp?ReportID=49359.

—— (2005e) 'Zimbabwe: Ruling Party Looks for Spiritual Support,' 26 June. Available from IRIN@irinnews.org.

—— (2006a) 'Zimbabwe: Army Enforces New Monetary Policy,' 7 August. Available at: http://www.irinnews.org. Accessed 9 August 2006.

—— (2006b) 'Zimbabwe: Opportunistic Money Is Creating a New Elite,' 10 July. Available from IRIN@irinnews.org.

—— (2006c) 'Zimbabwe: Ruralization Is the New Trend,' 26 July. Available from IRIN@irinnews.org.

United States Institute for Peace (2001) 'AIDS and Violent Conflict in Africa,' Special Report 75, Washington: USIP.

Unsworth, S. (2006) 'Getting Better Governance: Insights from new Research,' *Trócaire Development Review*, 17–35.

Unwin, T. (2004) 'Beyond Budgetary Support: Pro-Poor Development Agendas for Africa,' *Third World Quarterly* 25 (8), 1501–1523.

USAID (1996) 'Constituencies for Reform: Strategic Approaches for Donor-Supported Civic Advocacy Programs,' USAID Program and Operations Assessment Report No. 12, February, Washington, D.C.

—— (2004) 'What Conditions Favor the Success of General Budget Support: Mozambique Country Case Study.' Available at http://www.dec.org/pdf_docs/PNACU999.pdf. Accessed 21 April 2005.

US Department of State (2000) *African Crisis Response Initiative (ACRI)* website. Available at http://usinfo.state.gov/regional/af/acri/. Accessed 21 April 2006.

—— (2004) 'Extending and Improving the Lives of Those Living with HIV/AIDs.' Available at http://www.state.gov/s/gac/rl/fs/2004/33868.htm. Accessed 19 May 2005.

USEIA (United States Energy Information Administration) (n.d.) 'World Oil Transit Chokepoints.' Available at http://www.eia.doe.gov/emeu/cabs/choke.html. Accessed 21 April 2005.

Utstein Group (2005) 'Report of the Utstein Group Mission to the World Bank and IMF, January 2001, to Consider Poverty Reduction Strategy Papers.'

Available at http://www.nssd.net/references/PRSP/utsrprt.htm. Accessed 31 July 2005.

Uvin, P. (1998) *Aiding Violence: The Development Enterprise in Rwanda*, New York: Kumarian Press.

Valodia, I. (2000) 'Economic Policy and Women's Informal and Flexible Work in South Africa,' Paper Presented at the TIPS 2000 Annual Forum, Muldersrift, 18–20 September.

van Audenhove, L. (1999) 'South Africa's Information Society Policy: An Overview,' *Communication* 25 (1&2). Available at www.unisa.ac.za/dept/press. Accessed 20 June 2001.

van de Walle, N. (1999) 'Globalization and African Democracy,' in R. Joseph (ed.) *State, Conflict and Democracy in Africa*, Boulder: Lynne Rienner.

—— (2001) *African Economies and the Politics of Permanent Crisis, 1979–1999*, Cambridge and New York: Cambridge University Press.

—— (2003) 'Introduction: The State and African Development,' in N. van de Walle, N. Ball and V. Ramachandran (eds) *Beyond Structural Adjustment: The Institutional Context of Development*, New York: Palgrave Macmillan.

Van der Walt, T. and W. Blankley (1999) 'South African Strategies for the Promotion of Research and Technology Innovation: Towards Effective Collaboration and New Business Development,' *Industry and Higher Education*, February.

Van Rensburg, T. (1999) 'A Critical Assessment of Primary Listings of South African Companies on Offshore Stock Exchanges,' Paper Presented to the TIPS 1999 Annual Forum, Glenburn Lodge, Muldersdrift, 19–22 September.

Van Rooy, A. (1998) 'Civil Society As Idea: An Analytical Hatstand?' in A. Van Rooy (ed.) *Civil Society and the Aid Industry*, London: Earthscan.

—— and M. Robinson (1998) 'Out of the Ivory Tower: Civil Society and the Aid System,' in A. van Rooy (ed.) *Civil Society and the Aid Industry*, London: Earthscan.

Veltmeyer, H. and J. Tellez (2001) 'The State and Participatory Development in Bolivia,' in H. Veltmeyer and A. O'Malley (eds) *Transcending Neoliberalism: Community-Based Development in Latin America*, Bloomfield, CT: Kumarian Press.

Versi, A. (2003) 'At Last, a Win–Win Formula for African Business,' *African Business* 3 (285), 12–15.

—— (2004) 'Formula for Africa's Rapid Growth,' *African Business* 301 August/September, 16–23.

Villanger, E., S. Pausewang, A. Morten Jerve (2003) *The SAPRIN Report: An Assessment of the Empirical Analysis Supporting Main Conclusions*, Working Paper 2, Bergen: Chr Michelsen Institute.

Vines, A. and T. Cargill (2006) 'Le Monde Doit Nous Juger Sur L'Afrique,' *Politique Africaine* 1011, 132–147. Available at http://www.chathamhouse.org.uk/. Accessed 25 September 2006.

Volger, J. (1995) *The Global Commons: A Regime Analysis*, Chichester and New York: John Wiley.

Volman, D. (2003a) 'Oil, Arms and Violence in Africa.' Available at www.prairienet.org/acas/military/oilandarms.pdf. Accessed 17 March 2004.

—— (2003b) 'The Bush Administration and African Oil: The Security Implications of US Energy Policy,' *Review of African Political Economy* 98, 573–584.

—— (2003c) 'US Military Programs in Sub-Saharan Africa, 2001–2003.' Available at http://www.inwent.org/v-ez/lis/ghana/usmilafrica.pdf. Accessed 21 April 2006.

VonDoepp, P. (1996) 'Political Transition and Civil Society: The Cases of Kenya and Zambia,' *Studies in Comparative International Development*, 31 24–47.

WAAG Communications (2004a) 'Case for Developmental State,' *7 Days Update: Ethiopia* XI (26), 6 September, 1.

—— (2004b) 'How to Achieve Growth,' *7 Days Update: Ethiopia* XI (27), 10 September, 1.

Wade, R. (1990) *Governing the Market: Economic Theory and the Role of Government in the East Asian Industrialization*, Princeton, NJ: Princeton University Press.

—— (2001) 'Showdown at the Bank,' *New Left Review* 7, 124–137.

—— (2004) 'On the Causes of Increasing World Poverty and Inequality, or Why the Mathew Effect Prevails,' *New Political Economy* 9 (2), 163–188.

Wallace, T. (2003) 'NGO Dilemmas: Trojan Horses for Global Neoliberalism?' *Socialist Register*, 202–219.

Wallis, J. and D. Dollery (2001) 'Government Failure, Social Capital and the Appropriateness of the New Zealand Model for Public Sector Reform in Developing Countries,' *World Development* 29 (2), 245–263.

Wangwe, S. W. and F. Musonda (1998) 'The Impact of Globalization on Africa,' in A. S. Bhalla (ed.) *Globalization, Growth and Marginalization*, New York: St. Martin's Press.

Warren, M. E. (2001) *Democracy and Associations*, Princeton, NJ: Princeton University Press.

Washington Post Foreign Service (2006) 'In Africa, China Trade Brings Growth, Unease,' 13 June. Available at www.washingtonpost.com. Accessed 16 June 2006.

Watkins, K. (1999) 'G7 Summit Has Chance to End Debt and Close Obscene Rich, Poor Gap,' *The Irish Times*, 19 June.

Watts, M. (1983) *Silent Violence: Food, Famine, & Peasantry in Northern Nigeria*, Berkeley: University of California Press.

—— (1994) 'Oil as Money: The Devil's Excrement and the Spectacle of Black Gold,' in S. Corrbridge, R. Martin and N. Thrift (eds) *Money, Power and Space*, Oxford: Blackwell.

—— (2004) 'Antimonies of Community: Some Thoughts on Geography, Resources and Empire,' *Transactions of the Institute of British Geographers* NS 29, 195–216.

Webb, D. (1998) 'The Sexual and Economic Politics of (Re)Integration: HIV/AIDS and the Question of Stability in Southern Africa,' in D. Simon (ed.) *South Africa in Southern Africa: Reconfiguring the Region*. Athens, OH and London: Ohio University Press and James Currey.

Weber, H. (2004) 'Reconstituting the "Third World"? Poverty Reduction and Territoriality in the Global Politics of Development,' *Third World Quarterly* 25 (1), 187–206.

Webster, E. and G. Adler (1999) 'Toward a Class Compromise in South Africa's "Double Transition": Bragained Liberalisation and the Consolidation of Democracy,' *Politics and Society* 27 (3), 347–385.

Weekly Mail and Guardian (1997) 'Deft Juggling Gets Anglo Off the Hook,' 28 November. Available at www.sn.apc.org/wmail/issues. Accessed 15 October 2000.

Weeks, J. (1999) 'Stuck in low GEAR? Macroeconomic Policy in South Africa, 1996–1998,' *Cambridge Journal of Economics* 23, 795–811.

Weiner, D. (1988) 'Land and Agricultural Development,' in Colin Stoneman (ed.) *Zimbabwe's Prospects: Issues of Land, Class, State and Capital in Southern Africa*, London: Macmillan.

Weiss, L. (1998) *The Myth of the Powerless State*, Ithaca: Cornell University Press.

Wendt, A. (1999) *Social Theory of International Politics* Cambridge and New York: Cambridge University Press.

Whaites, A. (2002) 'Making PRSPs Work: Can Rhetoric and Reality Coincide?' in A. Whaites (ed.) *Masters of Their Own Development?: PRSPs and the Prospects for the Poor*, Monrovia, California: World Vision.

White, D. (2004) 'Stuck in Poverty after 40 Years of Aid: If Ghana Is Stalling, What Hope for Africa?' *Financial Times*, 25 November, p. 17.

White, G. (1993) 'Civil Society, Democratization and Development (II): Two Country Cases,' *Australian Journal of Chinese Affairs* 29, 63–87.

White, H. and T. Killick in collaboration with S. Kayizzi-Mugerwa and M. Savane (2001) *African Poverty at the Millennium: Causes, Complexities and Challenges*, Washington, D.C.: World Bank.

White, R. (2003) 'Financing the Transition to a Low-Carbon Future,' in Richard Sandbrook (ed.) *Civilising Globalisation: A Survival Guide*, Albany: SUNY Press.

Whitfield, L. (2003) 'Civil Society as Idea and Civil Society as Process: The Case of Ghana,' *Oxford Development Studies* 31 (4), 379–400.

Wilkinson, R. (1996) *Unhealthy Societies: The Afflictions of Inequality*, London: Routledge.

Willett, S. (1998) 'Demilitarisation, Disarmament and Development in Southern Africa,' *Review of African Political Economy* 77, 409–430.

Williams, D. and T. Young (1994) 'Governance, the World Bank and Liberal Theory,' *Political Studies* 42, 84–100.

Williams, G. (2004a) 'Evaluating Participatory Development: Tyranny, Power and (Re) Politicization,' *Third World Quarterly* 25 (3), 557–578.

—— (2004b) 'Towards a Repoliticization of Participatory Development: Political Capabilities and Spaces of Empowerment,' in S. Hickey and G. Mohan (eds) *Participation: From Tyranny to Transformation*, London: Zed Books.

——, M. Srivastava, S. Corrbridge and R. Véon (2003) 'Enhancing Pro-Poor Governance in Eastern India: Participation, Politics and Action Research,' *Progress in Development Studies* 3 (2), 165.

Williams, P. and I. Taylor (2000) 'Neoliberalism and the Political Economy of the "New" South Africa,' *New Political Economy* 5 (1), 21–40.

Winter, J. (2005) 'What Lies Behind the Zimbabwe Demolitions,' 17 June. Available at http://news.bbc.co.uk/1/hi/world/africa/4101228.stm. Accessed 24 June 2005.

Wisner, B. (1993) 'Disaster Vulnerability: Scale, Power and Daily Life,' *GeoJournal*, 30, 127–140.

Wolfensohn, J. (n.d.) Op-Ed on Fighting Terrorism and Poverty. Available at www.worldbank.org.cn/English/content/96m6286227.shtml. Accessed 21 June 2005.

—— (1997) 'The Challenge of Inclusion,' Annual Meeting speech. Available at www.worldbank.org/html/extdr/am97.

Wood, A. (2005) *World Bank's Poverty Reduction Support Credit: Continuity or Change*, Dublin: Debt and Development Coalition.

Wood, G. (1997) 'States without Citizens: The Problems of the Franchise State,' in D. Hulme and M. Edwards (eds) *NGOs, States and Donors: Too Close for Comfort?*, Basingstoke: Macmillan.

Woolcock, M. (1999) 'Managing Risks, Shocks and Opportunity in Developing Economies: The Role of Social Capital,' Washington, D.C.: World Bank. Unpublished Paper Available through the Social Capital Website.

—— (2002) 'Social Capital in Theory and Practice: Where Do We Stand?' in J. Isham, T. Kelly and S. Ramaswamy (eds) *Social Capital and Economic Development: On Well Being in Developing Countries*, Northampton, MA: Edward Elgar.

World Bank (n.d.) 'Private Sector Development for Black Businesses: Draft Issues Paper' (photocopied).

—— (1981) *Accelerated Development in Sub-Saharan Africa: An Agenda for Action*, New York: Oxford University Press for the World Bank.

—— (1990) *Making Adjustment Work for the Poor: A Framework for Policy Reform in Africa*, Social Dimensions of Adjustment Program, Washington, D.C.: World Bank.

—— (1991) *Co-operation between the Bank and NGOs: 1990 Progress Report*, Washington, D.C.: World Bank.

—— (1994) *The World Bank and Participation*, Operations Policy Department, Washington, D.C.: World Bank.

—— (1995) *Sri Lanka Poverty Assessment*, Washington, D.C.: World Bank.

—— (1996a) *Madagascar Poverty Assessment II: Main Report, Annexes*, Report 14044-MAG, Washington, D.C., South Central and Indian Ocean Department, Africa Regional Office: World Bank, unpublished document.

—— (1996b) *The World Bank Participation Sourcebook*, Environmentally Sustainable Development Publication Series, Washington, D.C.: World Bank.

—— (1996c) *World Development Report 1996: From Plan to Market*, Washington, D.C.: World Bank.

—— (1997a) 'Memorandum of the President of the International Development Association to the Executive Directors on a Country Assistance Strategy of the World Bank Group for the Republic of Zimbabwe, Report no. 16541-ZIM,' Washington, D.C.: World Bank.

—— (1997b) 'Staff Appraisal Report: South Africa: Industrial Competitiveness and Job Creation Project,' Report No. 16225-SA, photocopied.

—— (1997c) *World Development Report 1997: The State in a Changing World*, Oxford and New York: Oxford University Press.

—— (1998) *Knowledge for Development: World Development Report 1998/99*, New York: Oxford University Press.

—— (2000a) *Can Africa Claim the Twenty First Century*, Washington, D.C.: World Bank.

—— (2000b) *Entering the 21st Century, World Development Report 1999/2000*, Oxford: Oxford University Press.

—— (2000c) *World Development Report 2000/2001: Attacking Poverty*, Oxford and New York: Oxford University Press.

—— (2001a) *Adjustment from Within: Lessons from the Structural Adjustment Participatory Review Initiative*, A Contribution from the World Bank to the Second Global SAPRI Forum, 30–31 July. Available at http://www.worldbank.org/research/sapri/WB_SAPRI_Report.pdf.

—— (2001b) *Global Economic Prospects*, Washington, D.C.: World Bank.

—— (2002a) *Ethiopia: The Woreda Studies*, vol. 1, *The Study*, World Bank Country Office in Ethiopia, Country Department 6, Africa Region, Addis Ababa: World Bank.

—— (2002b) *Governance Matters II: Up-Dated Indicators for 2000–2001*, World Bank Policy Research Working Paper No 2772. Washington, D.C.: World Bank.

—— (2002c) *Sourcebook for Poverty Reduction Strategies*, Washington, D.C.: World Bank.

—— (2003a) *Annual Review of Development Effectiveness*, Washington, D.C.: World Bank.

—— (2003b) *Breaking the Conflict Trap: Civil War and Development Policy*, Washington, D.C.: World Bank.

—— (2004a) *Global Development Finance: Harnessing Cyclical Gains for Development*, Washington, D.C.: World Bank.

—— (2004b) *World Development Report 2005: A Better Investment Climate for Everyone*, New York: Oxford University Press.

—— (2004c) *Zimbabwe: Country Assistance Evaluation*, Operations Evaluation Department Report No. 29058, Washington, D.C.: World Bank.

—— (2005a) 'Chad-Cameroon Pipeline,' News Release, 30 July. Available from listserv dbobo@worldbank.org.

—— (2005b) 'Rationale for Decentralization,' World Bank Institute, Decentralization Briefing Note. Available at http://info.worldbank.org/etools/docs/library/128801/Ford%20Rationale%20for%20Decentralization.pdf. Accessed 24 June 2005.

—— (2005c) *Fragile States: The LICUS Initiative*. Available at http://web.worldbank.org. Accessed 21 June 2005.

—— (2005d) *Where is the Wealth of Nations: Measuring Capital for the Twenty-First Century*, Washington: World Bank.

—— (2005e) *World Development Report 2006: Equity and Development*, Oxford and New York: Oxford University Press.

Wrights Investor Service (2001) Internet site. Available at http://www.wisi.com. Accessed 19 April 2001.

WTO (World Trade Organization) 'South Africa.' Available at http://www.dti.gov.za/econdb/raportt/South%20Africawto.html. Accessed 29 July 2005.

Xinhua (2004a) 'China, S. Africa to launch free trade talks,' 7 January. Available at www2.chinadaily.com.cn. Accessed 18 September 2006.

—— (2004b) 'Chinese Vice President Calls for "Win–Win" China–Africa Cooperation,' June 30. Available at http://english.people.com.cn. Accessed 18 September 2006.

—— (2004c) 'S. Africa Seeks Opportunities in Emerging Oil Industry in Africa,' 9 March. Available through Business Source Premier at http://web22.epnet.com/.

Yates, J. and L. Okello (2002) 'Learning from Uganda's Efforts to Learn from the Poor: Reflections and Lessons from the Uganda Participatory Poverty Assessment Project,' in K. Brock and R. McGee (eds) *Knowing Poverty: Critical Reflections on Participatory Research and Poverty*, London: Earthscan.

Young, C. (1982) *Ideology and Development in Africa*, New Haven: Yale University Press.

—— (1994) 'In Search of Civil Society,' in J. W. Harbeson, D. Rothchild and N. Chazan (eds), *Civil Society and the State in Africa*, Boulder, CO: Lynne Rienner.

—— (2004) 'The End of the Post-Colonial State in Africa? Reflections on Changing African Political Dynamics,' *African Affairs* 103 (410), 23–49.

Young, T. (1993) 'Forcing Men be Free? Making Sense of the West's Agenda in the Third World: The Case of Mozambique,' Paper for 'Detraditionalization: Authority and Self in an Age of Uncertainty,' Lancaster University, July.

—— (1995) '"A Project to be Realized": Global Liberalism and Contemporary Africa,' *Millennium* 24 (3), 527–546.

Zacarias, A. (2003) 'Redefining Security' in M. Baregu and C. Landsberg (eds) *From Cape to Congo: Southern Africa's Evolving Security Challenges*, Boulder and London: Lynne Rienner.

Zakaria, F. (1997) 'The Rise of Illiberal Democracy,' *Foreign Affairs* 76, 22–43.

—— (2000) 'The New Twilight Struggle,' *Newsweek*, 23 October.

Zalik, A. (2004) 'The Niger Delta: "Petro Violence" and "Partnership Development,"' *Review of African Political Economy* 101, 401–424.

Zaman, M. (2002) 'Are We Getting Lost in Exclusive Anti-Poor, Adjustment Lending Policy Cycles? A Rapid Review of Preliminary Action Aid Engagement of Poverty Reduction Strategies in Kenya, Haiti, Uganda, Vietnam, Nepal, Rwanda and Malawi,' *Action Aid Policy Brief on PRSs*. Available at http://www.esrftz.org/ppa/documents/aa_1.pdf.

Zamponi, M. (2005) 'From Social Justice, to Neo-Liberalism, to Authoritarian Nationalism: Where is the Zimbabwean State Going?' in H. Melber (ed.) *Zimbabwe – the Political Economy of Decline*, Uppsala: Nordiska Afrikainstitutet.

ZCTU (Zimbabwe Congress of Trade Unions) (1996) *Beyond ESAP: Framework for a Long-Term Development Strategy in Zimbabwe*, Harare: ZCTU.

Zeilig, L. (2004) 'The Congo: Speculators and Thieves 1994–2000.' Available at http://www.voiceoftheturtle.org. Accessed 10 August 2006.

Zewde, B. (2002) 'Introduction,' in B. Zewde and S. Pausewang (eds) *Ethiopia: The Challenge of Democracy from Below*, Stockholm: Nordiska Afrikaininstitutet and Forum for Social Studies.

Zewdu, T. (2005) 'Ethnic Federalism and the Question of Democracy and Peace in Ethiopia,' Paper Submitted for Africa Module, M.A. in Globalization, Dublin City University, unpublished.

Zimbabwean, The (2005a) 'South Africa Buys Zimbabwe,' 20 May. Available at http://www.thezimbabwean.co.uk/20-may-2005/lead.html. Accessed 28 July 2005.

—— (2005b) '28 Die in SA's "Concentration Camp,"' 26 August –1 September, p. 1.

—— (2005c) 'Zimbabwe's Nuclear Ambition,' 29 April. Available at http://www.thezimbabwean.co.uk. Accessed 27 June 2006.

Zimbabwe Standard, The (1999) 'Old Mutual – The New Kid on the Block,' 11 July. Available at web7.infotrac.galegroup.com. Accessed 15 October 2000.

Zimplats, (n.d.) 'The History of Zimbabwe Platinum Mines.' Available at http://www.zimplats.com/about/about.htm. Accessed 31 July 2005.

Zwnews (2002) 'Jambanja,' 3rd December. Available at http://www.zwnews.com.

—— (2006) 'When in Doubt, Decorate,' Available at http://www.zwnews.com. Accessed 27 July 2006.

Index